Sefer BeMidbar as *Sefer HaMiddot*

Sefer BeMidbar as *Sefer HaMiddot*

The Book of Numbers as the Book
of Character Development

Rabbi Reuven Travis

FOREWORD BY
Paul Scott Oberman

WIPF & STOCK · Eugene, Oregon

SEFER BEMIDBAR AS SEFER HAMIDDOT
The Book of Numbers as the Book of Character Development

Copyright © 2018 Reuven Travis. All rights reserved. Except for brief quotations in critical publications or reviews, no part of this book may be reproduced in any manner without prior written permission from the publisher. Write: Permissions, Wipf and Stock Publishers, 199 W. 8th Ave., Suite 3, Eugene, OR 97401.

Wipf & Stock
An Imprint of Wipf and Stock Publishers
199 W. 8th Ave., Suite 3
Eugene, OR 97401

www.wipfandstock.com

PAPERBACK ISBN: 978-1-5326-4778-9
HARDCOVER ISBN: 978-1-5326-4779-6
EBOOK ISBN: 978-1-5326-4780-2

Chapter 3: Sharon Rimon, "The Nation and the Shekhina in the Wilderness," Israel Koschitzky Virtual Beit Midrash, http://etzion.org.il/en/nation-and-shekhina-wilderness. Yair Kahn, "Parshat Bamidbar—Not Just Numbers," Israel Koschitzky Virtual Beit Midrash, June 16, 2016, http://etzion.org.il/en/parshat-bamidbar-not-just-numbers. Amnon Bazak, "The Status of the Tribe of Levi," translated by Kaeren Fish, Israel Koschitzky Virtual Beit Midrash, http://etzion.org.il/en/status-tribe-levi. **Chapter 4:** Kevin Eikenberry, "Are You Observing or Judging?" Leadership and Learning with Kevin Eikenberry (blog). February 14, 2012, http://blog.kevineikenberry.com/leadership-supervisory-skills/are-you-observing-or-judging/, © (2012) All Rights Reserved, The Kevin Eikenberry Group. Pinchas Avruch, "Go for It! Parshas Vayakhel Pekudei." Torah.org. January 9, 2003. https://torah.org/torah-portion/kolhakollel-5762-vayakhel/. **Chapter 5:** Saul McLeod, "Nature vs. Nurture in Psychology," SimplyPsychology, 2015, https://www.simplypsychology.org/naturevsnurture.html. Mosheh Lichtenstein, "The Crisis of Leadership," Israel Koschitzky Virtual Beit Midrash, http://etzion.org.il/en/crisis-leadership. Yonatan Grossman, "Two Complaints of the Nation, and the Re-Appointment of Aharon," Israel Koschitzky Virtual Beit Midrash, http://etzion.org.il/en/two-complaints-nation-and-re-appointment-aharon. **Chapter 6:** Mosheh Lichtenstein, "Parashat Shelach," translated by David Silverberg, Israel Koschitzky Virtual Beit Midrash, http://etzion.org.il/en/shelach-0. Hershey H. Friedman and Abraham C. Weisel, "Should Moral Individuals Ever Lie? Insights from Jewish Law," Jewish Law, 2003, http://www.jlaw.com/Articles/hf_LyingPermissible.html. **Chapter 7:** Yair Kahn, "Parashat Korach: The Entire Nation is Holy," Israel Koschitzky Virtual Beit Midrash, http://etzion.org.il/en/parashat-korach-entire-nation-holy. Shira Smiles, "Freeing Yourself from Jealousy: Unlocking a Secret of the Tenth Commandment," aish.org, http://www.aish.com/sp/ph/Freeing_Yourself_from_Jealousy.html. **Chapter 8:** Alex Israel, "Is Bilam Evil?," Israel Koschitzky Virtual Beit Midrash, http://

etzion.org.il/en/bilam-evil. Gil Student, "Is Greed Good?," Torah Musings, May 11, 2011, https://www.torahmusings.com/2011/05/is-greed-good/. **Chapter 9:** Chanoch Waxman, "The Rise of Pinchas," Israel Koschitzky Virtual Beit Midrash, http://etzion.org.il/en/rise-pinchas. Zalman Baruch Melamed, "The Parameters of Pinchas' Zealotry," Yeshiva.co, https://www.yeshiva.co/midrash/shiur.asp?id=434. **Chapter 10:** Elchanan Samet, "The Sota (5:11–31)," translated by Kaeren Fish, Israel Koschitzky Virtual Beit Midrash, http://etzion.org.il/en/sota-511-31. Noson Weisz, "Sotah," Aish.com, http://www.aish.com/tp/i/m/48964791.html. **Chapter 11:** Amnon Bazak, "Why Are the Laws of the Nazir and the Sota Juxtaposed?," translated by Kaeren Fish, Israel Koschitzky Virtual Beit Midrash, http://etzion.org.il/en/why-are-laws-nazir-and-sota-juxtaposed. Bernie Fox, "Lessons from the Nazir," Torah New York, https://www.ou.org/torah/parsha/rabbi-fox-on-parsha/lessons_from_the_nazir/. **Chapter 12:** Daniel Shoag, "Reviving Religious Zionism," Harvard Israel Review, http://www.hcs.harvard.edu/~hireview/content.php?type=article&issue=spring04/&name=shoag. Ephraim Z. Buchwald, "Loving the Land of Israel," Rabbi Buchwald's Weekly Torah Message, 2002, http://rabbibuchwald.njop.org/2002/06/24/pinchas-5762-2002/. Ephraim Z. Buchwald, "The Daughters of Tzelafchad: Legitimate Feminist Claims," Rabbi Buchwald's Weekly Torah Message, http://rabbibuchwald.njop.org/2000/07/17/pinchas-5760-2000/.

Manufactured in the U.S.A.

In Memory of Martin Kahn
Beloved Husband, Father, and Grandfather

He embodied the best character traits
set forth by our sages.

Contents

Foreword by Paul Scott Oberman | ix
Preface | xi

Part One—A Complex Text
    Chapter 1—The Challenges of Teaching *Sefer BeMidbar* | 3
    Chapter 2—*Sefer BeMidbar* as *Sefer HaMiddot* | 22

Part Two—The Narrative of *Sefer BeMidbar*
    Chapter 3—The Census | 41
    Chapter 4—The Princes | 67
    Chapter 5—The People | 85
    Chapter 6—The Spies | 123
    Chapter 7—Korah | 171
    Chapter 8—Balaam | 198
    Chapter 9—Phinehas | 224

Part Three—The Legal Positings of *Sefer BeMidbar*
    Chapter 10—The Sotah | 259
    Chapter 11—The Nazirite | 294
    Chapter 12—The Daughters of Zelophehad | 320

    Final Thoughts | 357

Appendix—Sample Rubric for Middot *Essays* | 359
About the Author | 361
Bibliography | 363

Foreword

Rabbi Reuven Travis makes a compelling case that teaching *Sefer BeMidbar* (the book of Numbers) to high school students as a book of character development is very developmentally appropriate for this age group. For a group of budding adults searching for their own unique identity—trying on different character traits, learning to live in a world of gray instead of simple black and white, and embracing of a world where debate comes naturally—Rabbi Travis argues that a linear teaching of the text misses opportunities: connecting the dots, learning about themselves, and becoming better people.

Certainly anyone who knows teenagers will recognize the special challenge presented here. How do we as teachers connect with these high school students via a biblical text that is a mix of story and laws? (Some may ask, how do we connect with them at all . . .but not this author!) Rabbi Travis argues that the best way to teach this particular book is by examining each of the complex personality types and deciding whether the character traits as presented are positive ones or negative ones.

One unique aspect of *BeMidbar* is that it presents characters such as Korah, whose jealousy is absolutely relatable to teens, or Phinehas, whose actions are complex enough to argue, with issues that are real and relevant to teens. The strong actions taken by these characters forge an identity—an identity that conversely can be distilled from a unique, particularly strong action. Teenage students recognize that the choices they are making now can indeed craft the people they are becoming.

In this work, Rabbi Travis beautifully lays out an analysis of each of the character traits encountered and then provides lesson plans and supplemental readings which allow students to justify their judgments of each in turn. This approach models the way that research supports for students learning best: connecting what they are learning to their own lives.

Sometimes teens, perhaps because of their lack of decision-making power, complain about their circumstances. Sometimes teens are provocative, even deliberately so. Both of these are modeled by the Jewish people in *BeMidbar* and therefore can serve as prototypes for introspection. This can also lead to discussions of how God might respond to these behaviors, letting teens examine their own relationships with a higher being.

If you were to ask parents of high school students what they want for their children, or what they should look like upon high school graduation, almost all would include "good people" or perhaps the Jewish term "mensch." In fact, I once had a parent ask me to choose only one of the three positive traits she offered—happy, successful, or good—as my priority for the graduates of my school. The answer that I supplied, and that she sought, was "good." Rabbi Travis here proposes a vehicle for this sought-after character development, allowing teens to decide whether to emulate or avoid the character traits as seen in this book of the Bible.

In this light, his book makes a compelling argument for inclusion in any high school's curriculum. It uses the already existing Bible study, or Chumash, courses offered in religious high schools, and transforms the course into an analysis of and subsequent development of positive character traits, simultaneously teaching how to avoid negative character traits. I do not know of any parochial school that would not want such a course on character development as a jewel to be treasured in the center of their curriculum.

Paul S. Oberman, PhD
Head of School
Robert M. Beren Academy

Preface

OVER THE YEARS, MOST Bible classes I have attended as a student or have observed as mentor and colleague were taught in a linear fashion. In other words, teacher and students tackled the text chapter by chapter, verse by verse. Based on my personal experiences, this approach has two distinct drawbacks.

First, in terms of textual analysis, students who learn linearly are seeing snapshots of the biblical narrative (even if they are building linguistic skills by learning the text in its original Hebrew). These snapshots make it more challenging to see the big picture of each narrative or, more importantly, the distinct metaquestions that underlie each book of the Pentateuch.

Second, I believe that this linear learning limits teachers. All people are ultimately a composite of their individual experiences: where they grew up, where they went to school, their family backgrounds, mentors they have had throughout their careers, community service and involvement, and on and on. Teachers are no different, but the best teachers I have ever learned from or worked with all consciously used their life experiences to bring various perspectives and insights into their lessons. Unfortunately, teaching the Bible in a linear fashion makes it far more difficult for teachers to bring these other elements of themselves into their lessons.

I may represent a sample size of one, but here are the life and teaching experiences that inspired me to write this book.

I consider myself a successful teacher, and this is due in no small measure to my unusual background. Unlike the other Judaic studies teachers in my school, I did not grow up in a ritually observant home. I did not attend a Jewish day school as a child. In fact, I was in my twenties before I took my first real Bible class, and I did not become an ordained rabbi for another twenty-five years.

Instead, I went to a public high school and attended an Ivy League college, where I studied medieval French literature and political science (and even played on my college's football team). I then went on to work in advertising and marketing for fifteen years (not much use there for medieval French literature!) before becoming a school teacher some twenty years ago.

Each and every day since then, the experiences I had prior to becoming a teacher have regularly informed the way I structure and share information in my classrooms, not only in my Jewish studies courses, but in my American history and Advanced Placement U.S. government classes as well. My passion for history, political science, literature, Bible studies, and Hebrew language cross-pollinate within the curricula I develop. This explains why I am just as comfortable introducing a unit on the inauguration of the tabernacle in the Sinai wilderness with a talmudic dispute between Hillel and Shammai (see chapter 4 of this book) as I am beginning a unit on jealousy with a discussion of Shakespeare's *Othello* (see chapter 7) or teaching about Phinehas and zealotry via a history quiz (see chapter 9).

Here is the point of all this.

Teaching is about connecting the dots. That I can and do introduce Jewish ideas via non-Jewish sources should not be surprising given my eclectic background. But my life experiences have shown me the importance of helping students in my Bible classes see more than mere words on a page, or, in a Jewish day school setting, prodding them to go deeper than simply reading the commentaries on the pages of the printed Hebrew Bible.

As Ben Bag Bag says about the text of the Torah: "Turn it, and turn it, for everything is in it" (Pirqe Avot 5:22). And what's in it? Certainly the Bible teaches us big-picture beliefs about our Creator and how to serve Him. About our faith and how to act upon it. But it is replete with little picture lessons that are no less important. About visiting the sick and caring for the widow and the orphan. About being honest. About being charitable. In short, about how to be a better spouse, a better parent, a better child or sibling, or, quite simply, how to be a better person.

Teaching my students to be better people is something I strive to do every time I enter the classroom, and it is what underlies the analyses of and teaching pedagogy for the book of Numbers that I describe in this book. This pedagogy works, I think, for any teacher and any student (Jewish or otherwise) who sees in the biblical text a blueprint for self-improvement and self-actualization. But be aware that the Modern Orthodox orientation that shapes my religious and daily life colors my take on the book of Numbers, and this is something I discuss throughout this book, most intensely in chapter 12.

I hope that knowing these facts will help the reader understand my thoughts on the various stories in the book of Numbers. I am equally hopeful that, even if readers do not agree with all my analyses, they will not walk away from the main thrust of this book, namely, that the book of Numbers is about character development—and making students better people—and should be taught accordingly.

There is one additional and critical thing to remember. The curricular approach I propose in this work is not meant to be rigidly followed, with an instructor using only the materials I include here. To the contrary, the suggested commentaries and supplemental readings in the sample unit plans that follow each chapter below are simply ones I find interesting and have used to highlight different aspects of each narrative being studied. (To help clarify matters, I have included in the sample unit plans my thoughts on how to use these readings.) Of equal importance, I use these supplemental readings to show students that serious scholarship and interpretations of the biblical text are still being produced today within the Orthodox community.

Any instructor who opts to follow the curriculum found in this book might use some or none of these commentaries and suggested readings, and that's the point. As much as teachers of the Bible might desire well-crafted and insightful curricular materials, they still want the freedom to take ownership of them. And let me be clear about this. There have been years in which I have taught two classes on the book of Numbers to different groups of students, and the commentaries and readings I used in one were different from those I used in the other. That is what good teaching—and student-focused teaching—is all about.

There is a well-known talmudic dictum. Rabbi Hanina ben Dosa would say: "One who is pleasing to his fellow men is pleasing to God. But one who is not pleasing to his fellow men is not pleasing to God" (Pirqe Avot 3:10). To me, nothing makes us more pleasing to our peers and colleagues (and by extension to God) than a good character, and my sincerest hope is that this book will help Bible teachers inculcate proper character traits in their students.

In closing, I want to thank both Angela R. Erisman for the insights and suggestions she made while editing my manuscript and Jeff Sokolow for all his help in proofing the final version of the book. And I am deeply appreciative to the many authors who allowed me to include their Torah insights in the unit plans I crafted for teaching the book of Numbers.

Rabbi Reuven Travis

Part One

A Complex Text

Chapter 1

The Challenges of Teaching *Sefer BeMidbar*

THE BOOK OF NUMBERS, or *Sefer BeMidbar* as it is known in Hebrew, is a complex text, one whose narrative has been explicated in a variety of ways. An obvious but arguably simplistic approach to looking at this text is to see it as a story of a sinful people and a wrathful God. The God of this book certainly seems to see it this way.

> Nevertheless, as I live and as the Lord's Presence fills the whole world, none of the men who have seen My Presence and the signs that I have performed in Egypt and in the wilderness, and who have tried Me these many times [literally, ten times] and have disobeyed Me, shall see the land that I promised on oath to their fathers; none of those who spurn Me shall see it. (Numbers 14:21–23)[1]

What were these many times that the people disobeyed and provoked the Lord during their forty-year sojourn in the wilderness? Starting with chapter 14 of the book of Exodus and continuing through chapter 14 of the book of Numbers, the following ten incidents listed in the Babylonian Talmud, Erchin 15a seem to underscore the rebellious nature of the Jewish people in the Sinai desert.[2]

- The children of Israel, pinned against the Red Sea with the Egyptians in close pursuit, complained to Moses: "Was it for a lack of graves in Egypt that you took us to die in the wilderness?" (Exodus 14:11)

---

1. All translations of biblical texts and commentaries are from https://www.sefaria.org unless otherwise indicated.

2. It should be noted that there are no such incidents recorded in the book of Leviticus, as its narrative is limited to the laws of the sacrificial rites for the tabernacle (*mishkan* in Hebrew).

- After safely crossing the sea, Israel suspected that the Egyptians ascended on the opposite bank until God had the water spit them out: "Thus the Lord delivered Israel that day from the Egyptians. Israel saw the Egyptians dead on the shore of the sea." (Exodus 14:30)
- Complaining about the lack of water at Marah: "And the people grumbled against Moses, saying, 'What shall we drink?'" (Exodus 15:24)
- Complaining about the lack of food in the wilderness of Sin: "In the wilderness, the whole Israelite community grumbled against Moses and Aaron. The Israelites said to them, 'If only we had died by the hand of the Lord in the land of Egypt, when we sat by the fleshpots, when we ate our fill of bread! For you have brought us out into this wilderness to starve this whole congregation to death.'" (Exodus 16:2–3)
- Leaving over manna in defiance of the command not to leave the manna overnight: "But they paid no attention to Moses; some of them left of it until morning, and it became infested with maggots and stank. And Moses was angry with them." (Exodus 16:20)
- Searching for manna on the morning of the Sabbath: "Yet some of the people went out on the seventh day to gather, but they found nothing." (Exodus 16:27)
- Complaining about the lack of water at Rephidim: "From the wilderness of Sin the whole Israelite community continued by stages as the Lord would command. They encamped at Rephidim, and there was no water for the people to drink. The people quarreled with Moses. 'Give us water to drink,' they said; and Moses replied to them, 'Why do you quarrel with me? Why do you try the Lord?' But the people thirsted there for water; and the people grumbled against Moses and said, 'Why did you bring us up from Egypt, to kill us and our children and livestock with thirst'?" (Exodus 17:1–3)
- The sin of the golden calf: "When the people saw that Moses was so long in coming down from the mountain, the people gathered against Aaron and said to him, 'Come, make us a god who shall go before us, for that man Moses, who brought us from the land of Egypt—we do not know what has happened to him.' Aaron said to them, 'Take off the gold rings that are on the ears of your wives, your sons, and your daughters, and bring them to me.' And all the people took off the gold rings that were in their ears and brought them to Aaron. This he took from them and cast in a mold, and made it into a molten calf. And they exclaimed, 'This is your god, O Israel, who brought you out of the land of Egypt!' When Aaron saw this, he built an altar before it; and

Aaron announced: 'Tomorrow shall be a festival of the Lord!' Early next day, the people offered up burnt offerings and brought sacrifices of well-being; they sat down to eat and drink, and then rose to dance." (Exodus 32:1–6)

- The "mixed multitude" of nations which accompanied Israel complaining about the lack of meat, precipitating Israel's complaining as well: "The riffraff in their midst felt a gluttonous craving; and then the Israelites wept and said, 'If only we had meat to eat! We remember the fish that we used to eat free in Egypt, the cucumbers, the melons, the leeks, the onions, and the garlic. Now our gullets are shriveled. There is nothing at all! Nothing but this manna to look to!'" (Numbers 11:4–6)
- The sin of the ten spies, who gave a negative report about the land of Israel when they returned from spying it out, after which God refers to Israel as "having tested Me these ten times" (Numbers 13–14)

Given these, it is not surprising that many Christian preachers and teachers view the God of the Old Testament as a God of wrath compared to the God of the New Testament, who is seen as a God of love. Carl Olson, editor of *Catholic World Report* and *Ignatius Insight*, sums it up quite succinctly when he states that there is a "widespread and deeply ingrained" view among some Christians "that the God described in the Old Testament is, on the whole, quite angry and judgmental."[3]

Chuck Swindoll expresses a similar view. Swindoll is an evangelical Christian pastor, author, educator, and radio preacher who founded the publication *Insight for Living* and a radio program of the same name which airs on more than two thousand stations around the world. In his words, "More than just a history lesson, the Book of Numbers reveals how God reminded Israel that He does not tolerate rebellion, complaining, and disbelief without invoking consequences."[4]

As a last example, consider the views of David Lamb, author of *God Behaving Badly: Is the God of the Old Testament Angry, Sexist and Racist?* In a 2013 interview, Lamb was asked why he wrote this book. He responded in part:

> I was on a date with my wife Shannon recently, and we ended up chatting with our server. He says to me, "So what do you do?" I replied, "I teach the Bible, mainly the Old Testament." My response prompted him to ask, "The Old Testament—isn't that where God is always getting angry, smiting people, and

3. Olson, "'Angry God.'"
4. Swindoll, "Numbers."

destroying cities all the time?" I tell him, "Well, not exactly, but I get that question a lot because the God of the Old Testament has a bad reputation." I wrote *God Behaving Badly* for this server and for anyone who wonders about God's behavior in the OT (which is pretty much everyone). One of the biggest obstacles to moving atheists, agnostics, and skeptics toward God is the problematic passages of the Old Testament. I talk to people about the problem of God of the Old Testament all the time: my cardiologist, my postman, my son's soccer coach, my Sunday school class, and literally hundreds of college students. I wrote the book for them.[5]

In fairness, these people for whom Lamb wrote his book, as we have already seen, base their views about the God of the Old Testament upon large portions of the Torah narrative. To their credit, teachers and authors such as Olson, Swindoll, and Lamb work to disabuse the masses of this image of a wrathful and unforgiving God. Their efforts make great sense if one sees in the Old Testament theological underpinnings to the New Testament, and even a cursory perusal of the internet will show the extent to which Christian leaders strive to instill in their followers the notion that there is one God, one whose anger is tempered by mercy. As Swindoll writes, "Though the people failed many times, God showed His own faithfulness by His constant presence leading the way: through a cloud by day and a pillar of fire by night . . . . He taught His people how to walk with Him—not just with their feet through the wilderness, but with their mouths in worship, hands in service, and lives as witnesses to the surrounding nations."[6]

Jewish sages and scholars do not ignore the difficulties inherent in a text such as the book of Numbers, with its portrayal of an ostensibly wrathful God. How could they? The biblical canon has many examples of God's wrathful anger. Consider just a few examples:

- The divine anger kindled becomes "a fire [that] has flared in My wrath and burned to the bottom of Sheol, [that] has consumed the earth and its increase, [that has] eaten down to the base of the hills." (Deuteronomy 32:22)

- "So My fierce anger was poured out, and it blazed against the towns of Judah and the streets of Jerusalem. And they became a desolate ruin, as they still are today." (Jeremiah 44:6)

---

5. Quoted in Viola, "God Behaving Badly."
6. Swindoll, "Numbers."

- "Who can stand before His wrath? Who can resist His fury? His anger pours out like fire, and rocks are shattered because of Him." (Nahum 1:6)
- "God vindicates the righteous; God pronounces doom each day." (Psalm 7:12)

The talmudic sages went so far as to proclaim that "as long as the wicked exist in the world, there is wrath in the world" (Babylonian Talmud, Sanhedrin 111b). Nonetheless, the insights by Jewish scholars throughout the centuries into the narrative of Numbers have been driven and colored by the longstanding tradition of a God whose mercy is seemingly limitless and who far more often than not allows His mercy to trump both His anger and His desire to dole out strict justice.

There are many sources in the Torah itself and in the oral tradition that support the notion of a merciful God. One of the most important is found in the opening chapters of the book of Genesis. The book begins: "When God began to create heaven and earth."[7] Later, in the second chapter of Genesis, the verse reads: "These are the generations of the heavens and the earth when they were created, on the day that the Lord God made earth and heaven" (Genesis 2:4). Rashi, the most prominent of the medieval biblical commentators, is quick to note that the first chapter simply refers to God, whereas the second chapter refers to the Creator as the Lord God (Genesis 2:4).[8] In English, this linguistic change might not be significant. In Hebrew, it has great importance.

The term for the Creator in the opening verse of the Torah is אלהִים, or God. This name "God" is associated in the rabbinic tradition with the divine attribute of strict justice. In the second chapter, the appellation for the Creator now includes the four-letter name of the Creator, or Tetragrammaton (יהוה in Hebrew and YHWH in Latin script), which the scribes

---

7. The more familiar translation of this opening verse, found in the King James Bible, the American Standard Version, and the New American Standard Bible, among others, is: "In the beginning God created the heavens and the earth." Many Jewish commentators take issue with this translation and argue that this verse did not come to teach the sequence of creation. If it had meant to teach the order of creation, that is, which elements of creation came first, the verse should have read: "At first (בָּרִאשׁוֹנָה) He created the heavens and the earth." This is Rashi's explanation, and he continues: "For there is no רֵאשִׁית in Scripture that is not connected to the following word. Other examples include 'In the beginning of (בְּרֵאשִׁית) the reign of Jehoiakim' (Genesis 27:1); 'the beginning of (רֵאשִׁית) his reign' (Genesis 10:10); and 'the first (רֵאשִׁית) of your corn' (Deuteronomy 18:4). Here, too, the Hebrew reads בְּרֵאשִׁית בָּרָא אלהים, like בְּרֵאשִׁית בְּרֹא, in the beginning of creating."

8. Rashi is an acronym for Rabbi Shlomo ben Yitzhak, who lived in France from 1040 to 1105. His is the standard commentary on the biblical text.

who transmitted the Hebrew text instructed us to read as "Lord" in order to ensure that the divine name is never pronounced. The Tetragrammaton is associated with the divine attribute of mercy. By changing the Creator's name to "Lord God," the text teaches that the strictness of אלֹהִים must be tempered with the mercy associated with the Tetragrammaton. In his commentary on Genesis 1:1, Rashi explains this change as follows:

> It does not state 'ברא ה "The Lord (the Merciful One) created, because at first God intended to create it (the world) to be placed under the attribute (rule) of strict justice, but He realized that the world could not thus endure and therefore gave precedence to Divine Mercy allying it with Divine Justice. It is to this that what is written in (Genesis 2:4) alludes—"In the day that the Lord God made earth and heaven."

A second example is found in the early chapters of the book of Exodus. Moses's first encounter with Pharaoh does not go well. The Egyptian king orders that the Hebrew slaves no longer be supplied with straw, but that their daily quota of bricks not be reduced (Exodus 5:18–19). Moses, much distressed, in turn confronts God: "O Lord, why did You bring harm upon this people? Why did You send me? Ever since I came to Pharaoh to speak in Your name, he has dealt worse with this people; and still You have not delivered Your people" (Exodus 5:2–23). God's response is short but surprisingly complex in the original Hebrew: "And the Lord [the appellation connoting the attribute of divine justice] spoke to Moses saying to him, 'I am God' [the Tetragrammaton connoting the attribute of divine mercy]." The midrash in Exodus Rabbah on this verse notes that the divine attribute of justice wished to strike down Moses for his impertinence, to which God responds: "am I like one of flesh and blood in My attributes that I cannot be merciful?" Hence, the verse immediately adds "I am God" using the Tetragrammaton.

An even more striking example of God's unsurpassed mercy is found a bit later in Exodus in the verses describing the second set of tablets given to Moses. When Moses ascends Mount Sinai to receive the second set of tablets, God descends in a cloud and stands there with Moses, who in turn calls out with the ineffable name of God—that is, with the Tetragrammaton. The scene unfolds in a most unexpected manner:

> The Lord passed before him and proclaimed: "The Lord! The Lord![9] A God compassionate and gracious, slow to anger, abounding in kindness and faithfulness, extending kindness

9. The BabylonianTalmud (Rosh Hashanah 17b) famously understands this repetition of the Tetragrammaton as implying that "I am He before a person sins, and I am He after a person sins and repents."

to the thousandth generation, forgiving iniquity, transgression, and sin; yet He does not remit all punishment, but visits the iniquity of parents upon children and children's children, upon the third and fourth generations." Moses hastened to bow low to the ground in homage, and said, "If I have gained Your favor, O Lord, pray, let the Lord go in our midst, even though this is a stiff-necked people. Pardon our iniquity and our sin, and take us for Your own!" He said: "I hereby make a covenant. Before all your people I will work such wonders as have not been wrought on all the earth or in any nation; and all the people who are with you shall see how awesome are the Lord's deeds which I will perform for you" (Exodus 34:6–10).

This phrase "The Lord! The Lord! A God compassionate and gracious ..."[10] became in Jewish ritual the core component—the heart and soul, as it were—of communal worship during times of supplication and intense prayer.[11] While there is no explicit talmudic source for the inclusion of this phrase in Jewish penitential prayers, the Talmud addresses the concept of reciting the thirteen attributes in the context of a general discussion about God judging humanity in general and the Jewish people in particular on Rosh Hashanah (the Jewish New Year) and Yom Kippur (the Day of Atonement). There the Babylonian Talmud (Rosh Hashanah 17b) expounds on God's revelation of the thirteen attributes to Moses:

> "And the Lord passed by before him, and proclaimed . . ." Rabbi Yochanan said: Were it not written in the verse, it would be impossible to say it. This teaches that the Holy One, blessed be He, wrapped Himself like a prayer leader and showed Moses the structure of the prayer service. He said to him: "Whenever the Jewish people sin, let them act before Me in accordance with this prayer [that is, let them recite this prayer], and I will forgive them."

This talmudic text continues and proposes yet another powerful insight on the significance of reciting the thirteen attributes in penitential prayers:

> Rav Yehudah said: A covenant was made with the thirteen attributes that they will not return empty-handed [meaning that if one mentions them, he will certainly be answered], as it is stated: "Behold, I make a covenant" (Exodus 34:10).

---

10. The full phrase is commonly referred to in rabbinic and Jewish legal sources as the "thirteen *middot*" or "thirteen attributes" of God.

11. Rabbi Ezra Bick offers an extensive and insightful analysis of this prayer, called *selichot* in Hebrew, in his book, *In His Mercy*.

The importance of the thirteen attributes in Jewish thought, along with the notion of mercy tempering justice, is a topic to which rabbinic writers and aages return time and time again. One prominent example is found in the works of Rabbi Moshe Chaim Luzzatto.[12] In the fourth chapter of his highly regarded ethical treatise *Mesilat Yesharim* (*The Path of the Upright*), Rabbi Luzzatto writes:

> The Divine trait of mercy is the foundation of the world, which would not endure without it at all ... for according to the strict letter of the law, it would be proper that a sinner be punished immediately after sinning without any delay ... and there should not be any possibility to fix the sin at all, since in truth, how can one fix that which he distorted and the sin was already done? How could one mend murdering his friend or committing adultery? Is it possible to eradicate an act which was already performed? Nevertheless, the Divine trait of mercy allows for the reversal of three things: it grants the sinner time so he is not killed instantly after sinning, the punishment will not entirely annihilate the sinner, and repentance is given to the sinner with complete mercy, so that the uprooting of his desire to sin is considered like an uprooting of the action ... that the sin is totally removed from reality and retroactively uprooted through his regret and remorse for his actions. This is certain (Divine) benevolence which is not according to (Divine) strict justice.[13]

It is important to note that the mercy and forgiveness promised via the thirteen attributes are not, in the Jewish tradition, one-sided. For the person of faith, it is not sufficient to merely recite the thirteen attributes. "Our part of the 'bargain' is much deeper than that. Declaring the Thirteen Attributes—recognition of God's names of compassion—directly results in their manifestation in the world.... When we read these Attributes of Mercy, the *Shekhina*'s [Hebrew for God's presence] manifestation must, by necessity, take the form of mercy.... the very presence of these divine names in the mouths of humans constitutes the presence of mercy in the world."[14]

Notwithstanding this covenant and the assurances of mercy associated with the thirteen attributes, the rabbinic tradition strove to reconcile the rebellious behavior of the Jewish people in the wilderness (and the subsequent

---

12. Rabbi Luzzatto, who lived from 1707 to 1746, was an Italian rabbi, kabbalist, and philosopher who wrote many famous Torah works which are still studied today throughout the Jewish world.

13. Luzzatto, *Mesilat Yesharim*, chapter 4.

14. Bick, *In His Mercy*, xix–xx.

anger of and punishment by God) found in Numbers with the foundational principle of a merciful God.

For example, Sforno,[15] in his introduction to *Sefer BeMidbar*, makes clear that this book is largely about the interplay between strict justice and mercy. He writes that:

> (The Torah) makes mention of the merits of Israel by which they became worthy to enter the Land in this manner (i.e., without opposition) .... (However) they, in the manner of (fallible) mortals, transgressed His covenant and behaved treacherously in the episode of the Spies, thereby subverting their (own) interests. It was therefore decreed that they perish in the wilderness and that their children would go into exile for generations at the ordained time. As a result, their children encircled the lands of the nations for forty years and did not enter the land without a struggle. The third part (of this book) relates that, in spite of all this, the mercy of God did not cease in arranging the affairs of His children as much as possible, and He commanded regarding the libations of an offering made by an individual and the (separation of) *challah*,[16] and the goat (sacrifice) to atone for idolatry, all this instituted from (the time of) the (episode of) the Spies and beyond. He sanctified them unto Himself through the commandment of *tzitzit*.[17] In spite of all this, Korah and his congregation did not hesitate to rebel against His honored leaders. Indeed, they transgressed and were punished, (but) He had compassion on the rest of the masses and mended the breach, as symbolized by the firepans and the rod and the priestly gifts so that they should not revert to their reckless ways.[18]

This same synthesis between God's need to enforce strict justice in response to the rebelliousness of the people and His desire to be merciful is evident

---

15. Sforno is Rabbi Ovadyah Sforno, who lived in Italy from 1470 to 1550. Aside from being a proficient Torah scholar and halakhic authority, Sforno was also a physician and was educated in secular subjects. His commentaries were distinguished for their terseness, lucidity, and adherence to plain meaning, but they also contained short comments on the philosophical and ethical implications of the text. His commentary to this day is very popular with students and educators.

16. The Torah commands in Numbers 15:20: "From the first of your dough you shall set apart *challah*." In biblical times, this portion of the dough went to the priests who served in the tabernacle and later in the temple.

17. *Tzitzit* are specially knotted ritual fringes or tassels worn in antiquity by Israelites and today by observant Jews. *Tzitzit* are attached to the four corners of the *tallit* (prayer shawl) and *tallit qatan* (everyday undergarment).

18. Sforno, *Commentary*, 640–41.

in some of the well-known narratives in Numbers. Consider, for example, the episode involving the "mixed multitude" of nations which accompanied Israel complaining about the lack of meat and prompting the Israelites to complain as well (Numbers 11:4–6). The chapter begins by informing us that the "people took to complaining bitterly before the Lord. The Lord heard and was incensed: a fire of the Lord broke out against them, ravaging the outskirts of the camp."

In his commentary on this verse, Rashi notes how the people were deliberatively provocative; that is, they were seeking a pretext to turn away from the Omnipresent, and not just any pretext, but rather a pretext that was evil in God's ears, for they intended that it should reach His ears and provoke Him. Relying on midrashic sources, Rashi maintains that the people said something akin to "Woe is to us! How weary we have become on this journey! For three days, we have not rested from the fatigue of walking."

Sforno's commentary on this verse echoes Rashi's. Sforno argues that the people did not actually complain in their hearts, because they had nothing to complain about. They only voiced complaints as a form of testing God.

And how does God react to this deliberate provocation?

Yes, God becomes angry. And, yes, the fire of God burns in them, and it consumes the edge of the camp. However, in the end, "the people cried out to Moses. Moses prayed to the Lord, and the fire died down" (Numbers 11:2). The call for justice is tempered by God's mercy, which He extends in response to the cries of the people and the prayers of Moses.

Why does God give the Jewish people another chance? Why does He allow His thirteen attributes to overshadow His desire for strict justice? The answer is simple. God gives the people another chance so that they may prepare themselves properly for their next opportunity at redemption. In other words, "if and when God enacts His mercy, it is in order that we take advantage of this new opportunity to do what we should have done originally. This is what repentance is all about."[19]

There seems to be a consensus among the commentaries that the sinful activity at the beginning of chapter 11 is prompted by the mixed multitude that leaves Egypt along with the Jews during the exodus.[20] Their actions seem to have a strong impact on the rest of the people (who some-

---

19. Leibtag, "Tehillim Perek."

20. The text in Exodus 12:38 uses the expression "a mixed multitude." The identity of these people has been explained in a number of ways, including that they are Egyptian slaves who may or may not have believed in the God of the Hebrews, but who longed for freedom or the offspring of mixed marriages that took place in Egypt. Regardless of their identity, their adherence to Jewish practice and ritual was questionable at best.

how overlook the consequences of these actions). By the end of the chapter, the masses experience "a gluttonous craving" and begin weeping for meat. They say:

> "If only we had meat to eat! We remember the fish that we used to eat free in Egypt, the cucumbers, the melons, the leeks, the onions, and the garlic. Now our gullets are shriveled. There is nothing at all! Nothing but this manna to look to!" ... Moses heard the people weeping, every clan apart, each person at the entrance of his tent. The Lord was very angry, and Moses was distressed (Numbers 11:4-10).

Rather than immediately punish the people, God calls their bluff. He understands that there is more at play here than a desire for meat. He thus decides to give them meat, not for one day or two, or even five or ten or twenty days, but for "a whole month, until it comes out of your nostrils and becomes loathsome to you. For you have rejected the Lord who is among you, by whining before Him and saying, 'Oh, why did we ever leave Egypt!'" (Numbers 11:20).

In the end, God does punish the people. "The meat was still between their teeth, nor yet chewed, when the anger of the Lord blazed forth against the people and the Lord struck the people with a very severe plague" (Numbers 11:33). Yet even this severe plague is tempered by a form of mercy, as the Babylonain Talmud states in Yoma 75b:

> "While the meat was still between their teeth ..." [However, it also states: "You shall not eat it for only one day ...] but for an entire month [until it comes out of your nostrils and becomes loathsome to you" (Numbers 11:19-29)]. How can these texts be reconciled? The average people died immediately, but the wicked continued to suffer in pain for a month and then died.

This tempering of justice with mercy can be demonstrated again and again in the biblical text. It is consistent with both the Jewish belief in a merciful God and with the Christian belief that the God of the Old Testament is the same loving and merciful God of the New Testament. Moreover, it forms the basis for a reasoned and compelling understanding of the narrative of Numbers.

As a rabbi and a student of biblical texts, I understand and appreciate this approach to *Sefer BeMidbar*. Yet, as a high school teacher, I am troubled by it, for it is an approach that does not, as I have seen time and time again, resonate with my teenage students.

Let me explain.

Be they parents or educators (or both), individuals who deal with teens on a regular basis know how challenging the teen years can be. How teens rebel. Not only how they question the religious beliefs and practices of their parents, but also how they also struggle with issues relating to self. Who they are. Who they want to be. Where and how they fit in. Where and how God fits into all this.

Research shows that part of the challenge adults face when interacting with teens stems from the important changes that occur during adolescence in terms of development of the self-concept and the development of new attachments.[21] Whereas young children are most strongly attached to their parents, the important attachments of adolescents move increasingly away from parents and increasingly towards peers. As a result, parents' influence diminishes at this stage. And, based on my personal experience, the influence of teachers often diminishes as well.

Without doubt, the main social task teens face is the search for a unique identity—the ability to answer the question, "Who am I?" In the search for identity, a teen may experience role confusion, which involves balancing or choosing among identities, taking on negative or undesirable identities, or temporarily giving up looking for an identity altogether if things are not going well.

To help them work through the process of developing their identities, these young people may well try out different identities in different social situations. They may maintain one identity at home or at school and a different persona when they are with their peers. According to Dr. Les Parrott, a professor of psychology, teens demonstrate their struggles with identity in five common ways.[22]

Through status symbols. Adolescents try to establish themselves through prestige: wearing the right clothes and having the right possessions, from iPhones to the latest Nikes available online. These symbols help form teen identities by expressing affiliation with specific groups. This can be particularly challenging for teens in a school setting that has a dress code or a uniform, as a dress code inevitably restricts a teen's ability to showcase their status symbols.

Through forbidden behaviors. Teens often feel that appearing mature will bring recognition and acceptance. They begin engaging in practices they associate with adulthood, tabooed pleasures such as smoking, drinking,

---

21. "Adolescence," n.p. All discussions of this topic, unless noted otherwise, are culled from this book chapter.

22. As cited in Bellows, "Your Teen's Search." This is not to say that all teens manifest all five. They could show signs of some or of all. Parrott's point is that these are the five common categories for classifying teen struggles.

drugs, and sexual activity. From a ritualistic perspective, these forbidden activities for Jewish teens often involve breaking with dietary laws or the laws that govern Sabbath observance.

Through rebellion. Rebellion demonstrates separation. Teens can show that they differentiate themselves from parents and authority figures while maintaining the acceptance of their peers. In a religious school setting, this rebellion against and alienation from can extend even to God.

Through idols. Celebrities may become models for teens who are looking for a way of experimenting with different roles. (And as much as we may wish to the contrary, these role models too infrequently include teachers and religious leaders.) They may identify with a known figure, trying to become like that person and, in effect, losing hold of their own identities. This identification with a well-known personality gives teens a sense of belonging.

Through cliquish exclusion. Teens often can be intolerant in their exclusion of their peers. Because they are constantly trying to define and redefine themselves in relation to others, they do not want to be associated with anyone having unacceptable or unattractive characteristics. They try to strengthen their own identities by excluding those who are not like themselves. In a Jewish day school environment, this can mean excluding classmates from certain social settings and gatherings who are perceived to be more (or less) strict in their ritual observance.

In the face of all this, the traditional approach to understanding the narrative of *Sefer BeMidbar* seems ill-suited for the typical teen. Maybe not for all, but certainly for many of those I have been teaching for the past several years. Perhaps he reads Numbers and thinks, "I've done some bad stuff, nothing as bad as any of that. No need to back off or stay away from the things I've been doing." Maybe she thinks, "I know I've done wrong, and I'm glad I wasn't caught or punished. But doesn't God care enough to notice?" Worse still, it could be that the apparent lack of consequences calls into question her very belief in God.

Fortunately for educators like me who are struggling to find ways to make the biblical narrative come alive for high school students,[23] the Torah is a rich and nuanced text. This concept is beautifully explained by midrashic metaphor. Commenting on the dedication of the tabernacle and the offerings brought by the princes of each of the twelve tribes, each of which included a silver bowl weighing 130 shekels, the midrash in Numbers Rabbah 13:15 notes that:

---

23. As I hope will become clear in subsequent chapters, the methods I will expound for teaching the book of Numbers in modern times are appropriate for people of faith of any age who look to the Bible for inspiration and life lessons.

> "**One silver basin**" was brought as a symbol of the **Torah** which has been likened to wine, as it says: "And drink of the wine which I have mingled" [Proverbs 9:5]. Now because it is customary to drink wine in a basin, you may gather from the text, "that drink wine in bowls" [Amos 6:6]—he, on that account, brought a basin. "Of seventy shekels, after the shekel of the sanctuary" [Numbers 7:13]. Why? As the numerical value of (the Hebrew word for) wine is seventy, so there are seventy modes of expounding the Torah.

Reflecting on this midrash, I sometimes think Franklin Roosevelt was a high school teacher, or at least had aspirations to be one, given that he once famously quipped: "It is common sense to take a method and try it. If it fails, admit it frankly and try another. But above all, try something." [24] Like FDR, I admit that the more traditional approaches to the book of Numbers do not seem to work. And, like FDR and the midrash, I have tried others. One which particularly appeals to me is that of Ramban.[25]

In his introduction to *Sefer BeMidbar*, Ramban summarizes its general character and significance, placing it in the context of the arrangement of all the five books of the Torah.

> After having explained the laws of the offerings in the third book, He now began to set forth in this book the commandments which they [the Jewish people] are told with reference to the Tent of Meeting. Now He had already given a warning for all times about impurity relating to the Sanctuary and its holy things. Here He defined the boundaries of the Tabernacle while it was in the wilderness, just as He had set bounds for Mount Sinai when the Divine Glory was there.... Thus, He commanded how the Tabernacle and its vessels are to be guarded and how the people are to pitch round about it and how the people are to stand afar off and how "the priests who come near the Eternal" [Exodus 19:22] are to treat the Tabernacle when it is resting and when it is being carried and how they are to guard it. Now these are all signs of distinction and honor for the Sanctuary, just as the Rabbis of blessed memory have said: "A King's palace that

---

24. Roosevelt, "Address at Oglethorpe University."

25. Ramban is an acronym for Rabbi Moses ben Nachman, who was born in Spain in 1194, but who ultimately relocated to Israel and died there in 1270. He wrote legal codes; commentary on most of the Talmud; *Iggeret HaMussar*, an ethical epistle addressed to his son; and *Iggeret HaKodesh* on the sanctity and significance of marriage. Despite this vast array of writings, it is Ramban's commentary on the Torah which showcases his true greatness.

has guards over it cannot be compared to a palace that has no such guards."

We thus see that, according to Ramban, the tabernacle, which moved in the midst of the camp, was intended to replicate the Sinai experience, during which the Torah was given to the Jewish people. In this way, Mount Sinai accompanied the nation throughout their forty-year journey through the wilderness. "The Tabernacle was a mobile Sinai in the midst of them, the heavens and heavens of heavens, transplanted and brought down to earth."[26]

The insights of Ramban on the book of Numbers are in line with his holistic approach to biblical commentary, and I find them interesting and significant. Nonetheless, I believe that high school students in the twenty-first century have problems relating to this approach for a number of reasons. First, Ramban assumes that Numbers deals largely with commandments given with regard to the tabernacle, and the Jewish people have been without the successor to the tabernacle, the holy temple, for nearly two thousand years. Hence, most of my students have no feeling for or connection to the temple, which in turn means that teaching a book of the Torah based on the perspective of Ramban has little relevance for them. Second, this lack of relevance is compounded by the fact that Numbers, as noted by Ramban, primarily deals with those commandments which were meant only for a particular time, that is, the nation's forty-year sojourn in the wilderness. With few exceptions (a few commandments that pertain to the sacrificial rituals of the tabernacle), *Sefer BeMidbar* contains no commandments that are binding for all time.

Having tried and failed, I tried again, this time turning to the writings of Rabbi Joseph B. Soloveitchik,[27] referred to as "the Rav" by his students and disciples, for an approach to *Sefer BeMidbar* that might help my students relate to the text and its rich narratives. His approach is innovative and unique in its understanding of Numbers, and when the Rav presented it for the first time as a lecture on leadership in 1974, he shared with his listeners what I find to be perhaps the most amazing aspect of the talk, that

---

26. Leibowitz, *Studies in Bamidbar*, 2.

27. Rabbi Joseph Ber Soloveitchik was a major American Orthodox rabbi, talmudist, and modern Jewish philosopher who lived from 1903 to 1993. As a rosh yeshiva of Rabbi Isaac Elchanan Theological Seminary at Yeshiva University in New York City, the Rav ordained close to two thousand rabbis over the course of almost half a century. He served as an advisor, guide, mentor, and role model for tens of thousands of Jews, both as a talmudic scholar and as a religious leader. He is regarded as a seminal figure by Modern Orthodox Judaism.

its main points had occurred to him during the Torah reading on the previous Sabbath![28]

The Rav began his talk by focusing on a single weekly Torah reading—Beha'alotechah—as opposed to all of *Sefer BeMidbar*. He did so based on his thought that this reading is one of the most difficult to understand. As he noted, it is the number of seemingly diverse topics that are discussed, not the complexity of the commandments that are presented in the reading, that makes it so difficult to understand. Yet, as he argues throughout his lecture, understanding this reading is the key to a fuller understanding of all of *Sefer BeMidbar*.

At first glance, the many topics touched upon in this Torah portion appear to be unrelated to each other, and the Rav was searching for a common thread that runs through it. The Rav explained that when God commanded Moses to take the Jewish people out of Egypt, Moses was given a double mission in accordance with God's divine plan. The first was to physically take the people out of bondage in Egypt. The second was to build the tabernacle.

Moses's first mission was essentially completed in the Torah portion of Beshalach with the drowning of the Egyptians in the sea, thus closing the chapter of their bondage to and exodus from Egypt. The Torah tells us next about the process they went through to receive the Torah at Mount Sinai. This process was also the prelude to the construction of the tabernacle. With the completion of the tabernacle, Moses's two tasks were complete, and the Jewish people were ready for the fulfillment of the promise to march straight into the land of Israel.

Using this understanding of the mission of Moses as a trigger, the Rav went on to explain the overall flow of various weekly Torah portions. The book of Exodus begins with the story of the exodus itself, followed by the giving of the Torah to the Jewish people at Mount Sinai. The construction of the tabernacle is delayed by the episode of the golden calf. Leviticus continues with the details of the sacrifices to be offered in the tabernacle, all of which are included in the overall topic of its construction.

Turning to *Sefer BeMidbar*, the Rav observed that the book begins with the command from God to organize the tabernacle and the tribes into camps (four in total, with three tribes in each camp). The beginning of the book encompasses the dedication of the tabernacle itself by the tribal princes as well as the dedication of the sacred candelabra by Moses's brother Aaron. It also includes a description of the selection of the Levites to serve as the stewards of the tabernacle. This entire process had to be complete before Moses could turn to God and say that the Jewish people had done

---

28. Etshalom, Yitzchak. "Rav Soloveitchik's Lecture."

their part and that it is now up to God to fulfill His part and bring them into the land of Israel.

The people are now ready for their march into Israel, and the Torah tells us that the ark was traveling ahead of the people to prepare for their imminent arrival at Shiloh and Jerusalem. Unfortunately, as the Rav noted, events do not unfold as Moses hope they will. Had these events come to pass, had Moses been permitted to enter the land as the leader of the Jewish people, had he overseen the construction of the holy temple, Jewish history would have unfolded differently.

Think about it, said the Rav. The Jews never would have known exile, nor would the temple have been destroyed. The calamitous episode of the people crying the entire night following the return of the spies never would have happened. There would have been no need for seven years of battle to conquer the land in the time of Joshua.

In other words, everything was on track for an easy conquest of the land. Suddenly, something happened. Neither Moses nor anybody else expected it. What happened, asked the Rav? He argued that in the story of the golden calf, we know what happened. Concerning the spies, we know what happened. About Peor in Midian, forty years later, we know what happened. What happened here, once the narrative of Numbers reaches chapter 11?

> "The riffraff in their midst felt a gluttonous craving; and then the Israelites wept and said, 'If only we had meat to eat!'" (Numbers 11:4).

For the Rav, the Torah here is telling us that this seizure by desire was evil. It aroused the wrath of the Almighty. Moses also resented it, to the point that it is described for the first time as "evil" in his eyes! The Rav went on to explain what made it evil:

> This interrupted the great march—it has brought the march to an end. The vision of the Messiah, of the Land of Israel, of the redemption of the Jewish people, became a distant one, like a distant star on a mysterious horizon. It twinkled, but the road suddenly became almost endless. Why did Moses feel discouraged? Why didn't he offer prayers for the people as was his practice in past situations? Because [this] incident differed greatly from that of the Golden Calf. The making of the Golden Calf was the result of great primitive fright. The people thought that Moses was dead; they were afraid of the desert; they did not know what the future held in store for them; they were simply overwhelmed by a feeling of loneliness and terror. There were

mitigating circumstances—they wanted the Golden Calf to substitute for Moses.[29]

Far from mere gluttonous cravings, this incident in the eyes of the Rav is tantamount to idol worship. How so? In the Rav's words:

> When you speak about idol worship, you have to distinguish between idol worship as a ceremony/ritual and between the pagan way of life. In the Sage's opinion, an idol worshipper will also adopt the pagan way of life. But in this day and age, we know that it's possible for people to live like pagans even though no idolatry is involved. Paganism is not the worship of an idol; it encompasses more—a certain style of life. What is the pagan way of life, in contradistinction to the Torah way of life? The pagan cries for variety, for boundlessness, for unlimited lust and insatiable desire, the demonic dream of total conquest, of drinking the cup of pleasure to its dregs. The pagan way of life is the very antithesis of Judaism, which demands limitedness of enjoyment and the ability to step backwards if necessary, the ability to withdraw, to retreat.[30]

Unlimited desire is, in the Rav's worldview, the worst desire in humans. When people reach out for the unreachable, for the orgiastic and hypnotic, they do not violate the prohibition of idol worship. Rather, they adopt the pagan way of life, and the Torah hates the pagan way of life more than it hates the idol. This is the case in the narrative of the gluttons who crave meat. Again, in the words of the Rav, "the Torah describes so beautifully the way in which the pagan gathers, accumulates property—gathers the quail, how he gathers property, means of gratification for his hungry senses."[31]

Throughout the story of the cravings for meat, the people were mad with desire. There was no controlling or limiting element in their desire for vastness. Their imagination excited them, and their good sense was surrounded with a nimbus which was irresistible. Said differently, the pagan is impatient and insatiable, and that is what the Torah describes in the narrative of chapter 11.

Summarizing his analysis of this particular incident, the Rav argued that people who complain and agitate and lust after food are not ready to be ushered into the land of Israel. Their behavior thus caused a delay in their entry into the land. We do not know how long this delay lasted, said the Rav, but what we do know is that this episode is followed by the story

29. Etshalom, Yitzchak. "Rav Soloveitchik's Lecture."
30. Etshalom, Yitzchak. "Rav Soloveitchik's Lecture."
31. Etshalom, Yitzchak. "Rav Soloveitchik's Lecture."

of Miriam (and the delay of seven days until she was cleansed from her *tzara'at*).[32] However, once the entry was delayed, it became delayed with the subsequent sending of spies, causing the Jews to take a painful detour in the road of their historical destiny. There is much more to the Rav's analysis of the book of Numbers as set forth in this leadership lecture, but, at its core, *Sefer BeMidbar* is in his view a story of missed opportunity.

I must confess that while I never personally learned from the Rav, my teachers did, so I consider myself to be a student of the Rav by extension. Not surprisingly, I found this lecture remarkable in its depth and analysis, and it answered many questions I had about *Sefer BeMidbar*. More importantly, it answered many of my students' questions, despite the complexity of the Rav's analysis. They could and did relate to the notion of missed opportunity.

Why, then, did this lecture not solve my teaching dilemma? The answer is simple. Studying and discussing this lecture, even in great depth, typically takes two weeks—a worthwhile and exciting endeavor, but one that still left me with thirty-four weeks of the school year to fill.

By this point, my frustration should be apparent and understandable. I am regularly tasked with teaching *Sefer BeMidbar* to high school students, and most of the approaches I was taught, that I studied and parsed through, just did not meet the needs of my students. What I needed was something that my students would find interesting, something to which they could relate and which could fill an entire academic year.

I thought long and hard about that something, and what I came up with and have used successfully in my classes is described in the next chapter.

---

32. *Tzara'at* is commonly translated as "leprosy." While it is a skin disease, it most certainly is not leprosy. In the Bible, *tzara'at* is a skin disease that can take many different forms and can manifest itself on one's clothing, belongings, and house in addition to one's skin. According to the Talmudic Sages, *tzara'at* is caused by sin, specifically, tale bearing and gossip (*lashon hara* in Hebrew). This makes it a disease like no other—part medical condition, part spiritual pathology.

Chapter 2

Sefer BeMidbar as *Sefer HaMiddot*

Before I delve into the pedagogical approach I am proposing for teaching the book of Numbers to high school students and other people of faith, a bit of background is in order. The first involves the organization of the Bible itself.

Most students of the Bible are familiar with its system of chapters and verse numbers. This division, which has been universally adopted, was first made in the Latin Bible in the thirteenth century, most likely by Stephen Langston.[1] Langston's system was consequently employed in the concordances of the Vulgate, and this in turn gave Rabbi Isaac Nathan[2] the idea for the first Hebrew concordance. In it, Rabbi Isaac cites first by the number of the Vulgate chapter, and second by the number of the Masoretic[3] verse chapter, which remains to this day the standard format of the printed Hebrew Bible.

Yet the printed format of the Hebrew Bible is not the one used for ritual purposes. As part of Jewish prayer services on the Sabbath, different portions of the Torah are read each week.[4] These readings are commonly

---

1. Stephen Langton was an English cardinal of the Roman Catholic Church and Archbishop of Canterbury between 1207 and his death in 1228. The dispute between King John of England and Pope Innocent III over his election as archbishop was a major factor in the crisis which produced the Magna Carta in 1215.

2. Rabbi Isaac Nathan ben Kalonymus was a French Jewish philosopher who lived in the fourteenth and fifteenth centuries. In the introduction to his concordance, Rabbi Isaac wrote that he was completely ignorant of the Bible until his fifteenth year. Prior to that time, his studies had been restricted to the Talmud and religious philosophy.

3. In rabbinic Judaism, the Masoretic text is the authoritative Hebrew and Aramaic text of the Bible. It was primarily copied, edited, and distributed by a group of Jews known as the Masoretes between the seventh and tenth centuries CE. The Masoretic text—the oldest extant manuscripts of which date from around the ninth century—defines the Jewish canon and its precise text, with its system of vowels and accents known as the Masorah.

4. There are fifty-four such weekly portions, which means that a double portion is

referred to as the weekly *parashah* or *sedra*. Importantly, the starting and ending points of each *parashah* have nothing at all to do with Langston's system for organizing the Bible. Rather, they reflect the long-standing Masoretic tradition.

Another key feature of each weekly Torah portion is its name, which reflects the first distinctive word in the Hebrew text of the portion in question, a word which often comes from the first verse of the *parashah*. In *Sefer BeMidbar*, many of the weekly portions are named for individuals, such as Korah, Balak, and Phinehas. As will become evident below, the focus on individuals in the weekly portions from Numbers is highly salient to the pedagogical structure set forth in this chapter.

The second important bit of background needed to understand my proposed approach for teaching *Sefer BeMidbar* involves the literary style of the book itself. Rabbi Menachem Leibtag, an internationally acclaimed biblical scholar and pioneer of Jewish education on the Internet, is well known in the Jewish community for his essays on the weekly Bible portion. In his teachings, he points out that there are two distinct literary styles in the Torah.[5] There are passages (and indeed entire books) that tell stories, be it the story of creation or that of the exodus from Egypt; such texts have a narrative style of writing. The second literary style is legalistic, and examples include the text of the Ten Commandments or those that describe the construction of the tabernacle.

Rabbi Leibtag and some of his students, including Rabbi Alex Israel,[6] explore how these genres match the biblical books. They maintain that Genesis is solely narrative, made up of stories, whereas Leviticus, with its strict, formal legal style, is the opposite extreme. But *Sefer BeMidbar* is, in Rabbi Leibtag's view, more complex. It is characterized by a mixture of stories and laws. Its central thread is clearly narrative, as seen, for example, in its telling of the historic journey of the Jewish people to Canaan. However; there are many legal sections in this book, such as those found in chapters 5–7 and in chapters 15 and 18.

Determining and deciphering the relationship between these alternate literary genres is necessary if one is to gain a coherent understanding of the purpose of the book. Rabbi Leibtag has shown in his analysis of the book of Numbers that the legal sections generally support the central story of the narrative. In essence, he argues, the legal statements serve as an illustration,

---

read on some weeks.
    5. See generally "Parshat Naso."
    6. Israel, "Book of Bamidbar."

giving shape to the story at hand, and the legal sections at times fill in gaps in the story, redressing certain balances connected with the central narrative.

Rabbi Israel offers an excellent example of this, citing the legal list of all the gifts to the priesthood in chapter 18. He asks, why is this legal passage joined to the story of Korah? "Maybe, because particularly at this moment—in the aftermath of a direct attack to the priestly position—there is a pressing need to talk about the priesthood—its privileged position, and its benefits and responsibilities. The legal review reiterates the authority of the priestly laws providing a balance to the story text."[7]

Both Rabbi Leibtag and Rabbi Israel stress that the choice of certain legal sections and the weaving of these laws into the fabric of the story line expresses a deliberate purpose. The story line is highlighted by legal sections which inevitably reinforce a particular aspect of that story.

I cite Rabbi Leibtag's analysis at length to illustrate that the notion of separating *Sefer BeMidbar* into narrative and legal sections is not something I created or thought up. Indeed, I acknowledge that Rabbi Leibtag's characterizations are an important underpinning to my teaching pedagogy for the book of Numbers. The rationale is simple. High school students generally study various forms of literary analysis in their language arts classes. For them, looking at the biblical text through a literary filter, differentiating between narratives and legal sections, will make great sense to them. However, the challenge is this: The Torah is not a novel. It is a blueprint for life, one meant to enrich and better us, as the mishnah in Pirqe Avot 6:7 makes clear:[8]

> Great is Torah, for it gives life to its doers in this world and in the next world, as it is written: "For they [the teachings of the Torah] give life to those who find them and healing to all flesh" [Proverbs 4:22]. It also says: "Healing will it be for your flesh and marrow and for your bones" [Proverbs 3:8]. It also says: "It is a tree of life to those who take hold of it, and those who support it are fortunate" [Proverbs 3:18]. And it says: "They are a graceful garland for your head and necklaces for your throat" [Proverbs 1:9]. And it says: "It will give your head a graceful garland; it will provide you a crown of glory" [Proverbs 4:9]. And it says: "For in me [the Torah] will you lengthen days, and years of life will

---

7. Israel, "Book of Bamidbar."

8. Pirqe Avot, or Chapters of the Fathers, consists of the ethical teachings and maxims passed down to the rabbis, beginning with Moses. It is unique in that it is the only tractate of the Talmud that deals solely with ethical and moral principles. There is little or no legal discussion in Pirqe Avot, nor is there any rabbinic discussion (i.e., gemara) on the text of this mishnah.

be added to you" [Proverbs 9:11]. And it says: "Length of days in its right hand; in its left are wealth and honor" [Proverbs 3:16]. And it is written: "For length of days, years of life, and peace will they [the Torah's teachings] increase for you" [Proverbs 3:2].

The Torah is not just a text to be studied. It is meant to be lived. As such, using an analysis of literary structure is neither sufficient nor appropriate. The study of Torah should not be reduced to mental gymnastics of structure and form. Students need to see the biblical text, and especially that of the book of Numbers, as relevant, as having lessons to be incorporated into their lives.

This is why I use Rabbi Leibtag's methodology, compelling as it is, simply as a springboard for a broader and deeper pedagogical approach to teaching *Sefer BeMidbar*. While it is true that the Torah does relate important episodes in the history of the Jewish people, we think of the Torah as being much more than just a history book. Nonetheless, many students see the book of Numbers as little more than an extended history lesson, and they therefore question the rationale for including it as one of the five main books of the Torah.

Viewing Genesis as a history book makes sense. It tells of the creation of the heavens and earth and the foundational stories of the Jewish people. Even the book of Exodus, which relates the departure of the Jewish people from Egypt in exacting detail, has many legal sections. This raises the question among students: what exactly is the book of Numbers, and what role does it play in the overall narrative of the Torah?

After much reflection, I came to the conclusion that teaching *Sefer BeMidbar* as *Sefer HaMiddot*, that is, as the Torah's book of character traits and character development, would be a sound approach. I will touch upon the hows of this methodology shortly, but let us first consider the whys.

As I have noted, the teen years are a time for searching, a time for reflection about the type of person these young people can and ought to be. Their parents, their teachers, and even their friends make suggestions about (or criticisms of) their behaviors. This is a good thing. Keep doing it. This is a bad thing. How could you do it? Compounding (and perhaps confusing) matters, teens see different standards of acceptable behavior in the different spheres they inhabit. What is allowed at home may not be allowed at school. What they see at the mall or the grocery store or online is certainly not what they see in their houses of worship or their religion-oriented camps and youth groups.

How can the book of Numbers provide these young people with guidance in this area? Many of the behaviors and character traits teens wrestle with are treated in great detail in Numbers. However—and this is a key point for students to grasp—this treatment is often done in an indirect manner, that is, through a variety of character traits (sometimes good and sometimes bad) that themselves are presented via the diverse personality types who dominate the narrative of Numbers, such as Caleb, Korah, Balaam, Phinehas, and even the princes and the spies.

Another important point of emphasis—and here is where I tip my hat to Rabbi Leibtag—students need to realize that this focus on prototypical personality types is not limited to the narrative sections of *Sefer BeMidbar* but carries through to the sections of the book in which God gives commandments to the Jewish people (specifically, those involving the Sotah and the Nazirite). That the book of Numbers is intensely focused on prototypical personality types should be obvious as we circle back to the background points with which I opened this chapter.

Remember that the name of each weekly Torah portion typically reflects the first distinctive word in the Hebrew text of the portion in question. And, as we have seen, many of the weekly portions in *Sefer BeMidbar* are named for individuals. I do not believe this is coincidental. Rather, I believe that these weekly readings are named for individuals precisely so that we focus on their personalities and their behaviors. In short, I believe (and hope to demonstrate in subsequent chapters) that the various personages in the book of Numbers are meant to be prototypical representations of various *middot*, or character traits. The great challenge for students as they read and ponder the book is to determine if these character traits are ones the Torah is encouraging us to emulate or to avoid.

A focus on character traits can be considered a defining element of rabbinic thought and philosophy. Consider, for example, Rambam.[9] In his monumental legal code, the *Mishneh Torah*, Rambam devotes a major section to the topic of character traits, discussing how they are acquired by the individual and how they are to be cultivated and developed.[10] Reading

---

9. Rabbi Moses ben Maimon was born in Cordoba, Spain, in 1135. He was a rabbinic authority, codifier, philosopher, and physician. He died in 1204 and was subsequently buried in Tiberius, Israel. His tomb can be visited to this day and still bears the inscription penned at the time of his passing: "From Moses to Moses, there has never arisen one such as Moses."

10. Rambam's *Mishneh Torah* is, in the view of many scholars, the greatest and most comprehensive code of Jewish law ever produced. Its stated purpose, in the words of Rambam himself, is that "a person shall not need to have recourse to any other work in the world concerning any of the laws of Israel . . . that a person shall first read the Written Law and then this work and learn from it all of the Oral Law and shall not require to read any other work." Indeed, Rambam emphasized in his introduction that his code reflects the unbroken chain of transmission stretching back to Moses at Sinai and the validity of the laws of the Babylonian Talmud as being "incumbent on all Israel."

through the first chapter of his "Laws of Character Traits," one sees that Rambam believes certain traits to be inherited and others to be acquired or adopted by the individual.

Rambam's extensive examination of proper character traits is consistent with the sages' emphasis on the character and personality of the individual, a point well summarized by Rabbi Hanina ben Dosa in Pirqe Avot 3:9: "Any person whose good deeds exceed his wisdom, his wisdom will endure; but anyone whose wisdom exceeds his good deeds, his wisdom will not endure."

This highlighting of character development is the major guiding principle of the pedagogical approach to the teaching of the book of Numbers I set forth in the chapters that follow. Yet, serious students of the Bible could well push back at this point, and with some justification, by claiming that teaching character development via a book of the Bible should be and has already been done in the book of Genesis. Rabbi Sholom Noach Berezovsky, the Slonimer Rebbe, put forward this view quite cogently in his work entitled *Netivot Sholom*.[11] In his first discourse on the book of Genesis, Rabbi Berezovsky asks, as do many biblical commentators, why the Torah, which presumably is a book of laws, begins with the creation saga.[12] He cites the most commonly cited answer of the biblical commentators, that of Rashi:

> Rabbi Isaac said: The Torah, which is the Law book of Israel, should have commenced with the verse "This month shall be unto you the first of the months" [Exodus 12:2], which is the first commandment given to Israel. What is the reason, then, that it commences with the account of the Creation? Because of the thought expressed in the text "He declared to His people the strength of His works (i.e., He gave an account of the work of Creation), in order that He might give them the heritage of the nations" [Psalm 111:6]. For should the peoples of the world say to Israel: "You are robbers, because you took by force the lands of the seven nations of Canaan," Israel may reply to them: "All the earth belongs to the Holy One, blessed be He; He created it and gave it to whom He pleased. When He willed

---

11. Rabbi Sholom Noach Berezovsky, who lived from 1911 until 2000, served as Slonimer Rebbe from 1981 until his death. His Hasidic dynasty was virtually wiped out in the Holocaust, and, as part of his effort to rejuvenate Slonimer *chasidut*, Rabbi Berezovsky was responsible for collecting the oral traditions ascribed to previous Slonimer Rebbes (who did not commit their teachings to writing).

12. This question is prompted by the fact that the first commandment given in the Torah to the Jewish people *as a people* is that of the lunar calendar, found in chapter 22 of Exodus.

He gave it to them, and when He willed He took it from them and gave it to us."[13]

Rabbi Berezovsky correctly points out that Rashi's answer explains why the creation story appears at the start of Genesis, but he does not touch on the rest of the book's narrative, leaving unanswered why we need, for example, the story of Cain and Abel, of Noah and the flood, of the tower of Babel, and of the patriarchal families. For this reason, Rabbi Berezovsky puts forward the seemingly radical idea that proper *middot*, that is, character traits, are not part of the Torah's commandments because proper character traits are a necessary prerequisite to being a God-fearing, commandment-observing individual. Basing himself on the writings of Rabbi Chaim Vital,[14] Rabbi Berezovsky explains that proper character traits are not part of the Torah's commandments but form the basis for one's acceptance or rejection of them. This is why, he maintains, Genesis includes the story of Cain and Abel, to illustrate how far one may fall into the grasp of sin if overcome by jealousy.[15] The story of Noah and the flood, he believes, shows the injurious impact unchecked lust can have.[16] And, for him, the detrimental outcomes that result from the pursuit of excessive honor and glory is the point of the story of the tower of Babel and the dispersion of its builders. [17]

And what of the stories of the patriarchs (Abraham, Isaac, and Jacob) and the matriarchs (Sarah, Rebekah, Rachel, and Leah)? Their stories are essential in the view of Rabbi Berezovsky because they teach students of the Bible "the foundations of service of the Lord." In particular, these stories demonstrate how one can and should "purify" his or her character traits,

13. See Rashi's commentary on the phrase "in the beginning" from the opening verse of Genesis.

14. Rabbi Chaim Vital, who lived from 1542 to 1620, was a rabbi in Safed, Israel, and the foremost disciple of Rabbi Isaac Luria. He recorded much of his master's teachings. After Rabbi Vital's death, his writings spread and had a powerful impact on various circles throughout the Jewish world.

15. Genesis 4:5 states "but to Cain and his offering He paid no heed. Cain was much distressed and his face fell." Sforno quickly and correctly explains the Hebrew word for "much distressed relates to "his jealousy of his brother."

16. Genesis 6:12 states that "for all flesh had corrupted its ways on earth." Rashi, in a view adopted by many subsequent commentaries, explains that lust and sexual perversion was so pervasive that "even cattle, beasts, and fowl did not consort with their own species."

17. Genesis 11:4 states: "And they said, 'Come, let us build us a city, and a tower with its top in the sky, to make a name for ourselves; else we shall be scattered all over the world.'" In his commentary on this verse, Sforno, in his commentary on this verse, explains that "they hoped that the visibility of the Tower and its symbol on top would insure that they would be most highly esteemed among people all over the world, regardless of whether such people had become part of their city-state."

an action required not only to accept the commandments of God but also to specifically fulfill the maxim set forth in Deuteronomy 6:18: "to do that which is upright and good in the eyes of the Lord." It is thus not surprising that the Babylonian Talmud Avodah Zarah 25a refers to the book of Genesis as *Sefer HaYashar*, the Book of the Upright, and to the patriarchs and matriarchs as "the Upright Ones."

Viewing Genesis as the "Book of the Upright" makes perfect sense to me, and, in truth, I have made use of this approach when teaching this text to high school student. Nevertheless, just because this pedagogical method has already been used for Genesis does not mean that it is not the best or the right approach for teaching the book of Numbers. I would further argue that Numbers provides a more nuanced framework for teaching character development to teens. Consider Korah. Without a doubt, his rebellion against the leadership of Moses is driven by jealousy. Rashi, in his comments on Numbers 16:1, describes what drives Korah's jealousy as follows:

> He envied the chieftainship of Elizaphan the son of Uzziel whom Moses appointed as chieftain over the sons of Kohath by the [Divine] word. Korah claimed, "My father and his brothers were four [in number]" as it says: "The sons of Kohath were . . . " [Exodus 6:18]. Amram was the first, and his two sons received greatness—one a king [Moses] and one a High Priest [Aaron]. Who is entitled to receive the second [position]? Is it not I, who am the son of Izhar, who is the second brother to Amram? And yet, he [Moses] appointed to the chieftainship the son of his youngest brother!

Being snubbed for a position of leadership? Nepotism? These factors do not justify Korah's rebellion, but his issues seem very real. They seem like problems teens can relate to and understand. In comparison, Cain's jealousy and reactions are over the top and hard to relate to. Killing your brother because his offering was considered better, especially after the Lord offered such strong words of encouragement in Genesis 4:6–7: "And the Lord said to Cain, 'why are you annoyed, and why has your countenance fallen? Is it not so that if you improve, it will be forgiven you?'"

Then there is Phinehas. According to Rabbi Jonathan Sacks, "with Phinehas a new type enters the world of Israel: the zealot."[18] As Rabbi Sacks

---

18. Sacks, "Pinchas." Rabbi Jonathan Sacks is a British Orthodox rabbi, philosopher, theologian, and politician. He served as the chief rabbi of the United Hebrew Congregations of the Commonwealth from 1991 to 2013 and is now known as the emeritus chief rabbi. Rabbi Sacks was knighted by Her Majesty the Queen in 2005 and made a life peer, taking his seat in the House of Lords in October 2009. Since stepping down as chief rabbi, Rabbi Sacks has served as the Ingeborg and Ira Rennert Global

points out, there can be no doubt that Phinehas is a religious hero. He stepped into the breach at a time when the nation was facing religious and moral crisis and palpable divine anger. He acted while everyone else, at best, watched, and he risked his life by so doing. Nonetheless, the written and oral Torah are deeply ambivalent vis-à-vis the actions of Phinehas. God gives him "my covenant of peace" (Numbers 25:12), meaning that he will never again have to act the part of a zealot—not surprising given that, in Judaism, the shedding of human blood is incompatible with service at the sanctuary.[19]

Zealotry is a dangerous trait that can easily spin out of control. Jewish law is very aware of this, which explains why the talmudic sages held that had Zimri turned around and killed Phinehas, he would have been deemed innocent, because he would have acted in self-defense. Yet these very same sages thought that Phinehas's act of zealotry was lawful.[20] This moral ambivalence seems very compatible with modern times and our debates about stand-your-ground laws and chants of "Black Lives Matter."

Unlike Genesis, the character traits with which the key figures in *Sefer BeMidbar* wrestle are not black and white but very gray. For many of my high school students, one person's zealot is another person's hero. These same students struggle to understand when and how the strong sense of self needed to succeed in life can morph into an unhealthy arrogance and egotism. They ask: Is accepting one's lot in life a sign of contentment or of complacency?

At core, this is why I use the notion of *Sefer BeMidbar* as *Sefer HaMiddot*, the book of proper character development, when teaching this text to high school students. When doing so, I attempt to demonstrate which character trait the any given figure in the book of Numbers embodies and whether the character trait in question is a good one (and thus to be followed) or a bad one (and thus to be avoided). In the chapters that follow, I will elaborate on this pedagogy and also include sample activities teachers adopting this approach can use to help guide their students through this reflective process.

Allow me now to share some of these activities that I have used in the past to introduce the notion of *Sefer BeMidbar* as *Sefer HaMiddot*.

Distinguished Professor of Judaic Thought at New York University and the Kressel and Ephrat Family University Professor of Jewish Thought at Yeshiva University. He has also been appointed as Professor of Law, Ethics, and the Bible at King's College London.

19. Remember that King David was forbidden to build the temple for this reason in 1 Chronicles 22:8 and 28:3.

20. It must be noted that the sages placed limits on the lawfulness of Phinehas's action. Specifically, the Babylonian Talmud Sanhedrin 82b rules that had Phinehas asked a court of law whether he was permitted to do what he was about to do, the answer would have been no. The after-the-fact endorsement of his action is thus a rare example of the rule "It is a law that is not taught."

Sample Classroom Activities—Introduction and Overview

The tone and theme of the book of Numbers is set forth in a seemingly straightforward manner in its opening verse:

וַיְדַבֵּר יְהוָה אֶל־מֹשֶׁה בְּמִדְבַּר סִינַי בְּאֹהֶל מוֹעֵד בְּאֶחָד לַחֹדֶשׁ הַשֵּׁנִי בַּשָּׁנָה הַשֵּׁנִית לְצֵאתָם מֵאֶרֶץ מִצְרַיִם לֵאמֹר:

> On the first day of the second month, in the second year following the exodus from the land of Egypt, the Lord spoke to Moses in the wilderness of Sinai, in the Tent of Meeting, saying:

But is it? Is this just a book that chronicles the wanderings of the Jewish people in the wilderness of Sinai, or is there more to it than we think?

To answer this question, we need to first find out what *you* already know about *Sefer BeMidbar* (or at least what you think you know). In the table below, briefly write down three concepts, ideas, or themes you associate with *Sefer BeMidbar*. This should take no more than three minutes.

What I Know (Or Think I Know) about Sefer BeMidbar

1. _____

2. _____

3. _____

If your list included and focused on the events that transpired during the forty years the Jewish people spent in the wilderness of Sinai, you're not alone. Many of the traditional commentaries on the Torah focus on the same sort of happenings. Consider, for example, the writings of Rabbi Ovadyah (Sforno). In his introduction to *Sefer BeMidbar*, he writes as follows:

> In this fourth book it is related how, because He [God] desired to grant kindness [to the Jewish people], He arranged their flags similar to the Divine chariot as seen in the vision of His prophets, the intent being that just as they encamped, so would they journey, thereby entering the Land immediately without need to resort to weapons... therefore [the Torah] makes mention of the merits of Israel by which they became worthy to enter the land in this manner.... He then commanded regarding the trumpets which alerted the camps to journey, to battle and for other purposes. He then led them on three journeys in the great

> and awesome wilderness until Kadesh-barnea. However, they, in the manner of imperfect mortals, transgressed His covenant and behaved treacherously in the episode of the Spies, thereby subverting their own interests. It was therefore decreed that they perish in the wilderness and that their children would go into exile for many generations at the ordained time. As a result of this sin, their children encircled the lands of the nations for forty years and did not enter the land without a struggle.[21]

The great Rabbi Moshe ben Nachman (Ramban) also viewed *Sefer BeMidbar* as a book of limited scope, meaning that he saw it as describing events and *mitzvot* (commandments) unique to the forty-year period in the wilderness of Sinai. Here is how he describes it:

> Now this whole book deals only with those commandments which were meant only for a particular time, being the period when the Israelites stayed in the desert, and it deals also with the miracles which were done for them, in order to tell all the wondrous deeds of the Eternal which He wrought for them. It tells how He began to destroy their enemies before them by the sword, and He also commanded how the Land should be divided up among them. There are no commandments in this book which are binding for all times except for some commandments about the offerings which He had begun in the Book of Priests [Leviticus, or *Sefer Vayikra*], and whose explanation was not completed there. Therefore, He finished them in this book.[22]

Did your list include any of the events or commandments mentioned by either Sforno or Ramban? If so, write them below. If not, write three events or commandments these commentators noted that you see as being very important to understanding *Sefer BeMidbar*.

Items Included in My List and Noted by Sforno and Ramban

1. _____

2. _____

3. _____

---

21. Sforno, *Commentary*, 640–41.
22. Ramban, *Commentary*, 4.

Perhaps you are wondering why the Torah had to include a whole book which seems to be a history book. While it is true that the Torah does relate important episodes in the history of the Jewish people, we think of it as being much more than just a history book. This raises the question: What exactly is *Sefer BeMidbar*, and what roles does it play in the Torah?

I want to suggest a fundamentally different way to view *Sefer BeMidbar*, one which requires a brief introduction of the concept of *middot* (Hebrew for "character traits") as described by another of our great sages, Rabbi Moshe ben Maimon, otherwise known as Rambam.

In his monumental legal code, the *Mishneh Torah*, Rambam devotes a major section to the topic of character traits, discussing how they are acquired by the individual and how they are to be cultivated and developed. As you read through the text below (either in Hebrew or in the English translation), pay close attention to the section in which Rambam suggests that certain traits are inherited and others are acquired or adopted by the individual. You may even want to underline or highlight these so that you can easily refer back to them. (You'll see why shortly.)

Excerpts from the *Mishneh Torah* by Rabbi Moshe ben Maimon

The Laws of Character Traits	הלכות דעות
Chapter One	פרק א
Halakhah One	הלכה א

There are many character traits, all of which are different and each of which is distinct, and which are possessed by different people. There are people of angry disposition, who are always annoyed, and there are those who are even-tempered and are never angry, and if they do get angry, it is only slightly and rarely. There are people who are excessively haughty, and there are people who are excessively meek. There are those with many desires, who are never satisfied with what they receive, and there are those with a very pure heart and do not desire even the simplest things that the body needs. There are those with an open heart who would not be satisfied with even all the money in the world, as it is written: "He who loves silver shall not be satisfied with silver." And there are those with a short heart for whom small amounts are enough and sufficient, and will not persevere to fulfill all their needs. Then there are those who mortify themselves with hunger and collect by hand and will not even eat from a perutah [the ancient equivalent of a penny] of their own except with great suffering, and there are those who waste all their money without thinking. Other character traits, such as profligacy, mourning before the burial of the deceased, miserliness, nobility, cruelty, mercy, cowardice, courage, et cetera, also follow this pattern [of extremes].

דעות הרבה יש לכל אחד ואחד מבני אדם וזו משונה מזו ורחוקה ממנו ביותר יש אדם שהוא בעל חמה כועס תמיד ויש אדם שדעתו מיושבת עליו ואינו כועס כלל ואם יכעס יכעס כעס מעט בכמה שנים ויש אדם שהוא גבה לב ביותר ויש שהוא שפל רוח ביותר ויש שהוא בעל תאוה לא תשבע נפשו מהלוך בתאוה ויש שהוא בעל לב טהור מאד ולא יתאוה אפילו לדברים מעטים שהגוף צריך להן ויש בעל נפש רחבה שלא תשבע נפשו מכל ממון העולם כענין שנאמר אוהב כסף לא ישבע כסף ויש מקצר נפשו ודיו אפילו דבר מעט שלא יספיק לו ולא ירדוף להשיג כל צרכו ויש שהוא מסגף עצמו ברעב וקובץ על ידו ואינו אוכל פרוטה משלו אלא בצער גדול ויש שהוא מאבד כל ממונו בידו לדעתו ועל דרכים אלו שאר כל הדעות כגון מהולל ואונן וכילי ושוע ואכזרי ורחמן ורך לבב ואמיץ לב וכיוצא בהן:

Halakhah Two   הלכה ב

Between the extremes of each temperament are the intermediate character traits, each of which is also distinct. Of the character traits, there are those which one has from the moment of one's creation [and] according to the one's nature, and there are those character traits which direct one's nature and which one will quickly acquire in magnitudes greater than that of the other character traits. Then there are those character traits which one does not have from the moment of one's creation, but which one learns from others or which release themselves upon one depending upon one's thoughts or which one heard is a good temperament to have and which is fitting to follow and accustom oneself to until it becomes fixed in one's behavior.

ויש בין כל דעה ודעה הרחוקה ממנה בקצה האחר דעות בינוניות זו רחוקה מזו וכל הדעות יש מהן דעות שהן לאדם מתחלת ברייתו לפי טבע גופו ויש מהן דעות שטבעו של אדם זה מכוון ועתיד לקבל אותם במהרה יותר משאר הדעות ויש מהן שאינן לאדם מתחלת ברייתו אלא למד אותם מאחרים או שנפנה להן מעצמו לפי מחשבה שעלתה בלבו או ששמע שזו הדעה טובה לו ובה ראוי לילך והנהיג עצמו בה עד שנקבעה בלבו:

Now it's time for a group activity. Pick two of your classmates to work with. You will have ten minutes to brainstorm a list of character traits (either good or bad) that the three of you believe to be either inherited or acquired. (Remember how we told you to highlight in the text of Rambam where he discusses this point?) Each of you should write your list in the space provided below. Be sure to mark each character trait with either a "G" (for good) or a "B" (for bad).

Inherited Character Traits   *Acquired Character Traits*

_____   _____

_____   _____

_____   _____

_____   _____

_____   _____

Finished? Not quite. You and your partners should review your list once more, this time trying to group similar traits together. For instance, if your list included "lacking patience" and "quick to anger," you might consider grouping these together, as they are very closely related to each other. Take another five minutes or so for this and do try to come up with at least two groupings. Once you're done, you'll share your lists and groupings with the rest of the class.

Group 1 Character Traits

_____

_____

_____

_____

_____

Group 2 Character Traits

_____

_____

_____

_____

_____

Group 3 Character Traits

_____

_____

_____

_____

_____

Group 4 Character Traits

_____

_____

_____

_____

_____

You should know that many of the character traits you and your classmates listed are treated in great detail in *Sefer BeMidbar*. However, this is often done in an indirect manner—that is, these various character traits (again, sometimes good and sometimes bad) are presented via the diverse personality types in *Sefer BeMidbar*. These include Caleb, Korah, Balaam, Phinehas, and even the princes and the spies.

You should also know that this focus on personality types is not limited to the narrative sections (that is, the stories) of *Sefer BeMidbar* but carries through to the sections of the book in which God gives commandments to the Jewish people (e.g., the Sotah and the Nazirite).

Lastly, you should be aware that we, too, will emphasize this focus on character traits throughout our studies of *Sefer BeMidbar*, and, for this reason, we will refer to it as the Torah's *Sefer Middot*, or "book of Middot."

Our focus on *middot* as part of our studies of *Sefer BeMidbar* is very consistent with rabbinic tradition. Our sages have always understood the character and personality of the individual to be of the utmost importance. This is best summarized by Rabbi Hanina ben Dosa in Pirqe Avot (3:9) as follows and will be a major guiding principle for all we do in the course of our studies:

;הוּא הָיָה אוֹמֵר: כָּל שֶׁמַּעֲשָׂיו מְרֻבִּין מֵחָכְמָתוֹ חָכְמָתוֹ מִתְקַיֶּמֶת

וְכָל שֶׁחָכְמָתוֹ מְרֻבָּה מִמַּעֲשָׂיו אֵין חָכְמָתוֹ מִתְקַיֶּמֶת

Any person whose good deeds exceed his wisdom, his wisdom will endure;

but anyone whose wisdom exceeds his good deeds, his wisdom will not endure.

There is one final activity you will need to do for us to complete this introduction and overview to *Sefer BeMidbar*, or, as we are calling it, *Sefer Middot*.

Select one of the character traits from the list you compiled that compared inherited and acquired character traits. Specifically, select one which you think you possess. Now write two to three paragraphs in the space provided below explaining why you believe that you either were born with this trait or acquired it. This, too, will be shared with your classmates (unless you prefer otherwise).

The Character Trait I Acquired or Was Born With

_____

_____

_____

_____

Part Two

The Narrative of *Sefer BeMidbar*

Chapter 3

The Census

Having proposed a pedagogy that focuses on key figures in the book of Numbers as prototypes of various character traits, it is more than a bit ironic that I begin not with an individual but with an event—the census that opens the book and gives it its English name—that involves the entire Jewish people. However, there is a sound rationale for this. If students are to spend a year studying *Sefer BeMidbar* and reflecting on the various character traits portrayed therein, it seems reasonable to begin with a few basic questions: Is there such a thing as national character traits? Is it appropriate to consider such things, or are such discussions inherently prejudiced? Has the Torah, up to this point, given us any indications about the national character traits of the Jewish people?

Let us start with the first of these questions, that concerning national character traits. While at the National Institute on Aging, Antonio Terracciano and Robert R. McCrae conducted an extensive study that examined perceptions of the "typical American" from forty-nine cultures around the world.[1] Prior to examining the particularities of the typical American, Terracciano and McCrae pointed out that national character stereotypes are often dismissed as simple expressions of ethnocentric biases. They note that this is an old idea: Herodotus claimed that the Persians "look upon themselves as very greatly superior in all respects to the rest of mankind."[2] A simple and plausible theory of the origin of national stereotypes would hold that people everywhere attribute good qualities to themselves and perhaps to their allies, and hold negative evaluations of the citizens of competing or hostile nations. That this is true up to our time should surprise no one.

However, in considering how a particular people is viewed (by itself and by others), one must take into account the effect of significant historical events to see if world perceptions of a people are shaped by the actions

1. Terracciano and McCrae, "Perceptions."
2. Herodotus, *On The Customs of the Persians*.

of its government. Government policies, either foreign or domestic, might well be construed as an expression of national character. Consider these two examples. Terracciano and McCrae stated that there is some evidence that America's aid to postwar Europe through the Marshall Plan might have led Europeans to believe that Americans are a generous and compassionate people.[3] In contrast, the time period in which national character data were collected for the Personality Profiles of Cultures Project encompassed the American-led invasion of Iraq, an act to which world opinion responded strongly. Did the invasion reshape perceptions of American national character? Without doubt.

Terracciano and McCrae therefore concluded that answers to questions about a nation's profile or character traits would require valid measures of national character, that is, measures that accurately reflect perceptions of the traits typical of a country's citizens (even if those perceptions are themselves wholly illusory). This they did by assessing the American national character via a comprehensive Five-Factor Model (FFM) of personality. The FFM is a widely accepted hierarchical model with higher-order factors generally called Neuroticism, Extraversion, Openness, Agreeableness, and Conscientiousness. Using the FFM, these researchers discussed and documented key character traits associated with Americans: assertive, open minded, but antagonistic. In other words, they set forth what we might call an "American profile."

The idea of a national profile is not limited to America. In a piece a few years back, Fraser McAlpine, the lead writer for BBC America's blog for American Anglophiles, discussed five widely generalized characteristics of the British as a people that are, in his view, also broadly true.[4] These include "a rapier wit," the British reserve, and an obsession with class.

The Germans, too, are frequently thought of as having a national character.[5] Mention German, and certain phrases and adjectives quickly come to mind: direct, lover of rules and structure, punctual.

Now that we have reached the twenty-first century, and China has increased its reach and influence in the world, discussions of a Chinese profile have become more prominent and even the subject of academic studies. In one, "A Comparative Look at Chinese and American Stereotypes" by Lin

---

3. This article is summarized and included as a supplemental reading for this unit entitled "National Character Traits?" It follows the sample unit plan for this topic.

4. McAlpine, "Lost in Translation."

5. Schäferhoff, "9 German Stereotypes."

Zhu of the University of Massachusetts–Boston, Chinese individuals were said to be family oriented and collectivistic.[6]

It may seem that this focus on national stereotypes and character traits is a modern phenomenon, but it is not. God Himself understood that the Jewish people had certain common traits, most notably that they are "a stiff-necked people" (Exodus 32:9).[7]

Whether one believes that the social conditions under which people live tend to explain differences in behavior or one prefers to think that character traits are hereditary, the Jewish personality that has emerged since their forty-year experience in the wilderness has varied with time and culture. "While it is true that common elements may be found in the social position of all Jews since the Diaspora, these are insufficient to condition a universal Jewish prototype."[8] Anyone familiar with Jews in the world today would agree, for example, that the Yemenite Jew, the Israeli Jewish farmer, the Jew living in the former Soviet Union, and American Jews are essentially dissimilar.[9]

Wherever one comes out in this debate, a discussion about national character traits and whether there is such a thing a Jewish profile strikes me as a very appropriate way to begin teaching the book of Numbers. It should encourage students to reflect on what it means to be a Jew and how being a Jew has impacted and continues to impact who they are as individuals.

Before setting forth a sample unit plan on the census, a few words on methodology are in order. Over the years, I have found that framing a unit's objectives via a series of essential questions is most helpful. These questions help focus the students on the main points of the unit and also provide an opening for selecting and teaching classical commentaries on the text being studied. Here, then, are the essential questions I use in conjunction with the census. But know that, in the end, it is the students who shape the answers.

1. Is it even possible to talk about national character traits? Are such discussions inherently prejudiced?

6. Zhu, "A Comparative Look."

7. Various translation render the phrase "stiff-necked" as "stubborn and rebellious" and as "obstinate." Regardless of the translation, the sense is the same.

8. Orlansky, "Study of Man."

9. While it may be true that Jews around the world are dissimilar, Israelis are often seen as outspoken to the extent of being rude, loud, curt, and disdainful of rules. Their personality traits have been the subject of many parodies, and I believe the most humorous is the opening beach sequence in Adam Sandler's "You Don't Mess with the Zohan."

2. Has the Torah, up to this point, given us any indications about the national character traits of the Jewish people?
3. If the goal of the exodus from Egypt was to create a nation, why is the encampment still done by tribes?
4. Why does the tribe of Levi deserve (or need) a special status?

Once I introduce and contextualize the text via these essential questions, students read the text itself—for this unit, the first two chapters of the book of Numbers. In an ideal world, students are reading the text in the original Hebrew. This avoids the interpretations and spins that are present in every translation and thus enables students to unpack the text on their own. In doing so, they should strive to identify problematic words and phrases, what I call "red flag" verses that cry out for explanation and commentary.

Let me be clear. I well understand the challenges posed by learning the Bible in the original Hebrew. I am the product of a public high school and an Ivy League college (Dartmouth), neither of which offered Hebrew as one of its foreign language classes. Instead of Hebrew, I studied French in high school for four years and went on to major in French literature in college. I only learned Hebrew at the age of twenty-four after working on a kibbutz in Israel and attending a Hebrew language immersion program there.

I share all this because I did struggle with Hebrew when first studying biblical texts. To this day, I have students who struggle with Hebrew texts and have to rely on bilingual editions of the Torah. Yet, despite their linguistic struggles, my students do learn *Sefer BeMidbar* as *Sefer HaMiddot*, and they do have a deeper understanding of and affinity for the text because of this approach.

Sefer BeMidbar—The Census
Sample Unit Plan

Unit	Primary Source(s)	Supplemental Reading(s)	Timeframe
Census/ Encampment	Numbers 1	Nature vs. Nurture	three weeks
	Rashi 1:1		
Middah:	Rashi 1:2	Yeshivat Har	
National character trait?	Sforno 1:18	Etzion readings	
	Rashi 1:49	Not Just Numbers	
	Numbers 2	The Status of the	
	Rashi 2:2	Tribe of Levi	
	Kli Yakar 2:2		
	Rashi 2:3		
	Rashi 2:17		
	Hirsch 2:34		

Essential Question(s)

1. Is it even possible to talk about national character traits? Are such discussions inherently prejudiced?
2. Has the Torah, up to this point, given us any indications about the national character traits of the Jewish people?

3. If the goal of the exodus from Egypt was to create a nation, why is the encampment still done by tribes?
4. Why does the tribe of Levi deserve (or need) a special status?

Evaluating/Checking for Understanding

1. Daily discussions/student interactions

   Student questions and observations typically drive each day's discussion.

2. Occasional written reflections

   At the discretion of the teacher, a tool to foster further reflection on the unit's essential questions.

3. Character trait essay

   See appendix for assignment rubric.

4. Unit test

   Unit tests should, by definition, be crafted by individual teachers to meet the needs of their specific students. The Understanding by Design *framework created by Grant Wiggins and Jay McTighe is an excellent tool for the development of appropriate tests and assessments, as its emphasis on backward design forces teachers to consider in advance the assessment evidence needed to document and validate that the targeted learning goals have been achieved.*

Primary Source Texts

1. *BeMidbar* chapter 1: Read text and seek to identify problematic (what I will call "red flag") words and phrases (with teacher's guidance, of course). These red flag words and phrases will likely vary from class to class depending on the sophistication and linguistic abilities of the students, coupled with the background and interests of the teacher.

2. Consider the unit's essential questions (especially the first two) and how they are to be understood/explained in light of commentaries A–D.

3. Read/discuss the selected readings from the teachers at Yeshivat Har Etzion that follow in the Supplemental Readings section and tie these readings into a consideration of the possibility of national character traits—that is, does it even make sense to argue that they do exist and if they do, how do we define them?

4. *BeMidbar* chapter 2: Read text and seek to identify problematic (what I will call "red flag") words and phrases (with teacher's guidance, of course). These red flag words and phrases will likely vary from class to class depending on the sophistication and linguistic abilities of the students, coupled with the background and interests of the teacher.

5. Consider the unit's essential questions (especially the last two) and how they are to be understood/explained in light of commentaries E–I.

6. Supplemental readings for each unit are intended to demonstrate that serious scholarship about and explanations of *Sefer BeMidbar* are not limited to the classical medieval commentators but continue to our time. The supplemental readings for this portion of this unit include "Not Just Numbers," which discusses the importance of tribal units and why they were preserved, and "The Status of the Tribe of Levi," which focuses on the importance of complementary character traits.

Sefer BeMidbar—The Census

Primary Sources

A. Rashi 1:1

> "And [God] spoke [to Moses] in the desert of Sinai . . .
> on the first day of the [second] month"

Because they were dear to him, He counts them every now and then: when they went forth from Egypt He counted them (Exodus 12:37), when many of them fell in consequence of their having worshipped the Golden Calf. He counted them to ascertain the number of those left (cf. Rashi Exodus 30:16); when he was about to make His Shechinah dwell amongst them (i.e., when He commanded them to make a Tabernacle), He again took their census; for on the first day of Nisan the Tabernacle was erected (Exodus 40:2) and shortly afterwards, on the first day of Iyar, He counted them.

B. Rashi 1:2

> "By the house of their fathers"

One whose father belongs to one tribe and his mother to another tribe shall take his stand with the tribe of his father (cf. Bava Batra 109b).

C. Rashi 1:18

> "They declared their pedigrees after their families"

They brought the records of their pedigree and witnesses to confirm the prevalent presumption regarding their parentage, so that each might establish his pedigree with regard to the particular tribe (cf. Yalkut Shimoni on Torah 684).

D. Sforno 1:18

"They convoked the whole community"

Seeing the purpose of the count was to know who would have to join the ranks of those going to war, it was important to have genealogically pure men, not any who were the product of forbidden unions. Knowledge that they were the children of unblemished parentage would protect them when exposed to the dangers present in any war and battle. We find a similar thought expressed in Kidushin 76 that "the credentials of people recorded in the king's register need not be investigated any further." We also find the statement (on folio 70 of the Talmud there) that God's presence does not rest protectively except over genetically "pure" families.

E. Rashi 2:2

"Every man of the children of Israel shall encamp by his own standard with the signs"

Each banner shall have a different sign—a piece of colored cloth hanging on it, the color of the one not being the same as the color of another, but the color of each tribe shall be like that of his stone that is fixed in the breastplate (cf. Exodus 28:21), and by this means everybody will be able to recognize his banner. Another explanation is: by the signs which their father Jacob gave them severally when they carried him out from Egypt, as it is said (Genesis 50:12), "And his sons did unto him exactly as he had commanded them." For he had commanded that Judah, Issachar and Zebulun should carry him, having their position at the east side of the bier, Reuben, Simeon and Gad at the south side, etc.,—as it is related in Tanchuma on this section. (Midrash Tanhuma, Numbers 12; cf. Rashi on Genesis 50:12)

F. Kli Yakar 2:2

"Each with his standard, under the banner of his ancestral home"

The following background information will help students better understand the thrust of the Kli Yakar's commentary. It is important that each camp consisted of three tribes, and each camp had its own unique banner. The first banner was led by Judah, who represented wisdom or Torah. Judah was the *Nasi* (head of the central judiciary) and *Reish Galusa* (head of the exile community) who set the policies of the Torah. Issachar learned Torah, and Zebulun supported him, making Zebulun an equal contributor to the acquisition of Torah wisdom. They camped in the east where the sun rays first emanate in the morning, to symbolize that Torah also goes out from the east, from Zion. The second banner was that of Reuben, who represented modesty. He was not embarrassed to admit his mistake and do repentance for moving Jacob's bed. Along with him is Simeon, a tribe comprised of teachers, scribes, and poor people. This latter group is usually more modest than all others. Gad led the battles in the land of Israel even though his territorial inheritance was to the east of the Jordan River. He led not out of haughtiness but out of humility. They camped in the south, or *darom* in Hebrew, which is interpreted as *dar rom*, living on high since God lifts up all those who lower themselves. The third banner was that of Ephraim, who was joined by Manasseh and Benjamin. Collectively, these three tribes represent strength, as the verse in Psalms (80:3) says: "Before Ephraim, Benjamin, and Manasseh arouse Your might, and it is for You to save us." They camped in the west where the sun sets, since strength wanes with time. The last banner was that of Dan, who represented wealth. In fact, the members of this tribe were so wealthy that their abundance of gold led them to worship idols. Asher was wealthy as well, and so was Naphtali. The attribute of wealth, as portrayed in the commentary of Kli Yakar, was the least important of the tribes' character traits, so the banner of Dan traveled last. Below are translations of key parts of a long commentary.

We find in several midrashim the topic of the banners discussed at length and explained in the context of the verse from Psalm 20:6: "May we shout for joy in your victory, arrayed by standards in the name of our God." For at the time of the giving of the Torah the Jewish people saw the angels with their banners and greatly desired to have banners like they had. And in regard to the verse in the Song of Songs 6:10—"Who is she that shines through like the dawn, Beautiful as the moon, Radiant as the sun Awesome as bannered hosts?"—the midrash says that the nations of the world looked upon the greatness of the Jewish people with wonder, and they said: "Turn back, turn back, O maid of Shulem!" (Song of Songs 7:1).

The crux of the desire of the Jewish people was to show to all the nations that God's name was upon them and as such they (the nations of the world) would fear them. And for this reason, they raised their banners, victorious, in the four directions of the world so as to demonstrate that they (the Jewish people) were surrounded on all sides by God's presence. And the ark was in the center and all (that is, the respective camps) were turned towards it.[1]

---

1. Translation mine.

G. Rashi 2:3

"In front"

Which is expressed by קדם; and which side is it? The east side (מזרחה), and accordingly the west is termed אחור, the back side of the world.

H. Rashi 2:17

"And the tent of meeting shall set forward"

After these two divisions (those of Judah and Reuben), as is shown by the position of this statement in the narrative.

"As they encamp so shall they journey"

Just as I have explained (v. 9): their positions when marching shall be the same as when encamping—each division marches on that side that is assigned to it.

I. Rabbi Samson Raphael Hirsch 2:34

"The Children of Israel did"

If we picture to ourselves the grouping of the Jewish people according to camps as directed in these verses, we will see, in the front, to the east, under the standard of Judah, the tribes of Judah, Issachar, and Zebulun. To the right, in the south, under the standard of Reuben, are the tribes of Reuben, Simeon, and Gad. To the left, in the north, under the standard of Dan, are the tribes of Dan, Asher, and Naphtali. In the rear, opposite Judah, under the standard of Ephraim, are the tribes of Ephraim, Manasseh, and Benjamin.

Each of the three tribes of the camp of Judah was noted for two qualities. Already the patriarch Jacob, on his deathbed (Genesis 49:8–10), visualized Judah as the leader striding at the head, with a ruler's scepter and a lawmaker's stylus. Issachar was the tribe of agriculture, with sufficient leisure also to engage in learning (ibid., 49:14–15). Zebulun (ibid., 49:13) was the tribe of commerce; at the same time according to the Song of Deborah (Judges 5:14), his sons produced literature. Thus, the camp of Judah, which traveled in the lead, united all the basic elements on which the material and spiritual welfare of the nation depends: the scepter and the law, agriculture and scholarship, commerce, and literature.

These two factors, the spiritual, and the material, united in leading camp, are divided into two subordinate camps, which follow the leading camp on either side.

Reuben, Simeon, and Gad comprise Judah's right hand, as it were. Reuben is endowed with all the intellectual gifts and with a keen sense of justice, but the softness of his character makes him unfit for national leadership. Assigned to flank him are Simeon, the impetuous avenger of honor, and Gad, the avenger of unprovoked attacks (see Genesis 49:3–7 and 19). These, then, are the attributes represented by the tribes on Judah's right: the courage to fend off insults and attacks, but all under the aegis of gentle mercy.

Marching at Judah's left were Dan, the tribe of adroit cunning (ibid., 49:16–17); Asher, representing refinement of taste (ibid., 49:20); and Naphtali (Genesis 49:21), representing eloquence. Thus, on the left side, under the aegis of Dan, there was rich side, under the aegis of Reuben, there was development in the direction of strength and force.

The tribes camped to the west, under the standard of Ephraim, opposite the camp of Judah in the east, were Ephraim, Manasseh, and Benjamin. Their national significance is not characterized as clearly as that of the other tribes. Actually, Ephraim and Manasseh together represent the tribe of Joseph. But what Jacob said on his deathbed with regard to Joseph (ibid., 49:22ff.) refers to Joseph personally, more than to the tribe. What Jacob said (ibid., 48:19) about Ephraim and Manasseh indicates an unfolding of power; particularly of Ephraim, Jacob said that he would become very great and that his descendants would become the "armor" reinforcing the defenses of the other tribes.

Thus, in the camp of Ephraim we should look for strength and courage, which, for the national well-being, were positioned facing the camp of Judah in the lead. Judah was in the east and Ephraim in the west. Thus, too, the Song of Asaph (Psalm 80:2–3) sees Israel's salvation as depending on the achievements of Joseph.[2]

---

2. Hirsch, *Pentateuch*, 21–22.

Sefer BeMidbar—The Census

Supplemental Reading

Excerpt from "The Nation and the *Shekhina* in the Wilderness"

—Rabbanit Sharon Rimon

Connection between the Nation and the *Shekhina*

Let us now look at some of the subjects that appear in *Sefer BeMidbar* and see how the sefer describes the connection between the nation and the *Shekhina*. *Sefer BeMidbar* (1:2–3) opens with the census:

> Take a count of all of the congregation of the Israelites by their families, by their fathers' houses, according to the number of names; every male by their tally. From twenty years old and upward, all who go out to war in Israel—you and Aaron shall count them by their hosts.

What is the purpose of this census? This is not a mere recording of the total number of people eligible for combat; rather, it is a count of the people "by their families, by their fathers' houses, according to the number of names; every male by their tally." This verse is repeated no less than fourteen times in chapter 1. The repetition serves to emphasize that the purpose of the census is not just to know what the total population is. Every person is counted by name, then by his father's house, then the family to which the father's house belongs, and finally—which tribe they are part of.

In other words, the census is not counting the total population, nor even the number comprising each tribe. The purpose of the census is to record the lineage of each person, in order to organize them by tribe. *Sefer*

BeMidbar, describing the nation that journeys with the *Shekhina* in its midst, starts off with a census detailing all of the people. The emphasis is on a nation that is made up of its constituent individuals.

Following this census, which groups the people by their tribes, comes the next stage, described in chapter 2 (v. 2):

> Each person among the Israelites shall encamp by his flag, with the signs of the house of their fathers; they shall encamp at a distance around the Tent of Meeting.

Once every person has been traced to his family and his tribe, the nation can be ordered by tribes, and the camp as a whole can take shape. The purpose of the census in chapter 1, aside from military and administrative needs, is to register the tribes, and chapter 2 describes the location of each tribe once the entire camp is arranged around the *Mishkan*. The arrangement of the Camp of Israel is not an arbitrary matter, but rather a reflection of sanctity: the *Mishkan* is located at the center of the camp, at the center of the life of the tribes, with each tribe situated at an equal distance from the *Mishkan*.

Each camp (i.e., each group of three tribes, located on one of the sides of the *Mishkan*) has a flag with a drawing symbolizing its tribes. According to the Midrash,[1] these were the four images of the *Merkava* (Chariot) in Ezekiel's vision (1:10): a lion, a man, an ox and an eagle. The camp of Israel is arranged into four forces, corresponding to the four creatures comprising the Chariot of the *Shekhina*.

What is the significance of this symbolism? The Camp of Israel represents a chariot for the *Shekhina*. When God's Presence is in the heavens, the cherubim and other spiritual bodies serve as His chariot. When His *Shekhina* is on earth, God's throne, as it were, is the cherubim of the *Mishkan*, and the entire camp of Israel is His chariot.[2]

If the entire Camp of Israel is a chariot for the *Shekhina*, then the conduct of this camp is of acute importance. There is significance to the actions of the people and to their spiritual level. *Sefer BeMidbar* describes first the arrangement of the camp and then its conduct.

Chronologically speaking, chapters 7–9 come before the census. Why, then, does the sefer open with the census and the ordering of the camp? Perhaps because of the principle we have explained here: the census describes the nation, which stands at the center of *Sefer BeMidbar*, while the arrangement of the camp testifies to the manner of the journey through the

---

1. *BeMidbar Rabba* 2; *Pesikta Zutreta BeMidbar* 81b; Ibn Ezra on *BeMidbar* 2:2.
2. For a detailed discussion of this, see Grossman, "'How Good Are Your Tents?'"

wilderness. The *Mishkan* is the heart of the camp, and the camp as a whole is the chariot of the *Shekhina*.

Sefer BeMidbar uniquely combines the description of the nation's humanity with the great ideal of the *Mishkan* and *Shekhina*. The Israelite camp in the wilderness is a human camp with God dwelling in its midst, and the *sefer* opens with a description of this special nexus.[3]

Rabbanit Sharon Rimon is a freelance teacher and author of Torah. She has an MA in Tanach from MaTaN and the University of Baltimore and earned her BA from Michlalah. Rabbanit Rimon teaches at the Efrat Women's Beit Midrash and has taught mother-daughter Bat Mitzvah classes. She is also the author of a series of online Torah *shiurim* for the Virtual Beit Midrash of Yeshivat Har Etzion. Rabbanit Rimon and her husband live in Alon Shvut with their daughters.

---

3. For the sake of brevity we have not discussed chapters 3–4, concerning the Levites, nor chapters 5–6, which present a series of commandments. These chapters, too, give expression to the connection between the nation and the *Mishkan*, with the *Shekhina* in its midst. The Levites are the Israelites' representatives in the *Mishkan* service, and the commandments set forth in chapters 5–6 are laws that clearly reflect the mutual interaction of the camp and the *Mishkan*, with the *kohanim*, at its center.

Sefer BeMidbar—The Census

Supplemental Reading

Excerpt from "Not Just Numbers"

—Rav Yair Kahn

Harmony vs. Uniformity

At this point, we should note the composition of *machane Yisrael*. It is interesting that the tribal units were retained, not only at this stage, but even later when the Israelites enter Canaan. Indeed, we find the division into tribal units in Ezekiel's prophesy of the future *Mikdash* (chapters 47–48). Theoretically, one could have imagined that at this juncture, the tribal system should be abolished and replaced, as the Israelites form a national entity. Instead, we find that the nation is actually comprised of those tribal units. This point is instructive insofar as it describes the nature of the nation being formed. The *machane* is not developed at the expense of the individual tribes. There is no evidence of a nation-wide melting pot creating a homogeneous entity, which suppresses any expression of non-conformity. The Israelites form a harmonious society, not a uniform one. Each of the tribes is encouraged to express its singular qualities and unique characteristics. They are nurtured and woven together in perfect balance to form a magnificent multi-colored garment. Indeed, our Sages viewed the number twelve as expressing the completeness and perfectness formed by the sons of Jacob. (See our *shiur* on Parashat Vayeshev.)

The tribal unit was not the only institution that was preserved. We find that each individual was recorded according to his family and paternal household. These subdivisions are additional support for our thesis that the *machane* was intended as a harmonious entity based on the pre-existing social structure, not as a melting pot.

Furthermore, the Torah stresses that every person was counted *le-gulgilotam*, by his head—that is, as an individual. In other words, the singular characteristics exclusive to each individual are not to be suppressed and destroyed, but protected and only then integrated into the national whole. The ideal of *machane Yisrael* rejects both individualism, in which the particular denies his communal obligations and responsibilities, as well as uniformity, which forces the individual to conform and thereby deadens his singular characteristics and qualities.

The sum total of individuals that form the holy nation of Israel is *shishim ribo*—600,000. This number mysteriously repeats itself. The Israelites number approximately 600,000 when they leave Egypt. A year later, this number appears again at the beginning of our *parasha*. When the people are counted for the final time in the Torah, at the end of the forty years in the wilderness, once again the number settles around 600,000. Our Sages considered *shishim ribo* as the sum total of distinct individual personalities.

> One who sees masses of Israel [Rashi—a great host of 600,000) says: "Blessed the wise one of secrets." (Berakhot 58a)

Ramban is more explicit.

> Our Sages received a tradition that only 600,000 faces were created, and this number includes all personalities. Therefore, the Torah was given to this number. They said that the Torah needed to be given to be acceptable to all personalities, and since the Creator knows the personality of all creatures and creates the minds of all, therefore we make this blessing. (*Torat Hashem Temima*).

Based on the above, we can further clarify the significance of the *pekudim* that open and set the tone of *Sefer BeMidbar*.

> Take a census ("raise the heads") of the whole Israelite community by their families and ancestral houses, listing the names, every male, head by head. (Numbers 1:2)

The head of each individual is "raised" as he is counted and awarded his specific role within the *machane*. Unique characteristics are not suppressed, but recognized and utilized in the formation of the nation. Conformity, which celebrates the lowest common denominator, is rejected in favor of harmony, which delicately combines the genius found in specific individuals who combine to form the community.

Rav Yair Kahn (YHE '77), head of the Overseas Students Program, has been a Ram at Yeshivat Har Etzion since 1987. He teaches an Israeli *shiur*, one into which the overseas students integrate comfortably. Rav Kahn has been the coordinator of the Virtual Beit Midrash Gemara Iyun Shiur for several years. Originally from New York, Rav Kahn studied at Chaim Berlin, Yeshiva University, and Yeshivat Har Etzion. Rav Kahn is also the editor of the *Shiurei Hagrid* series published by the Toras Horav Foundation and Mossad Harav Kook.

Sefer BeMidbar—The Census

Supplemental Reading

The Status of the Tribe of Levi

—Rav Amnon Bazak

I. Why Are the Levites Not Counted amongst the Israelites?

[The Book of Numbers] begins with a description of the census taken throughout the tribes of Israel. God commands Moses and Aaron to count all the men eligible to serve in the army, aged 20 and up. Twelve princes, "a man of each tribe," are named to assist in conducting the census (1:4–16). This list of princes omits any representative of the tribe of Levi, and it therefore comes as no surprise that the census does not include the tribe of Levi,[1] as indeed we are told explicitly at the conclusion:

> But the Levites, by the tribe of their fathers, were not counted among them. (1:47)

This is followed, right at the end of the chapter, by a surprising command:

> God spoke to Moses saying: "Only the tribe of Levi you shall not count, nor shall you number them among the Israelites. (1:48–49)

Immediately thereafter, in chapter 2, the text describes the camp of Israel, and at its conclusion, the same message is emphasized once again:

---

1. To preserve a count of twelve tribes, Ephraim and Menashe are counted as two separate tribes.

> But the Levites were not counted amongst the Israelites, as God had commanded Moses. (2:32)

The reason for this verse's appearance here is understandable: since God had commanded not to count the Levites, it makes sense for the text to note that this command had been fulfilled. The verses at the end of chapter 1, however, are puzzling from two angles: on the one hand, why is the command not to count the Levites recorded after the census rather than prior to it, which would seem to make more sense? On the other hand, if Moses and Aaron understood on their own that the Levites should not be counted because no prince of the tribe had been appointed to count them, then why is there any need for an explicit command—since they had already been left out of the census in any case?

Ramban notes this problem and explains that Moses had indeed understood on his own that the Levites should not be counted, since no prince of the tribe had been appointed for this purpose, but he remained "in doubt concerning the Levites, and did not know what to do in their regard." Therefore, when the census was complete, "God stipulated that he should not count them amongst the Israelites, but should count them separately." However, this answer fails to answer the question: if Moses understood, correctly, that the Levites should not be counted as part of the census, then what is the meaning of his "doubt concerning the Levites"? Why was another command required, stating that they were not to be counted along with the other tribes?

It seems that the answer to our question lies in a different direction. Chapters 1 and 2 would appear to express two different reasons for the non-inclusion of the tribe of Levi in the census. In chapter 1, the emphasis is on counting "all in Israel who are able to go forth to war" (1:3).[2] For this reason, the names of the Princes of the tribes are noted—with the exception of the prince of the tribe of Levi. From the perspective of this chapter, there was no need to count the Levites because they were not eligible to go out to war, while the whole point of this census was to determine the size of the fighting forces prior to the planned entry into the land. Since the issue here is essentially a technical matter, there is no need for a special command not to count the Levites—and had they been counted, this would not have transgressed any prohibition; at most, it would have been a pointless

---

2. For this reason, the text notes explicitly in the count of each and every tribe, "... according to the number of names, from twenty years and upwards—all who were able to go forth to war." The word *tzava* ("host, army, war") appears 14 times in this chapter, in the usual manner of key words, which appear in multiples of 7.

exercise that might introduce some confusion among the commanders of the army.

However, in the second description, we find that the Levites are left out of the census of the Israelites not only because of what this tribe does not do, but also because of what it does do:

> Only the tribe of Levi you shall not count (*lo tifkod*), nor shall you number them among the Israelites. But you shall appoint (*hafked*) the Levites over the Sanctuary of Testimony, and over all of its vessels ... (1:49–50)

The Torah uses this root—*p-k-d*—over and over again to emphasize the unique role of the Levites:

> And you shall appoint (*tifkod*) Aaron and his sons, and they shall keep their priesthood. (3:10)

> ... overseeing (*pekudat*) those who keep the charge of the Sanctuary. (3:32)

> And the oversight (*pekudat*) of the charge of the sons of Merari ... (3:36)

In other words, the Levites are not counted (*nifkadim*) amongst the Israelites because they are charged (*mufkadim*) with the Sanctuary of the Testimony, and as Rashi states, "It is proper for the King's guard to be counted separately." This entails an actual prohibition on including the Levites in the census, for this would show a lack of respect for their special status and role.

Thus, the Levites are not included in the census for two reasons: because they do not go out to war and because of their special role.

There is another aspect to the uniqueness of the tribe of Levi. The census of the Israelites includes "every male from the age of 20 and up," while the census of the tribe of Levi includes "every male from the age of one month and up" (3:15). The reason for this difference is that the census of the Israelites is a functional one, aimed at ascertaining the size of the army, while the count of the Levites testifies to their unique essence, and therefore includes any infant who has survived the first month and is considered as having value.[3]

At the same time, the Torah emphasizes later on that the function of the Levites should also be regarded as a "host" or "army." In chapter 4, we find repeated mention of "all who enter the host (*tzava*), to perform work in

---

3. Recall that in the context of a vow dedicating the personal value of a human being to the Temple, this assessment can be made from the age of one month (Leviticus 27:6).

the Tent of Meeting."[4] We may therefore amend our prior conclusion and state that the Levites are not counted along with the other tribes because they are not part of their "host" or "army" (*tzava*); rather, they are a host in their own right—the host of the Sanctuary service.[5]

II. The Special Status of the Tribe of Levi

From here we may proceed to another surprising duality in the special status of the Levites. Twice our parasha defines their special duties. Let us examine the two descriptions, alongside each other:

Numbers 1:48–53	Numbers 3:5–10
God spoke to Moses, saying: "Only the tribe of Levi you shall not count, nor shall you number them among the Israelites. But you shall **appoint the Levites over the *Mishkan* of the Testimony**, and over all its vessels, and over all that belongs to it; they shall carry the Tabernacle and all its vessels, and **they shall minister to it**, and they shall encamp around the Tabernacle. And when the Tabernacle journeys on, the Levites shall take it down, and when the *Mishkan* is to be pitched, the Levites shall set it up, **and the stranger who comes near shall be put to death**. And the Israelites shall encamp by their respective camps, and each by their banner, according to their hosts. **But the Levites shall encamp around the *Mishkan* of Testimony, so that there will be no wrath upon the congregation of the Israelites. And the Levites shall keep the charge of the *Mishkan* of Testimony**."	God spoke to Moses, saying: "Bring near the tribe of Levi, and **present them before Aaron, the Kohen**, that they may minister to him. And they shall keep his charge, and the charge of the whole congregation, before the Tent of Meeting, to perform the work of the *Mishkan*. And they shall keep all the vessels of the Tent of Meeting, and the charge of the Israelites, to perform the service of the *Mishkan* And you shall give the Levites to Aaron and to his sons; they are wholly give to him from the Israelites. And you shall appoint **Aaron and his sons, and they shall keep their priesthood, and the stranger who comes near shall be put to death**."

4. This phrase appears in the chapter (with slight changes) six times, but in one instance we find: "All who enter in to join the host (*litzvo tzava*), to perform the work in the Tent of Meeting" (verse 23), such that the root *tz-v-a* appears a total of 7 times.

5. It would seem that the Torah regards the host of the Levite service more highly than the host of Israel, since the latter are counted "from twenty years" with no upper limit, while the Levites are counted "from thirty years and up, until fifty years" (4:3), such that only men in their prime are included. (Further on, in 8:24, we find: "This is as pertains to the Levites, from twenty-five years and up they shall enter in to join the host in the work of the Tent of Meeting"—see the commentators there.)

Both commands note the role of the Levites in keeping the charge of the *Mishkan* (1:53; 3:7) and their responsibility for its vessels (1:50; 3:8). However, chapter 1 notes explicitly (verse 53) that their role is to encamp around the *Mishkan*, thereby preventing God's wrath from consuming the Israelites, while chapter 3 would seem to suggest that this role is meant for Aaron and his sons (verse 10). What is the meaning of these discrepancies?

Apparently, there are two different aspects to the selection of the Levites. Chapter 3 places the kohanim—and Aaron, specifically—at the center. The roles of the Levites are explained in this chapter right after a genealogical list of Aaron and his sons (3:1–4). Once God has dedicated the Kohanim to the priestly service, He takes the Levites and gives them to Aaron:

> Bring near the tribe of Levi, and present them before Aaron, the Kohen, that they may minister to him ... And you shall give the Levites to Aaron and to his sons; they are wholly give to him from the Israelites.

The Levites here serve only as assistants to the Kohanim; they have no special identity of their own. The giving of the Levites to Aaron and his sons, the Kohanim, raises a question as to the source of the sanctity of the Levites: what makes them worthy of serving in the *Mishkan*? Here, the Torah explains that their sanctity arises from their replacement of the firstborn, who were originally dedicated to God following the plague of the firstborn in Egypt:

> God spoke to Moses, saying, "And I—behold, I have taken the Levites from among the Israelites, instead of all the firstborn who open the womb of the Israelites, such that the Levites are Mine. For all the firstborn are Mine: on the day that I smote all the firstborn in the land of Egypt, I dedicated to Me all the firstborn in Israel, both man and beast; they shall be Mine, I am the Lord." (3:11–13)

The Torah does not elaborate as to why the firstborn were replaced by the Levites.[6] From the context of the chapter, it would appear that the reason is that the Levites are related, by family ties, to the Kohanim. In any event, chapter 3 contains no expression of the idea that the Levites have any

---

6. Rashi explains, based on Chazal, that the Levites had no share in the sin of the Golden Calf, and were therefore chosen in place of the firstborn, who had sinned. We shall address the Golden Calf below, but as regards the exchange of the firstborn, the text itself does not offer the slightest hint that it had anything to do with that episode. Moreover, the very fact that the Levites require the redemption of the firstborn as the source of their sanctity indicates that the choice of the Levites did not arise from any special virtue on their part.

special status; on the contrary, in order to confer a special status upon them, it is necessary to "borrow" the special status of the firstborn, by redeeming them with the Levites.

In chapter 1, in contrast, no mention is made of the Kohanim, and the Levites are awarded an independent status, with no connection to the firstborn. This is especially apparent when we compare the following two verses:

1. But you shall appoint the Levites over the *Mishkan* of the Testimony, and over all its vessels, and over all that belongs to it; they shall carry the *Mishkan* and all its vessels, and they shall minister to it. (1:50)

2. Bring near the tribe of Levi, and present them before Aaron, the Kohen, that they may minister to him. (3:6)

Both verses tell us that the role of the Levites is to minister, but in chapter 1 they minister to the *Mishkan*, while in chapter 3 they minister to Aaron, the Kohen, and help him with the charge of the *Mishkan*. For this reason, we read in chapter 1 that the Levites encamp "around the *Mishkan*"—i.e., they have a camp of their own. This idea appears again in chapter 2, as a direct continuation of what we have seen in chapter 1:

> The Tent of Meeting shall journey forth, with the camp of the Levites in the midst of the camps; as they encamp, so shall they journey—each in his place, by their banners. (2:17)

However, from chapter 3 onwards, no further mention is made of the Levite camp.

Our parasha thus presents two different aspects of the selection of the Levites. In chapter 1, there is a direct selection of the Levites to minister in the *Mishkan*; in chapter 3, there is a selection of the Levites as replacements for the firstborn, and they minister to the Kohanim and help them in their service. This gives rise to a further question: Chapter 3 addresses at length the source of the Levite status—their replacement of the firstborn. In chapter 1, on the other hand, there is no mention of any source for their special status. What, then, is the source for the selection of the Levites in chapter 1?

It seems that chapter 1 expresses a different angle of the selection of the Levites as recounted in *Sefer Shmot*, in circumstances that are altogether different—immediately after the description of the festivities held before the Golden Calf:

> Moses stood at the gate of the camp and he said, "Who is on God's side? Let him come to me." And all the sons of Levi gathered themselves to him. And he said to them, "So says the Lord God of Israel: Let every man place his sword at his side; go to

and from gate to gate in the camp, and kill every man his brother, and every man his neighbor, and every man his friend." And the sons of Levi did according to Moses's word, and there fell of the people on that day about three thousand men. And Moses said, "Consecrate yourselves today to the Lord, every man against his son and against his brother, that He may bestow a blessing upon you today." (Exodus 32:26–29)

The readiness of the tribe of Levi to kill even members of their own families earned them a blessing and a special new role: "Consecrate yourselves today to the Lord." The term "consecration" (milui yadayim) is familiar to us from the priesthood; indeed, in every other instance, the term applies to the Kohanim commencing their duties. For example:

> You shall dress them—Aaron, your brother, and his sons with him, and you shall anoint them and consecrate them (u-mileita et yadam) and sanctify them, that they may minister to Me. (28:41)

Thus, there was also a direct selection of the Levites for their role, by virtue of their devotion to God's service, as proven in their deeds after the sin of the Golden Calf.

We therefore conclude that our parasha reflects two different aspects of the selection of the Levites. The first selection, described in chapter 1, arises from the sanctity of the tribe of Levi as a whole, as it was sanctified for God's service in the wake of the sin of the Golden Calf. From this perspective, the Levites serve in the *Mishkan* with no connection to the Kohanim, and they have a camp of their own, surrounding the *Mishkan*. According to the other perspective, as reflected in chapter 3, the source of the holiness of the Levites is actually the prior selection of the firstborn; the Levites are simply the replacement for the firstborn. This perspective diminishes the role and status of the Levites; they are considered merely as ministering to the Kohanim and aiding them in the service of the *Mishkan*.

In conclusion, let us briefly consider how this duality with regard to the Levite status is expressed in the description of their actual dedication for their role in chapter 8. There, we again find two clearly defined parts. The first part reads:

> You shall bring the Levites before the Tent of Meeting, and you shall gather the whole assembly of the Israelites. And you shall bring the Levites before the Lord, and the Israelites shall place their hands upon the Levites. And Aaron shall offer the Levites

before the Lord for a wave offering of the Israelites, that they may carry out God's service. (8:9–11)

This emphasizes the selection of the Levites in their own right, to "carry out God's service." Aaron shows them as a wave offering before God, as befitting people who have been chosen directly for their role by virtue of their inherent sanctity.

The second part of chapter 8 returns to the second aspect in our parasha:

> And afterwards the Levites shall go in to perform the service of the Tent of Meeting, and you shall purify them and show them for a wave offering. For they are wholly given to Me from among the Israelites; as replacement for those who open every womb, the firstborn of all of the Israelites, have I taken them for Me. For all the firstborn of the Israelites are Mine, both man and beast; on the day that I smote every firstborn in the land of Egypt, I sanctified them for Myself. And I have taken the Levites instead of all the firstborn of the Israelites, and I have given the Levites as a gift to Aaron and to his sons, from among the Israelites, to perform the service of the Israelites in the Tent of Meeting and to make atonement for the Israelites, so that there will be no plague among the Israelites when the Israelites approach the Sanctuary. (8:15–19)

Here again, there is mention of the "wave offering" made of the Levites, but not "before the Lord." In this section, which emphasizes the sanctity of the Levites as arising from their replacement of the firstborn, their role is not "to perform God's service," as in the previous unit, but rather a more minor and modest role: "to perform the service of the Israelites."

Rav Amnon Bazak is a *Shiur Bet Ram* at Yeshivat Har Etzion and teaches Bible and Oral Law at the Herzog College and at the Women's Beit Midrash in Migdal Oz. He completed his Hesder army service in the military rabbinate and was later ordained as a rabbi and received his BEd degree at Herzog College for Teacher Training. Rav Bazak has authored several books on Bible study.

Chapter 4

The Princes

THE BABYLONIAN TALMUD, IN discussing the question of how one ought to dance before a bride, brings a fascinating dispute between the students of Shammai and those of Hillel in Ketubbot 16b–17a. At issue is what one recites while dancing at a wedding when the bride is not considered particularly attractive (or, in the legal construct under consideration in the Talmud, when she is either lame or blind, which in those times would have rendered the bride undesirable). In other words, do the wedding guests have an obligation to praise her beauty knowing that this is false praise? The students of Shammai say that one recites praise of the bride as she is—that is, one should emphasize her good qualities without commenting on her physical appearance. In response, the students of Hillel maintain that one praises her as a "fair and attractive" bride, for there is truth in this statement. How so? The groom, having opted to marry this woman, clearly sees her as fair and attractive.

The point of this debate, at least for me, is that there is always more than one perspective when examining the events of our lives, and this goes beyond "beauty is in the eyes of the beholder." When analyzing another's actions and the character traits that underlie them, there are always multiple ways of viewing things. Yet, regardless of outcomes, Judaism inclines us to look for the good. This is epitomized in the teaching of Hillel: "Do not judge your fellow until you have stood in his place" (Pirqe Avot 2:4). Rabbi Natan Sternhartz, in his book, *Sefer Eitzot Yesharot*, expands on this concept and argues that when we look for the good in other people, when we judge their seemingly negative actions in a positive light, we are emulating God's attribute of mercy. In doing so, we act in accordance with the commandment of "and you shall do that which is righteous and good" (Deuteronomy 5:18).[1]

---

1. Rabbi Natan Sternhartz, who lived from 1780 to 1844, was the primary student of the great Hasidic master, Rabbi Nachman of Breslev.

This is the challenge when teaching the narrative of the princes: recognizing and remembering that there are multiple ways to understand their actions while, at the same time, looking for the good (or perhaps, just some good) in what they do. The starting point of our discussion is the actions of the princes during the dedication of the tabernacle, as we read in Numbers 7:1–3:

> On the day that Moses finished setting up the Tabernacle, he anointed and consecrated it and all its furnishings, as well as the altar and its utensils. When he had anointed and consecrated them, the chieftains of Israel, the heads of ancestral houses, namely, the chieftains of the tribes, those who were in charge of enrollment, drew near and brought their offering before the Lord: six drawn carts and twelve oxen, a cart for every two chieftains, and an ox for each one.

This seemingly nondescript account of the gifts of the princes gave birth to a heated debate in rabbinic literature regarding the motivations underlying their gifts. One school of thought focuses on their ostensibly lethargic attitude toward the building of the tabernacle. The midrash in Numbers Rabbah 13:16 offers these observations:

> Why were the Princes quick to sacrifice first, whereas regarding the building of the Tabernacle they were lazy and only brought the onyx stones and the stones to be set in the *efod*[2] at the end? Because when Moses said, "Whoever is of a willing heart, let him bring it, an offering of the Lord" [for the work of the tabernacle, Exodus 35:5], he did not say anything to the Princes. It was wrong in their eyes that he did not tell them to bring anything. They said: "Let the people bring what they will bring, and whatever is missing, we will fill in." All of Israel rejoiced in the work of the Tabernacle and gladly and quickly brought all [their] offerings.... And in two days they brought all [their] offerings.... After the second day, the Princes wished to bring their offering, but they were unable to do so, for Moses had already issued a command: "And they caused it to be proclaimed throughout the camp saying, 'Let neither man nor woman do any more work for the offering of the sanctuary'" [Exodus 36:6]. And the Princes were distressed that they did not merit contributing to the Tabernacle. They said: "Since we did not merit contributing to the Tabernacle, let us give to the garments of the High Priest" ... The Holy One, blessed be He, said: "Regarding

---

2. The ephod was an elaborate garment worn by the high priest and upon which the *hoshen*, or breastplate containing Urim and Thummim, rested.

My sons who were quick, it shall be written that they brought 'too much'" [Exodus 36:7]. But regarding the Princes who were lazy, He removed one letter from their name, for it is written "ve-hanesim," [the Princes] in a defective manner, without [the letter] yod.

Numbers Rabbah is not alone in its critical attitude toward the princes. Consider the commentary of Rabbi Samson Raphael Hirsch on Exodus 35:27:[3]

> It speaks of the Princes felt themselves somewhat slighted in their office by the call for gifts being made direct to the people, and accordingly held back from the offering in the expectation that the people's contribution would not be sufficient for all the work, and they would then, in all honor, step in and make up the deficit. But they had not reckoned on the enthusiasm of the people, so that, in the end, nothing remained for them to contribute except the precious stones for the garments of the High Priest and the oil and fragrant spices for the incense and the anointing oil.[4]

In short, argues Rabbi Hirsch, the princes are deserving of criticism because they felt "that their office placed them preferably above the people and representing the people, rather than as being in the midst of the people." This arrogance was not what one expects from the princes of the people.

A much sharper rebuke of the princes is set forth in Midrash ha-Gadol, which initially brings the opinion of Rabbi Shmuel:

> R. Shmuel said: When Moses came to Israel and said to them, "The Holy One, blessed be He, said to me, 'Make for Me a sanctuary,'" the Princes said to him: "Let us make the sanctuary from our [money], and let Israel not participate." He said to them: "This is not what the Holy One, blessed be He, commanded me, but rather: 'Speak to the children of Israel, that they bring Me an offering'" [Exodus 25:2]. They [the princes] immediately withdrew and did not participate with the community.

In the end, at least in the view of this midrash, the princes understood the error of their ways. They brought materials for the priestly garments (even

---

3. Rabbi Samson Raphael Hirsch, who lived from 1808 to 1888, was a German Orthodox rabbi best known as the intellectual founder of the *Torah im Derech Eretz* school of contemporary Orthodox Judaism. Occasionally termed "Neo-Orthodoxy," his philosophy, together with that of Azriel Hildesheimer, has had a considerable influence on the development of Orthodox Judaism.

4. Hirsch, *Pentateuch*, 678.

though they did not contribute to the building of the tabernacle itself). Understandably, Moses was unwilling to accept any contributions from the princes because of their attitude, so it took the intervention of God Himself, when He said "Take it of them" (Numbers 7:5), for Moses to acquiesce and accept the offerings of the princes.

Midrash ha-Gadol goes on to offer a second perspective on the princes:

> R. Chinena bar Chanina said: A great miracle was performed on Moses' behalf in the Tabernacle. When the Holy One, blessed be He, said to him, "And they shall make Me a sanctuary" [Exodus 25:8], the Princes said: "Let us establish it from our own [money]." He said to them: "It was said to me, 'of every man'" [Exodus 25:2]. They immediately withdrew and said: "Now you will see that you need us." When they came to the priestly garments, they needed onyx stones and stones to be set in the *efod*, and the community was unable to provide them. A miracle was performed, and the clouds of Glory brought him precious stones and jewels. And thus it says: "And the Princes (*nesi'im*) brought"—it is written "nesi'im," as it is written: "He causes clouds (*nesi'im*) to ascend from the ends of the earth'" [Psalm 135:7].[5]

Again, we see the seeming arrogance of the princes; rather than give them their fifteen minutes of fame, God precludes the princes' participation and causes a miracle to make up the shortfall. Ultimately, it is the people and God, not the princes, who contribute to the construction of the tabernacle.

What is the commom thread that connects these two midrashim (as well as the above-cited commentary by Rabbi Hirsch)? "Both of these midrashim bestow special meaning upon the word 'nesi'im,' understanding the term as denoting the pride with which the Princes lorded over the people or the miracle that God performed so that their contribution would be unnecessary. Owing to this, Moses did not want to accept the sacrifices that they brought on their own initiative for the dedication of the Tabernacle until God favorably accepted their offering, saying, 'Take it of them.'"[6]

A second approach to the actions of the princes is far more positive, and it stems from the idea of equality that is reflected in the identical gifts the princes ultimately offered. Thus, for example, section 6, number 84 of the Sifrei Zuta notes:

---

5. Note that the English transliteration makes the two words seem identical, whereas in the original Hebrew, they are not. Rather, they share the same root letters and are thus simply related linguistically.

6. Levy, "Shiur #27."

What is taught by [the phrase] "from the Princes of Israel?" This teaches that they contributed on their own initiative and that the offering of each of them was the same in length, in width, and in weight. R. Shimon says: What is taught by "from the Princes of Israel?" This teaches that they contributed on their own initiative, and that the offering of each was the same and that one did not offer more than his fellow, for had one offered more than his fellow, none of the offerings would have set aside [the laws of] Shabbat [which normally would prohibit these activities]. God said to them: "You showed honor one to the other, and I will show honor to you." As it is stated: "And the Lord said to Moses, 'They shall offer their offering, each prince on his day.'"

The rabbinic sages expounded upon the tallying of the sacrifices in a similarly positive fashion in Numbers Rabbah 14:12:

> [The verse states] "This was the dedication of the altar, in the day when it was anointed." Did the entire dedication of the altar take place on the day that it was anointed? But surely the dedication of the altar did not end until twelve days had passed! Rather, Scripture comes to teach you that all the tribes are equal and equally dear to the Holy One, blessed be He. For Scripture related to them as if they had all offered [their sacrifices] on the first day, to fulfill that which is stated: "You are all fair, my love; there is no blemish in you" [Song of Songs 4:7].

Another (but certainly not last) source that reflects this positive point of view is the commentary of Ramban on Numbers 7:2–5:

> The Holy One, blessed be He, shows honor to those who fear Him, as it is stated: "Those that honor Me I will honor" [1 Samuel 2:30]. Now, all of the Princes brought this offering that they had agreed upon together on the same day, and it would have been impossible for the one not to precede his fellow. And so, He honored those who come first with their banners that they should come first with their sacrifices. But He wanted to mention them all by name and to spell out their sacrifices and to mention the day of each one, and not that he should mention and honor the first one, "This is the offering of Nahshon the son of Amminadab," and say: "And so the Princes offered sacrifices, each one on his own day," because this would have been a diminishment of the honor of the others. Afterwards, He put them all together to say that they were equal before Him, may He be blessed. And similarly, they said there in the Sifrei (Sifrei

Numbers, section 53). Scripture teaches that just as they were all the same in one counsel, they were also all the same in merit.

Regardless of which perspective one prefers, it is quite clear that the actions and motivations of the princes are not so black and white. One can argue that their reticence in contributing to the construction of the tabernacle is a reflection of an undesirable character trait, namely, arrogance. Conversely, one could posit that the sense of equality all the princes felt toward one another flowed from their humbleness, and this humility (clearly a positive character trait) led them to delay their offerings until the people could bring all they could afford.

These shades of gray in considering the motivations of the princes stand in stark contrast to the examples of the patriarchs and the matriarchs set forth in the book Genesis, the *Sefer HaYashar* in the eyes of the talmudic rabbis. Thus, in our pedagogical model, the princes illustrate why the book of Numbers can and ought to be used with teens to elicit in them serious discussions of what defines a positive character trait and what a negative one. This should lead in turn to a discussion of which character traits they should strive to inculcate in themselves. By engaging in such a discussion, the students will be acting in accordance with the aggadic maxim: "Consider your actions, to have them accord with good manners, and you will be well rewarded for whatever you do" (Derekh Eretz Zutra 3).[7]

---

7. Aggadah (or as an adjective, aggadic) refers to non-legal exegetical texts in classical rabbinic literature, particularly as recorded in the Talmud and various collections of midrash.

Sefer BeMidbar—The Princes
Sample Unit Plan

Unit	Primary Source(s)	Supplemental Reading(s)	Timeframe
The Princes	Numbers 7	Are You	two weeks
	Rashi 7:1	Observing or Judging?	
Middah:	Ramban 7:1		
Worth of actions	Rashi 7:2	Go for It!	
as subjective	Sforno 7:3		
	Rashi 7:3		
	Rashi 7:9		
	Rashi 7:11		
	Rashi 7:12		
	Rashi 7:13		
	Rashi 7:16		
	Rashi 7:89		

Essential Question(s)

1. Why such divergent views regarding the actions of the Princes?
2. Is there an objective way to judge actions after the fact, or are such judgments always subjective?

Evaluating/Checking for Understanding

1. Daily discussions/student interactions

   Student questions and observations typically drive each day's discussion.

2. Occasional written reflections

   At the discretion of the teacher, a tool to foster further reflection on the unit's essential questions.

3. Character trait essay

   See appendix for assignment rubric.

4. Unit test

   Unit tests should, by definition, be crafted by individual teachers to meet the needs of their specific students. The Understanding by Design *framework created by Grant Wiggins and Jay McTighe is an excellent tool for the development of appropriate tests and assessments, as its emphasis on backward design forces teachers to consider in advance the assessment evidence needed to document and validate that the targeted learning goals have been achieved.*

Primary Source Texts

1. As a general introduction to this unit, students will read and discuss two articles that follow this unit plan: "Nature vs. Nurture in Psychology" and the blog on judging versus observing that follow.

2. *BeMidbar* chapter 7: Read text and seek to identify problematic (what I will call "red flag") words and phrases (with teacher's guidance, of course). These red flag words and phrases will likely vary from class to class depending on the sophistication and linguistic abilities of the students, coupled with the background and interests of the teacher.

3. Consider the unit's essential questions and how they are to be understood/explained in light of commentaries A and B, beginning with how Moses's actions/attitudes compare with those of the princes.

4. The remaining commentaries we will study and discuss in this chapter (C–K) will help us resolve this unit's essential questions: Why such divergent views regarding the actions of the princes? Is there an objective way to judge actions after the fact, or are such judgments always subjective?

5. Supplemental readings for each unit are intended to demonstrate that serious scholarship about and explanations of *Sefer BeMidbar* are not limited to the classical medieval commentators but continue to our time. The supplemental readings for this unit give tips on how to determine what is really driving one's actions and how to avoid complacency. The readings are a blog entitled "Are You Observing or Judging?" and an article entitled "Go For It!" by Rabbi Pinchas Avruch.

Sefer BeMidbar—The Princes

Primary Texts

A. Rashi 7:1

> *"Moses had finished"*

Bezalel and Oholiab and all the wise-hearted men made the Tabernacle (cf. Exodus 36:1), but Scripture attributes it to Moses (describes it as his work), because he devoted himself wholeheartedly to it, to see that the shape of each article was exactly as He had shown him on the mountain—to show the workmen how it should be made; nor did he err in a single shape.—A similar thing do we find in the case of David: because he devoted himself to the building of the Holy Temple,—as it is said, (Psalms 132:1—5) "Lord, remember David, and all his affliction: How he swore unto the Lord . . . [I will not give sleep to mine eyes . . . until I find out a place for the Lord . . .]," therefore it is called by his name, as it is said (1 Kings 12:16), "Now see your own house, David" (Midrash Tanhuma, Nasso 13).

> *"And it came to pass on the day] that Moses had finished setting up [the Tabernacle]"*

But it is not said, "on the day Moses set up," this teaches us that during each of the seven days of installation Moses used to erect and dismantle it (the Tabernacle), but on that day (the eighth) he erected it but did not again dismantle it; for this reason it is said: "on the day that (Moses) finished setting up"—i.e., on that day his several erections of it came to an end.—It was the New Moon (the first day) of Nisan, on the second the Red Heifer was burnt, on the third they (the Levites) were sprinkled for the first time with the water in which its ashes were mingled, and on the seventh day, after having been again sprinkled, they shaved their bodies and were ready to enter on their duties (cf. 8:6–7).

B. Ramban 7:1

"On the day that Moses finished setting up the Tabernacle"

Scripture does not say "on the day that Moses set up." This teaches us that on each of the seven days of initiation Moses erected and dismantled the Tabernacle, and on that day he erected it but did not dismantle it. Therefore, it says, "on the day that Moses had finished setting up the Tabernacle," since it was on that day that he finished all his erections. This happened on first of Nisan. On the second day, the Red Heifer was burnt. On the third day, they sprinkled the first sprinkling, and on the seventh day, the Levites were shaven." This is Rashi's language on the basis of the words of our Rabbis of blessed memory. But it is not a complete proof, for the expression "on the day that he had finished" is not connected with the word "setting up" but [its meaning is rather as follows]: "on the day that Moses had finished setting up the Tabernacle" and anointing and sanctifying it, and the altar and all the vessels thereof—the Princes offered their offerings, when all this was done. Nonetheless, it was on the eighth day [of the initiation of the priests].

This section was written here because on the first day of the initiation "He called unto Moses out of the Tent of Meeting and God spoke to him," all the sections from the beginning of the Book of Leviticus until the section of "And it was on the eighth day," which all deal with the laws of the offerings. From that eighth day on Moses was told all the sections beginning with "These are the beasts which you may eat," which contain the laws of forbidden and permitted foods, since they are all related to the subject of the offerings, and these topics continued in their correct order up to this place as I have explained.

Thus, when He had completed the commandments which Moses was ordered to say to Israel, all of them being laws of the Divine Service and the offerings, the charge of the Tent of Meeting and its service. He reverted here afterwards to tell of the freewill offerings of the Princes, which took place from the eighth day until the nineteenth day of Nisan or until the twelfth day of the month in accordance with the words of our Rabbis.

C. Rashi 7:2

"These are the leaders of the tribes"

They were the officers [appointed] over them in Egypt, and they were beaten on account of them, as it says (Exodus 5:14), "The officers of the children of Israel were beaten" (Sifre Numbers 45).

D. Sforno 7:3

"A cart for every two chieftains"

The reason that they shared a cart each was not that they were stingy, but that they wanted to demonstrate that there was no rivalry between them, but that, on the contrary, they felt like brothers one toward the other. Such sentiments have been recorded in the Torah in Deuteronomy 33:5, "Moses was king in Yeshurun when all the people gathered together" [a king is not someone aloof, in an ivory tower, but his distinction becomes relevant only in his being part of his people, יחד, together]. The opposite is reported in Hosea 10:2, "when its collective heart is divided, this is they their guilt."

E. Rashi 7:3

"And they brought them before the Tabernacle"

Because Moses would not accept them (the gifts) at their (the Princes') hands until he was so bidden by the mouth of the Omnipresent (cf. v. 5).— Rabbi Nathan said: What reason had the Princes to give their contributions here first of all the people, whereas at the work of the Tabernacle they were not the first but the last to contribute? But—he replied—the Princes spoke thus: "Let the community in general contribute all they wish to give and then what will then be lacking we shall supply." As soon as they saw that the community gave everything needed in its entirety (lit., that the community completed everything)—as it said (Exodus 36:7), "For the stuff they had was enough [for all the work to make it]"—the Princes asked, 'What can we now do'? Therefore they brought the onyx stones, and stones for setting for the Ephod and for the breast plate. That is why they were here the first to contribute" (Sifre Numbers 46:1).

F. Rashi 7:9

"[But to the sons of Kohath he gave none (no wagons)] because the belongs unto them"

[Not the service of the Sanctuary devolved upon them, but the service in connection with] carrying the most holy objects: the ark, the table, etc. was incumbent upon them, therefore they should carry upon their shoulders (not in wagons).

G. Rashi 7:11

"They shall offer their offering, [each prince on his day] for the dedicating of the altar"

But Moses did not yet know how they were to bring their offerings—whether according to the order of their birth (i.e., according to the order in which the sons of Jacob after whom the tribes were named were born, in which case the prince of the tribe of Reuben would have offered first), or according to the order in which they moved off on the journeys (when Judah would be the first), until he was told by the mouth of the Holy One, blessed be He: "according to the order on the journeys shall they offer"—yet each prince on his day (and not three together as they actually journeyed).

H. Rashi 7:12

"[Nahshon the son of Aminadab,] of the tribe of Judah"

By these words Scripture merely states his genealogy after his tribe, and they do not mean that he collected the offerings from his tribe and offered them on their behalf. Or perhaps it does state "of the tribe of Judah" only to intimate that he collected the offerings from his tribe and then brought them? Scripture, however, states (v. 17): this was the offering of Nachshon—he brought it of that which was his own (Sifre Numbers 48).

I. Rashi 7:13

"Both of them were full of fine flour"

For a free-will meal-offering.

J. Rashi 7:16

"One kid of the goats for a sin-offering"

To make expiation for uncleanness caused by a grave in the depths of the earth (i.e., one that is not known to exist and it might therefore be assumed that people passed over it and thereby unwittingly became unclean), which was only a doubtful uncleanness (one about which there exists a doubt as to whether it actually has been incurred or not) (cf. Sifre Numbers 51).

K. Rashi 7:89

> "And when Moses came [into the tent of meeting . . . then he heard the voice speaking unto him from off the covering that was upon the ark of the testimony]"

When two Scriptural verses apparently contradict each other there comes a third and reconciles them. We have got such a case here: one verse says (Leviticus 1:1), "[And the Lord called unto Moses] and spoke unto him out of the appointed tent," which was outside the Vail, and another verse says (Exodus 25:22), "And I shall speak unto you from off the Ark-lid", thus within the Vail—then this (our verse) comes and reconciles them: Moses entered the appointed tent, and there he heard the Voice which came from above the Ark-lid, from between the two Cherubim—the Voice issued from Heaven unto the space between the two Cherubim, and from there it issued into the appointed tent where it was heard by Moses (Sifre Numbers 58 1).

Sefer BeMidbar—The Princes
Supplemental Reading

Are You Observing or Judging?

—Kevin Eikenberry

Yesterday, I was thinking about observation and judgement, and how it relates to effective communication and coaching. It reminded me of a particular incident that took place a few years back—an incident I had previously written about on the blog for my book *Remarkable Leadership*.

We were driving somewhere as a family and, in conversation, I made some comment (about which I don't remember, and it isn't relevant anyway). In reply, my son Parker, probably about 15 at the time, commented that his mother and I were being judgmental.

My immediate response was that I wasn't judging, but making an observation. This led to a spirited conversation in our car about the differences between observation and judgement. The differences are huge and we see them every day.

Here are some examples.

"He has long hair."—observation

"His hair is too long" or "His hair needs to be cut."—judgments

"The table is black."—observation

"The table is ugly."—judgement

"She is very skilled."—observation, if based on truly observing the skills being discussed

"She is better than I am."—judgement, unless there is factual measurement on a criteria [sic] that all agree defines "better."

The conversation we had in our car was more than wordplay or a dictionary challenge. It defines an important concept that we often miss by not thinking clearly. As a leader, when communicating, coaching, developing others, giving feedback, or making decisions, we need to be crystal clear on our judgements and our observations—and which are which.

What are You Doing?

Are you passing judgement on people and their behavior? Whether positive or negative, spoken or unspoken, those judgements will have an impact on people's performance (so if you are going to judge, make it positive).

When giving feedback, are your statements largely observational or judgmental? If you try to pass judgement off as fact, you risk being wrong and setting a stage for defensiveness, resistance, or worse.

There is nothing necessarily wrong with making judgments. Decisions are judgments. But even then, it is important to separate observation from assumption and judgement. Doing so will help you make better decisions.

The differences between judgement and observation can get cloudy, but it need not be. When we speak or think from a place of observation, there is no assignment of right or wrong, or degree of goodness. Observations are like reflecting a mirror on a situation—simply reporting what we see. Being more observant, and being able to state our observations are important to our ability to effectively communicate, influence, and lead.

Kevin Eikenberry is an American author, speaker, and trainer. He has a BS from Purdue University. He is the chief potential officer of The Kevin Eikenberry Group and is the current president of the Purdue Agricultural Alumni Association.

Sefer BeMidbar—The Princes

Supplemental Reading

Go For It!

—Rabbi Pinchas Avruch

The Torah portions of the last three weeks have given vivid descriptions of the component parts of the *Mishkan*, its utensils and the clothes worn by the priests during their service within. This week's double portion relates the actual donation and collection of the needed materials and their manufacture.

The masses responded generously to the appeals for the myriad of different colored yarns needed for the tapestries, and they supplied all the needed gold, silver, copper and acacia wood. By the time the Princes of the twelve tribes responded, all that was left to be donated were the precious stones for the high priest's garments and the oil and spices for the service in the *Mishkan*. The Hebrew word for Princes, *Nesi'im*, usually contains the letter *yud* in the suffix that transforms the singular *nasi* to the plural *Nesi'im*. While the letter is not needed for the word to be pronounced *Nesi'im*, it appears in compliance with the rules of grammar. Yet, in the verse, "The *Nesi'im* brought the onyx stones and the stones for the settings for the Ephod and Breastplate" (Exodus 35:27), the word *Nesi'im* is missing the *yud*. Knowing the axiom that every letter in the Torah, whether additional or missing, is significant, what is the meaning of the missing *yud*?

Rashi explains with a Midrash relating to the *Mishkan*'s inauguration. At that time, each of the Princes voluntarily came forward with a celebratory offering. Why did the Princes display such alacrity at that time but at the time of the original donations they were last? The Midrash answers that when the general appeal was made for building materials they wanted to allow the Jewish people to respond to the best of their ability, while the Princes intended to compensate for any shortfall. But in the end, there was very little for them to give. Learning from their earlier missed opportunity, they offered enthusiastically when the inauguration came. But, concludes the Midrash, because of their laziness at the original collection (the episode of our Parsha) their title is written deficiently, lacking the *yud*.

Many contemporary commentaries note the Midrash's choice of verbiage in calling the Princes "lazy." The Midrash itself explains the very logical rationale for the wait: to give the people a chance to give. But the commentaries concur that the Midrash's critique is predicated on the understanding that had the Princes shared the enthusiasm of the masses to be contributors, they would not have let themselves be held back from participating. They would have been clamoring to give like the others, all rationales to the contrary notwithstanding. This laziness is the root of the loss of the *yud* in their name.

On the other hand, the Chofetz Chaim (Rabbi Yisrael Meir HaKohen Kagan of Radin; 1838–1933; author of basic works in Jewish law, philosophy and ethics and renowned for his saintly qualities) uses this same axiom to answer a perplexing phenomenon in the narration of the Inauguration. Each of the twelve Princes brought the exact same gift, and while they are absolutely identical, the Torah itemizes each facet of each Prince's donation (Numbers 7:12–83). Rabbi Kagan clarifies that while the Torah could just as well have listed the six-verse sequence once and noted that all twelve Princes brought these gifts, each gift is enumerated because God treasures people who do mitzvot with enthusiasm, as a united group without jealousy and competition. More so, the Chofetz Chaim emphasizes, when the Princes, in their laziness, separated themselves from the masses, they lost only ONE LETTER; but when they came together to serve God with fervor, not only were no letters missing but the Torah added SIXTY SIX VERSES! Such is God's value of a mitzvah done with passion and zeal!

Rabbi Pinchas Avruch is the executive director at Bais Yaakov Academy of Queens

Chapter 5

The People

PERHAPS THE MOST DIFFICULT and challenging aspect of *Sefer BeMidbar* is how to explain the behavior of the Jewish people throughout this book's narrative. The Jewish people witness God bring ten devastating plagues in order to liberate them from enslavement at the hands of the era's most powerful nation. They are saved from the pursuing Egyptian army when God splits the sea for them. They are brought to Mount Sinai where, as a nation, they experience a direct revelation from God. Subsequently, they are miraculously sustained in their treks through the wilderness with bread from heaven (the manna) and with water from the well of Miriam.[1] Yet the talmudic sages famously taught that "with ten trials did our forefathers try the Holy One, blessed be He: two at the sea, two because of water, two because of manna, two because of the quails, one in connection with the Golden Calf, and one in the wilderness of Paran" (Erchin 15a).

How are we to reconcile the miracles the people experienced with what seems to be a lack of faith and a heightened sense of self-pity? This is a key question in *Sefer BeMidbar* when it comes to examining and explaining the actions of the people. Throughout the book, the Jewish people come across as a self-pitying, whiny lot, a nation frequently bereft of gratitude for the wondrous and miraculous deeds done for them by God. Is this reflective of their true nature? Is it a normal and expected outcome of the difficult circumstances incumbent with life in the wilderness? Or perhaps it is both,

---

1. The description in Numbers of the death of Miriam is immediately followed by the episode of the waters of Meribah: "Miriam died there .... The community was without water" (20:1–2). The rabbis learn from this juxtaposition that Miriam's death resulted in a dearth of water. How so? Throughout their many years in the wilderness, the Jewish people drew water from a well that accompanied them due to the great merits of Miriam. According to the rabbis, this well was one of the things created on the eve of the Sabbath at twilight (Pirqe Avot 5:6) and was wondrous in that it flowed from itself, like a rock full of holes (Sukkah 3:11).

which would be consistent with more recent research on the topic of nature versus nurture.

The origin of the nature versus nurture debate dates back thousands of years and subsequently occurs in many cultures.[2] The Greek philosopher Galen theorized that personality traits are the result of a person's relative concentrations of four bodily fluids, or humors: blood, phlegm, yellow bile, and black bile. The term "nature–nurture" comes from Sir Francis Galton's 1874 publication, *English Men of Science: Their Nature and Nurture,* in which he argued that intelligence and character traits came from hereditary factors. His beliefs were in clear opposition to earlier scholars such as philosopher John Locke, who is well known for the theory that children are born a blank slate, and that their traits develop completely from experience and learning.

For most of the 1900s, the two dominant schools of thought when it came to human behavior and psychiatric symptoms were *behaviorism,* which emphasized the importance of learning principles in shaping behavior, and *psychoanalysis,* which developed from the ideas of Sigmund Freud and focused on the ways that unconscious sexual and aggressive drives were channeled through various defense mechanisms. Despite the fact that these two perspectives were often in opposition to each other, both shared the view that the environment and a person's unique experiences, that is, nurture, were the prevailing forces in development.

From about the 1970s to the end of the twentieth century, a noticeable shift occurred as direct knowledge of the brain and genetics started to swing the pendulum back to an increased appreciation of nature as a critical influence on a person's thoughts, feelings, and behavior. Research studies from this time period made it increasingly difficult to argue for the supremacy of either nature or nurture as the primary driver of behavioral traits and disorders. Although many experts acknowledged the importance of both nature and nurture, the two were generally treated as being quite independent.

Today, most scientists who carefully examine the ever-expanding research base have come to see nature and nurture as inextricably interwoven with one another. Genes have an influence on the environments we experience. At the same time, a person's environment and experience can directly change the level at which certain genes are expressed, which in turn alters both the physical structure and activity of the brain.

Given this modern understanding, some maintain that the question of nature versus nurture ceases to even make sense in many ways. Nonetheless,

---

2. My discussion and analysis of the topic of nature versus nurture is culled from Rettew, "Nature versus Nurture."

for the traditional biblical commentators, the question of nature versus nurture, even if not articulated in these terms, was very much on their minds as they examined the repeated complaints of the Jewish people in the wilderness. To see the extent to which this is true, it is appropriate to consider two distinct episodes set forth in *Sefer BeMidbar*: the people's dietary complaints about the manna they ate daily and about their lack of meat (chapter 11) and the people's reaction to the report of the spies (chapter 14).

Chapter 11, with its dietary complaints, is arguably the more perplexing of the two episodes. The chapter itself opens with only the vaguest hint of the people's actions: "The people took to complaining bitterly before the Lord. The Lord heard and was incensed: a fire of the Lord broke out against them, ravaging the outskirts of the camp" (Numbers 11:1). This vagueness spurs a debate among the commentators as to the underlying causes of the people's complaints. Do they reflect the outlook and personality of the people (nature), or are they caused by the harsh circumstances of their lives in the wilderness (nurture)?

Some, such as Rashi, attribute these complaints to nature. In his commentary on Numbers 11:1, he uses the term "wicked men" and argues that they were simply seeking a pretext for distancing themselves from God.[3] Others, such as Ramban, see circumstances (that is, nurture) as the root cause of these complaints:

> The correct explanation seems to me to be that when they distanced themselves from Mount Sinai, which was almost like a permanent encampment, and then, after their first journey, found themselves in the vast terrifying wilderness, they made themselves uncomfortable. They said, "What will we do? How will we live in this wilderness? What will we eat and drink? How can we handle this oppression? When will we leave [this wilderness]? (Ramban on Numbers 11:1)

The authors of *Daat Zekenim* echo the approach of Ramban in their commentary on Numbers 11:1 but give a slightly different read on the circumstances that drive their complaints: "The people were already mourning the potential casualties they would incur when going into battle against the

---

3. It is important to note that Rashi does not view the entire nation as wicked, but only a subset of them—the "mixed multitude" who left Egypt along with the Jews—as he makes clear in his commentary to Numbers 11: 4. Rashi adopts this same approach, namely, seeing the rabble-rousers as a subset of the nation as opposed to the entire nation, in his commentary on the narrative of the golden calf.

Canaanites in order to conquer their land. They were lacking in faith and dreading warfare."[4]

Nevertheless, other commentators seem to reflect the modern view that nature and nurture function in tandem. Consider, for example, Sforno's commentary on Numbers 11:1, where he sees the complaints as a result "of the difficulties of the journey." Yet he goes on to say that the people "had nothing to complain about. They only voiced complaints as a form of testing God." Could not a desire to test God be seen as part and parcel of their personality traits?

The struggle to understand the complaints of the people and the role specific circumstances play in prompting these complaints is one that continues to our times. One prominent scholar, Rabbi Mosheh Lichtenstein of Yeshivat Har Etzion, has written a rather detailed analysis of the narrative of chapter 11.[5] In his analysis, Rabbi Lichtenstein points out that the story of the Jewish people's journey through the wilderness after the exodus is laden with complaints and quarreling over the lack of rations in the wilderness and the hardships of travel (nurture). The uncertainty of daily sustenance brings the nation to constant quarrels with Moses. The nation argues with Moses and challenges God in a continuous cycle of complaints (Exodus 15:22—17:7). After a period during which they receive law while camped at Mount Sinai, narrated at the end of Exodus, through Leviticus, and into the beginning of Numbers, *Sefer BeMidbar* tells of their depature from the mountain, when the complaints and protests surface once again. The Jewish people grumble over the manna, they desire meat, they reject the promised land, and they continuously rebel to the point where Moses testifies that "from the day that you left the land of Egypt until you reached this place, you have been defiant toward God" (Deuteronomy 9:7). Rabbi Lichtenstein argues that this shift in narrative tone reveals a fundamental difference between the situation in Exodus and that which transpires in Numbers, a difference reflected in God's reactions to the nation's complaints in the two books. In Exodus, God does not respond harshly, and we may even describe His attitude as forgiving. Matters change dramatically in the book of Numbers. Almost immediately after the first complaint (set forth in chapter 11), God unleashes punishment. While the content of the complaint itself is not specified, the Torah still describes the nature of the complaint itself as רע ("evil"), an adjective with no parallel in the accounts of the people's complaints in Exodus.

---

4. *Daat Zekenim* is a Torah commentary compiled by later generations of scholars from the Franco-German (*Ba'alei HaTosafot*) school in the thirteenth century.

5. Lichtenstein, "Crisis."

As we noted at the outset of our discussions of *Sefer BeMidbar*, God is often angered in the Numbers narrative. Yet, in Exodus, God is never described as reacting angrily to the people's grumbling, nor does He smite them in response. Even in the episode involving the waters of Massah and Meribah in Exodus 17:1–7, the Lord does not punish. Instead, he instructs Moses to provide the people with water, without any rebuke or condemnation. Rabbi Lichtenstein asks, how can we explain this striking difference?

In answering this question, Rabbi Lichtenstein maintains that the difference in God's responses to the nation's complaints in Exodus and Numbers stems from the very dissimilar underpinnings to the complaints themselves. In Exodus, we see a people troubled by legitimate dilemmas, ones that require resolution. True, the nation falls short of the proper level of trust in the Lord who leads them into the wilderness, but this does not reflect any significant spiritual weakness on their part. Their sustenance in the arid desert is not self-evident, and even after learning of God's plan to provide them with a daily ration, most people cannot easily rely on supernatural means for their basic needs. Hence, the Jewish people's concerns and appeals to Moses arises out of genuine concern for their fate and that of their children.

Rabbi Lichtenstein demonstrates that things become more complex in *Sefer BeMidbar*. The Jewish people no longer fear survival in the wilderness, and their complaints do not flow from their concern for their basic needs. Already at this stage, after the manna has fallen daily for a full year without exception, the nation knows that God can and will provide them with food. Their complaints now are not about sustenance but are, as Rabbi Lichtenstein so aptly describes, about the menu. They cannot satiate their desire for food, and they have no possibility of fulfilling their culinary dreams. We deal here not with the guarantee of physical sustenance but with the pursuit of fantasy. In Rabbi Lichtenstein's view, the Torah identifies desire as the motive behind their protest, and their complaint in Numbers 11:4 makes this clear: "We remember the fish that we used to eat free in Egypt, the cucumbers, the melons, the leeks, the onions, and the garlic." So where does this analysis leave us? Nature? Nurture? Both? It's hard to say, but I imagine that different readers of the text of chapter 11 will come to different conclusions.

Let us move on to the people's reactions to the report of the spies sent out by Moses to scout out the land of Canaan as described in chapter 14. The story of the spies themselves, as detailed in chapter 13, is much discussed and debated. What were the motivations of the spies? How could men of such standing—Numbers 13:2 describes them a "one man from each of their ancestral tribes, each one a chieftain among them"—have sinned so grievously? Where was the truth in the report? Where were the lies? Less often discussed, to the point of sometimes being left out of certain curricula, is the narrative of chapter 14. It is here that we again see the Jewish people as wallowing in self-pity and lacking in gratitude:

> All the Israelites railed against Moses and Aaron. "If only we had died in the land of Egypt," the whole community shouted at them, "or if only we might die in this wilderness! Why is the Lord taking us to that land to fall by the sword? Our wives and children will be carried off! It would be better for us to go back to Egypt!" And they said to one another, "Let us appoint a leader and return to Egypt" (Numbers 14:2–4).

The frustrations of the people are not solely directed towards God. According to Sforno in his commentary on Numbers 14:2, the people here were claiming that all the actions of Moses and Aaron during and subsequent to the exodus from Egypt were undertaken only in order to deliver the people into the hands of the Amorites. In his commentary on Numbers 14:3, Sforno goes on to explain that the people further challenge Moses and Aaron by asking: "What sin did we commit against God that He made the effort to bring us to this crisis by using you two as His instruments?" Per this view, the people thought their present troubles were all in retribution for the abominable things they had done while in Egypt. Or perhaps these troubles arose on account of some other cause they were not aware of which had caused God to hate them.

Their self-pity kept them from seeing any culpability on their part, from their acceptance of the "calumnies [the spies had spread] among the Israelites about the land they had scouted" (Numbers 13:32) to the anger they unjustifiably displayed toward Moses and Aaron, evident in the fact that "the whole community threatened to pelt them with stones" (Numbers 14:10). Not surprisingly, God was quickly and fiercely provoked in this instance by the people:

> And the Lord said to Moses, "How long will this people spurn Me, and how long will they have no faith in Me despite all the signs that I have performed in their midst? I will strike them with pestilence and disown them, and I will make of you a nation far more numerous than they!" (Numbers 14:11–12)[6]

---

6. Due to the intervention and pleas of Moses, God refrains from destroying the people and starting anew with Moses. Nonetheless, this generation is punished and condemned to wander in the wilderness until all the men aged twenty and above, save for Joshua and Caleb, perish (see Numbers 14:13–24).

Unlike the narrative of chapter 11, in which the text and the commentaries seem split on the motivations underlying the actions of the people (that is, was it nature or nurture), here there seems little ambiguity. One could argue with some confidence that the people's true nature was on display.

In the end, how does the debate about nature versus nurture in the context of the people's actions fit in with the metanarrative we are arguing for in the study of *Sefer BeMidbar*? Quite well actually, for, as we have seen and will continue to see, Numbers is a book about gray. Rarely is it about black and white.

More fundamentally, our basic premise is that *Sefer BeMidbar* is a logical teaching tool for fostering among students deep reflection about proper character trait development. Any pushback by students who might say "that is not in my nature" when considering one or another character trait can be deflected by the above analysis of the actions of the Jewish people in the wilderness and the extent to which their actions were driven by circumstances (that is, nature) and not by nurture. Clearly, as demonstrated by the actions of the Jewish people in the book of Numbers, proper character traits (or, sadly, improper ones) can be learned and acquired.

Sefer BeMidbar—The People
Sample Unit Plan

Unit	Primary Source(s)	Supplemental Reading(s)	Timeframe
The People	Numbers 11	Nature vs. Nurture	three–four weeks
	Rashi 11:1		
Middah:	Sforno 11:1	Erchin 15a	
Lack of gratitude	Ramban 11:1		
Self-pity	Daat Zekenim 11:1	The Crisis of Leadership	
	Rashi 11:4		
	Rashi 11:10		
		Two Complaints of the Nation	
	Numbers 14		
	Sforno 14:2	Mt. Sinai: Their Finest Hour	
	Sforno 14:3		
	Rashi 14:12		
	Rashi 14:18		
	Rashi 14:27		
	Rashi 14:33		
	Rashi 14:37		

Essential Question

Do the frequent complaints of the people reflect their true nature or the circumstances of the wilderness experience?

Evaluating/Checking for Understanding

1. Daily discussions/student interactions

   Student questions and observations typically drive each day's discussion.

2. Occasional written reflections

   At the discretion of the teacher, a tool to foster further reflection on the unit's essential questions.

3. Character trait essay

   See appendix for assignment rubric.

4. Unit test

   Unit tests should, by definition, be crafted by individual teachers to meet the needs of their specific students. The Understanding by Design *framework created by Grant Wiggins and Jay McTighe is an excellent tool for the development of appropriate tests and assessments, as its emphasis on backward design forces teachers to consider in advance the assessment evidence needed to document and validate that the targeted learning goals have been achieved.*

Primary Source Texts

1. As a general introduction to this unit, students will read the article "Nature vs. Nurture in Psychology" that follows this unit plan.

2. *BeMidbar* chapter 11: Read text and seek to identify problematic (what I will call "red flag") words and phrases (with teacher's guidance, of course). These red flag words and phrases will likely vary from class to class depending on the sophistication and linguistic abilities of the students, coupled with the background and interests of the teacher.

3. Prior to studying various commentaries on this chapter, students will learn Erchin 15a (a copy of which follows this sample unit plan), and the discussion of it should focus on what actually constituted the ten times the Jewish people tested God in the wilderness.

4. Then, consider the unit's essential question and how it is to be understood/explained in light of commentaries A–E.

5. As a supplement to these commentaries, students will read and discuss two contemporary analyses about the issues in this chapter: "The Crisis of Leadership" by Harav Mosheh Lichtenstein and "The Complaints of the Nation and the Re-Appointment of Aaron" by Rav Yonatan Grossman. Both readings examine Moses's reactions to the complaints of the people and why his reactions are so different in this episode compared to others in *Sefer BeMidbar*.

6. Students will next move on to *BeMidbar* chapter 14: Read text and seek to identify problematic (red flag) words and phrases (with teacher's guidance, of course). These red flag words and phrases will likely vary from class to class depending on the sophistication and linguistic abilities of the students, coupled with the background and interests of the teacher. That said, some important examples of red flag words and phrases in this chapter appear in commentaries F–L.

7. Supplemental readings for each unit are intended to demonstrate that serious scholarship about and explanations of *Sefer BeMidbar* are not limited to the classical medieval commentators but continue to our time. The supplemental reading for this part of the unit on the people is "Mt. Sinai—Their Finest Hour" found in a book by Rabbi Abraham Besdin entitled *Reflections of the Rav: Volume One*. It should foster further discussion on how a people worthy of engaging God at Mount Sinai could so soon thereafter begin to test and test and test Him.

Sefer BeMidbar—The People

Primary Texts

A. Rashi 11:1

"And the people were complaining"

The term "the people" always denotes wicked men. Similarly it states (Exodus 17:4), "what shall I do unto this people? [yet a little and they will stone me]," and it further states (Jeremiah 13:10), "This evil people [which refuses to hear my words]." But when they are worthy men who are spoken of they are called "My people," as it is said (Exodus 5:1), "Let My people go"; (Micah 6:3) "O My people, what have I done unto you."

B. Sforno 11:1

"were complaining"

On account of the difficulties of the journey. They did not actually complain in their hearts as they had nothing to complain about. They only voiced complaints as a form of testing God.

C. Ramban 11:1

"And the people were like 'mitonenim'"

Ibn Ezra explained: "It is the same language as 'evil,' like it is used in the phrase 'your evil thoughts' (Jeremiah 4:14) ... that is, they spoke evil words." But this is not correct. For why would the Torah hide their sin instead of telling us explicitly, like in every other place? The correct explanation seems to me to be that when they distanced themselves from Mount Sinai, which was almost like a permanent encampment, and then, after their first journey, found themselves in the vast terrifying wilderness, they made themselves uncomfortable. They said, "What will we do, how will we live in this wilderness? What will we eat and drink? How can we handle this oppression? When will we leave [this wilderness]? [*Mitonenim*, then] is like in the verse "What should a living man complain (*yitonen*) of? Each of his own sins" (Lamentations 3:39), meaning the pain and suffering one brings upon himself. Similarly, "the child of my pain (*oni*)," (Genesis 35:18); also in "The fisherman will lament (*anu*) and mourn" (Isaiah 19:8). Since the text says that the people were in pain and sorrow, it mentions and tells us their sin [explicitly], as they were speaking from the bitterness of their souls like people who are in pain do. And this was wicked in the eyes of God, for they should have followed Him with joy and good spirit from all of the good that God had bestowed upon them. Instead, they were like people being forced, like people in pain, like people who were annoyed at their poor situation. This is also why the Torah tells us a second time (in verse 4) that the Children of Israel returned and cried. Their first sin was that they were annoyed that they lacked enjoyable things in the wilderness. They then repeated this sin instead of receiving message of the fire of God that burned among them [after the first sin].

D. *Daat Zekenim* 11:1

> "*The people were like murmurers*"

The people were already mourning the potential casualties they would incur when going into battle against the Canaanites in order to conquer their land. They were lacking in faith and dreading warfare.

E. Rashi 11:10

> "*[Then Moses heard the people] weep throughout their families*"

That is, the members of each family gathered together and wept in order to display their discontent in public. Our Rabbis, however, said that "throughout their families" means "the people wept because of family affairs"—because of the intermarriage of blood-relatives that had been forbidden to them.

F. Sforno 14:2

"All the Israelites railed against Moses and Aaron"

[These] who were God's delegates charged with taking them out of Egypt and with saving them from fear of death in the desert; they claimed that all that Moses and Aaron had done was only in order to deliver the people into the hands of the Amorite.

G. Sforno 14:3

"Why is the Lord taking us . . ."

What sin did we commit against Him that He made the effort to bring us to this crisis by using you two as His instruments? They thought that these present troubles were all retribution for the abominable things they had been doing while in Egypt, or on account of some other cause they were not aware of which had caused God to hate them. We know that they had concluded that God must hate them from their own words in Deuteronomy 1:27: "because God hates us He took us out of Egypt in order to deliver us into the hands of the Amorite."

H. Rashi 14:12

"and disown them"

[This] is an expression for "driving out" (here, driving out from the world, destroying).—And if you ask what I will do regarding the oath I have sworn to the Patriarchs (i.e., to give the Land to their children; cf. Exodus 6:3–4), then I reply:

"I will make of you a great nation"

[whereby My oath will be fulfilled] since you are one of their descendants.

I. Rashi 14:18

"The Lord! Slow to anger"

[The Lord is long suffering] towards both the righteous and the wicked. When Moses ascended to Heaven to receive the Law he found the Holy One, blessed be He, engaged in writing: "The Lord is long-suffering." He asked,

"Surely only to the righteous?" The Holy One, blessed be He, answered him, "To the wicked also!" Whereupon Moses said: "The wicked—let them perish!" He (the Lord) replied to him: "I swear by your life that you shall eventually need this thing (the extension of My mercy also to the wicked)." When the Israelites sinned at the incident of the Golden Calf and at that of the Spies, Moses offered prayer before Him, with mention of God's attribute of His being long suffering. The Holy One, blessed be He, then said to him: Did you not say, "Surely only to the righteous!?" Whereupon Moses replied, "But did You not tell me, 'To the wicked also'?" Let then—Moses added—the strength of My Lord be great [even as Thou didst say]—by fulfilling Thy statement and not mine!

J. Rashi 14:27

"[How long shall I bear] with this evil congregation"

This refers to the Spies (not to the whole congregation); from here we learn that "a congregation" is technically a gathering of at least ten persons (Megillah 23b).

K. Rashi 14:33

"[And your children shall wander in the desert] forty years"

None of them was to die younger than 60 years old (Bava Batra 121b). For this reason a period of forty years was decreed for their wanderings in order that those who were at that time 20 years old (and only those from twenty years old and upwards came under this decree; cf. v. 29) should reach the age of sixty. The first year that they were in the wilderness was included in the forty although it preceded the sending forth of the Spies (which took place in the second year), because from the moment they made the Golden Calf this decree entered the mind of God, but He waited for them (postponed their punishment) until their measure of sin should be full. This is the meaning of what is stated (Exodus 32:34), "And in the day when I shall visit—viz., at the incident of the Spies—I shall visit their sin (that of the Golden Calf) upon them." And, here, indeed, it states (v. 34), "ye shall bear your iniquities" (in the plural) suggesting two sins; that of the Calf and that of the murmuring.—In the calculation it (Scripture) regards in the years of their lives a part of the year (of the sixtieth year) as the whole of it, and as soon as they entered their sixtieth year those who were now twenty years old died.

L. Rashi 14:37

"[Even those men died . . .] by the plague before the Lord"

By that death which was fitting for them—measure for measure. They had sinned with their tongue, therefore their tongue grew long extending right down to their navels, and worms came from their tongue and entered their navels. This is the reason why it states, they died by "the" plague, and not by "a" plague; this, too, is the meaning of the words "before the Lord" (they died by the plague which was before the Lord)—by that plague which was fitting for them according to the methods of the Holy One, blessed be He, Who metes out "measure for measure."

Sefer BeMidbar—The People
Supplemental Reading

Excerpt from "Nature vs. Nurture in Psychology"

— Saul McLeod

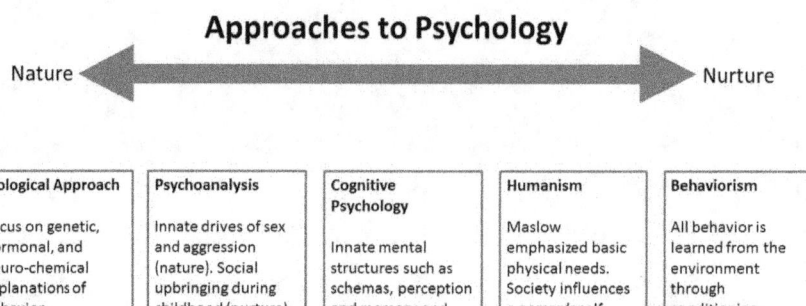

It has long been known that certain physical characteristics are biologically determined by genetic inheritance. Color of eyes, straight or curly hair, pigmentation of the skin and certain diseases (such as Huntingdon's chorea) are all a function of the genes we inherit. Other physical characteristics, if not determined, appear to be at least strongly influenced by the genetic make-up of our biological parents.

Height, weight, hair loss (in men), life expectancy and vulnerability to specific illnesses (e.g., breast cancer in women) are positively correlated between genetically related individuals. These facts have led many to speculate as to whether psychological characteristics such as behavioral tendencies, personality attributes and mental abilities are also "wired in" before we are even born.

Those who adopt an extreme heredity position are known as **nativists**. Their basic assumption is that the characteristics of the human species as a whole are a product of evolution and that individual differences are due to each person's unique genetic code. In general, the earlier a particular ability appears, the more likely it is to be under the influence of genetic factors.

Characteristics and differences that are not observable at birth, but which emerge later in life, are regarded as the product of maturation. That is to say we all have an inner "biological clock" which switches on (or off) types of behavior in a pre-programmed way. The classic example of the way this affects our physical development are the bodily changes that occur in early adolescence at puberty. However, nativists also argue that maturation governs the emergence of attachment in infancy, language acquisition and even cognitive development as a whole.

At the other end of the spectrum are the environmentalists—also known as **empiricists** (not to be confused with the other empirical/scientific approach). Their basic assumption is that at birth the human mind is a **tabula rasa** (a blank slate) and that this is gradually "filled" as a result of experience (e.g., behaviorism).

From this point of view psychological characteristics and behavioral differences that emerge through infancy and childhood are the result of learning. It is how you are brought up (nurture) that governs the psychologically significant aspects of child development and the concept of maturation applies only to the biological.

For example, when an infant forms an attachment, it is responding to the love and attention it has received, language comes from imitating the speech of others and cognitive development depends on the degree of stimulation in the environment and, more broadly, on the civilization within which the child is reared.

Examples of an extreme nature positions in psychology include Bowlby's theory of attachment, which views the bond between mother and child as being an innate process that ensures survival.[1] Likewise, Chomsky proposed language is gained through the use of an innate language acquisition device.[2]

---

1. J. Bowlby, *Attachment. Attachment and Loss: Vol. 1. Loss* (New York: Basic Books, 1969).

2. N. Chomsky, *Aspects of the Theory of Syntax* (MIT Press, 1965).

Another example of nature is Freud's theory of aggression as being an innate drive (called thanatos).

In contrast Bandura's social learning theory states that aggression is a learnt from the environment through observation and imitation.[3] This is seen in his famous bobo doll experiment.[4] Also, Skinner believed that language is learnt from other people via behavior shaping techniques.[5]

In practice hardly anyone today accepts either of the extreme positions. There are simply too many "facts" on both sides of the argument which are inconsistent with an "all or nothing" view. So instead of asking whether child development is down to nature or nurture the question has been reformulated as "How much?" That is to say, given that heredity and environment both influence the person we become, which is the more important?

This question was first framed by Francis Galton in the late 19th century. Galton (himself a relative of Charles Darwin) was convinced that intellectual ability was largely inherited and that the tendency for "genius" to run in families was the outcome of a natural superiority.

This view has cropped up time and again in the history of psychology and has stimulated much of the research into intelligence testing (particularly on separated twins and adopted children). A modern proponent is the American psychologist Arthur Jenson. Finding that the average I.Q. scores of black Americans were significantly lower than whites he went on to argue that genetic factors were mainly responsible—even going so far as to suggest that intelligence is 80% inherited.

The storm of controversy that developed around Jenson's claims was not mainly due to logical and empirical weaknesses in his argument. It was more to do with the social and political implications that are often drawn from research that claims to demonstrate natural inequalities between social groups.

Galton himself in 1883 suggested that human society could be improved by "better breeding." In the 1920s the American Eugenics Society campaigned for the sterilization of men and women in psychiatric hospitals. Today in Britain many believe that the immigration policies are designed to discriminate against Black and Asian ethnic groups. However, the most chilling of all implications drawn from this view of the natural superiority of one race over another took place in the concentration camps of Nazi Germany.

---

3. A. Bandura, *Social Learning Theory* (Englewood Cliffs, NJ: Prentice Hall, 1977).

4. A. Bandura, D. Ross, & S. A. Ross, "Transmission of Aggression through the Imitation of Aggressive Models," *Journal of Abnormal and Social Psychology* 63 (1961): 575–82.

5. B. F. Skinner, *Verbal Behavior* (Acton, MA: Copley, 1957).

For many environmentalists there is a barely disguised right-wing agenda behind the work of the behavioral geneticists. In their view part of the difference in the I.Q. scores of different ethnic groups is due to built-in biases in the methods of testing. More fundamentally they believe that differences in intellectual ability are a product of social inequalities in access to material resources and opportunities. To put it simply children brought up in the ghetto tend to score lower on tests because they are denied the same life chances as more privileged members of society.

Now we can see why the nature–nurture debate has become such a hotly contested issue. What begins as an attempt to understand the causes of behavioral differences often develops into a politically motivated dispute about distributive justice and power in society. What's more this doesn't only apply to the debate over I.Q. It is equally relevant to the psychology of sex and gender where the question of how much of the (alleged) differences in male and female behavior is due to biology and how much to culture is just as controversial.

However, in recent years there has been a growing realization that the question of "how much" behavior is due to heredity and "how much" to environment may itself be the wrong question. Take intelligence as an example. Like almost all types of human behavior it is a complex, many-sided phenomenon which reveals itself (or not!) in a great variety of ways. The "how much" question assumes that the variables can all be expressed numerically and that the issue can be resolved in a quantitative manner. The reality is that nature and culture interact in a host of qualitatively different ways.

This realization is especially important given the recent advances in genetics. The Human Genome Project for example has stimulated enormous interest in tracing types of behavior to particular strands of DNA located on specific chromosomes. Newspaper reports announce that scientists are on the verge of discovering (or have already discovered) the gene for criminality, for alcoholism or the "gay gene."

If these advances are not to be abused then there will need to be a more general understanding of the fact that biology interacts with both the cultural context and the personal choices that people make about how they want to live their lives. There is no neat and simple way of unraveling these qualitatively different and reciprocal influences on human behavior.

Saul McLeod is a psychology (BSc) tutor at The University of Manchester while also working there on his PhD. Previous to this, he taught A-level psychology at Wigan and Leigh College for ten years. He has a degree in psychology and an MA in research.

Sefer BeMidbar—The People

Supplemental Reading

Erchin 15a

Rabbi Yehudah said: "Our ancestors tested Holy One, blessed be He, with ten trials as follows: two at the sea, two in relation to water, two in relation to the manna, two in relation to the quails, one in connection with the Golden Calf, and one in the wilderness of Paran."

Two at the sea: one at the going down, the other at the coming up.

At the going down, as it is written: "Was it because there were no graves in Egypt that you brought us to the desert to die?" (Exodus 14:11) At the coming up: That is in accord with what R. Huna taught, as he said: The Israelites of that generation were among those of little faith. Rabbah b. Mari expressed it thusly: It is written: But they were rebellions at the sea, even at the Red Sea. Nevertheless, He saved them for His name's sake. This teaches that Israel were rebellious at that very hour, saying: Just as we go up from this side, so will the Egyptians go up from the other side. The Holy One, blessed be He, said to the Prince of the Sea: Cast them out on the dry land! He answered: Sovereign of the Universe, is there a slave to whom his Master gives a gift and then takes it away from him again? He said to him: I shall give you [afterwards] one and a half times as many of them. He said before Him: Sovereign of the Universe, is there any slave who can claim anything against his master? He said: The brook of Kishon shall be surety. At once he cast them on the dry land, as it is written: "And Israel saw the Egyptians dead on the seashore." (Exodus 14:30)

Twice because of water: at Marah and at Rephidim.

At Marah, as it is written: "And when they came to Marah, they could not drink" (Exodus 15:23), and it is written: "And the people murmured against Moses" (Exodus 15:24).

At Rephidim, as it is written: "They encamped in Rephidim and there was no water to drink," (Exodus 17:1), and it is also written: "Wherefore the people strove with Moses" (Exodus 17:2).

Twice because of the manna.

They were command not to go out and collect it on the Sabbath; yet they did (Exodus 16:4–5). Similarly, they were commanded not to leave any over until the next day; yet they did (Exodus 16:19).

Twice because of the quails: with regards to the first and second quails.

With the first, the people complained and said, "There [in Egypt] we sat around pots of meat and ate all the food we wanted, but you have brought us out into this desert to starve this entire assembly to death" (Exodus 16:3).

With the second, the people, prompted by the mixed multitude, reacted thusly, "[they] began to crave other food, and again the Israelites started wailing and said, if only we had meat to eat!" (Numbers 11:4).

With the Golden Calf: as it happened (Exodus 32).

In the wilderness of Paran: as it happened in the episode of the spies (Numbers 13–14).

Sefer BeMidbar—The People

Supplemental Reading

The Crisis of Leadership

—Rav Mosheh Lichtenstein

A. Kibroth-hattaavah

The verses in *Sefer BeMidbar* (Numbers) 11:10–15, which appear in the heart of the account of "Kibroth-hattaavah" (where the Israelites expressed an inappropriate desire for meat), mark a fundamental transformation in the relationship between Moses and the Israelites. Moses, the teacher of Israel, the man who led and guided the nation throughout their long, winding journey, who defended them in the wilderness and after the incident of the calf, feels that he cannot go on. Here, for the first time, Moses breaks, and he feels the need to ask for help in leading the people. Moses transforms from the leader who had once declared his supreme dedication—"Now, if You will forgive their sin [well and good]; but if not, erase me from the record which You have written!" (Exodus 32:32)—into a figure pleading for assistance in his leadership role: "I cannot carry all this people by myself, for it is too much for me. If You would deal thus with me, kill me rather, I beg You, and let me see no more of my wretchedness!" (Numbers 11:14–15). Moses senses that he no longer possesses the strength, and he also does not see himself obliged to continue his job: "Did I conceive all this people, did I bear them, that You should say to me, 'Carry them in your bosom as a nurse carries an infant'?!" (Numbers 11:12).

Several difficult questions immediately arise: What's the problem? What changed? What caused such a drastic transformation in Moses's attitude? How did it happen that such a dedicated leader is suddenly filled with despair and frustration, and how did such a sharp, emotional break, as screams forth from the verses, develop?

In addition, we must consider the location of this parasha within the framework of *Sefer BeMidbar*. On the surface, it would appear more reasonable to separate the incident of the Kibroth-hattaavah from the appointment of the seventy elders (which occurred in response to Moses's plea). The Torah could have completed the story of the complaints and their ensuing punishment as a single unit, and subsequently presented all the details of the elders' appointment and the enigmatic prophecy of Eldad and Medad, without elaborating on these incidents in the midst of the account of the nation's sin. The interweaving of the elders' appointment between the complaint and its ensuing punishment requires an explanation.

As often occurs in instances such as these, we are not surprised to discover that the answer to the first question lies in the second. Indeed, an inherent connection exists between the leadership crisis and the sin, and the Torah therefore did not separate the stories, but rather bound them together. The sin is the cause of Moses's crisis, and his asking the Almighty to liberate him from his responsibility. Seeing the Israelites's conduct, Moses was overcome by frailty and fatigue, and therefore sought to extricate himself from his leadership role. Yet, this still requires further explanation. It is not the actual complaint itself or the nation's sin that brings Moses to frustration and despair. After all, this marks not the first nor the second problem that Moses faces since he began his term of leadership. Many sins, including the particularly grave incident of the Golden Calf, have occurred without causing the shepherd of Israel an emotional breakdown. A comparison of Moses's reaction to the Golden Calf with his response at Kibroth-hattaavah clearly demonstrates that it was not the Israelites' sin in and of itself, but rather the nature and character of this sin that caused this transformation in Moses's attitude towards the nation.

To properly understand this issue, we must consider the broader picture by assessing that which occurs in *Sefer Bemidbar* in general, and comparing it with parallel situations in *Sefer Shmot*.

B. From Mount Sinai to the Wilderness of Sinai

The transition from *Sefer Shmot* to *Sefer BeMidbar* is marked by a transition from success to failure. Even the leadership of Moshe Rabbenu is not as successful in the Book of Numbers as in the Book of Redemption. Whereas the sin of the calf transpires in Moses's absence and ends immediately upon his return to the Israelite camp, the sin of the Spies occurs with Moses present, and as a result of an action that had earned his support. Moses reacts to the Golden Calf with the self-confidence and determined resolve of one who understands his constituency and controls it with firm authority. In the debacle of the scouts, by contrast, we find a leader who is mistaken in his assessment of the nation and does not succeed in steering them away from the path of sin, a leader who falls on his face. From the Golden Calf to the Spies, Moses moves from confidence to confusion, from proactive involvement to silence and stammering. Moreover, whereas Moses's prayer in the aftermath of the calf is successful, with the revolt of the scouts his prayer cannot annul the decree of, "In this wilderness your carcasses shall drop."

We thus have an exceptionally sharp distinction between these two books, both in terms of the Israelites' success in achieving their spiritual and historical goals, and with respect to Moses's ability to lead them towards the realization of these aspirations.

The beginning of *Sefer BeMidbar* does not deal with failure, but rather presents us with the ideal picture of Israel dwelling tribe by tribe, encamped around the Tabernacle, each with its standard in proper formation. The *Mishkan* is erected, God's glory dwells in its midst, the Princes of Israel dedicate it on the day of its anointing, and the nation prepares for a life of sanctity and purity in the wilderness. Situated at the foot of Mount Sinai, the Jews learn from Moses the Torah that he had recently brought down from the heavens.

However, this description depicts only the nation's existence before the cloud rose and the journey to the Land got underway. From the moment the transition occurs from the static life after Matan Torah to the renewed entry into a dynamic, historic existence, we come upon a different picture entirely. As soon as the nation departs from the Mountain of God on their way to the Promised Land, their path is laden with mishaps. We now hear nothing besides grumbling and complaints, weeping and desperation; we proceed from the *mit'onenim* (complainers) to the *mit'avim* (who desired meat), to the Spies, to the *mapilim*, to Korah's rebellion. The nation lacks the strength necessary to confront challenges and bring to realization their destiny in the world of history; they confront the historical realm by turning their backs to it.

The transition from the opening chapters of the sefer, which deal with the wilderness of Sinai, to the chapters describing Israel's attempt to proceed to the Land, marks the central dividing line in this sefer, which brings in its wake a fundamental change in the system of national leadership. Until that point, the nation is destined to enter the Land with Moses and Aaron as their leaders, and with the Almighty bestowing His *Shekhina* upon them in order to bring them to His sacred borders and chosen mountain. From this point, we find revolt and dissent.

Truth be told, this dividing line is so significant that Chazal viewed it as a central cleft which splits the sefer into different units. Chazal viewed the two sections as so distinct that they counted the beginning and continuation of *Sefer BeMidbar* as different *sefarim* of the Chumash. The first book, which contains the parshiyot from the beginning of chapter 1 until the section of *Va-yehi bi-nso'a ha-aron* (1:1—10:34), discusses the Israelite camp in the wilderness, in which reality and vision go hand-in-hand. The second speaks of the journey to the Land on the wings of the *Shekhina*, and contains merely the eighty-five letters of the parasha, *Va-yehi bi-nso'a* (10:35-36). The third sefer (11:1—36:13), meanwhile, which opens with the account of the *mit'onenim* and continues through the conclusion of *Sefer BeMidbar*, describes the sins on whose account the destiny of that generation was not realized.

Our focus here is on the final section. What is the background to this failure, what factors led to this disappointment, and why was Moses's leadership incapable of stopping the nation from their constant rebelliousness?

C. "You Have Been Defiant Towards God"

The story of the Israelites' journey through the wilderness after the Exodus is laden with complaints and quarreling over the lack of rations in the wilderness and the hardships of travel. The uncertainty of daily sustenance brings the nation to constant quarrels with Moses. The nation argues with Moses and challenges God, in a continuous cycle of complaints, as documented in the second half of Parashat Beshalach (Exodus 15:22—17:7). Things become more stable afterward, the nation calms and we hear of no other complaints through the remainder of *Sefer Shmot* or in the beginning of *Sefer BeMidbar*.

Suddenly, when we come to Parashat Beha'alotekha, when the nation embarks from Mount Choreb, the complaints and protests surface once again. The Israelites grumble over the manna, they desire meat, reject the Promised Land, and continuously rebel to the point where Moses testifies that "from the day that you left the land of Egypt until you reached this place, you have been defiant toward God" (Deuteronomy 9:7).

Careful consideration of the text reveals a fundamental difference between the situation in *Sefer Shmot* and that which transpires in *Sefer BeMidbar*. There is a basic difference in God's reactions to the nation's complaints in the two books. In *Sefer Shmot*, He does not respond harshly, and we may even describe His attitude as forgiving. In the Book of Numbers, by contrast, this is clearly not the case. Already after the first complaint, God unleashes punishment instantaneously: "The people took to complaining before the Lord, and it was evil in the ears of the Lord. The Lord heard and was incensed: a fire of the Lord broke out against them, ravaging the outskirts of the camp" (Numbers 11:1). The Torah even describes the complaint itself—the content of which is not specified—as *ra* (evil), an adjective with no parallel in the accounts of the people's complaints in *Sefer Shmot*.

In the following incident, as well, that of Kibroth-hattaavah, God is angered and the people's conduct is described as *ra* ("and it was evil in the eyes of Moses," Numbers 11:10). Yet, in *Sefer Shmot*, God is never described as reacting angrily to the people's grumbling, nor does He smite them in response. Even in Massah and Meribah, so named because "the Israelites quarreled and because they tested God, saying, 'Is the Lord present among us, or not?'" (Exodus 17:7), the Almighty does not punish. He rather instructs Moses to provide the people with water, without any rebuke or condemnation.

D. Survival and Comfort

This difference between the two books with respect to God's response to the nation's complaints evolves from the fundamentally different roots of the complaints themselves. In *Sefer Shmot*, we speak of people troubled by a legitimate dilemma requiring resolution. True, the nation falls short of the proper level of trust in the Almighty who leads them into the wilderness, but this does not reflect any significant spiritual weakness on their part. Their sustenance in the arid desert is not self-evident, and even after learning of God's plan to provide them with a daily ration, a human being cannot easily rely on supernatural means for his basic needs. Thus, the Israelites' concerns and appeals to Moses arose out of genuine concern for their fate and that of their children.

Not so in *Sefer BeMidbar*. Here the Israelites no longer fear survival in the wilderness, and their complaints do not evolve from their concern for their basic needs. Already at this stage, after the manna has fallen daily for a full year without exception, the nation knows that God can and will provide them with food. They complain now not about food, but about the menu. They cannot satiate their desire for food and have no possibility of fulfilling their culinary dreams. We deal here not with the guarantee of physical sustenance, but with the pursuit of fantasy. The Torah identifies DESIRE as the motive behind their protest, "The riffraff in their midst felt a gluttonous craving" (Numbers 11:4). Their complaint makes this clear: "We remember the fish that we used to eat free in Egypt, the cucumbers, the melons, the leeks, the onions and the garlic" (Numbers 11:5).

The nation's conduct during this episode of Kibroth-hattaavah, from the pathetic nostalgia for the delicacies of the country that oppressed them (which they likely never tasted), down to their demand for meat and fish, all signify boredom and idleness, the precursors of an obsessive pursuit of pleasure and desires. As they were assured sufficient rations to survive, we can interpret their demands only as an expression of a craving for luxury.

Released from the spiritual tension they had experienced since Matan Torah, the nation now goes through a stage of pursuit of comfort and enjoyment. How profound, painful, and rooted in the peshat are Chazal's comments describing the departure from Sinai:

> They journeyed from the Mountain of God on a three-day trip like a child leaving school, who runs away and leaves. So did they flee from Mount Sinai on a three-day journey, for they studied much Torah at Sinai. (Cited in Tosefot, Masekhet Shabbat 116a s.v. *pur'anut*)

The manna can therefore no longer provide their needs as it did in the past. So long as the nation worried about its very survival, the manna's descent was a perfect solution. The moment they begin focusing on enjoyment, rather than sustenance, they can no longer appreciate or feel content with the manna.

Whereas God can accept with understanding the nation's concerns in *Sefer Shmot*, He does not react with the same sympathy to their pursuit of luxury in *Sefer BeMidbar*. God responds to the complaints of *Sefer BeMidbar* with fury and punishment.

E. "It Was Evil in Moses's Eyes"

Let us now return to the question why Moses responds to the people's complaints with such despair. The answer lies in the unique nature of this sin that sets it apart from all its predecessors. The sin of Kibroth-hattaavah, which at its very essence involved the pursuit of pleasure, not only evokes a harsh response from both the Almighty and Moses, but also leads to Moses's dissociation from the people. The Almighty cannot proceed with His plan when physical desire is what dictates the nation's agenda, and Moses has no interest in devoting himself to defend and provide the needs of people who subjugate themselves to the consumption of meat and other delicacies. The consequence of "it was evil in Moses's eyes" is his request to divest himself of the burden of leadership.

Beyond his disappointment in the people, Moses claims that he lacks the wherewithal to supply them with what they desire: "Where am I to get meat to give to all this people, when they whine before me and say, 'Give us meat to eat!' I cannot carry all this people by myself, for it is too much for me" (Numbers 11:13–14). In light of this we can readily understand why God appoints seventy spiritual leaders to come to his assistance in educating the people. This appointment was meant as an educational measure necessitated by the particular nature of this incident.

Several questions, however, remain. The first involves God's formulation in issuing this command: "Gather for Me seventy men from the elders of Israel, whom you know to be the elders of the nation and its officers" (11:16). What does He mean by, "seventy men from the elders of Israel whom you know to be the elders of the nation"? If these men rank among the "elders of Israel," then clearly, they are "the elders of the nation."

The key to understanding this verse must lie in the fact that these men were *zekeinim* (elders) and *shoterim* (officers). We should also interpret the term, *ziknei ha-am* (elders of the nation), which contrasts with the earlier expression, *ziknei Yisrael* (the elders of Israel), as referring not to age, but, similar to *shoterim*, to a position of communal leadership. God here instructs Moses to appoint those among *ziknei Yisrael* (the elderly population) who are also leaders. Since the need for leadership qualities for this position is obvious, the emphasis of this verse must involve the requirement that they be elderly as well.

A second, more central question relates to the elders' lack of success. From the moment of their appointment through the calamity of the scouts and the incident of Korah, we detect no sign of improvement in the nation's behavior. To the contrary, the sin of the Spies occurs immediately following Kibroth-hattaavah. Is this lack of success due purely to the utter lack of faith on the nation's part, or does it testify to the failure of the elders? Or, in simpler terms, are the elders indeed qualified for the responsibility cast upon them?

To understand the role assigned to the elders as prophets who assist Moses in leading the nation, we must discuss the story of Eldad and Medad, who prophesy at this point without having Moses's spirit bestowed upon them (as do the seventy elders).

F. Eldad and Medad

> Two men, one named Eldad and the other Medad, had remained IN THE CAMP; yet the spirit rested upon them—they were among those recorded, but they had not gone out to the Tent—and they prophesied in the camp. A youth ran out and told Moses, saying, "Eldad and Medad are prophesying in the camp!" Joshua the son of Nun, Moses's attendant from his youth, spoke up and said, "My lord Moses, imprison them!" But Moses said to him, "Are you wrought up on my account? Would that all the Lord's people were prophets, that the Lord put His spirit upon them!" Moses then reentered the camp together with the elders of Israel (11:23–30).

A careful examination of these verses reveals that location constitutes a central component of the story of Eldad and Medad. The verses tells us little about Eldad and Medad; it omits information such as who they are, what exactly they prophesied, and why Joshua reacted so angrily. The text does, however, emphasize the location of their prophecy—in the camp, and they had not "gone out into the Tent."

Whereas they remain among the people in the camp, the assigned elders separate from the camp and leave to the Tent of Meeting, situated outside the camp: "Bring them to the Tent of Meeting and let them take their place THERE with you. I will come down and speak with you THERE . . ." (11:16–17). Throughout this parasha, a clear distinction is drawn between "here"—the camp, where Eldad and Medad are situated—and "there"—the Tent of Meeting, where Moses takes the elders.

In light of this, we must understand the phrase, "Two men . . . had remained in the camp" to mean that Eldad and Medad made a conscious decision on principle to remain in the camp with the nation, rather than leaving with the elders outside the camp. Their having remained in the camp involves not a geographic issue, but rather an expression of their stance regarding spiritual and political leadership.

In order to understand what exactly the "camp" signifies and Eldad and Medad's insistence on its decisive importance, we must resort to Chazal's comments in identifying the content of Eldad and Medad's prophecy. According to one view in the Midrash (accepted by Rashi in his commentary), they foresaw that "Moses will die and Joshua will bring them into the land."

Chazal likely based their comment on the juxtaposition between this account and the story of the Spies, which resulted in the death of that generation in the wilderness. This will not, however, answer our question unless we presume a thematic—beyond simply chronological—connection between Kibroth-hattaavah and the scouts on the one hand, and the approach of Eldad and Medad to these sins, on the other.

G. Generation Gap

This question brings us to the point where the various plots that transpire simultaneously in chapter 11—the sin of Kibroth-hattaavah, the leadership crisis, Moses's despair and the prophecy of Eldad and Medad—all blend together.

Eldad and Medad sense a developing gap between Moses and the people. Now that the pursuit of physical gratification, rather than weakness and skepticism, motivate [sic] the nation's complaints, Moses can no longer bear the burden. He cannot understand this attitude and condemns it entirely. It is this widening gap between Moses and his flock that troubles Eldad and Medad.

The appointment of the elders, in the view of Eldad and Medad, will only make matters worse. The *zekeinim*, too, will not lend an ear to the wailing of the people longing for delicacies. These elders, Moses's contemporaries, belong to the generation of leaders and fighters who participated in the struggle against Pharaoh. The Egyptian bondage, the yearning for freedom and the struggle for its achievement, is what forged their spiritual image. They never considered personal comfort or luxuries.

These elders cannot understand the younger generation, the generation that was not among the founders, the generation that seeks comfort and relaxation rather than struggle and challenge. We have here a generation gap between the generation of Egypt and the younger generation of the wilderness. The appointment of the elders will not solve the problem that led Moses to despair, as they belong to the same generation as he.

Chazal expressed this idea beautifully by identifying these *shoterim* as the Jewish overseers who suffered beatings in their brethren's stead at the hands of the Egyptian taskmasters. Their self-sacrifice speaks for itself of the superior spiritual level of the *shoterim*. However, the sympathy they afforded their fellow sufferers in Egypt will not apply to the younger generation of the wilderness, whose spiritual world differs so drastically from that of the generation of slavery. The verse therefore emphasizes the age of the elders, for their belonging to the older generation is the critical factor in understanding the rift that has been created in the nation.

Eldad and Medad express their position with the prophecy, "Moses will die and Joshua will bring them to the Land." Joshua belongs to the younger generation; he is therefore capable of bringing the new generation into the Land. For the same reason, Eldad and Medad remain in the camp, with the people, rather than leaving the camp with the elders. They maintain that the leadership must remain with the people, despite and because of the pursuit of physical gratification they have undertaken.

Along these lines we may explain Chazal's comment that the other elders never prophesied again, whereas Eldad and Medad continued to prophesy. Their prophecy, which is directed towards the younger generation, will continue to bear relevance and meaning in the future, beyond the limited context of Kibroth-hattaavah. The elders, by contrast, are detached from the spiritual world of the generation of the wilderness, and their prophecy was but a one-time effort to lighten the burden on Moses's shoulders.

Chazal's comment, that the elders did not prophecy again, is well-grounded in the *peshat*. After this episode, we never again hear of the elders except in one context. When Moses goes to confront Dathan and Abiram, who conspired with Korah against his authority, the elders accompany him (Numbers 16:25). Dathan and Abiram were not from the younger generation, but rather members of Moses's generation. Here the spiritual world of the elders enter [sic] the struggle. Throughout the other parshiyot, however, when Moses does not battle against the nation but rather tries to lead them, the elders cannot serve in an educational capacity, and their prophecy ceases.

(At first glance, this attempt at describing the elders as unfit for leadership seems untenable, given the fact that God Himself selected them. In truth, however, God's purpose here is not to designate new leaders for the nation, but rather to strengthen Moses in his personal crisis by lightening his yoke. To this end, therefore, the men selected are specifically those who resemble Moses, as Chazal emphasize in several places. See Sanhedrin 17a; Numbers Rabbah 15:25; Tanhuma, Beha'alotekha 22.)

H. "Moses Reentered the Camp"

Moses responds to Eldad and Medad by accepting their criticism and taking concrete action to correct the error that they noted. Beyond his comments to Joshua praising the proliferation of religious expression, he also leaves the Tent, together with the elders, and enters the camp: "Moses reentered the camp together with the elders of Israel" (11:30). The policy of positioning the Tent outside the camp, which was adopted in the wake of the Golden Calf, is ended. From now henceforth Moses will work within the camp, he will listen and deal with the people's feelings and demands.

However, whereas Moses's policy was intended to improve the situation, the exact opposite occurred. Immediately after his reentry into the camp, Moses and the nation experience the awful tragedy of the scouts. Moses's dreams, hopes, and personal and national aspirations are at once destroyed. The "crying for naught" of that bitter night brought an end to the generation of the wilderness; the situation worsens, rather than improves.

Of course, here one will reasonably ask: did the sin of the Spies transpire despite Moses's return to the camp, or perhaps, Heaven forbid, because of it? Was the implementation of Eldad and Medad's idea simply "too little, too late," or perhaps this very decision accelerated the negative progression of the people?

Rav Mosheh Lichtenstein immigrated to Israel with his family in 1971. He studied at the Netiv Meir High School in Jerusalem and thereafter spent a year studying with Rabbi Joseph B. Soloveitchik. From 1979 to 1985, Rav Mosheh did *hesder* at Yeshivat Har Etzion, serving in the Armored Corps. He received *semicha* from the *rabbanut* and a degree in English literature from Hebrew University. Rav Mosheh began teaching at Yeshivat Har Etzion in 1992, and, in 2008, he was inaugurated as Rosh Yeshiva, alongside his father Harav Aharon Lichtenstein, Harav Yaakov Medan, and Harav Baruch Gigi. He is married to Dr. Michal Lichtenstein and has three daughters.

Sefer BeMidbar—The People
Supplemental Reading

Two Complaints of the Nation, and the Re-Appointment of Aaron

—Rav Yonatan Grossman

There's an old joke about a Rabbi who could only give derashot about parashat Korah, and so when it came time to give his derasha on the weekly parasha he would find weird and wonderful ways of connecting any parasha in the Torah to the story of Korah. Indeed, some of Chazal's teachings on this parasha are quite curious, and among later commentators, too, there are some particularly interesting ideas which arise in the context of our parasha—particularly with regard to Korah's words, "the entire congregation is holy." However, even a simple and literal rendition of the text presents difficulties.

In this shiur we shall concentrate on two central complaints which appear in this week's parasha, one after the other, both aimed against Moses and Aaron.

Let us first recall the story: First, Korah, Dathan and Abiram, On ben Peleth and two-hundred and fifty other notables complained against Moses and Aaron: "For the entire congregation is holy, and God is among them; why then do you lord it over God's congregation?" (16:3). In the wake of this questioning of Moses and Aaron's leadership, it is decided to conduct a test to determine whom God has chosen. Anyone desiring to serve in the *mishkan* is required to offer incense (*ketoret*): And Moses said to Korah:

> "You and your whole congregation shall be before God, you and they and Aaron, tomorrow. And each person shall take his

> incense pan and shall place incense upon it, and shall offer it before God tomorrow, each person and his incense pan—two hundred and fifty incense pans—and you and Aaron, each with your incense pan." And each person took his incense pan and put fire in it, and placed incense upon it . . . (Numbers 16:16-8).

The *ketoret* serves as a TEST to determine the person whom God has chosen to serve in the *mishkan*.

Parallel to this test, Korah, Dathan and Abiram receive a punishment—the earth swallows them up. This particular punishment would seem to be connected to an additional complaint: "Is it not sufficient that you took us up out of a land flowing with milk and honey to make us die in the desert; you also make yourself a prince over us? Nor have you brought us to a land flowing with milk and honey . . ." (16:13-14). While challenging Aaron's priesthood, they simultaneously raise a most serious accusation, reminiscent of the second complaint of the Israelites in their journey from Egypt to Mount Sinai (the complaint in the wilderness of Sin, Exodus 16)—but here the wording of the complaint is particularly strong. Using the phrase "a land flowing with milk and honey" to describe the land of Egypt is certainly a pointedly sarcastic reference to Moses's promise to take the nation to a land he described in the same way. Dathan and Abiram deliberately and explicitly use the same language. Their words hence contain a harsh criticism of Moses and Aaron's leadership—not only with regard to the priesthood, but in regard to the entire exodus of the nation into the desert.

It appears that this additional complaint is what justifies the special punishment which singled them out from amongst the group of complainers, those who offered up the *ketoret*. Only after the earth swallows them up do we read of the punishment of the others: "And a fire went out from before the Lord, and it devoured the two hundred and fifty men who had offered incense" (16:35).

But even after the "incense test" indicated that Aaron was chosen for the priesthood, the nation was not appeased. They now accuse Moses and Aaron of responsibility for the death of the 250 who had offered incense. This was a most serious accusation, with the implication that in order to hold onto their high office they had put 250 people to death.

In order to deal with this complaint a further test is proposed (the twelve staffs placed before God). Again Aaron is clearly chosen. This time the test is acceptable to the nation, and their reaction is the complete opposite of their original claim—they no longer wish to be among those who serve in the *mishkan*; now they fear approaching the *mishkan* at all:

And the Israelites said to Moses saying, "Behold, we shall perish and die; all of us shall die. Anyone who approaches—who approaches God's sanctuary will die; shall we perish altogether?" (17:27-8).

The style of the description of this cry is distinctly lyrical in character (the translation does not do justice to the poetical qualities of the Torah's language here). The lyrical motifs reflect the nation's fear, giving us the impression that their great terror leads them to stuttering ("who approaches—who approaches") and confusion. The solution to the problem raised by the nation is, "And God said to Aaron, 'You and your children and your father's house with you will bear the responsibility of the mikdash'"—and thus the Torah returns to the beginning of the story and closes the cycle. In the beginning the nation (or a part thereof) complained about the selection of Aaron for the priesthood, in the end this very situation is presented as the solution to the problem raised by the nation and in response to their fears.

However, this reading gives rise to a number of problems concerning the development of the story. Let us focus on three of them:

Firstly, what is the result of the first test, the offering of the incense? We see no evidence of God choosing one incense pan in preference over the others.

Secondly, the nation's second complaint revolves around the accusation that "you have put God's nation to death." The reaction to this should include a proof that it was God Who put those who offered incense to death, and not Moses and Aaron. Instead, all we find is yet another test related to the original complaint—the selection of God's chosen.

Thirdly, why does the nation's fear of approaching the *mishkan* appear following the selection of Aaron's staff? This test involved no punishment or death; their terror would have seemed more appropriate after the devouring of the 250 men by fire!

Let us deal with the first question. What is the result of the first test? How does the offering of the *ketoret* clarify who is worthy of the priesthood? The basic assumption underlying this test is that "one who is not of the seed of Aaron the priest" (16:5), who comes to offer *ketoret*, will die—because only the *kohen* chosen by God is permitted to offer *ketoret*. In other words, this test arranged by Moses does not merely indicate the chosen priest, it is based on that choice itself. Only the person who is chosen may offer *ketoret*, and obviously he will live on after this sacrifice, but if you were not chosen by God and you still chose to offer *ketoret*, your penalty is death. And so, the results of the test are to be discerned in the fire which "went out from before God and devoured the two hundred and fifty men who offered *ketoret*"

(16:35). This is not merely the punishment for the complaint, but rather a genuine clarification of the claim. Anyone who came to offer incense "in competition" with Aaron endangered himself, for if he was not truly worthy of priesthood then he would pay for this attempt with his life. This wording—"and a fire went out from before God and devoured . . ."—recalls the punishment of Nadab and Abihu on the eighth day of the consecration of the *mishkan*: "And a fire went out from before God and devoured them, and they died before God" (Leviticus 10:2). The connection between the two events is clear; in both cases those who offer foreign incense without being so commanded are burned. This is not necessarily a punishment for something that they have done, but rather a direct consequence of the actual offering of the incense.

When the nation complains to Moses and Aaron that they have put God's nation to death, this is not merely another complaint, but rather a rejection of the proof of God's choice. The fundamental assumption of the test of the *ketoret* was that anyone not worthy of offering it would die by God's hand. If it was Moses and Aaron who had put the 250 men to death, however, then nothing had been proven, and Aaron was not shown to have been chosen. Therefore—and this answers our second question—further clarification is brought for the original complaint. The additional test comes not to respond directly to the claim that Moses and Aaron had put the 250 men to death, but rather to prove once again Aaron's selection, since the nation refused to accept the result of the first test.

The way in which the Torah emphasizes that we are returning here to the original test, and that this did not represent proof of anything new, is to draw a clear parallel between the first complaint—"the entire congregation is holy"—and the second—"you have put God's nation to death." All the motifs of the first complaint appear in the second one, too. Let us briefly compare them:

a. **The complaint:** "And they GATHERED to Moses and to Aaron and said to them, 'It is too much for you; for the entire congregation—all are holy and God is among them; why then do you elevate yourselves over GOD'S CONGREGATION" (16:3);

"And all the congregation of the Israelites complained the next morning to Moses and to Aaron saying, 'you have put GOD'S CONGREGATION to death. And it was, when the congregation GATHERED to Moses and Aaron . . ." (17:6-7).

b. **Moses's response:** "And Moses heard and fell upon his face" (16:4);

"And they fell upon their faces" (17:10).

c. **Revelation of God's glory in the Ohel Mo'ed:** "And Korah GATHERED the whole congregation to them to the entrance of the OHEL MO'ED. And God's glory appeared to the whole congregation";

"And it was, when the congregation GATHERED to Moses and Aaron and they turned to the OHEL MO'ED, and behold—a cloud covered it, and the glory of God was visible" (17:7).

d. **God's words:** "'Separate yourselves from this congregation and I shall devour them in an instant'—and they fell upon their faces" (16:21);

"Rise up from amongst this congregation and I shall devour them in an instant'—and they fell upon their faces" (17:10).

In both instances Moses and Aaron attempt to cancel the evil decree—the first time by prayer, and the second time by Aaron's atonement for the people by means of the *ketoret*.

e. **The test for the chosen one:** As already discussed, in both instances there is a test in which Aaron prevails over his adversaries and it is proved that he is the one worthy and chosen for priesthood.

f. **Memorial of the test:** "And he lifted the incense pan from the midst of the burning and scatter the fire outwards …' and it was A SIGN TO THE ISRAELITES … a memorial to the Israelites" (17:2–5);

"Place Aaron's staff before the ark of testimony as a keepsake, AS A SIGN TO THE REBELLIOUS PEOPLE."

g. **In fact, if we take this comparison further we see that corresponding to the nation's complaint following the taking of the incense pans as a memorial,** "You have put God's nation to death," we later find "See, we shall perish, we shall die; all of us shall die." The death which serves as the topic of the complaint against Moses and Aaron now serves as the reason for the great fear on the part of the nation to approach the kodesh.

Now we are able to answer the third question. Why was it only after the second test—the blossoming of Aaron's staff, involving no death—that the people fear to approach the *mishkan*? As mentioned, this fear would have seemed more appropriate following the first test, when more than 250 people lost their lives. But in light of our discussion, it is only in the wake of the second test that it becomes clear to the nation that the 250 indeed lost their lives because they offered incense without being permitted to do so. At first, the nation suspected Moses and Aaron of having put "God's nation" to death, and so they had no reason to fear approaching the *kodesh*. It was only after Aaron's selection was clearly and openly displayed that they understood that their second claim simply had no substance, and that the *kodesh* itself consumed those who entered without authorization. Now the nation experiences the full awe and fear of approaching the *kodesh*, which brings death to those who are not permitted to be there.

Rav Yonatan Grossman is a graduate of Yeshivat Har Etzion and has earned a PhD from Bar Ilan University. He is an instructor at Herzog College and Bar Ilan University and also teaches at Har Etzion and Migdal Oz. He is the son of famed Israeli historian, Dr. Avraham Grossman.

Chapter 6

The Spies

A FEW YEARS AGO, *Forbes* magazine ran a column listing ways to identify bad leaders. Among the traits common among bad leaders is the failure of leaders to "lead themselves." As the article notes, "A leader who lacks character or integrity will not endure the test of time. It doesn't matter how intelligent, affable, persuasive, or savvy a person is, if they are prone to rationalizing unethical behavior based upon current or future needs, they will eventually fall prey to their own undoing." Another problematic trait identified by *Forbes* as typical of poor leaders is a know-it-all attitude: "The best leaders are acutely aware of how much they don't know. They have no need to be the smartest person in the room, but have the unyielding desire to learn from others." A third trait that caught my attention was the notion that it's all about them. "If a leader doesn't understand the concept of 'service above self' they will not engender the trust, confidence, and loyalty of those they lead .... An over-abundance of ego, pride, and arrogance are not positive leadership traits."[1]

What does this *Forbes* article have to do with the story of the spies, which is found in chapter 13 of *Sefer BeMidbar*? If we skip to the end of that story, just about everything. Look at the conclusion of the story: the spies themselves are struck down by God in a plague (Numbers 14:37), and the nation is condemned to wander for forty years in the wilderness (Numbers 14:34). Talk about bad leadership!

Yet the opening of the story of the spies is both vastly different and quite positive:

> The Lord spoke to Moses, saying, "Send men to scout the land of Canaan, which I am giving to the Israelite people; send one man from each of their ancestral tribes, each one a chieftain among them." So Moses, by the Lord's command, sent them out from

---

1. Myatt, "15 Ways."

the wilderness of Paran, all the men being leaders of the Israelites (Numbers 13:1–3).

These verses are unequivocal about the strong leadership qualifications of this band of spies, and, if that were not sufficient, several traditional commentators step forward to emphasize and reinforce the high-caliber nature of these men. For example, Sforno makes clear in his commentary on Numbers 13:2 that the selection of these men, who by necessity must be of sterling character, is too important a task to be left to the people themselves. Rashbam, a grandchild of Rashi and a highly regarded commentator in his own right, also sees the positive in the spies and offers the following observations regarding the language of verse 2 in his commentary on Numbers 13:2:[2]

> The principal meaning of the verse is as follows: you should take as the twelve representatives, one of each tribe, men whose hearts were set on going on to the Holy Land. You should select volunteers, willing to act as spies. From among all these volunteers, you are to select the ones who appear most suitable to you.

Presumably, Moses, God's most trusted servant, would have had the knowledge and insight to pick the right men for the job. Nonetheless, based on the outcome of their mission, it would seem that these twelve men were not the leaders all assumed them to be.

Or were they?

Any consideration of the spy story must necessarily address two fundamental questions. First, how could the spies, who were "men of distinction" and all "heads of the children of Israel," sin so badly? Second, if their report was truthful (an issue we will consider at length below), what was their sin? Answering these questions will allow us to focus on the character traits that these men embody and determine whether these are admirable or to be avoided.

There is sharp disagreement about what motivates the spies. Rashi, for example, argues in his comment on Numbers 13:3 that the spies started out with good intentions: "these men [although they later sinned] at that time [when they were appointed] were worthy men." However, even Rashi concedes that their good intentions dissipated quickly. As he notes, the spies, upon their return, opted not to report to Moses and Aaron but instead shared their findings directly with the people (Numbers 13:26). Reflecting on the phrase "and they went and came" in his commentary on this verse,

---

2. Rabbi Samuel ben Meir was a leading French tosafist. His commentary on the Torah is renowned for its stress on the plain meaning of the text.

Rashi asks, what is the intent here of emphasizing their "coming" and "going"? He answers that "it is intended to compare their 'going' with their 'coming' to Moses. How was their coming to Moses? With an evil plan. So, too, was their 'going' on the journey with an evil plan."

Another source, the Zohar, steps in to address the issue of what motivates the Spies.[3] According to the Zohar, it is little more than blatant self-interest:

> Moses sent them. They were all men. They were righteous prominent leaders of Israel, but their words caused terrible calamity. What made them do this? Rather, they said: "If Israel enters the land, Moses will cause us to be replaced, for we can only lead in the desert, but in the land we will not lead" (Zohar Shlach 158a).[4]

The Zohar here paints a picture of leaders who are more concerned with their own positions of power than with the good of their constituents. In essence, they guarantee their own standing by preventing a situation which would have caused their removal from power.

According to this view, the spies are motivated by greed and perhaps even by arrogance. Yet this is not the only or even the most prevalent opinion. In their report, the spies proclaim that "we looked like grasshoppers to ourselves, and so we must have looked to them" (Numbers 13:33). According to one midrashic explanation, God rebukes the spies for this claim: "I take no objection to your saying: 'We looked like grasshoppers to ourselves,' but I take offense when you say 'So we must have looked to them.' How do you know how I made you look to them? Perhaps you appeared to them as angels!" (Numbers Rabbah 16:11). Does this not sound like fear? Rashi seems to think so and opines in his comment on Numbers 13:33 that the spies reported overhearing the giants talking to one another, saying: "There are ants in the vineyard that resemble human beings." Why does Rashi shift the metaphor from grasshoppers to ants? Perchance he is trying to emphasize their lack of confidence, for an ant is smaller and more easily crushed than a grasshopper.[5]

Rabbi Jonathan Sacks expounds on this shift of metaphors and asks how the spies were to know the people's strength.[6] By merely looking at

---

3. The Zohar is a group of books including commentary on the mystical aspects of the Torah and scriptural interpretation as well as material on mysticism, mythical cosmogony, and mystical psychology.

4. Translation from "Shlach (Numbers 13–15): The Spies."

5. Loevinger, "Seeing Beneath the Surface."

6. Sacks, "Parshat Shelach."

their cities to see if they were unwalled or fortified? Should the spies have assumed that if the inhabitants of the land lived in unwalled cities, they were strong and trusted in their own strength? Or maybe they should have assumed that if these people live in fortified cities, they were weak and insecure?

Basing himself on Rashi and midrashic commentaries, Rabbi Sacks concludes that the spies correctly noted and reported that the cities were fortified, but that they drew the wrong conclusion:

> Clearly, the sight of the cities made a deep impression on the Spies. This makes psychological sense, and it accords with historical fact. The cities in ancient Canaan were indeed surrounded by high and thick walls which made them seem impregnable. It is easy to enter into the mindset of the Spies. They had been living in the wilderness, in fragile, temporary dwellings. They had not seen a city for some time. The fortifications surrounding towns like Jericho must have been awe-inspiring. But they did not stop to consider what this might mean in terms of the strength of the opposition they faced. According to the Midrash, they drew precisely the wrong conclusion: the cities are strong; therefore the people are strong. In fact, the opposite was the case: the cities are strong; therefore the people are weak. People who are strong do not have to live behind defensive walls.[7]

Rabbi Hayyim ben Moshe ibn Attar, also known as the Or HaChaim, brings yet another perspective. He asks: if the twelve spies were all initially righteous and went to scout out the land with God's approval, what caused them to become corrupt? He suggests a fascinating answer: In his view, when a person represents another individual as his agent, he is affected by the mindset and thoughts of that person so much so that he is acting totally in the capacity of the one who appointed him. The *BeMidbar* narrative to this point makes clear that the Jewish people are suspicious and distrustful of God and His willingness to take them to the promised land, and consequently, the spies were impacted by this negative intent. In other words, it was the very negativity of the Jewish people that corrupted the spies.

The common theme in these divergent views is that the spies were evil or misguided or corrupt, that they had bad intentions, possibly even from the outset of their mission. However, there are those who bring a countervailing argument. Consider the view of Rabbi Yeshayahu Horowitz, more commonly referred to as Sh'lah HaKadosh. He explains that, indeed, all the spies were great men, but the consideration of the spies was that they wished

---

7. Sacks, "Parshat Shelach."

to remain in the desert with their beloved leader Moses. "They did not reject the Land of Israel, but preferred to learn Torah from Moses in exile. They appreciated that the Land was, indeed, a holy land, a special land, but they believed that the Jews needed to earn their entry into the Land. They knew that the Land of Israel would 'vomit out' any who were undeserving."[8]

A corollary to this—and arguably an even more positive perspective on the actions and motivations of the spies—derives from the role of the spies as leaders of the people.[9] Precisely because they were leaders, they were afraid to enter the land. As leaders, they felt responsibility for the well-being of the people. They were afraid that entering the land would constitute a step down from the spiritual level that they were accustomed to in the desert—a life in which they were visibly directed in their travels by God Himself—where their thirst was sated by the miraculous well of Miriam, and where their physical needs were satisfied by Heavenly bread (the manna). From this perspective, who could blame the spies for wanting to remain in the wilderness? Yet, who could not help but see the arrogance underlying their actions, to think that they knew better than Moses (or perhaps even better than God Himself) which destiny was best for the Jewish people?

This being the book of Numbers, a lack of clarity about the motivations of the spies, and even regarding the character trait most logically associated with them, is not surprising. And for this reason, this is one of my favorite units when teaching *Sefer BeMidbar*. There is so much for students to consider and to focus on, and different students will inevitably latch onto one or another of these differing views when discussing and debating the actions of the spies.

There is one aspect of the spie's story that is not lacking in clarity, and this involves the false nature of their report to the people. The false and misleading elements of their report transcend their motivations, and Jewish perspectives on truth can and should be an important aspect of this unit, especially when coupled with lessons on leadership.

The views of the talmudic sages here are clear and unequivocal. Rabban Shimon ben Gamliel said: "The world endures because of three things: justice, truth, and peace" (Pirqe Avot 1:18). Rabbi Hanina said: "Truth is the seal of the Holy One, blessed be He" (Babylonian Talmud, Shabbat 55a). The Babylonian Talmud perhaps sums it up best in Pesahim 113b: "The Holy One hates him who says one thing in his mouth and another in his heart."

For the talmudic sages, the God of truth is found wherever there is truth, and His absence is felt wherever there is falsehood. Various biblical

---

8. Quoted in "Shlach."
9. See generally Katz, "Sin."

texts echo and reinforce this notion. The prophet declares: "The Lord God is truth" (Jeremiah 10:10). So, too, does the psalmist: "Your Torah is truth" (Psalm 119:142).

This allegiance to truth extends even to promises a God-fearing individual makes in their heart, an axiom illustrated in the tale of Rav Safra in the Babylonia Talmud, Makkot 24a. Rav Safra once had a particular item for sale. An individual came to him and offered Rav Safra a price which suited him. What the individual did not realize when making his offer was that Rav Safra was immersed in prayer and could not interrupt to signal his consent. The prospective buyer, under the impression that the rabbi's silence was a sign that he had rejected the bid, kept increasing his offering price. In the end, Rav Safra insisted on concluding the sale at the original price to which he had consented "in his heart."

This commitment to truth and the impact it has on communal leaders is not limited to the biblical or talmudic eras. Modern scholars continue to proclaim its relevance. Take, for example, Chaya T. Halberstam, who, in the introduction to her book *Law and Truth in Biblical and Rabbinic Literature*, writes that:

> The eschatological vision of the eleventh chapter of Isaiah envisages the ideal leader in these terms: "The spirit of YHWH shall alight upon him: a spirit of wisdom and insight, a spirit of counsel and valor.... He shall sense the truth by his reverence for YHWH: he shall not judge by what his eyes behold, nor decide by what his ears perceive" (2–3). Looking, listening—these human senses, we are told, often steer decision makers in the wrong direction. But the spirit of YHWH imparts the truth, and it is through the truth that the ideal leader "shall judge the poor with justice, and decide with equity for the meek of the earth" (11:4).[10]

Let us now circle back to the spies and their use of deceit and falsehood as a tool for convincing the people that conquest of the promised land was beyond them. The spies begin their report innocently enough: "We came to the land you sent us to; it does indeed flow with milk and honey" (Numbers 13:27). Rashi is quick to point out in his comment on this verse that they stated this because "no fabricated statement in which one does not say at least some true words at first can in the end be maintained."

Ironically, the spies in this instance seem to set the template for the "big lie" technique employed and mastered by the Nazi propaganda machine of the twentieth century. This should be obvious to the informed reader, but

---

10. Halberstam, *Law and Truth*, 1.

many high school students may require some review and reinforcement of this concept. Hitler himself is the source of this technique, as he wrote in the tenth chapter of *Mein Kampf*:

> All this was inspired by the principle—which is quite true within itself—that in the big lie there is always a certain force of credibility; because the broad masses of a nation are always more easily corrupted in the deeper strata of their emotional nature than consciously or voluntarily; and thus in the primitive simplicity of their minds, they more readily fall victims to the big lie than the small lie, since they themselves often tell small lies in little matters, but would be ashamed to resort to large-scale falsehoods. It would never come into their heads to fabricate colossal untruths, and they would not believe that others could have the impudence to distort the truth so infamously. Even though the facts which prove this to be so may be brought clearly to their minds, they will still doubt and waver and will continue to think that there may be some other explanation. For the grossly impudent lie always leaves traces behind it, even after it has been nailed down, a fact which is known to all expert liars in this world and to all who conspire together in the art of lying.[11]

In contrast to the championing of the "big lie" by the Nazis, the Torah's view on lying seems clear cut.[12] A sampling of verses demonstrates the point: "You shall not bear false witness" (Exodus 20:16); "You shall not steal, you shall not deny falsely, and you shall not lie one to another" (Leviticus 19:11); and "Distance yourself from a false matter" (Exodus 23:7). These verses notwithstanding, there are discussions among Jewish legal authorities as to whether the prohibition against lying in a non-judicial context is biblically or rabbinically based. Some halakhic decisors are of the opinion that the Torah only explicitly forbids lying by judges and witnesses, whereas others apply this prohibition universally.[13] Legal technicalities aside, the talmudic rabbis in general come out forcefully against lying. For instance, basing themselves on the verse "You shall have just scales, just weights, a just *ephah* [a dry measure], and a just *hin* [a liquid measure]" (Leviticus 19:36), the sages homiletically translate *hin* as "yes" based on the similarity of the word *hin* to the Aramaic word meaning yes (*hen*). According to the

---

11. Hitler, *Mein Kampf*, volume 1, chapter 10.

12. For a more extensive examination of this topic, see Friedman and Weisel, "Should Moral Individuals Ever Lie?"

13. Friedman and Weisel, "Should Moral Individuals Ever Lie?," 2.

Babylonian Talmud, Bava Metzi'a 49a, the phrase "a just *hin*" teaches us that an individual's "yes" should be as just (in the sense of righteous) as his "no."

In any discussion about character traits, be it in the context of the spie's story or any other aspect of the book of Numbers, staying clear of lying is perhaps the only exception (or, at the very least, among the most important ones) to the grayness of *Sefer BeMidbar*.

Sefer BeMidbar—The Spies
Sample Unit Plan

Unit	Primary Source(s)	Supplemental Reading(s)	Timeframe
The Spies	Numbers 13	Parshat Shelach	two weeks
	Rashi 13:2		
Middah:	Kli Yakar 13:2		
Arrogance	Rashi 13:16		
	Sforno 13:16		
	Rashi 13:22	Should Moral Individuals Ever Lie? Insights from Jewish Law	
	Rashi 13:26		
	Hirsch 13:26		
	Rashi 13:30		

Essential Questions

1. How could the spies, who were "men of distinction" and all "heads of the children of Israel" sin so badly?
2. If their report was truthful, what was their sin?
3. What is the power of "but?"

Evaluating/Checking for Understanding

1. Daily discussions/student interactions

   Student questions and observations typically drive each day's discussion.

2. Occasional written reflections

   At the discretion of the teacher, a tool to foster further reflection on the unit's essential questions.

3. Character trait essay

   See appendix for assignment rubric.

4. Unit test

   Unit tests should, by definition, be crafted by individual teachers to meet the needs of their specific students. The Understanding by Design *framework created by Grant Wiggins and Jay McTighe is an excellent tool for the development of appropriate tests and assessments, as its emphasis on backward design forces teachers to consider in advance the assessment evidence needed to document and validate that the targeted learning goals have been achieved.*

Primary Source Texts

1. *BeMidbar* chapter 13: Read text and seek to identify problematic (what I call "red flag") words and phrases (with teacher's guidance, of course). These red flag words and phrases will likely vary from class to class depending on the sophistication and linguistic abilities of the students, coupled with the background and interests of the teacher. That said, some important examples of red flag words and phrases in this chapter appear in commentaries A–H.

2. Supplemental readings for each unit are intended to demonstrate that serious scholarship about and explanations of *Sefer BeMidbar* are not limited to the classical medieval commentators but continue to our time. As part of this unit's analysis of the character traits embodied by the spies, students will read "Parashat Shelach" by Rav Mosheh Lichtenstein and discuss his insights into the motivations and the actions of the spies.

3. To conclude our discussions of the spies, a "stand alone" mini-unit on lying should include these two supplemental readings: "Truth and Lies in the Jewish Tradition" and "Should Moral Individuals Ever Lie?—Insights from Jewish Law."

Sefer BeMidbar—The Spies
Primary Texts

A. Rashi 13:2

"Send thou men"

Why is the section dealing with the Spies put in juxtaposition with the section dealing with Miriam's punishment? To show the grievousness of the Spies' sin: because she (Miriam) was punished on account of the slander which she uttered against her brother, and these sinners witnessed it and yet they did not take a lesson from her.

"Send you (lit., for thyself)"

That is, according to your own judgement: I do not command you, but if you wish to do so send them.—God said this because the Israelites came to Moses and said. "We will send men before us etc.," as it is said (Deuteronomy 1:22): "And you approached me, all of you, [saying, We will send men, etc.]," and Moses took counsel with the Shechinah (the Lord), whereupon He said to them, I have told them long ago that it (the land) is good, as it is said (Exodus 3:17): "I will bring you up out of the affliction of Egypt . . . [unto a land flowing with milk and honey]." By their lives! I swear that I will give them now an opportunity to fall into error through the statements of the Spies, so that they should not come into possession of it (the land).

B. Kli Yakar 13:2

"Send thou men"

According to that which the Jewish people said (Deuteronomy 1:22), "Let us send men ahead of us so that they will search out the land for us." "For us," that is to say, for our benefit and for our good. Said the Holy One, blessed be

He to Moses, "Send for yourself and not for them, for the benefits and the good that comes from this mission will be specifically for you. But for them, no good will come of it, for because of this mission, death will be decreed upon them." As for Moses, this [mission] resulted in him living another 40 years, because it had already been decreed concerning Moses that he would not see that which would be done to the seven nations [then inhabiting Canaan, that is, Moses would not be allowed to enter the land with the people]. Thus due to the sin of the Spies, Moses life was extended by 40 years. [In other words, were it not for the sin of the Spies, the people would have soon entered the Promised Land, and Moses would have died.]

C. Rashi 13:16

"And Moses called Hoshea [the son of Nun Jehoshua]"

By giving him this name יהושע which is a compound of יה and הושע "God may save," he in effect prayed for him: "May God save you from the evil counsel of the Spies."

D. Sforno 13:16

"And Moses called Hoshea [the son of Nun Jehoshua]"

The Torah means that this man was known as a man of valor by the name of Hoshea among the members of his tribe. The fact that he has been referred to as "Joshua" already in Numbers 11:28 is because in his capacity as Moses's personal valet. Moses had changed his name in the form of a prayer asking that he be the instrument of his own salvation and that of others.

E. Rashi 13:22

"[And they went up by the south] and he came unto Hebron"

Caleb alone went there and prostrated himself on the graves of the Patriarchs, offering prayer that he might be helped not to give way to the enticement of his colleagues and join them in their counsel. You may see that it was Caleb who went there, for so indeed it (Scripture) states (Deuteronomy 1:36), "[Save Caleb the son of Jephunneh, he shall see it] and unto him will I give the land upon which he hath trodden!" and it is written (Judges 1:20), "And they gave Hebron unto Caleb."

F. Rashi 13:26

"And they went and came [to Moses]"

What is the force of "they went" (we have been informed that they had returned; why afterwards make any reference to their going on the journey)? It is intended to compare their "going" with their "coming" to Moses! How was their coming to Moses? With an evil plan! So, too, was their "going" on the journey with an evil plan (i.e., that when they were travelling they had already resolved to bring back an evil report)!

G. Rabbi Samson Raphael Hirsch 13:26

"And they went and came [to Moses]"

At their return they had already decided beforehand not to go first to Moses and Aaron, but to give the result of their investigations immediately to the people. And just thereby they showed the malevolence of their behavior. Had their intentions been good, whatever conclusions they might have arrived at, they would first have made their report to Moses and Aaron and sought advice and instructions. But that was just what they did not want. They thought that the only means for their own and the people's salvation lay in opposition to Moses and Aaron. Their report took the form at once of an accusation against Moses and Aaron in the presence of all the people and a call to these latter to save themselves from the ruin with which they were threatened by Moses and Aaron's intentions.

H. Rashi 13:30

"to Moses"

This means he silenced them that they should hear what he was going to say about Moses. He cried aloud saying: "Is this the only thing the son of Amram has done to us?!"—One who heard him thus speaking believed that he was about to speak to his disparagement, and because they had something in their mind against Moses through the Spies' statements, all of them kept silent to hear his disparagement. He, however, said: "Did he not divide the Red Sea for us, and bring down the Manna for us, and collect the quails for us?!"

Sefer BeMidbar—The Spies

Supplemental Reading

Parashat Shelach

—Rav Mosheh Lichtenstein

Last week, in our study of Parashat Beha'alotekha, we saw that in response to the prophecy-criticism of Eldad and Medad, Moses changes course with respect to his leadership of the Israelites. Whereas until then he had remained "outside the camp," detached from the nation's petty murmuring and gluttonous yearnings for meat, he now "reentered the camp" (11:30). He is now prepared to work with the nation from within, rather than condemning their complaints from without. We then asked, why was this decision ineffective? Why was this new policy of Moses followed by the nation's continued deterioration, culminating with the sin of scouts, as we read in Parashat Shelach?

A. The Spies

In order to answer this question, we must conduct a careful study of the episode of the Spies. Among the more surprising features of this incident is the list of people chosen for the spy mission. Besides Joshua, we have not encountered any of the scouts earlier in Chumash. We thus deal with an inexperienced, unknown team charged with this task. We could have perhaps easily explained this in light of the simple fact that the scouts embarked on a purely military scouting mission, involving no communal function. There was no need, then, to select for this job known leaders, but rather professional military men. However, the crisis that surfaces upon their return is due precisely to the fact that this constituted not a standard, routine survey of territory, but rather a mission of a communal nature, that was composed in accordance with its nature and communal function. After all, Moses did not dispatch a small group of secret spies, but rather a delegation consisting of representatives from all the tribes, men whose tribes saw them as respected leaders, as the text itself testifies: "send one man from each of their ancestral tribes, each one a chieftain among them" (13:2). Additionally, a point was made to select men who had earned the respect of the entire nation: "all the men being leaders of the Israelites" (13:3). Needless to say, these considerations are hardly suitable as criteria for a surveillance unit sent to collect information, but rather for a representative delegation. The question thus arises, who are these unknown individuals, whom the Torah describes as "chieftains" and "leaders of the Israelites"?

I would suggest that the scouts were selected specifically because they were unknown. Whereas until know [sic] the leadership has come from the elders, in the wake of Eldad and Medad's call for a transition to a younger leadership Moses appoints men from Joshua's generation to participate in the scouting delegation. In place of Nahshon, the senior chieftain of the tribe of Judah, came the younger leader, Caleb, and so with each of the twelve tribes.

It would appear that this replacement of the older leadership with a younger group more in tune with the state of mind of the new generation contributed to the failure of the scouts. To substantiate this claim, we must examine the components of *chet ha-meraglim* (the sin of the Spies) and the function played by the leadership in this tragic incident.

B. The Mission

The commentators raise two basic approaches as to the purpose of dispatching the scouts: 1) it served as a military mission to assist in the conquest of the land; 2) to foster an attachment of the Jewish people to the land. Both these elements appear in the assignment with which Moses charges them:

> See what kind of country it is. Are the people who dwell in it strong or weak, few or many? Is the country in which they dwell good or bad? Are the towns they live in open or fortified? Is the soil rich or poor? Is it wooded or not ... (13:18–20)

As we emphasized, however, the composition and nature of the delegation itself seem more suitable for the second purpose, which, apparently, appeared to be the central function as Moses saw it. Following the incident of Kibroth-hattaavah and the Israelites' state of mind that it revealed, this mission was dispatched in an attempt to impress upon the nation the goodness of the land and to endear it to them, by showing them its fruit and describing it to them. The more the Israelites would sense that they would soon leave the wilderness and enter their new land, they could expect fewer problems along the way. For this purpose Moses sent the scouts after the debacle of Kibroth-hattaavah.

In effect, the message demanded from the scouts to encourage the nation had to be a two-tiered one. First, they would have to show the goodness that awaits them in the land; secondly, that they are fully capable of seizing it. Without the first message, the people will have no desire to continue forward towards the land; without the second, they would despair and make no attempt at the conquest. The need for both these messages flows from the same root—the nation's inability and unwillingness to take upon itself challenges and objectives. Struggle, confrontation and responding to the need of the hour without expecting to taste of the fruits of the land do not speak to the hearts of the weary nation. They want fruit. Endearing the land to them thus entails emphasizing its agricultural qualities and fertile soil.

Yet, the tragic irony of this situation is that specifically the personality and approach of the elders would have better suited this task. True, the scouts, who belonged to the new generation, indeed felt genuine appreciation for the goodness of the land and its fruit; however, they also confronted the challenge of capturing the land and displacing its inhabitants. The land, its quality and fruits are indeed impressive, but so is the might of its inhabitants and their fortified cities. The scouts are seized with terror when confronting this challenge, and this fear is conveyed to the people. Despairing of the possibility of capturing the land, and not a lack of appreciation, lies at the heart of the *chet ha-meraglim*. They do not reject the beautiful land itself, but rather the effort required to occupy it. This point emerges clearly from both the verses in *Sefer BeMidbar* describing the events as they unfold, as well as from Moses's analysis of the incident years later, from a more distant perspective:

> They told him and said: "We came to the land you sent us to; it does indeed flow with milk and honey, and this is its fruit. However, the people who inhabit the country are powerful, and the cities are fortified and very large; moreover, we saw the children of giants there. Amalekites dwell in the Negev region; Hittites, Jebusites and Amorites inhabit the hill country; and Canaanites dwell be the sea and along the Jordan." Caleb hushed the people before Moses and said, "Let us by all means go up, and we shall gain possession of it, for we shall surely overcome it." But the

men who had gone up with him said, "We cannot attack that people, for it is stronger than we." They spread calumnies among the Israelites about the land they had scouted, saying, "The country that we traversed and scouted is one that devours its settlers. All the people that we saw in it are men of great size; we saw the Nefilim there, giants among the Nefilim, and we looked like grasshoppers to ourselves, and so we must have looked to them" (Numbers 13:27–33).

They took some of the fruit of the land with them and brought it down to us. And they gave us this report: "It is a good land that the Lord our God is giving to us." Yet you refused to go up, and flouted the command of the Lord your God. You sulked in your tents and said, "It is because the Lord hates us that He brought us out of the land of Egypt, to hand us over to the Amorites to wipe us out. Where are we going? Our kinsmen have taken the heart out of us, saying, 'We saw there a people stronger and taller than we, large cities with walls sky-high, and even giants'" (Deuteronomy 1:25–29).

The deep despair that flows from the people's general spiritual state arises very clearly from the bottom-line consensus that the scouts convey to Moses and the people: "we looked like grasshoppers to ourselves, and so we must have looked to them."

Paradoxically, specifically with this spiritual danger, the elders, who led the struggle in Egypt, were far better suited to deal. They, who harbored no fear towards Pharaoh's taskmasters as they suffered as slaves under the whip, who did not hesitate to oppose the Egyptian oppressors, would certainly not have been deterred by the military might of the Canaanite peoples. On the other hand, though, we may assume that sending the elders would not have helped significantly in enlisting the people for the effort required or convincing them of the goodness of the land. A dilemma with no solution has evolved. Dispatching the elders would have deepened the national crisis and the gap between the leadership and the public, which would not have been convinced of the very need to enter the land. Conversely, selecting a younger delegation could be effective in impressing upon the nation the quality of the land, but could also bring them to despair. There was no choice, then, other than selecting outstanding individuals from the younger generation in the hope that they could rise to the challenge and bring the nation along with them. If they had not become frightened as a result of their lack of trust in God, if they had not been dragged along by the people's loss of resolve, they would have been the only ones capable of changing the picture. As Eldad and Medad claimed, the older leadership would have no impact on those who longed for meat and comfort, the ones who set the tone for the rest of the nation. Only a fresh leadership from within this layer could tap the slumbering reservoirs of strength and bring about the necessary transformation. But instead of awakening the nation, the scouts were frightened, and they engendered despair and terror.

It turns out, then, that the selection of the young scouts in response to the sin of Kibroth-hattaavah contributed tragically to the birth of *chet ha-meraglim* and its severe consequences. In order to bring the nation into the land, there was no choice but to select "chieftains" with leadership potential from within the younger generation; and this is exactly what Moses did. Moses did not, however, realize that they were not prepared to meet the challenges that stood before them. He thus allowed them to embark on this fateful mission, thereby contributing to the tragic result.

C. Caleb and Joshua

> They said one to another, "Let us make a captain and return to Egypt." Then Moses and Aaron fell on their faces before all the assembled congregation of the Israelites. Joshua son of Nun and Caleb son of Jephunneh, of those who had scouted the land, rent their clothing and exhorted the whole Israelite community: "The land that we traversed and scouted is an exceedingly good land" (Numbers 14:4–7).

The response to the sin of the Spies also illustrates the gap that has developed between the generations. Moses, Aaron and the elders cannot oppose the nation or deal with them; they simply "fell on their faces." Caleb and Joshua, meanwhile, members of the younger generation, stand up to the people and try to uplift their spirits. Belonging to the younger stratum, the generation of the wilderness, Caleb and Joshua are not taken aback, they don't feel hopeless in opposing the nation, as do Moses and Aaron.[1] Caleb, who demonstrates courage and the preparedness to oppose the despair and spiritual fatigue of his generation, expresses the leadership qualities that his

---

1. In effect, this response of Moses marks the culmination of a process. After the Israelites' first complaint in *Sefer BeMidbar*, not only is Moses not disheartened, but he prays on their behalf (Numbers 11:2); in response to the second complaint (Kibroth-hattaavah), he turns to the Almighty for assistance, whereas here, in the incident of the Spies, Moses is simply paralyzed and cannot react. This is not just a gradual progression; rather, each time the severity of the complaint increases and even encompasses broader sectors within the nation. Correspondingly, Moses's ability to handle these problems gradually diminishes.

colleagues were to embody. But given that the rest of the entire delegation do not support their position, but rather seek to undermine it, their efforts are futile and destined for failure from the outset.

In this context, it is worth noting the distinction between Caleb and Joshua in their reaction to their colleagues. As we can see from the narrative, only Caleb speaks out forcefully against the scouts, even when Joshua remains silent: "Caleb hushed the people and said, 'Let us by all means go up, and we shall gain possession of it, for we shall surely overcome it'" (13:30). True, they both rend their garments and together express their positive stance:

> Joshua son of Nun and Caleb son of Jephunneh, of those who had scouted the land, rent their clothing and exhorted the whole Israelite community: "The land that we traversed and scouted is an exceedingly good land. If the Lord is pleased with us, He will bring us into that land, a land that flows with milk and honey, and give it to us; only you must not rebel against the Lord. Have no fear then of the people of the country, for they are our prey: their protection has departed from them, but the Lord is with us. Have no fear of them!" (14:6–9)

Nevertheless, Caleb opposes the nation more directly and overtly. He is not inhibited by them at all; he expresses his view with force and pride, without softening his words. This approach, however, will not succeed under the conditions that have emerged. Joshua therefore does not join him, trying as much as possible to avoid a direct confrontation with the nation. Both he and Caleb face the same dilemma as Aaron and Hur encountered during the worship of the Golden Calf. Is it preferable to preach the absolute truth while confronting an unrestrained, incited mob, or should one avoid confrontation as much as possible, in order to preserve the possibility of positive influence changing the situation that has emerged? (See Babylonian Talmud, Sanhedrin 7a.) Caleb's confrontational approach resembles that of Hur, whereas Joshua foregoes on the direct confrontation out of a desire and hope to allow for positive influence in the future.

This distinction between Joshua and Caleb is expressed in the Torah's explanation of the merits by which they are permitted to enter the land. Whereas Caleb is presented as earning entry into the land because of his praiseworthy leadership during the incident of the Spies, Joshua does not enter for this reason. Rather, he enters because he is the leader of the generation that would enter Eretz Yisrael. This point is made very clear towards the beginning of *Sefer Devarim*:

> "The Lord heard the sound of your words and He was angry and vowed: Not one of these men, this evil generation, shall see the good land that I swore to give to your fathers—none except Caleb son of Jephunneh; he shall see it, and to him and his descendants will I give the land on which he set foot, because he remained loyal to the Lord. Because of you the Lord was incensed with me, too, and He said: You shall not enter it either. Joshua son of Nun, who attends you, he shall enter it. Imbue him with strength, for he shall allot it to Israel. Moreover, your little ones who you said would be carried off, your children who do not yet know good from bad, they shall enter it; to them will I give it and they shall possess it" (Deuteronomy 1:34–39).

In this passage, Moses clearly distinguishes between Caleb and Joshua. Only Caleb inherits the land as reward for his action during the incident of the Spies. Joshua, by contrast, earns entry not as reward, but due to his role as leader of the next generation. The verses therefore separate the two men from one another. It mentions Caleb's merit in the same breath as the fate of the generation of the wilderness, since his fate, too, results from that event. Joshua's fate, however, is mentioned in conjunction with that of Moses, since his future follows from Moses's death in the wilderness, and not the decree resulting from *chet ha-meraglim*.

In effect, Caleb earns his portion in the land as reward for the devotion he demonstrated; his portion was thus given to him and his offspring as a personal gift. He receives his portion not as part of the Israelites' general inheritance of the land, but rather as a private bequest. These verses therefore emphasize that the portion is bequeathed to Caleb and his children, and the designation of "the land on which he set foot" as his personal portion—despite the fact that the land has yet to be apportioned among the tribes. Joshua, on the other hand, was not sentenced to die in the wilderness, but neither did he earn the right to enter the land as a special privilege. Joshua's entry or barred entry depends on the generation to which he will belong. If he will be counted among the generation of the wilderness, then he will die a natural death—not as a punishment—in the wilderness. If, however, he will be considered a member of the generation entering the land, he will enter with them. The Torah therefore does not designate any specific area for his allotment, for before the general distribution of the land we cannot speak of certain places earmarked for given individuals. For the same reason the Torah makes no mention of Joshua's offspring, for we deal here not with a private grant that becomes a family estate, but rather part of the Israelites' inheritance of the land as a whole.

In *Sefer BeMidbar*, too, we detect a distinction between Joshua and Caleb in terms of their portions in the land. In discussing the generation of the meraglim and their fate, the Torah mentions only Caleb as the one from that generation who earned entry into the land. In this context, no mention is made of Joshua:

> "Nevertheless, as I live and as the Lord's Presence fills the whole world, none of the men who have seen My Presence and the signs that I have performed in Egypt and in the wilderness, and who have tried Me these ten times and have disobeyed Me, shall see the land that I promised on oath to their fathers; none of those who spurn Me shall see it. But My servant Caleb, because he was imbued with a different spirit and remained loyal to Me—him will I bring into the land that he entered, and his offspring shall hold it as a possession" (Numbers 14:21-24).

When, however, the Torah emphasizes not only the barred entry of the scouts, but also the entry of the next generation into the land, Joshua is then mentioned together with Caleb as among those permitted to enter Canaan:

> "Say to them: 'As I live, says the Lord, I will do to you just as you have spoken in My ears. In this very wilderness shall your carcasses drop. Of all of you who were recorded in your various lists from the age of twenty years up, you who have muttered against Me, not one shall enter the land in which I swore to settle you—except for Caleb son of Jephunneh and Joshua son of Nun. Your children who, you said, would be carried off—these will I allow to enter; they shall know the land that you have rejected'" (Numbers 14:28-32).

In conclusion, Caleb wages a tenacious, head-on confrontation against the Spies, bringing about a public Kiddush Hashem (sanctification of God's Name); for this he receives a reward from the Almighty for himself and his offspring for all time. Joshua, on the other hand, calculated his steps such that he could rehabilitate the nation and lead the next generation in the aftermath of the crisis. Through the efforts of both, an absolute Chillul Hashem (desecration of God's Name) was avoided, allowing for the infrastructure that would facilitate the entry of the next generation into the land.

Rav Mosheh Lichtenstein immigrated to Israel with his family in 1971. He studied at the Netiv Meir High School in Jerusalem and thereafter spent a year studying with Rabbi Joseph B. Soloveitchik. From 1979 to 1985, Rav Mosheh did *hesder* at Yeshivat Har Etzion, serving in the

Armored Corps. He received *semicha* from the *rabbanut* and a degree in English literature from Hebrew University. Rav Mosheh began teaching at Yeshivat Har Etzion in 1992, and, in 2008, he was inaugurated as Rosh Yeshiva, alongside his father Harav Aharon Lichtenstein, Harav Yaakov Medan, and Harav Baruch Gigi. He is married to Dr. Michal Lichtenstein and has three daughters.

Sefer BeMidbar—The Spies

Supplemental Reading

Should Moral Individuals Ever Lie?
Insights from Jewish Law

—Hershey H. Friedman and
Abraham C. Weisel

Indubitably, truth is important for the welfare of society. The famous dictum by Rabbi Shimon ben Gamliel (Babylonian Talmud, Avot 1:18) proclaims "the world endures on three things: justice, truth, and peace." It is difficult to imagine a society surviving for long if no one cares about honesty. Are there situations where one is permitted, or even obligated, to lie? This is a question that has been of great interest to theologians, philosophers, and religious leaders.

It appears that Aristotle in his *Ethics* feels that it is never permissible to prevaricate. Plato, on the other hand, in his *Republic*, is of the opinion that there are situations when one is indeed permitted to lie. For instance, he allows physicians to lie to patients if it is for their own good and statesmen to deceive if it is for the welfare of the public. Similarly, Christian thinkers and modern philosophers have also divided into two camps: Those who take an absolutist position on lying, whereby it is always forbidden, and those who believe that falsehoods are sometimes necessary, and accordingly, permissible.

In *De Mendacio* (On Lying), written c. 395 C.E., Augustine takes an absolutist approach to lying.[1] Citing Psalms (5:6–7) he rhetorically queries:

---

1. Augustine, *De Mendacio*, New Advent, <http://www.newadvent.org/fathers/1312.htm>.

How can one ever prevaricate if the Lord abhors liars and will destroy them. Accordingly, Augustine does not agree with those that favorably point to the two Hebrew midwives, Shiphrah and Puah, who risked their lives by lying to the Pharaoh in order to save the newborn Israelite babies in Egypt (Exodus 1:19–21), as proof that it may be praiseworthy to be dishonest. To Augustine, lies are abhorrent, even if for a good purpose. Augustine, however, espouses a hierarchy among eight types of lies, ranging from falsehoods "in religious doctrine" (the worst) to lies that do not hurt anyone. Similarly, Thomas Aquinas (*Summa Theologia*, Part II, Question 110) also took an absolutist approach to lying and believed that "every lie is a sin" yet he too, makes distinctions among falsehoods.[2] Jocose (made in jest) and officious (for the benefit of others) lies are not mortal sins and "the greater the good intended, the more is the sin of lying diminished in gravity." Unsurprisingly, injurious, hurtful lies that are harmful to others are deemed mortal sins.

Immanuel Kant also took the absolutist position and claimed that a lie is a "crime of man against his own person" and must therefore be shunned regardless of the costs. He also took the position that one is never permitted to lie even if there is a murderer at the door looking for his victim's room.

Some religious leaders did not agree with the absolutist view on falsehoods. St. John Chrysostom believed that lying in order to benefit others is permitted. Cassian and Origen felt that sometimes lies are necessary but they should be used the way we use medicine, something we do with distaste but out of necessity.[3] Martin Luther also felt that lying for the sake of the Christian church would not be a sin.

Grotius, the seventeenth century Dutch theologian and legal scholar, by many considered "the father of modern international law," also rejects the absolutist position and asserts that falsehoods are only a problem if it violates the right of the individual who hears it.[4] Suppose the individual telling the lie has wicked intentions, then s/he forfeits the right to hear the truth. Similarly, children are too young to have acquired this right and thus may be lied to.

---

2. Thomas Aquinas, *The Summa Theologica*, translated by Fathers of the English Dominican Province (Benziger Bros. Edition, 1947), online at Christian Classics Ethereal Library, http://www.ccel.org/a/aquinas/summa/home.html.

3. Thomas Slater, "Lying," *Catholic Encyclopedia* (New York: Robert Appleton Company, 1910), vol. 9, online at New Advent, http://www.newadvent.org/cathen/09469a.htm.

4. Hugo Grotius, *On the Law of War and Peace*, translated by F. Kelsey (Indianapolis, IN: Bobbs-Merrill, 1925).

Sidgwick makes the argument that if we may kill to defend ourselves, why should we not be able to lie if this will provide us with a better means of protection. He asserts the following:

> Where deception is designed to benefit the person deceived, Common Sense seems to concede that it may sometimes be right: for example, most persons would not hesitate to speak falsely to an invalid, if this seemed the only way of concealing facts that might produce a dangerous shock: nor do I perceive that any one shrinks from telling fictions to children, on matters upon which it is thought well that they should not know the truth.[5]

Bok feels that there are several conditions that may excuse a falsehood.[6] A "test of publicity" should be used to determine whether a lie is justifiable. The test asks: "Which lies, if any, would survive the appeal for justification to reasonable persons. It requires us to seek concrete and open performance of an exercise crucial to ethics: the Golden Rule, basic to so many religious and moral traditions."[7]

Bok suggests that, as part of the test, one should first consult with her own conscience and ask how she would feel if roles were reversed and she were lied to. Also, will this lie encourage others to lie or even change the personality of the individual who has been untruthful so that she now finds it easy to lie, even when it is not justifiable? After introspection, one should consult with a small but representative group of people to see how they feel about the lie and would they approve of it. Clearly, lying to the murderer looking for his victim or to the Gestapo seeking Jews in hiding would easily pass the "test of publicity" and would be permissible.

According to Nietzsche, "lying is a necessity of life." Stiegnitz contends that lying starts with "how are you?" a question for which no one really cares to hear the answer. Stiegnitz believes that telling falsehoods are "an essential part of survival in everyday life" and "as necessary to life as air and water."[8] Nyberg also believes that without lying, it would be virtually impossible to

---

5. Henry Sidgwick, *The Methods of Ethics* (New York: Dover Publications, 1966), 313–16. Originally published in 1907.

6. Sisella Bok, *Lying: Moral Choice in Public and Private Life* (New York: Vintage, 1999), 90–106.

7. Bok, *Lying*, 93.

8. James Geary, "Deceitful Minds: The Awful Truth About Lying," *Time Europe* 155, no. 10 (2000): 56-61 and John Walsh, "So, How Many Lies Have You Told Today?" *The Independent—London*, January 17, 2001.

have a relationship. Society could not survive if we all felt compelled to always tell the truth.[9]

Intuitively, it appears obvious that truth can be quite hurtful. Some secular writers seem to align themselves with the anti-absolutist position:

> "A truth that's told with bad intent
> Beats all the lies you can invent" [William Blake]
> "Tis not enough your counsel still be true;
> Blunt truths more mischief than nice falsehoods do"
>
> [Alexander Pope]
>
> "The truth is an awful weapon of aggression.
> It is possible to lie, and even to murder, with the truth"
>
> [Alfred Adler]

The Jewish View on Lying

The Torah seems to be unequivocal with regard to lying: "Thou shall not bear false witness" (Exodus 20:16), "Thou shall not steal, thou shall not deny falsely, and thou shall not lie one to another" (Leviticus 19:11), and "Distance yourself from a false matter" (Exodus 23:7). The first verse clearly applies to witnesses in a court; the second has been defined as a prohibition against swearing in order to avoid returning someone else's property (see Sefer HaHinukh 226). A closer perusal of the latter verse reveals that the Torah is regulating in the context of a Jewish court of law. As such, there is much dispute as to whether the proscription of lying in a non-judicial context is Biblically or Rabbinically based. Some halachic decisors are of the opinion that the Torah only explicitly forbids lying by judges and witnesses, whereas others apply this prohibition universally. For the former, the prohibition against lying to cause another financial harm derives from the verse (Leviticus 19:36): "You shall have just scales, just weights, a just ephah (a dry measure), and a just *hin* (a liquid measure)." The Rabbis homiletically (Babylonian Talmud, Bava Metzi'a 49a) translate *hin* to mean "yes" based on the similarity of the word *hin* to the Aramaic word meaning yes (*hen*). According to the Talmud, the verse "a just *hin*" teaches us that an individual's "yes" should be just as should be his "no."

As far as lying in situations where no harm results, there is a dispute among the commentaries as to whether it is prohibited by the Torah. Yabrov

---

9. David Nyberg, *The Varnished Truth: Truth Telling & Deceiving in Ordinary Life* (Chicago: University of Chicago Press, 1993).

provides an extensive treatment and concludes that the majority of decisors are of the opinion that the verse "Distance yourself from a false matter" includes all kind of lies.[10] We shall see, however, that the Talmud does not take an absolutist position on lying and permits and even encourages lying in certain situations.

There are four important Talmudic texts that deal with the issue of permissible deceptions. The first is the following (Babylonian Talmud, Yevamot 65b).

> Rabbi Ille'a said in the name of Rabbi Elazar son of Rabbi Shimon: It is permitted for a person to deviate from the truth in the interest of peace, as it says (Genesis 50:16–17): "Your father [Jacob] commanded before his death, saying: So shall you say to Joseph, 'O Please forgive the offense of your brothers and their sin for they have treated you so wickedly.'"
>
> Rabbi Nathan said it is a commandment [to deviate from the truth in the interest of peace], as it says (1 Samuel 16:2): "And Samuel said, 'How can I go? If Saul hears of it, he will kill me.'"
>
> At the Academy of Rabbi Yishmael it was taught: Great is the cause of peace, seeing that for its sake, even the Holy One, blessed be He, changed the truth, for at first it is written (Genesis 18:12), 'My lord [i.e., husband Abraham] is old, while afterward it is written (18:13), "And I am old."

The case dealing with Joseph's brothers is as follows. After Jacob's death, Joseph's brothers feared that Joseph would retaliate against them and get even for what they had done to him. They therefore fabricated a story that Jacob begged Joseph to forgive his brothers for having sold him into slavery. There is no record of such an instruction and the Talmud assumes that the brothers invented the story in the name of peace.

The second case is where God Himself suggests to the prophet Samuel to bring a heifer and say that he came to sacrifice it, though the prophet's true mission was to anoint David as a successor for King Saul. The commentaries note that even though Samuel did indeed bring a sacrifice, the deception was in implying that this was the only purpose of his trip to Bethlehem.

Rabbi Yishmael's proof is from the story of Abraham and Sarah. When Sarah overheard one of the three "guests" telling Abraham that she would have a son by the following year she laughed and said to herself that her husband was old. God gets angry and asks Abraham why Sarah laughed in

---

10. Nochum Yabrov, *Niv Sefasayim* (Jerusalem: Self-Published, 2000), 1–5.

disbelief saying *she* was old, i.e., too old to have children. Seemingly, God altered the truth in order to spare Abraham's feelings.

It should be noted that Rabbi Nathan not only agrees that one is permitted to lie in the name of peace, he believes that it is a *mitzvah* (commandment) to lie if this will bring peace.

It appears that normative halacha agrees with the ruling of Rabbi Nathan.[11]

The second text (Babylonian Talmud, Ketubbot 16b–17a) discusses the problem of what praises to say before a bride at her wedding.

> The Rabbis taught: How does one dance before the bride [i.e., what does one say in praise of her]? The School of Shammai says: We praise the bride as she is. The School of Hillel says: We say that she is a beautiful and graceful bride. The School of Shammai said to the School of Hillel: If she was lame or blind, does one say about her that she is a beautiful and graceful bride? But the Torah said (Exodus 23:7): "Distance yourself from a false matter." The School of Hillel said to the School of Shammai: According to your opinion, if someone made an inferior purchase in the marketplace, should one praise it or deprecate it in his eyes. Surely, one should praise it. From here [the latter statement of the Hillel School] the Sages said: A person's disposition should always be pleasant with people.

Tosafot notes that the School of Shammai agrees that if someone makes a bad purchase, others should laud the item. However, in the case of a bride, the Sages should not institute a general rule that forces everyone to lie, given the Torah's aversion of falsehoods. Rabbi Isaiah diTrani (Tosefot RI"D) also notes that the opinion of the Sages is that one has to be pleasant with people even if it means that he has to lie. The Ritva (Rabbi Yomtov ben Abraham), in his discussion of the above Talmudic passage, states in an unambiguous manner that wherever one has to be concerned about "the ways of peace" there is no prohibition of "Distance yourself from a false matter." This would probably include such statements as "you look good," "nice to see you," "thanks for the wonderful gift," "I really had a wonderful time," "You haven't aged a bit," or "I missed you." Being told by friends that "You look terrible," "I couldn't care less whether I saw you," "I hate your gift," "I had a lousy time," "Boy, did you age," or "I did not miss you at all" would not further the cause of peace.

The above passage regarding "how one dances before the bride" also appears in another tractate of the Talmud (Babylonian Talmud, Kallah

---

11. Yabrov, *Niv Sefasayim*, 23.

Rabbati 10). There, however, the Talmud notes that the School of Hillel connects the proscription (Exodus 23:7) of "Distance yourself from a false matter" with the end of the verse that states "And the innocent and righteous do not slay." The verse, therefore, is speaking of testifying falsely and thereby causing an innocent person to be executed. The Talmud concludes that the Hillel School believes that when the lie preserves life, e.g., strengthening the bond between bride and groom, lying is acceptable.

The third text (Babylonian Talmud, Bava Metzi'a 23b–24a) describes three situations when even scholars may lie.

> Rabbi Yehuda stated in the name of Shmuel: In the following three matters it is the practice of the rabbis not to tell the truth: In matters of a tractate, a bed, and hospitality.

If a rabbi is asked whether he is familiar with a certain tractate, he may, for the sake of humility, answer in the negative even if he is knowledgeable in that tractate. Of course, one should not disclaim knowledge of a particular tractate if one asks because he seeks help. According to Rashi, the meaning of "bed" is that if a rabbi is asked whether he engaged in sexual relations with his wife, he may, for the sake of modesty, answer that he has not. Tosafot, does not accept this explanation since people do not normally ask someone whether or not he slept with his wife. Tosafot offers an alternative explanation. One may lie if he was asked whether or not he slept in a particular bed. The bed may be stained from an emission and this could be embarrassing. "Hospitality" refers to a situation where one is asked whether a host was hospitable or not. If one is too effusive in his praise, especially in front of ne'er-do-wells, he may cause problems for his host. It is therefore better to lie and downplay how good his host was.

The fourth case (Babylonian Talmud, Nedarim 27b) describes where lies to thieves are permitted in order to protect oneself from financial harm.

One is permitted to make a vow to murderers, plunderers, and [corrupt] tax collectors that the produce they wish to seize is *terumah* [which is only permitted to be eaten by priests and therefore of little value; an alternative explanation is that even murderers and robbers would not violate the prohibition against using *terumah*], even if it is not *terumah*, or that the property they wish to seize belongs to the Royal House, even if it does not.

We have a situation where one is dealing with immoral people and the victim has no other recourse. It should be noted that the dishonest tax collector discussed in the Talmud is an individual who pays the ruler a fee for the right to collect taxes, and then imposes exorbitant and inequitable taxes (the Talmud refers to this as "taxes without a limit") on the public. In a similar vein, later in the same tractate, (Babylonian Talmud, Nedarim 62b),

Rava relates that a Torah scholar is permitted to declare that he is a "servant of fire" in order to evade paying communal taxes—the pagan priests of the fire-worshippers were exempt from taxes. The two justifications given by the commentaries are: (1) it is clear that the purpose of this declaration is to avoid a tax and not to suggest that one is renouncing his belief in God; (2) the term "servant of fire" could refer to God who is compared in the Torah (Deuteronomy 4:24) to a "consuming fire." Moreover, the Ran explains that this law applies to every Jew and is not limited to Torah scholars.

Thus, there are several circumstances where one is permitted or sometimes required to lie:

- Lying to preserve the cause of peace, not to hurt another person's feelings, or to provide comfort.
- Lying in a situation where honesty might cause oneself or another person harm.
- Lying for the sake of modesty or in order not to appear arrogant.
- Lying for the sake of decency, i.e., not telling the truth about intimate matters.
- Lying to protect one's property from scoundrels.

Lying to Preserve the Cause of Peace or in Order Not to Hurt Another Person's Feelings

Aaron the High Priest, brother of Moses, was known in Talmudic and Midrashic literature as a lover of peace. The following passage indicates that one may use deception in order to bring peace between people who are quarreling (Avot de Rabbi Nathan 12:3; Babylonian Talmud, Pereq Hashalom).

> When two people had a dispute, Aaron [the High Priest] went and sat near one of them and said to him: "My son, see what your friend is doing? He is beating his heart and tearing his clothing saying: "Woe is me. How can I lift up my eyes and look at my friend. I am ashamed of myself since I was the one who offended him." Aaron would sit with him until he removed the hatred from his heart. Aaron would then go and sit next to the other and say to him: "My son, see what your friend is doing? He is beating his heart and tearing his clothing saying: "Woe is me. How can I lift up my eyes and look at my friend. I am ashamed of myself since I was the one who offended him." Aaron would sit with him until he removed the hatred from his heart.
>
> When the two met, they hugged and kissed each other.

The above story about Aaron makes it quite apparent that Jewish law recognizes that lying to bring peace is a commandment. Indeed, Aaron is praised in the Talmud as the lover and pursuer of peace (Babylonian Talmud, Avot 1:12).

The Talmud and Midrash (Jerusalem Talmud, Sotah 1:4; Leviticus Rabbah 9:9) relate that a certain woman was wont to attend the lectures given by Rabbi Meir. One evening, the lecture ended late, and upon arriving home, the woman's husband vowed to her that she would not be permitted to reenter his house until she spat in the face of the lecturer. Upon hearing of the woman's dilemma, Rabbi Meir devised a ruse whereby he pretended to be afflicted by an eye ailment that necessitated someone spit in his eye. After she spat in his eye seven times, Rabbi Meir told her to return to her husband and tell him that she had bested his requirement by spitting in the lecturer's eye seven times, not just once.

The patriarch Jacob dissembled when he pretended not to believe Joseph's dream and even rebuked Joseph and said to him (Genesis 37:10): "What kind of dream is this that you have dreamt! Shall we come—I, your mother, and your brothers—to bow down to you on the ground?" Rashi notes that Jacob did this in order to "remove the jealousy from the heart of the brothers." It appears that Jacob was not entirely honest with Joseph's brothers in order to preserve the peace. Unfortunately, the ruse did not help since the next verse notes: "His brothers envied him; while his father kept the matter in his mind."

Judah prevaricated when he said to the Viceroy of Egypt, who was actually Joseph, (Genesis 44:20): "and his brother [Joseph] is dead." Judah was the one who, 22 years earlier, convinced his brothers to sell Joseph as a slave. Rashi and other commentaries feel that Judah lied because he was afraid that he would be asked to produce Joseph if he had said that he was alive. However, a Midrash (quoted in Torah Shleimah, Genesis 44:20) notes that Judah lied in the interest of peace. We assume that this refers to the possibility that the truth would cause additional problems for the family, i.e., Benjamin would have to remain a slave until Joseph is produced.

The Talmud (Babylonian Talmud, Eruvin 53b) relates that Rabbi Yehoshua once stayed at a certain inn. The hostess served beans on the first and second day and he ate them. On the third day, she burned the beans and he did not eat them. When she asked him why he did not eat the beans, he politely told her that he had already eaten during the daytime. This story also demonstrates that in order to spare the feelings of another person, it is permissible to tell a falsehood.

There is evidence that even Heaven uses deception in order to protect the feelings of others. The Talmud (Babylonian Talmud, Berakhot 28a) relates that when Rabbi Gamliel was the *Nasi* [President of the Sanhedrin], a proclamation was issued that "any scholar whose inside is not as his outside" [i.e., of perfect character] may not enter the house of study. This proclamation was nullified when Rabbi Elazar ben Azariah became the *Nasi*; the Talmud notes that either 400 or 700 benches had to be added to the academy. Rabbi Gamliel felt bad about this and was afraid that he was responsible for withholding Torah from good students. He was subsequently shown in a dream white casks full of ashes, indicating that the new students were not worthwhile. The Talmud concludes that this was not the case and the students were actually of high caliber. Evidently, Heaven did this to spare Rabbi Gamliel's feelings.

Fish cites numerous sources that state that one may lie in order to comfort another person.[12] One proof he cites is from the Talmud (Babylonian Talmud, Nedarim 50a). There the story is told of how impoverished Rabbi Akiva and his wife, the daughter of the wealthy Kalba Sevuah, were. Kalba Sevuah disinherited his daughter when he heard that she was going to marry the poor, ignorant shepherd, Akiva. They were so impecunious that they had to sleep on straw. Elijah the Prophet disguised himself as a mortal and pretended to need straw for his wife who had given birth. Rashi and the Ran both note that Elijah did this in order to comfort them and make them realize there were people in the world in greater poverty.

Rabbi Meir's two sons died on the Sabbath. Beruriah, wife of Rabbi Meir, lied to her husband when he asked where they were, and said the two boys were at the house of study. She waited until he made *Havdalah*, the prayer signaling the end of the Sabbath, and had to deceive a second time about his son's whereabouts. After Rabbi Meir ate something she broke the news to him very gently by comparing their children's lives to an object deposited with someone for safekeeping. The owner took back what belonged to him. She concluded by citing the verse (Job 1:21): "The Lord has given, the Lord has taken, May the name of the Lord be blessed (Yalkut Shimoni, Proverbs 31). Apparently, Beruriah did what was proper since the Midrash refers to her as "a capable wife" and relates this story in that regard.

The Talmud (Babylonian Talmud, Sanhedrin 11a) enumerates several stories where someone prevaricated in order to prevent the humiliation of another person. For instance, once Rabbi Gamliel asked that seven scholars join him the following morning in the upper chamber for the purpose of intercalating the year [i.e., proclaiming a leap year]. The next morning, they noticed that there was an extra person there. Rabbi Gamliel asked: "Who is the one who came up without permission?" Jewish law mandates that the

---

12. Yaakov Fish, *Titen Emes L'Yaakov* (Jerusalem: Self-Published, 1981), 62–63.

year may be intercalated only by a court whose members were specifically designated for that purpose the previous evening. Rabbi Shmuel Hakatan arose and declared: "It was I who came up without permission. My purpose was not to participate in the intercalation, but to learn how the law is applied in practice." The Talmud states that Rabbi Shmuel Hakatan was actually invited to join in the intercalation, but stated a falsehood in order not to cause embarrassment for the intruder.

Something similar happened when Rebbi was delivering a lecture and the strong odor of garlic caused a disturbance. Rebbi said: "Let the person who has eaten the garlic, please leave." Rabbi Chiya arose and left; then all the disciples arose and left. Again, it turned out that Rabbi Chiya had not eaten garlic, but left in order not to shame the true perpetrator.

The Talmud (Babylonian Talmud, Sanhedrin 11a) relates another story in the same vein. To understand this story one must know how marriage worked in Talmudic times. In those days, the first stage of marriage known as *erusin* was followed a year later by the final stage known as *nesuin*. *Erusin*, could technically be done via cohabitation, but this method was strongly frowned upon. A woman appeared at the academy of Rabbi Meir and said that one of the students betrothed her [i.e., *erusin*] by cohabitation. Apparently, the woman did not remember which of the students betrothed her. The woman wanted the student to either complete the marriage [*nesuin*] or give her a divorce. Even though Rabbi Meir was not the guilty one, he gave her a bill of divorce and then all of the students gave her one as well.

Shechaniah also told an untruth in order not to embarrass others. Shechaniah told Ezra (Ezra 10:2): "We have trespassed against our God and have married foreign women of the peoples of the land." Shechaniah included himself in the sin of intermarrying with pagan women living in Judea. Actually, he had not committed the misdeed of intermarriage but included himself in order not to embarrass the others who had.

Fish uses the famous story of how Rabbi Shimon ben Shetach (Jerusalem Talmud, Hagigah 2:2; Rashi; Babylonian Talmud, Sanhedrin 44b) captured 80 sorceresses who lived in Ashkelon and brought them to trial as evidence that one may lie to eradicate evil.[13] In the story, Rabbi Shimon had 80 of his students hide dry clothing in a jar. During a downpour, he went with them to the cave where the sorceresses lived and had the young men hide nearby. Rabbi Shimon entered the cave and told them that he was a sorcerer who had the power to make 80 young people magically appear in dry clothing, despite the strong rain. Arguably, eradicating evil is another way of bringing peace to the world.

13. Fish, *Titen Emes*, 199.

Lying in A Situation Where Honesty Might Cause Oneself or Another Person Physical Harm

Abraham asked his wife Sarah to lie and say that she was his sister because he was traveling with her to ancient Egypt, a place known for its lack of morality (Genesis 12:10–13). Ramban believes that Abraham unintentionally committed a "great sin" and endangered his wife's virtue because he should have had faith that God would save him and his family. After all, it was God who told Abraham to leave the land of his birthplace. However, even Ramban would have to agree that, where one does not have the personal assurance of God, one should be permitted to lie. In fact, Abraham used the same ruse again when sojourning in Gerar (Genesis 20:1–3). Isaac also used the same lie when traveling in lands where the morality of the inhabitants is questionable and claims that his wife Rebekah is his sister (Genesis 26:7).

According to the Midrash (Midrash Tanchuma, Lech Lecha 5), Abraham hid Sarah in a locked box when traveling to Egypt. When the Egyptian customs officials asked him what was in the box, he tried to convince them that it contained barley. When the officials did not believe him and said that it might contain wheat, Abraham offered to pay the tax on wheat. The officials then claimed that it might contain pepper, so Abraham offered to pay the tax on pepper. They then claimed that it might contain gold. Eventually, they opened the box and found Sarah. This Midrash also demonstrates that lying is permitted in order to protect someone from harm.[14]

The two midwives in Egypt, Shiphrah and Puah, undoubtedly did the right thing by lying to Pharaoh and thereby not take part in the attempt to murder newborns. There is no question that Jewish law obligates one to prevaricate in order to save one's own life or the life of another person. Rahab the harlot prevaricated in order to save the life of the two Jewish spies sent by Joshua to Jericho (see Joshua 2). The Midrash (Pirka de Rabeinu Hakadosh 15) notes that Rahab told a lie yet inherited life in this world and in the world to come. In fact, eight prophets descended from her (Babylonian Talmud, Megillah 14b).

The following involves a deception over a remedy (Babylonian Talmud, Avodah Zarah 28a) and deals with a considerably more complex ethical situation.

> Rabbi Yochanan suffered from *tzafdina* [a dangerous disease of the gums or teeth] and went to a certain heathen lady who made a remedy for him to use on Thursday and Friday. He said to her: "What should I do tomorrow [the Sabbath]"? She replied: "You

---

14. Fish, *Titen Emes*, 110.

will not need the treatment." Rabbi Yochanan said: "But what if I do need it?" She replied: "Swear to me that you will not reveal the remedy to anyone." Rabbi Yochanan swore to her: "To the God of Israel I will not reveal it." She then disclosed the remedy to him and the next day he taught it in his public lecture.

The Talmud asks: But did he not swear to her not to reveal it? The Talmud answers: He swore that he would not reveal it to the God of Israel, but to His people, Israel, he would reveal it. The Talmud asks: But is this not a profanation of the name of God? [when a Jew commits a misdeed, especially something as serious as swearing falsely, it causes people to denigrate Judaism and the Torah]. The Talmud answers: That from the beginning he revealed to her that his oath was not binding [and that he wanted to help the public].

The above story is problematic since deception (*geneivat da'at*) is prohibited, even with an idolater. The loophole that Rabbi Yochanan employed does not take away from the fact that he deceived her. I believe the answer to this question is that to save a life, even one's own life, one is permitted to lie. *Tzafdina* was a deadly disease and Rabbi Yochanan wanted to save the lives of many people who were afflicted with this malady. It is interesting to note that the above story is also told in the Jerusalem Talmud. There the Talmud has two opinions as to what happened to the heathen woman. One opinion was that she committed suicide. Another opinion was that she converted to Judaism presumably because she was impressed with Rabbi Yochanan's decision to go public with the cure rather than trying to enrich himself by selling the remedy. Rabbi Akiva (Babylonian Talmud, Kallah Rabbati 2) used Rabbi Yochanan's approach to deceive a Jewish woman. He was trying to determine the status of her son who impudently uncovered his head in front of the Sages.

In a converse situation, Shmuel (Babylonian Talmud, Shabbat 129a) deceived Ablat, a pagan because he did not want him to learn about the value of sunbathing at certain times of the year. Instead, he told Ablat that he was sunbathing because he had just been engaged in bloodletting. This story is used by Fish to prove that one is permitted to deceive a wicked person and thereby not provide him with a medical remedy.[15]

Jewish law generally allows one to commit a sin if one's life is at stake. There are three serious transgressions, however, where a Jew is required to give up his life rather than violate Jewish law (*yehareg v'al ya'avor*): idolatry, illicit sexual relations with an *ervah* (e.g., adultery or incest between very close relatives), and murder (Babylonian Talmud, Sanhedrin 74a; Shulchan

---

15. Fish, *Titen Emes*, 82.

Aruch, Yoreh Deah, 157a). Jewish law does not obligate one to give up his or her life for other transgressions. Thus, if a Jew is told to desecrate the Sabbath or be killed, s/he should desecrate the Sabbath. (It should be noted that one may be obligated to become a martyr for a "lesser" transgression if the individual is told to violate the law publicly or if it is an epoch of forced conversion.) Lying is not, however, one of the three "serious" transgressions for which a Jew is obligated to become a martyr. There is however one possible exception to this rule. Is a Jew permitted to lie and say he is not Jewish in order not to be killed? Rabbi Abin mentions (Jerusalem Talmud, Avodah Zarah, 2:1) that a Jewish woman may save her life in a time of danger by saying that she is not Jewish. The Rosh, however, explains this passage differently and states that a Jew is not permitted to state that s/he is not Jewish, even to save one's life since this is tantamount to denying one's religion. According to him, the above passage is talking about a Jewish woman dressing in a manner so that people believe that she is not Jewish in order to save herself. This would be permitted. The discussion by the commentaries over whether a Jew may lie and say he is not Jewish in order to save his life is very complex and beyond the scope of this paper.

Naaman the Aramean accepted monotheism after he was cured of his leprosy by the prophet Elisha (2 Kings 5). He indicated, however, to Elisha that he would have to bow to the pagan deity, Rimon, when he accompanied his master to the House of Rimon since his master would lean on him while he prostrated himself. Elisha told him (2 Kings 5: 19) to "go in peace" and, in effect, condoned the simulation of idol worshipping. Naaman was permitted to deceive his master rather than die for his beliefs since he had not converted to Judaism and thus only had the status of a Noachide who observes seven precepts (Babylonian Talmud, Sanhedrin 74b-75a).

According to the Talmud, Jacob distorted the truth when his brother Esau offered to accompany him (Genesis 33:12-16). Jacob, realizing that it might not be wise to travel with Esau, who might still harbor resentment over what happened regarding Isaac's blessing, told Esau (Genesis 33:14): "Let my lord go on ahead of his servant; while I will travel slowly at the pace of the work and at the pace of the children, until I come to my lord at Seir [Esau's land]." Of course, Jacob never went to Seir. The Midrash (Genesis Rabbah 78:14, cited by Rashi) notes that Jacob will one day go to Seir—in Messianic times. The Midrash is trying to show that Jacob did not actually lie.

The Talmud, however, derives an interesting principle from the above story that does permit lying in a potentially dangerous situation. The Talmud (Babylonian Talmud, Avodah Zarah 25b) states that one should always "broaden the journey" when speaking to idolaters [or anyone who could be a possible highwayman]. When asked about a destination, one should reply that he is traveling to a town that is actually well beyond his actual destination. The reason: If the idolater has plans to rob him along the way, he may wait until the Jewish traveler is near the end of the trip and by then the Jew will have already arrived at his destination. In fact, the Talmud notes that this stratagem saved the students of Rabbi Akiva from some armed robbers.

When Rabbi Eliezer was arrested by the authorities on suspicion of being a heretic, he saved himself by using a white lie involving some double talk (Babylonian Talmud, Avodah Zarah 16b–17a). The governor asked him: "How can a wise man such as you occupy himself with such nonsense?" Rabbi Eliezer replied: "I acknowledge the Judge as being right." The "Judge" Rabbi Eliezer referred to was God, not the judge who was interrogating him. The ruse worked and the governor said to him: "Because you have acknowledged me as being right, by *his* [the idol that the governor worshipped] mercy I am acquitting you."

There is another type of deception that is permitted where one's life may be in danger. Rabbi Shimon ben Pazi states (Babylonian Talmud, Sotah 41b) that "It is permitted to flatter wicked people in this world." He derives it from a verse in Isaiah (32:5) that refers to the Hereafter: "The vile person shall no longer be called generous, nor shall a deceitful person be said to be noble." Rabbi Shimon ben Lakish agrees but derives this ruling from a statement made by Jacob to Esau (Genesis 33:10): "for therefore I have seen your face, which is as though I had seen the face of a Divine being." This appears to contradict numerous negative statements about flattering evildoers such as "Every individual in whom there is flattery will fall into Hell," and "Whoever flatters the wicked [some texts have "his fellow human"] will eventually fall into his hand." (Babylonian Talmud, Sotah 41b). Tosafot explains this apparent contradiction by asserting that it is permitted to flatter the wicked in a dangerous, life-threatening situation. He provides proof for his view by citing a story involving Ulla who traveled with two people from Chozae to Israel (Babylonian Talmud, Nedarim 22a). One of his fellow travelers slaughtered the other and asked Ulla: "Did I do well?" Ulla replied in the affirmative and felt guilty but was later assured by Rabbi Yochanan in Israel that what he did was permitted since he said it to save his life.

The Talmud (Babylonian Talmud, Sanhedrin 29b) avers that "a person is accustomed not to make himself appear sated with wealth." This Talmudic principle is used to explain the reason that if an individual claims to owe another party money, we do not necessarily consider this as a true admission; this is why the "creditors" must furnish additional proof. Many people do not wish to arouse the envy of others so they pretend to be debtors.

Lying for the Sake Of Modesty or in Order Not to Appear Arrogant

There is an interesting story in the Talmud (Babylonian Talmud, Ketubbot 77b) that supports the principle that one may utter a falsehood for the sake of modesty. When Rabbi Yehoshua ben Levi passed on to the next world, he was asked by Rabbi Shimon ben Yochai whether or not a rainbow ever appeared during his lifetime. A certain type of rainbow is a sign that the world actually deserves to be destroyed but is not because of God's promise to Noah after the Great Flood (see Genesis 11:12). Rabbi Yehoshua ben Levi responded in the affirmative. Rabbi Shimon ben Yochai replied: "Then you are not the son of Levi" since the merit of one true saint is sufficient to protect the entire world. The Talmud concludes, however, that the rainbow did not appear during Yehoshua ben Levi's lifetime. The reason he did not tell the truth was that "he did not want to boast about himself."

Another story in the Talmud (Babylonian Talmud, Ta'anit 23b) about Abba Chilkiyah also demonstrates that one may lie because of humility. The rabbis sent scholars to Abba Chilkiyah during a drought to ask him to pray for rain. While the scholars were waiting for Abba to finish his meal, he surreptitiously went to the roof with his wife and prayed for rain. Clouds immediately appeared and it began to rain. He went back to the scholars and asked them why they had come, knowing very well the reason. Abba tried to convince the scholars that the rain came on its own accord, and not because of his (and his spouse's) prayer. The scholars, however, knew what had caused the rain to come.

Judaism also commands the converse of the above insofar as one is obligated to ensure that he does not benefit from others' misconception about his status or scholarship. The Talmud (Jerusalem Talmud, Makkot 2:6) states that if one is being honored by the public as a scholar who is proficient in two tractates but only knows one, he is obligated to disabuse the misconception and explicitly state "I am only knowledgeable in one tractate, and no more." Similarly, the Talmud earlier discusses the case of the scholar who is exiled to the city of refuge owing to his unintentional murder of another person. Should the people of the city wish to honor him, the scholar is duty-bound to proclaim that he is in town because he has taken a life.

Lying for the Sake of Decency

The following story/parable (Babylonian Talmud, Sanhedrin 97a) demonstrates the harm that may result from a lie for the sake of decency.

Rava said: At first I used to say that there is no truth in the world [i.e., that no person speaks the truth all the time]. Whereupon one of the Rabbis said to me, and Rabbi Tavus was his name, and some say Rabbi Tavyome was his name, that even if he would be given all the wealth in the world, he would not tell a lie. He related the following story: Once, I came to a certain town called Kushta [this name means truth in Aramaic] whose inhabitants would never tell a lie and no person ever died before his time.

He married a woman from among them and had two sons from her. One day his wife was sitting and washing her hair when a neighbor came and knocked on the door. Thinking to himself that it was not proper [to tell the neighbor that his wife was washing her hair], he said to the neighbor, "she is not here." His two sons died [as a punishment for his lying]. The people of the town came to him and asked, "What is the cause of this?" He related to them what had happened. They said to him: "We beg you to leave our town and do not incite death against us."

Rabbi Yaakov Emden explains why Rabbi Tavus was punished if one is permitted to lie for the sake of decency. In this case, Rabbi Tavus could have simply told the truth to the neighbor who would have understood and left; the white lie was totally unnecessary (Hagahos Yaakov Emden). Not all commentaries take the above story literally (e.g., Maharal).

Jacob's Deception of His Father

One of the more difficult cases of dishonesty to explain is Jacob's deception of his blind father, Isaac (Genesis 27). Was Jacob permitted to deceive his father and pretend to be Esau? Some commentaries take the approach that Jacob did not actually lie. When asked by his father who he was (Genesis 27:18), he replied: "I am Esau your firstborn." Rashi and other commentators try to show that this was not really a falsehood. They say that Jacob responded as follows: "I am [the one who is bringing you the savory meats]; [whereas] Esau is your firstborn." Ibn Ezra does not accept this interpretation and points out that other prophets had to resort to deceptions. This difference of opinion also affects the explanation of a later verse (Genesis 27:35), when Isaac tells Esau: "your brother came with *mirmah* and took your blessing. Rashi interprets *mirmah* as wisdom; Ibn Ezra apparently translates it in the usual way, "deceit," because his comment on the word is that Jacob did not tell the truth. One important law that can be derived from the above is that if one does find himself or herself in a situation where they must lie, the correct way to do this is to use words that may have another meaning, vague statements, or through the use of half-truths (Hofetz Hayyim, Hilkhot Issuer Rechilut 1:8; Sefer Hasidim 642). This is somewhat similar to the "mental reservation" loophole discussed by Bok.[16] A mental reservation works as follows: "If you say something misleading to another and merely add a qualification to it in your mind so as to make it true, you cannot be responsible for the 'misinterpretation' made by the listener."

Nehama Liebowitz asserts that even the Sages who take the side of Jacob "detect the workings of strict justice which is no respecter of persons, in what had befallen Jacob."[17] She cites the following Midrash Tanchuma that describes what happened after Laban switches Leah for Rachel. Laban promised Jacob the hand of his beloved Rachel after seven years of labor.

All that night Leah pretended to be Rachel. When Jacob arose in the morning and saw that it was Leah, he said to her: "Daughter of the deceiver! Why did you deceive me? Leah said to him: And you, why did you deceive your father? When he said to you: "Are you my son Esau?" You replied (Genesis 27:19): "I am your son Esau." Yet you say to me, "why did I deceive you?" Did not your father say about you (Genesis 27:35): "Your brother came with guile."

It should be noted that the expression that Jacob uses when speaking to Laban after he switched Leah for Rachel is (Genesis 29:25): What is this that you have done to me? Was it not for Rachel that I served you? Why have you deceived [*rimitony*] me? The word used by Jacob is very similar to the word used to describe what Jacob had done to Esau. In fact, other commentators note that the words used in this passage "deceit," "younger," and "elder/firstborn" serve the purpose of reminding the reader of the similarity of the two situations, except that it is now Jacob who is being deceived by a substitution. Jacob is deceived several more times in his life. Laban switches his compensation several times (Genesis 31:7) and his children deceive him into believing that his beloved Joseph was dead. Whether Jacob was justified or not in deceiving his father, his entire life is turned upside down by deception.

Frimer uses a Midrash (Yalkhut Shimoni, Genesis 29:12, Section 124; Genesis Rabbah 70:13) to make an interesting observation about dissembling.[18] The Midrash, cited by Rashi, is on the following verse (Genesis 29:12): "And Jacob told Rachel that he was her father's brother [i.e., relative]

---

16. Bok, *Lying*, 35–36.

17. Nehama Liebowitz, *Studies in Shemot*, translated by Aryeh Newman (Jerusalem: World Zionist Organization, 1985), 322–23.

18. Norman Frimer, "A Midrash on Morality or When is a Lie Permissible," *Tradition* 13 (Spring–Summer 1973): 23–34.

and that he was Rebecca's son; then she ran and told this to her father." There is an obvious redundancy in this verse, hence the Midrash: "If he comes to cheat, I am his brother in deceit; If he is an honorable man, then I am the son of Rebekah [i.e., a man of integrity]." The Talmud (Babylonian Talmud, Bava Batra 123a; Megillah 13b) has a slightly different explanation: Jacob declares to Rachel that "I am his brother [match] in deceit." Rachel suspected that her father would try to deceive Jacob and try to make a substitution. The Talmud asks whether the righteous may indeed engage in deceit? The Talmud answers with the following verse (2 Samuel 22:27): "with an honest person, act honestly; and with a corrupt person act perversely." Although this verse speaks of God, the Talmud is homiletically interpreting this verse to teach us that one may use guile when dealing with a cheat.

Frimer notes that Jacob tried his best to deal with Laban as honestly as possible (see Genesis 31:6-7).[19] Moreover, Laban had a reputation for engaging in fraud. His reputation was so renowned that even his own daughter warned Jacob that her father was a cheat. Frimer therefore requires the following five conditions before allowing the honest person to "act perversely":

1. The antagonist's record of general conduct is negative.

2. There is adequate motivation and testimony to justify one's anticipated concern in the immediate and specific condition.

3. The intended victim is acting only in self-defense and after the attack has been initiated.

4. There appears to be no alternative to one's present course of action. Other options have been tried or are judged not to be viable.

5. That which is at stake has tremendous seriousness to the intended victim involving a high investment of one's person or property.

Lying to Protect One's Property From Scoundrels

Frimer proves his position that deception is permitted when the above five conditions are met by citing the following case (Shulchan Aruch, Hoshen Mishpat 335:5 based on Babylonian Talmud, Bava Metzi'a 75b):[20]

> When does this principle [that workers may quit their job] apply? Where the loss is irreparable [*davar ha'avud*]. If the loss is irreparable, for example, if one hires laborers to remove his flax from the steeping water or hires a donkey-driver to bring flutists

---

19. Frimer, "Midrash."
20. Frimer, "Midrash."

for the dead or for a bride, or something similar, then neither a laborer not a contractor may quit his job unless there has been an emergency such as sickness or if he heard that there has been a death in the family.

The Shulchan Aruch states that if the worker, however, does attempt to quit when the loss is irreparable, and a replacement worker cannot be found, then the employer has a right to deceive the employee. This deception involves promising the laborer a much higher wage to continue working and then only paying the wage originally agreed upon after the work is completed. This is a case where the employer has much at stake (spoiled flax or a ruined wedding) and has no alternative (no replacement workers); therefore Jewish law allows one to be dishonest.

Fish maintains that Rabbis Elyashiv, Fisher and Kanievsky were of the opinion that one may write "glass" on a package in order to ensure that it is handled properly, even if it does not contain glass.[21] As proof, Rabbi Kanievsky cites the Talmudic view (Babylonian Talmud, Yevamot 115b) that people would sometimes write "*terumah*" (consecrated to the priests) on a jar that did not contain unconsecrated produce as a means of protecting it, i.e., to ensure that people would not take it.

Daat Zekenim M'Baalei Tosafot (Genesis 25:34) quotes Rabbi Yehuda HaChasid and states that one is permitted to deceive a wicked person who has a Torah scroll or another item used for a *mitzvah*. This principle is derived from Jacob who "tricked" Esau into selling his birthright to him (Genesis 25) for some lentils. According to the *Daat Zekenim*, Esau was abusing the birthright even before Jacob purchased it from him.

Habitual Lying

Dratch claims that even when prevaricating is permissible, habitual lying will still be forbidden.[22] He uses the following Talmudic passage to support his position (Babylonian Talmud, Yevamot 63a):

> Rav was constantly tormented by his wife. When he asked her to prepare him some lentils, she would prepare peas. When he asked for peas, she would prepare lentils. When Chiya, Rav's son, grew up, he would reverse his father's request. Once, Rav said to Chiya: "Your mother has improved." Rabbi Chiya replied: "It is I who reversed your requests to her." Rav remarked to Chiya: "This is what people say, 'Your own offspring teaches

21. Fish, *Titen Emes*, 66.
22. Mark Dratch, "Nothing but the Truth," *Judaism* 37, no. 2 (Spring 1988).

you reason.'" However, you should not continue to do so, for it says (Jeremiah 9:4): "They have taught their tongues to speak lies."

It is interesting to note that Rabbi Zera (Babylonian Talmud, Sukkot 46b) uses the same verse from Jeremiah (9:4) to make the point that one should not promise to a child that he will give him something and then not give it to him, because this will teach the child to lie.

Deceptions in Business

Lest one think that Jewish law is very flexible about lying for financial gain, the following is just a small sample of what one has to be concerned with. The Talmud has special rules about *geneivat da'at* (literally, theft of one's mind, thoughts, wisdom, or knowledge), i.e., fooling someone and thereby causing him or her to have a mistaken assumption, belief, and/or impression. The Sages believed that there are seven types of thieves and, of these, the most egregious is the one who "steals the minds" of people (Tosafot Bava Qamma 7:3). "Shmuel asserts (Babylonian Talmud, Hullin 94a-b): It is forbidden to steal the mind of anyone, even idolaters."

Geneivat da'at includes situations that result in someone getting undeserved goodwill (Babylonian Talmud, Hullin 94a), something considerably weaker than an outright lie. Thus, a person should not urge his friend to dine with him knowing that he will refuse. One should not offer gifts to another person knowing that the latter will not accept them. In a business setting, this would include misleading customers into thinking that the quality of the item they purchased is much better than it really is or making people believe they are getting a special deal when they are not. For additional information, see Friedman.[23]

Other kinds of deceptions that are prohibited include "deceiving the eye" by placing the better quality items in a bin on top in order to make it appear that the merchandise is of uniformly high quality throughout; soaking meat in water to make it appear fatter; and painting animals or utensils so that a buyer will think they are younger or newer (Babylonian Talmud, Bava Metzi'a 60a-b).

It is obvious that there are few situations where dissembling would be permitted in a business setting as a way of increasing one's profits. Rabbi Yonah (Shaarei Teshuvah 3:178-86) describes nine types of liars and states explicitly that the businessperson who cheats others out of money is the

---

23. Hershey Friedman, "Geneivat Da'at: The Prohibition Against Deception in Today's World," *Jewish Law* (March 2003), http://www.jlaw.com/.

worst of all. Another category of liar (third worst) is one whose prevarications cause someone to lose out on a future benefit or profit. For instance, making someone believe that a business deal is a bad idea when it really has excellent profit potential.

One situation that occurs quite frequently in business is where one party agrees to sell a product at a certain price. When the buyer shows up with the money, the seller changes his mind and asks for a higher price. Sometimes this occurs because market conditions have changed, i.e., prices have gone up or down. There is an argument in the Talmud (Babylonian Talmud, Bava Metzi'a 49a) as to whether a verbal commitment alone (i.e., no money has changed hands) to engage in a transaction obligates one from an ethical point of view to go through with the deal. Rav states that the individual who changes his mind is "not lacking in honesty." Rabbi Yochanan disagrees and says that the individual is "lacking in honesty." It is not clear whether this passage refers to a situation where market prices have changed.

The Shulchan Aruch (Hoshen Mishpat 204:7) states that an individual who has made a verbal commitment, even if no money has changed hands, should stand by his word. People who retract after making a verbal commitment are "lacking in trustworthiness" and "the spirit of the Sages is not pleased with him." There is a disagreement among the commentaries as to whether a person who changes his mind because the market price has changed is considered "lacking in trustworthiness." Several (e.g., Rosh, Tur) believe that a change in the market price is a legitimate reason for retracting and does not cause one to be considered as "lacking in honesty." The Remah (204:11) remarks that individuals who make verbal commitments to buy or sell—even if no *kinyan* (act of acquisition when title actually transfers) has taken place—should abide by their word; the "spirit of the Sages is not pleased" with those who retract. If, however, the market price has changed, the individual who changes his mind about the deal is not considered "lacking in honesty."

The Aruch Hashulchan (Hoshen Mishpat 204:8) asserts that if the market price has changed, and the seller therefore changes his mind about the selling price, he is not considered "lacking in honesty." It is, however, considered "the way of the pious" not to retract from a verbal agreement even if the market price has changed.

In Jewish law, title does not change hands until a *kinyan* (an act of acquisition) has been made by the acquirer. One example of a *kinyan* for a moveable object is *meshichah*, the act of pulling the object towards oneself. Suppose one party purchases an object from another party, money has changed hands, but there has been no *kinyan*. There is a public curse that may be proclaimed by the aggrieved party. The curse is as follows: "The One who punished the people of the generation of the Flood, the people of the generation of the Dispersion, the people of Sodom and Gomorrah, and the Egyptians in the sea, He will punish the person who does not stand by his word" (Babylonian Talmud, Bava Metzi'a 48a).

The Talmud lauds Rabbi Safra for his exemplary behavior in business and claims the verse (Psalm 15:2) "speaks truth in his heart" refers to individuals such as he. The Talmud (Makkot 24a, see commentary of Rashi) relates that one day, while Rabbi Safra was in the midst of prayer, a man offered to buy some merchandise from him. He made an offer, but Rabbi Safra was praying and could not respond. The prospective buyer mistakenly thought that Rabbi Safra was holding out for more, and kept increasing his bid. When Rabbi Safra finished his prayer, he told the buyer that he would sell the item at the original price because he had "agreed in his heart" to this price and his silence was misconstrued. Legally, of course, making up one's mind does not constitute a binding agreement but demonstrates an unusually high level of ethical behavior.

Rabbi Yehuda HaChasid (Sefer Hassidim, 311) states that merchants are prohibited from misleading customers by falsely claiming that another party wishes to pay so much for the item or by stating how much that they paid for the merchandise when it is not true. Regarding these type of deceptions the verse (Zephaniah 3:13) avers: "The remnant of Israel shall do no wrong, and not speak falsehood, and a deceitful tongue shall not be found in their mouths."

Rabbi Yehuda HaChasid (Sefer Hassidim, 395) tells a story of a businessman who wanted to know how to gain the World-to-Come (i.e., Paradise) if he had no time for studying Torah, except for the Sabbath. He was told by a rabbi to conduct his business as follows: giving something extra to the buyer when weighing out the merchandise, being honest in business with Jew and Gentile, doing business with a friendly disposition, not losing one's temper, not being overly trusting (by lending money without witnesses one may tempt others to steal), and paying one's debts on time. "If you heed the above principles," the rabbi stated, "then I wish that my share in the World-to-Come would be equivalent to yours."

Fish discusses the question as to whether one may lie in order to get back money that was stolen from him.[24] He uses the following story from the Talmud (Babylonian Talmud, Yoma 83b) to prove that it is permissible. Before the Sabbath, Rabbi Yehuda and Rabbi Yosi asked their host, Kidor, to hold their money for safekeeping. When the Sabbath ended, they asked Kidor to return their money; he denied ever having been given anything.

---

24. Fish, *Titen Emes*, 79–80.

Subsequently, they saw him outside with lentils on his moustache. They surmised that he had eaten lentils. They went to his house and told his wife that her husband requested that she return their money and as a sign that they were telling the truth, he told them to tell her that he had eaten lentils for his meal.

Other Situations Involving Lying

The Talmud (Babylonian Talmud, Kallah Rabbati, 2) relates that Rabbi Tarfon was wealthy but did not give as much to charity as he was capable. Rabbi Akiva offered to purchase some cities for him and he was given four thousand gold *dinarim*. Rabbi Akiva took the money and distributed it to poor people. When Rabbi Tarfon asked where the cities were, Rabbi Akiva took him to the house of study and brought a schoolchild who read the verse from Psalms (112:9) "he [the righteous person] distributed widely to the impoverished." Some use this story to prove that deception may be permitted in some situations involving charity collection to help the impoverished.[25]

Fish cites several sources that indicate that one should lie to an individual who is very ill when the truth could demoralize the person and possibly hasten his death.[26] Thus, one should not tell a sick person that his friend has died, if he asks how the person is doing, especially if the individual passed away from the same illness.

The Talmud (Babylonian Talmud, Shabbat 116a–b) relates a story of how Imma Shalom and her brother Rabbi Gamliel pretended to be involved in a dispute in order to expose a heretical judge. The judge had an undeserved reputation for honesty and they went to him to settle their "dispute" over the division of their deceased father's estate. The judge ended up taking bribes from both of them. Apparently, they felt that the situation called for lying, in order to expose the corrupt judge.

In an example of the Sages' concern for potentially conveying an appearance of falsehood, the Talmud (Babylonian Talmud, Sanhedrin 30a) rules that when a judicial verdict is handed down via majority (not unanimously), the decision is proclaimed "through the words of the Court, so and so was found not liable." This is the opinion of Rabbi Elazar and is the *halacha*. Rabbi Yochanan's opinion was that the verdict is written simply as "not liable" since Rabbi Yochanan was concerned with the problem of gossip mongering (prohibited by the Torah—see Leviticus 19:16). Revealing how the individual judges voted is tantamount to gossip mongering. After

---

25. Fish, *Titen Emes*, 54–55.
26. Fish, *Titen Emes*, 197.

all, little good can come from the losing party knowing which judges voted against him. Resh Lakish disagrees with Rabbi Yochanan and says the wording must indicate which judge voted to acquit and which judge found the defendant liable; otherwise, the verdict will appear to be untrue. The view of Rabbi Elazar protects the truth and, at the same time, does not violate the prohibition against gossip mongering.

There is a problematic story in the Talmud (Babylonian Talmud, Berakhot 43b) that suggests that Rabbi Pappa fabricated a legal statement in order to avoid embarrassment. The Talmud first discusses the dispute between the Schools of Shammai and Hillel as to which blessing is made first when one is given oil and myrtle at the end of a meal (fragrant oil was used to clean off the food odors and the myrtle was smelled for its pleasant scent). The School of Shammai states that the blessing is first made over the oil and then over the myrtle; the School of Hillel disagrees and says that the benediction over the myrtle is made first. Rabbi Gamliel said that he would "decide" the issue and favors the opinion of the School of Shammai (since oil has two uses whereas the myrtle only has one). Rabbi Yochanan (in a later generation) asserted: "the law is in accordance with the decider."

Rabbi Pappa was at the house of Rabbi Huna ben Ika and they brought oil and myrtle before him and he made the blessing on the myrtle before the oil. Rabbi Huna was surprised and asked: "Does not the master hold that "the law was in accordance with the decider." The Talmud then states that Rabbi Pappa was ashamed of having done something wrong so he told a falsehood and claimed that Rava had stated that the law is agreement with the School of Hillel, a statement that Rava had never made. This story presents many difficulties. However, according to Tosafot and Rif there is an error in the text and they delete the phrase that says Rabbi Pappa made up the statement of Rava. Those who delete the phrase obviously believe that lying about a legal matter in order to avoid embarrassment is not allowed. This is clearly true. An alternative explanation, however, of the above story is that Rabbi Pappa did not agree with the view of Rabbi Yochanan and rather than stating that he did not agree and that the law is in accordance with the School of Hillel, he attributed the statement to his teacher, Rava (see Rama MiPano). According to this view, if one is absolutely sure of a law, one, because of modesty, may attribute it to someone else.

Conclusion

This paper demonstrates that Jewish law does not take an absolutist approach to prevaricating and, indeed, will obligate the individual to lie in various circumstances, for instance, lying to save a life or to bring peace. This, by no means, makes light of the seriousness of lying. The Talmud is replete with statements that stress the importance of truth-telling and remarks that "the seal of God is *emet* [truth]" (Babylonian Talmud, Shabbat 55a); "God hates one who speaks one thing with his mouth and another thing in his heart" (Babylonian Talmud, Pesahim 113b); "Whoever breaks his word is regarded as though he has worshipped idols" (Babylonian Talmud, Sanhedrin 92a); and "liars will not receive the Divine Presence (Babylonian Talmud, Sotah 42a)." The extreme importance of honesty is appropriately summed up by the Talmudic belief that the first question a person is asked in the hereafter at the final judgment is (Babylonian Talmud, Shabbat 31a): "Have you been honest in your dealings?" Despite all this, the Talmud recognizes that there are situations where one may be untruthful.

Chapter 7

Korah

ONE NEED NOT BE an accomplished Bible scholar to hear envy and jealousy pour out of the mouth of Korah when he confronts Moses: "You have gone too far! For all the community are holy, all of them, and the Lord is in their midst. Why then do you raise yourselves above the Lord's congregation?" (Numbers 16:3). It is a given that teaching the Korah narrative will involve a unit built around the topic of jealousy, and this is a theme that lends itself quite well to an interdisciplinary approach. Over the years, I have found that interdisciplinary units offer a change of pace that often draws students more quickly into the material being covered. Here is just one example of an interdisciplinary approach to Korah's rebellion.

Anyone who is a product of the American education system, whether a graduate of public or private school, at some point probably studied the works of William Shakespeare. We can debate which is his best play or which is our favorite, but all would agree *Othello* is the one that most intensely focuses on the dangers of jealousy.

As is typical of Shakespeare's tragedies, the main character in *Othello* is besieged and overcome by a weakness that leads him to ruin. Wherein lies his weakness? On the surface, he may appear confident, even outwardly arrogant at times, but the reality is that he lacks self-esteem. In truth, Othello is actually quite insecure. This helps explain why in act 1, scene 3 he accepts the villain Iago's suggestion that Desdemona is somehow abnormal or strange when she chooses him as a husband.

Another factor underlying his insecurity is that he is an outsider in Venetian society. He lacks insight into and experience with Venetian women and therefore believes Iago's assertion that they secretly cheat on their husbands: "In Venice they do let heaven see the pranks they dare not show their husbands" (act 3, scene 3). Othello is arguably most insecure about his wife. His greatest fear? That his rich, beautiful, aristocratic, white wife does not truly love him. "Perhaps he all too quickly believes the lies Iago tells him about his wife because he secretly believes that the racist majority in Venice are right: maybe a black man is an unattractive creature, not quite human, unworthy of love."[1]

Othello's lack of self-esteem is exploited by Iago, who insinuates that Desdemona is unfaithful. In response, Othello becomes intensely jealous, and this becomes dangerously obvious to his once-beloved wife in act 5, scene 2, where she utters these words shortly before she is murdered by Othello:

> That death's unnatural that kills for loving.
>
> Alas, why gnaw you so your nether lip?
>
> Some bloody passion shakes your very frame:
>
> These are portents; but yet I hope, I hope,
>
> They do not point on me.

Othello is not the only character in the play racked by jealousy. Iago is jealous of Othello's success and of the fact that Othello made Cassio a lieutenant.

> One Michael Cassio, a Florentine,
>
> A fellow almost damned in a fair wife,
>
> That never set a squadron in the field,
>
> Nor the division of a battle knows
>
> More than a spinster—unless the bookish theoric,
>
> Wherein the togèd consuls can propose
>
> As masterly as he: mere prattle, without practice
>
> Is all his soldiership. But he, sir, had the election;
>
> And I, of whom his eyes had seen the proof
>
> At Rhodes, at Cyprus and on other grounds
>
> Christian and heathen, must be beleed and calmed
>
> By debitor and creditor. This counter-caster,
>
> He, in good time, must his lieutenant be.

In this speech from act 1, scene 1, Iago claims he hates Othello because Othello passed him, Iago, over for a promotion, giving "one Michael Cassio" the job as his military lieutenant instead. Iago claims he is far more qualified

---

1. O'Connor, "Othello."

than Cassio, who lacks Iago's experience on the field of battle. It is hard not to see Iago's jealousy in his words.

In the play and in these characters, Shakespeare has expertly brought to life four stages of jealousy.[2]

Stage 1—Identification: Jealousy is a three-part emotion that encompasses the jealous party and two others. These emotions are typically driven by a person feeling that he or she is losing someone—a friend, spouse, lover—to someone more intelligent, more attractive, or with greater wealth. Conversely, envy pops up when one looks around and thinks: "I want what you have, and I hate that you have what I want." Envy is akin to anger, anger that someone else possesses and enjoys something you desire.

Stage 2—Confrontation: This is the stage at which negative thoughts morph into envy. Thoughts such as "I'm so jealous when he looks at her" seem to indicate love for the person. What is instead conveyed is that the individual is afraid of losing his or her love object.

Stage 3—Redirection: Individuals here derive fun and pleasure out of attacking others. They might think, "Do you know what my new car cost?" Such words provide clues to their unconscious feelings of envy. Here, envy can come about as a form of competitiveness. At this stage, the jealous individual must ask for help to change his or her negative thoughts and perspectives into positive ones. The goal in redirecting such thoughts is to arrive at a stage where one can say, "What do I want? What do I do well? And how do I go about achieving it?"

Stage 4—Medea:[3] At this stage, the power envy has over the individual appears almost irreversible. This Medea dimension is strongest in individuals who are in dead-end relationships or who suffer from feelings of low self-esteem or being devalued. Their hatred toward the world and others dominates their thinking. They cannot see themselves ever becoming successful and leading content, happy lives.

I believe there are clear echoes of Iago and of each of these four stages of jealousy in the story of Korah (found in chapter 16 of *Sefer BeMidbar*), which is why I see an interdisciplinary approach employing Shakespeare as so appropriate for teaching it. However, before delving into the details of this story and how it might be taught, we should contextualize the story by considering a few Jewish sources on jealousy.

Let's start with the Torah itself, which specifically alludes to jealousy in the last of the Ten Commandments: "You shall not covet your neighbor's

---

2. The summary that follows is based on Hailparn and M. Hailparn, "Four Dimensions of Envy."

3. The naming of this phase derives from the play *Medea* by Euripides, in which Medea is a woman scorned, rejected by her husband Jason, and seeking revenge.

house: you shall not covet your neighbor's wife, or his male or female slave, or his ox or his ass, or anything that is your neighbor's" (Exodus 20:14). In his enumeration of the 613 commandments traditionally said to be found in the Torah, Rambam codifies Negative Mitzvah 266 as "It is forbidden to envy other people's possessions" based on this biblical verse.[4] He notes that the Jewish people are specifically commanded not to be jealous or envious of other people's belongings.

The view of the talmudic sages on jealousy is equally unambiguous. "Rabbi Elazar HaKappar said: Jealousy, lust, and the [pursuit of] honor remove a person from the world" (Avot 4:21). The sages further observed that envy and jealousy, born out of discontent with one's portion in life, lead a person to begrudge the good fortune that has come to others. Indeed, Rabbi Eleazar went so far as to offer this daily prayer: "May it be acceptable before You, O Lord my God and God of my fathers, that no hatred against us may enter the heart of any man, that no hatred of any man enter our heart, that no envy of us enter the heart of any man, nor the envy of any man enter our heart" (Jerusalem Talmud, Berakhot 7d).

A parable from Shabbat 152b in the Babylonian Talmud further reinforces this point. According to the story, some workers were digging on land belonging to Rav Nachman. In their labors, they happened upon a grave, disturbing the dead man's peace. They were frightened by the man's shriek from within the grave and, running in fear, went to inform Rav Nachman that "a deceased man scolded us!" Hearing this news, Rav Nachman hurried with the workers to the grave. There, he leaned toward the grave and inquired as to the deceased man's name.

"I am Achai son of Yoshiya."

Rav Nachman looked back at the cowering workmen and then faced the grave. "Didn't Rav Meri teach that even the bodies of the righteous will disintegrate in their graves?" He asked. "How is it that your body did not disintegrate?"

"Who is Rav Meri? I don't know who he is."

"You may not know who Rav Meri is but surely you are familiar with the verse in *Ecclesiastes*: '... and the dust returns to the earth as it was' (Ecclesiastes 12:2)."

"Whoever taught you this verse clearly did not teach you the verse from *Proverbs*: 'the rotting of the bones—envy' (Proverbs 14:30). That is,

---

4. The tradition that 613 is the number of commandments in the Torah, began in the third century CE, when Rabbi Simlai mentioned it in a sermon that is recorded in the Babylonian Talmud, Makkot 23b. Although there have been many attempts to codify and enumerate the commandments contained in the Torah, the most commonly cited is that of the Rambam.

he who lives with jealousy in his life will turn to dust when he dies, but he who bears no jealousy, his bones will not disintegrate. Now, the verse in *Ecclesiastes* speaks to the majority of people who conduct their lives driven by jealousy, but when I was alive, I did not bear jealousy in my heart, and so my bones did not rot."

Rav Nachum was much impressed with the explanation, and in fact, the Talmud concludes the narrative with him reaching out and touching Achia's body to find that it was whole. Even the flesh had not rotted.

Rabbi Eliyahu Safron summarized the point of this parable as follows: "Jealousy eats at the essence of our being. It eats at us as we live. What's more, it causes us to rot after we are in the grave."[5] Interestingly, Rabbi Safron continues and quotes his grandfather, who argued that perhaps there can be a positive outcome to jealousy.[6] "But my grandfather taught that there could be a positive side to jealousy, to envy. When we are jealous, we want things we should not. However, it is possible to be envious of a fellow's kindness, his sensitivity, his decency, understanding, knowledge, and diligence. In other words, to envy these positive attributes, we might be motivated to attain those same positive attributes for ourselves. That type of envy may well enhance one's behavior and serve as a motivator for self-improvement."[7] The envy and jealousy displayed by Korah, however, brought about no good at all—not to him and not to his followers.

Korah makes no effort to mask his envy and his jealousy of Moses: "You have gone too far! For all the community are holy, all of them, and the Lord is in their midst. Why then do you raise yourselves above the Lord's congregation?" (Numbers 16:3). It is thus left to the commentators, most notably Rashi, in his comment on Numbers 16:1, to highlight the reasons for Korah's jealousy.

> And what induced Korah to quarrel with Moses? He was envious of the princely dignity held by Elzaphan the son of Uzziel whom Moses had appointed prince over the sons of Kohath although this was by the express command of God. Korah argued thus: "My father and his brothers were four in number—as it is said, 'and the sons of Kohath were [Amram and Izhar and Hebron and Uzziel]' (Exodus 6:18). As to Amram, the eldest, his two sons have themselves assumed high dignity, one as king and the other as High Priest. Who is entitled to receive the second (the rank next to it)? Is it not I who is the son of Izhar, who

---

5. Safran, "Jealousy Rots."

6. This teaching is most likely based on the statement in Babylonian Talmud, Bava Batra 22a that "the envy of Torah scholars increases wisdom."

7. Safran, "Jealousy Rots."

was the second to Amram amongst the brothers? And yet he has appointed as prince the son of his (Amram's) brother who was the youngest of all of them! I hereby protest against him and will undo his decision." What did Korah do? He arose and assembled 250 men, fitted to be heads of the Sanhedrin, most of them of the tribe of Reuben, who were his neighbors.

A more complicated question involves the tribe of Reuben. What prompted them to join Korah's rebellion?[8] Rashi simply ascribes it to proximity in his commentary on Numbers 16:1: "Because the tribe of Reuben had their place, when they encamped, in the South, thus being neighbors of Kohath and his sons, who, too, encamped in the South, they joined Korah in his quarrel. 'Woe to the wicked, woe to his neighbor!'" Ramban offers a more practical reason. Members of the tribe of Reuben join the rebellion for a very simple reason. They were afraid of dying in the desert, a fear they expressed with great passion: "Is it not enough that you brought us from a land flowing with milk and honey to have us die in the wilderness, that you would also lord it over us?" (Numbers 16:13). Only the commentary of *Daat Zekenim* on Numbers 16:1 suggests that jealousy plays a role in their decision: "Seeing that he was from the tribe of Reuben, Jacob's firstborn whom his father had deprived of the privileges of the birthright, Korah thought he had reason to join his rebellion."[9]

And what is Moses's reaction to all this? Initially, as Rashi notes in his commentary on Numbers 16:4, he prays to God to forgive yet another transgression of the people against the Lord. He then becomes angry and directs this anger towards Korah and his followers:

> Is it not enough for you that the God of Israel has set you apart from the community of Israel and given you access to Him, to perform the duties of the Lord's Tabernacle and to minister to the community and serve them? Now that He has advanced you and all your fellow Levites with you, do you seek the priesthood too? Truly, it is against the Lord that you and all your company have banded together. For who is Aaron that you should rail against him? (Numbers 16:9–11)

---

8. Interestingly, there are no similar questions about Dathan and Abiram's involvement with Korah's rebellion. In fact, it is almost a given that they would be involved. The rabbinic view of these two individuals is summed up nicely in the commentary of *Daat Zekenim*. This source notes that Dathan "flouted Jewish law" and that Abiram "prevented his heart from repenting."

9. It should be noted that Ramban specifically rejects this rationale in his commentary on this verse.

Despite his anger, Moses tries reconciliation, sending messengers to Dathan and Abiram in an effort to assuage their grievances, but to no avail (Numbers 16:12). Ultimately, he expresses his exasperation in the presence of the rebels, their followers, and the rest of the nation:

> And Moses said, "By this you shall know that it was the Lord who sent me to do all these things, that they are not of my own devising: if these men die as all men do, if their lot be the common fate of all mankind, it was not the Lord who sent me. But if the Lord brings about something unheard of, so that the ground opens its mouth and swallows them up with all that belongs to them and they go down alive into Sheol, you shall know that these men have spurned the Lord" (Numbers 16:28–30).

We all know how the story ends. "The earth opened its mouth and swallowed them up with their households, all Korah's people and all their possessions" (Numbers 16:32).

What is the enduring lesson for those looking to *Sefer BeMidbar* as a guide to character development? Simply this: In the pristine world of the talmudic house of study, jealousy could be imagined as a tool for self-improvement. In the reality of Korah's rebellion, it is an instrument of his downfall and of his followers as well.

Sefer BeMidbar—Korah
Sample Unit Plan

Unit	Primary Source(s)	Supplemental Reading(s)	Timeframe
Korah	Numbers 16	The Entire Nation is Holy	two weeks
	Rashi 16:1		
Middah:	Rambam 16:1		
Jealousy	Rashi 16:3	Freeing Yourself from Jealousy	
	Rashi 16:4		
	Kli Yakar 16:4		
	Ramban 16:4		
	Rashi 16:12		
	Ramban 16:12		
	Rashi 16:19		

Essential Questions

1. Who was Korah and why did he feel entitled to a leadership position?
2. What were the grievances of his co-conspirators?
3. How would Jewish society have changed if Korah had prevailed with his argument that "all of them are holy"?
4. What are we to make of Moses's reactions to the rebellion throughout this chapter?

Evaluating/Checking for Understanding

1. Daily discussions/student interactions

   Student questions and observations typically drive each day's discussion.

2. Occasional written reflections

   At the discretion of the teacher, a tool to foster further reflection on the unit's essential questions.

3. Character trait essay

   See appendix for assignment rubric.

4. Unit test

   Unit tests should, by definition, be crafted by individual teachers to meet the needs of their specific students. The Understanding by Design *framework created by Grant Wiggins and Jay McTighe is an excellent tool for the development of appropriate tests and assessments, as its emphasis on backward design forces teachers to consider in advance the assessment evidence needed to document and validate that the targeted learning goals have been achieved.*

Primary Source Texts

1. *BeMidbar* chapter 16: Read text and seek to identify problematic (what I call "red flag") words and phrases (with teacher's guidance, of course). These red flag words and phrases will likely vary from class to class depending on the sophistication and linguistic abilities of the students, coupled with the background and interests of the teacher. That said, some important examples of red flag words and phrases in this chapter appear in commentaries A–I.

2. Supplemental readings for each unit are intended to demonstrate that serious scholarship about and explanations of *Sefer BeMidbar* are not limited to the classical medieval commentators but continue to our time. The supplemental readings for this unit focus on the notion of whether the entire nation could be holy (and the implications of this if it is true) as well as various suggestions for overcoming jealousy. These readings are: "All the Nation is Holy" by Rav Yair Kahn and "Freeing Yourself from Jealousy" by Shira Smiles.

Sefer BeMidbar—Korah

Primary Texts

A. Rashi 16:1

"And Korah took"

He betook himself on one side with the view of separating himself from out of the community so that he might raise a protest regarding the priesthood to which Moses had appointed his brother. This is what Onkelos means when he renders it by ואתפלג—"he separated himself" from the rest of the community in order to maintain dissension. Similar is, (Job 15:12) "Why doth thy heart take you aside (יקחך)," meaning, it takes you aside to separate you from other people (Midrash Tanhuma, Korah 2).—Another explanation of ויקח קרח is: he attracted (won over) the chiefs of the Sanhedrin amongst them (the people) by fine words. The word is used here in a figurative sense just as in (Leviticus 8:2) "Take (קח) Aaron"; (Hosea 14:3) "Take (קחו) words with you" (Midrash Tanhuma, Korah 1).

"[Korah] the son of Izhar, the son of Kohath, the son of Levi"

It does not, however, make mention of Levi being "the son of Jacob," because he (Jacob) offered prayer for himself that his name should not be mentioned in connection with their (the Korahites') quarrels, as it is said (Genesis 49:6), "with their assembly, my glory be thou not united." And where is his name mentioned in connection with Korah? In the passage in Chronicles where their (the Korahites') genealogy is traced in connection with the "Duchan" (properly the platform—the place on which the Levites were stationed for the service of song in the Temple), as it is said, (1 Chronicles 6:22–23) "the son of Ebiasaph, the son of Korah, the son of Izhar, the son of Kohath, the son of Levi, the son of Israel."

"And Dathan and Abiram"

Because the tribe of Reuben had their place, when they encamped, in the South, thus being neighbors of Kohath and his sons, who, too, encamped in the South, they (the Reubenites) joined Korah in his quarrel. "Woe to the wicked, woe to his neighbor!"—And what induced Korah to quarrel with Moses? He was envious of the princely dignity held by Elzaphan the son of Uzziel whom Moses had appointed prince over the sons of Kohath although this was by the express command of God (Numbers 3:30). Korah argued thus: "My father and his brothers were four in number—as it is said (Exodus 6:18), "and the sons of Kohath were [Amram and Izhar and Hebron and Uzziel]."—"As to Amram, the eldest, his two sons have themselves assumed high dignity, one as king and the other as High Priest; who is entitled to receive the second (the rank next to it)? Is it not "I" who am the son of Izhar, who was the second to Amram amongst the brothers? And yet he has appointed as prince the son of his (Amram's) brother who was the youngest of all of them! I hereby protest against him and will undo his decision."—What did he do? He arose and assembled 250 men, fitted to be heads of the Sanhedrin, most of them of the tribe of Reuben who were his neighbors, viz., Elizur the son of Shedeur, and his colleagues, and others of a similar standing,—for here it states (v. 2) that they were "princes of the congregation, those who were called to the assembly (קראי מועד)," and there (in another passage) it states (Numbers 1:16), "these were they who were called to the congregation (קרואי העדה)" (amongst whom was also Elizur the son of Shedeur),—and he attired them in robes of pure purple wool. They then came and stood before Moses and said to him, "Is a garment that is entirely of purple subject to the law of *tzitzit* or is it exempt"? He replied to them: "It is subject to that law." Whereupon they began to jeer at him: "Is this possible? A robe of any different colored material, one thread of purple attached to it exempts it, and this that is entirely of purple should it not exempt itself (i.e., ipso facto be exempt) from the law of *tzitzit*?"

B. Ramban 16:1

"And Korah took"

A correct interpretation by way of homiletic exposition is that Korah became angry because of the status of prince bestowed [by Moses] upon Elizaphan, as our Rabbis have said, and he was also jealous of Aaron, as it is said, "And seek you the priesthood also!" (Numbers 16:10) Dathan and Abiram were attracted to Korah, but not because of the [loss of their] birthright, for it was their father Jacob who had deprived Reuben of it and given it to Joseph. However, they, too, voiced their complaint [by saying that Moses had taken the people out of Egypt] "to kill us in the wilderness" (Numbers 16:13), and "moreover you have not brought us into a land flowing with milk and honey" (Numbers 16:14). Now, as long as Israel was in the wilderness of Sinai, no evil happening befell them, for even after the incident of the Golden Calf, which was a serious and well-known sin, those who died were few, and the people were saved by Moses' prayer when he "fell down before the Eternal the forth days and forty nights" (Deuteronomy 9:15). Thus, they loved Moses as [they loved] themselves, and they obeyed him, so that had anybody rebelled against Moses at that time, the people would have stoned him. Therefore, Korah endured the greatness of Aaron, and the firstborn accepted [without protest] the high status of the Levites, and all [the other] acts of Moses. But when they came to the wilderness of Paran and [some people] were burnt in Taberah, and many died in the incident of the quails (see Numbers 11:34), and when after sinning [in the matter of] the Spies Moses did not pray on their behalf, so that the decree against them was thus not annulled, and the Princes of all the tribes "dies by the plague before the Eternal" (Numbers 11:37), and it was decreed that the whole people would be consumed in the wilderness and there they would die, then the mood of the whole people became embittered, and they said in their hearts that mishaps occur to them through Moses' words. Therefore, Korah found it an opportune occasion to contest Moses's deeds, thinking that the people would listen to him.

C. Rashi 16:3

"[For] all [the congregation] are holy"

They all heard the utterances on Sinai from the mouth of the Almighty.

"Why then lift you up yourselves [above the assembly of the Lord]"

If you have taken royal rank for yourself, you should at least not have chosen the priesthood for your brother—it is not you alone who have heard at Sinai: "I am the Lord thy God," all the congregation heard it!

D. Rashi 16:4

"[And when Moses heard it,] he fell upon his face"

Because of the rebellion, for this was already the fourth offence on their part: when they sinned by worshipping the Golden Calf, it states (Exodus

32:11), "And Moses besought [the Lord]"; in the case of the "people who complained" (Numbers 11:1), it states: "and Moses prayed"; at the incident of the "spies" (Numbers 14:13), "And Moses said unto the Lord, 'When the Egyptians shall hear it . . . [and now I beseech You etc.]"; but now at the rebellion of Korah, his hands sank down (he felt himself powerless) A parable! This may be compared to the case of a prince who sinned against his father and for whom his (the father's) friend gained forgiveness once, twice, three times. When he offended for the fourth time the friend felt himself powerless, for he said, "How long can I trouble the king? Perhaps he will not again accept advocacy from me!"

E. Kli Yakar 16:4

"[And when Moses heard it,] he fell upon his face"

In the Tractate Sanhedrin (110a) they said, "What sayings [in the sense of rumors] did he [Moses] hear? This teaches us that they [the rebels] suspected Moses of adulterous relations (with their wives), as it is said (Psalm 110:16), "And there was envy of Moses in the camp." Each one (of the rebels) was envious of Moses with regards to his wife (that is, they suspected him of having adulterous relations with her). Such a thought is beyond comprehension. And this oral tradition (that the rebels suspected Moses) can only be applied to these specific set of circumstances because there is nothing in this verse that hints to it. Therefore I say that the one who brought down this oral tradition wanted to explicate the verse "For all the community are holy, all of them, and the Lord is in their midst. Why then do you raise yourselves above the Lord's congregation?" What does holiness ("for all the community is holy") have to do with leadership ("why then do you raise yourselves above the Lord's congregation")? And should you wish to say that there is a connection between them, that holiness is an appropriate prevention again haughtiness (that is, raising oneself above the community), why then does the verse not say "why do you raise yourself about this holy community?" Rather, this is certainly what Korah said to Moses according to that which we find in Tractate Sotah (4b): "Rabbi Yochanan says: Any person who has arrogance within him will eventually stumble by sinning with an adulteress." And it further says (in this same source), "Rabbi Hama bar Hanina says: Any person who has arrogance within him is considered as if he engaged in sexual intercourse with all of those with whom relations are forbidden." And it is well-known that in the Biblical texts wherever there is mention of holiness one finds warnings (literally, fences) about forbidden sexual relations, because such relations profane holiness. Thus Korah reasoned that if the entire congregation is holy and thereby girds itself against forbidden sexual relations why would Moses (and Aaron and the other leaders) raise themselves up over the community? Because by doing so they will surely stumble when it comes to forbidden sexual relations and there will hence profane the holiness of the people! Thus he refers to "the congregation of God" and not "this holy congregation" because he thought that after the haughtiness of the leaders there can no longer be any holiness . . . . and through this Moses understood that Korah suspected him of adulterous relations. This is why the verse states, "And when Moses heard it, he fell upon his face."

F. Ramban 16:4

"[And when Moses heard it,] he fell upon his face"

(It says, "he fell") and not "they fell." Because Aaron because of his sanctify [in accordance with his position as high priest] he was at all involved in this dispute. This is why Aaron was silent and a reflection of his agreeing that Korah had greater standing than him. But he (Aaron) acted in accordance with the words of Moses and fulfilled the decrees of the king.

G. Rashi 16:12

"And Moses sent [to call Dathan and Abiram]"

From here we may learn that one should not persist in strife, for, you see, Moses sought them out in order to conciliate them by peaceful words.

H. Ramban 16:12

"And Moses sent [to call Dathan and Abiram]"

Since Dathan and Abiram were tribal leaders, Moses assumes that they were more important than On son of Peleth, and if they would reconcile with him, On would follow their lead. Therefore, he (Moses) did not send emissaries to him. Thus he did not come and was not with them or with the congregation of Korah for he left them. And when Dathan and Abiram went and joined Korah, he did not return with them, for he (On) had already taken the advice of his wife (who thereby saved him), as our Sages explain (Sanhedrin 109b). For the verse does not mention that he (On) was swallowed up by the earth along with Dathan and Abiram, nor was he among those who appear with firepans before the Lord (verses 16–18) because there were only 250 such individuals (apart from the four originally mentioned at the beginning of the chapter).

I. Rashi 16:19

"And Korah convened [all the congregation] against them"

By means of scoffing language: that whole night he went round to all the tribes and tried to win them over: "Do you really think that I care for myself alone? It is only for all of you that I have a care! These men come and occupy every high office: royal rank for himself, for his brother the priesthood!"—until in the end all of them submitted to his persuasion.

Sefer BeMidbar—Korah

Supplemental Reading

The Entire Nation is Holy

—Rav Yair Kahn

I. The Aftermath of the Rebellion

The story of Korah's rebellion is a fascinating drama, full of passion and intrigue. Although the Torah is grudgingly silent regarding the background and details of these events, Chazal, utilizing various nuances and hints in the Biblical texts, managed to weave together a tale that reflects both human realities and philosophical dilemmas.

In sharp contrast to this narrative brevity, the aftermath of the rebellion, which at first glance appears insignificant, is treated with surprising detail. This epilogue is quite uncharacteristic of Biblical narrative. The Torah records numerous occasions when the Jewish People failed and were subsequently reprimanded and sometimes even punished, but at that point, the episode ends. In contrast, the story of Korah inexplicably seems to linger on. It is only after Korah and his followers are destroyed, the people continue to complain, bringing disaster upon themselves.

Let us consider one of the major points of contention—the authority of Moshe Rabbeinu. In response to the challenge presented by Korah, the divine sanction of Moses's rule was clearly established when the earth opened up its mouth to swallow Dathan and Abiram. If this issue has been resolved, how are we to understand the people's subsequent verbal assault on Moses and Aaron: "YOU murdered God's people" (17:6)? The use of the term "you" in this context indicates that Moses and Aaron were being held personally responsible for the deaths of the insurgents. Did the people still believe that Moses was acting out of personal vengeance? Were they totally oblivious to the most essential message indicated by the divine sign they had just witnessed: "Hereby you will know that God sent me to perform all these acts, as they were not [done] of my own mind" (16:28)? Was the mouth of the Earth, which our Sages say was created at twilight on the Friday of creation, created for naught? Let us not ignore the fact that most of the casualties occurred during the plague that took place only at this point, and not during the actual rebellion!

However, the story does not end even at this point. The Korah saga continues, as the people once again turn to Moses, complaining in the wake of the plague:

> "Behold, we die, we perish, we are all perishing! Everyone who approaches the sanctuary of God dies; have we stopped dying?" (17:27–28)

This complaint is enigmatic. Did the people really believe that God killed at random? Were they unaware that Korah and his followers had committed a grave sin? Moreover, why do they continue to complain after seeing the tragic consequences of their initial complaint? Was one plague insufficient? Why don't they learn from their mistakes?

Based on the above, it seems obvious that far more emphasis should be placed on the events that followed the rebellion. The Torah is trying to draw our attention to this section of the story, and a complete understanding of the Korah rebellion cannot be attained without deciphering the significance of the epilogue.

II. Philosophical Skepticism or Emotional Reaction

In my opinion, these events implicitly address a basic problem raised by Korah that was never explicitly treated: "For the entire congregation is holy and God dwells in their midst; why then do you raise yourselves above the congregation of God?" (16:3). Regardless of the impurity of Korah's personal motives, the problem he raised seems legitimate—the question of equality. This question is never specifically addressed, nor adequately resolved. Although we trust Moses's assertion that Korah was interested only in his personal status (see 16:10), we are nevertheless left to ponder the Jewish caste system that separates *kohanim* from the rest of the nation.

Let us take a closer look at the events leading to the plague. The people blamed Moses and Aaron for the death of Korah and his followers. But was Moshe Rabbeinu completely in error when he claimed, "Hereby you shall know that God sent me" (16:28)? As we mentioned before, it is difficult to assume that the people were totally oblivious to the divine proof indicating that Moses and Aaron were merely implementing God's will.

I believe that the people WERE convinced by the divine sign. Korah's claim that Moses was not representing God's will was laid to rest when the earth miraculously swallowed the insurgents. The people's argument was not rooted in philosophical skepticism; rather, it was a human reaction generated by sorrow and pain. Devastated by the death of public leaders, friends and relatives, they turned to Moses and Aaron full of grief: "Was there no other way to prove your point? Did all these people have to be destroyed? Are we short of orphans and widows?" It was an emotional outburst, not a rational argument. However, if my interpretation is correct, the severity of God's response seems incomprehensible: "Remove yourselves from amongst this congregation and I will destroy them in an instant" (17:10).

It would be instructive to glance at a similar divine reaction, which is the precursor of this one. When Korah goes to the sanctuary with his two hundred and fifty followers, he gathers the entire nation to witness the outcome. God's severe response to the nation's curiosity is startling: "Separate from amongst this congregation and I will destroy them in an instant" (16:21). Again, we find God's response totally out of proportion to the severity of the infraction. It is true that the people should not have harbored even the slightest doubt regarding the divine nature of Moses's authority, but is this curiosity punishable by death? Although in the end Moses managed to deflect the danger of destruction, we are left to ponder the significance of the threat.

At this point, I would like to suggest an approach radically different from the one assumed until now. The plague was not the deserved punishment for a specific sin; rather, it was the almost inevitable result of a new situation created by the rebellion. Korah attacked the institution of *kehuna* (priesthood). He claimed that the entire nation was holy and therefore there was no need for a separate priestly class. According to his argument, anyone could enter the sanctuary and bring the incense offering. Although the Israelites did not challenge Moses's authority, they nonetheless identified with Korah's argument. They did not understand why they could not fully participate in the Sanctuary worship. After all, were they not a "kingdom of priests" (Exodus 19:6)? Why should they be considered *zarim* (strangers), who may not enter the Temple? Why should a barrier separate them from the Sanctuary?

However, this barrier was not unilaterally imposed upon the Israelites by God; it was erected with the implicit consent of the people, when *machane Yisrael* was set up. Once the Israelites accepted the premise of

Korah's argument and rejected the barrier separating the sacred and the mundane, they found themselves faced with a new situation—the barrier was abolished. There was no longer any division between the people and the Sanctuary. The line separating "the camp of the Shekinah" from "the Levite camp" and "the Israelite camp" became blurred. The entire camp became enveloped within the context of the *Mishkan* and the presence of the *Shekinah*.

Of course, being in the presence of the Almighty, as it were, is quite demanding. Behavior deemed acceptable under usual circumstances, becomes intolerable within the context of the Sanctuary. As it is written in Qoheleth, "Take heed when you walk in the house of Hashem" (4:17). Normal human reactions of anger and grief must be suppressed; emotional outbursts are unacceptable.

> When Nadab and Abihu were destroyed, Aaron and his remaining sons were commanded not to mourn: Let not the hair of your heads go loose, neither rend your clothes, lest you die ... but let your brethren, the whole house of Yisrael, bewail the burning which Hashem has kindled. And you shall not go out from the door of the tent of meeting, lest you die; for the anointing oil of Hashem is upon you. (Leviticus 10:6–7)

Since they were in the *Mishkan*, Aaron and his remaining sons must suppress the basic human emotion of mourning. Similarly, the Kohen Gadol cannot leave the sanctuary to attend the funeral services of even his closest relatives (see Leviticus 21:11–12).

When the people gathered to witness the outcome of the Korah–Moses controversy, they did not necessarily harbor deep-rooted doubts regarding the divine nature of Moses's authority. Perhaps they were driven by simple human curiosity. It is even possible that they were rooting for Korah not due to wavering faith, but merely because it is human nature to root for the underdog. Even if we concede that the Israelites identified with Korah's populist campaign slogan, were they cognizant of the philosophical ramifications? Weren't they merely acting human?

The answer is that human frailties are inexcusable within God's presence. While standing within the framework of the *Mishkan*, which now enveloped the entire camp, human behavior must be impeccable. Had Moses not pleaded on behalf of the nation, a lethal plague would have devastated the camp.

Mourning the death of Korah and his followers, the people approached Moses and complained. Their reaction was understandable as an emotional outburst of grief, sorrow and pain. They did not challenge Moses's authority; they merely let off steam. Again, their reaction, though acceptable under normal situations, was intolerable once the barriers had collapsed. The presence of the Shekinah demands restraint and self-control (see Leviticus 10:3); there is no room within the *mishkan* for such passionate outbursts of anger. Once the people protested, there was nothing left for Moses to do but to send Aaron to stop the spread of the plague.

III. The Final Stage

In sharp contrast with the argumentative tone of the emotional outburst that led to the plague, the complaint that followed seems like a pathetic whimper. Frustrated and desperate, the people return to Moses and say, "Behold, we are all dying!" (17:27). After the plague, they finally understood the severity of their situation. They realized that the plague was not a punishment for sin, but a result of the total breakdown of barriers that they had brought upon themselves—"Everyone who approaches the Sanctuary of God dies; have we stopped dying?" (17:28).

After initially identifying with Korah's campaign and rejecting the barriers separating the Sanctuary from the nation, the people are now ready to appreciate why division is necessary. They understand that, to a certain extent, "a holy nation" is a contradiction in terms. Sanctity demands separation, a departure from the mundane. Frailties typical of the human condition are incommensurate with holiness. Normal societal conditions are replete with passion and competition, arguments and jealousy. Although these are unavoidable within a normal human framework, they are intolerable in the presence of God. Nationhood and holiness appear to be mutually exclusive.

Now, the time is ripe to re-introduce the institution of *kehuna*. A Sanctuary for the entire nation can be established within their midst on one condition—there must be barriers. A *Mishkan* can be established within a human context; however, the priests who are to serve within it must be separated from the mundane routine of life, which is full of tension and strife. The remainder of the nation can continue to lead a normal life, and nevertheless the *Mishkan* in their midst becomes the focus which invests their life with direction and meaning.

This, in fact, is God's response to the people's second complaint:

> And Hashem said to Aaron: "You and your children and your father's house with you shall bear the iniquity of the Sanctuary and you and your children with you shall bear the iniquity of your priesthood . . . and to the consecrated vessels and the altar they will not approach and neither they nor you will perish." (18:1–3)

The Israelites finally appreciate the institution of *kehuna*. They finally understand why barriers are necessary for the realization of that great vision—to become a kingdom of priests and a holy nation. At this point, the institution of *kehuna* could finally be re-established, and the barriers rejected due to Korah's rebellion could be rebuilt with the entire nation's consent. Upon the ruins of a fragmented society divided by a sense of inequality, a harmonious community based upon separation of roles and mutual respect was built.

IV. When Did the Rebellion Take Place?

At the beginning of *Sefer BeMidbar*, we read:

> But the Levites shall pitch round about the Tabernacle of the Testimony, that there be no *ketzef* (wrath) upon the *eida* (congregation) of the the Israelites. (1:53)

When the division of the various camps was initially established, it was to prevent *ketzef* from the *eida*. When Hashem threatens to destroy Israel after Korah gathers the entire *eida*, Moses and Aaron plead with Hashem not to have *ketzef* on the *eida* because of the transgressions of one person (16:22). After the people complain and the plague begins, Moses sends Aaron into the *eida* because the plague has begun due to Hashem's *ketzef* (17:11). After the people complain for the second time and lament their sorry condition, the division of the machane is re-established and the Levites are charged with guarding the holy places so that Yisrael should not be struck by *ketzef* (18:5).

The Ibn Ezra notes that Korah attacked the structure that was established at the beginning of *Sefer BeMidbar*. Applying the principle that the Torah does not necessarily correspond to chronological order, he argues that the Korah rebellion preceded the meraglim. The Ramban counters that Dathan and Abiram's attack on Moses ("You have brought us up out of a land flowing with milk and honey, to kill us in the wilderness.... Moreover, you have not brought us into a land flowing with milk and honey, nor given us inheritance of fields and vineyards" [16:13–14]) is a clear reference to the decree following the *chet ha-meraglim*.

A straightforward reading of the Torah supports the position of the Ramban, that the rebellion took place after the *meraglim*. However, the Ibn Ezra correctly notes that the issue at stake is the original structure of the *machane*, which was established at the beginning of *Sefer BeMidbar*. Perhaps Korah was unable to attack Moses as long as he was popular and success seemed just around the corner. The devastating decree of the *meraglim* afforded the opportunity to attack.

The understanding that Korah attacked the *machane* structure established at the beginning of *BeMidbar* is significant in appreciating the flow of the sefer. In our study of *Sefer BeMidbar*, we have traced the development of the multifaceted *machane*. We began with its birth, so full of promise and hope, as described in the opening chapters. We began to note troublesome signs of deterioration as the Israelites began their epic journey from Sinai to Canaan. We watched in horror as the *machane* collapsed upon the return of the *meraglim*. Until this point, the decline affected the masses as well as the political leadership; the institutions of *kehuna* and *leviya* somehow remained intact. Here, we witness the collapse of these institutions as well.

Thus, our parasha describes the continuation of the disintegration of the machane. This process, which began in *BeMidbar* 11 and peaks with the episode of the Spies, continues with the rejection of *kehuna* and *leviya*. However, Parashat Korah is also the turning point. *Kehuna* and *leviya* are re-established, and the process of rebuilding has begun. In next week's shiur, we will continue to trace this rebuilding process.

Rav Yair Kahn [YHE '77], head of the Overseas Students Program, has been a Ram at Yeshivat Har Etzion since 1987. He is currently teaching a third-year Israeli shiur. Rav Kahn has been the coordinator of the Virtual Beit Midrash Gemara Iyun Shiur for several years. Originally from New York, Rav Kahn studied at Chaim Berlin, Yeshiva University, and Yeshivat Har Etzion. Rav Kahn is also the editor of the Shiurei Hagrid series published by Mossad Harav Kook.

Sefer BeMidbar—Korah

Supplemental Reading

Freeing Yourself from Jealousy: Unlocking A Secret Of The Tenth Commandment

—Shira Smiles

At a first glance of the Ten Commandments, the average person would find most of them both logical and feasible. After all, who could disagree with rules such as "You shall not kill" and "You shall not steal"? The last commandment, however, might leave one a bit apprehensive: "You shall not covet the home of your fellow, nor his spouse or servants or animals, or anything that belongs to your fellow" (Exodus 20:14).

Nowadays, servants and animals might not be the coveted items, but we can certainly relate to envying our neighbor's new car or fancy china plates. Desire is a feeling that seems to come almost unbidden. It is an emotion that tends to overwhelm one's entire being. An obvious question arises: how can God ask us to control a feeling? We think to ourselves, Of course, I would never steal my neighbor's new crystal vase, but I can't even *secretly want it*? How can we be expected to uphold this commandment?

Let us first define what the Torah identifies as "desire." The Ten Commandments are listed in the Torah in two different places: once in the Book of Exodus and again in Deuteronomy. Interestingly, their wording is not identical. In Exodus, the tenth commandment reads, "You shall not covet" *(lo tach'mod)* while in Deuteronomy, it reads "You shall not desire" *(lo tita'veh)*.

Jealousy is an impulsive, natural reaction. How can we avoid it?

This discrepancy clarifies the two parts of the commandment. Desire means wanting another's possession and designing a mental plan for acquiring it for oneself. Coveting is defined as pursuing that plan of getting the desired item. Technically, this commandment does not prohibit the undeveloped general thoughts of craving someone else's belongings. These thoughts, however, are the catalyst for one's formulation and execution of a plan to acquire the item he wants.

Negative thinking that precedes desiring and coveting is nothing less than jealousy. The Talmud says that "jealousy, desire and honor remove a person from the world" (Avot 4:21). Jealousy is such a destructive emotion that often misleads us to act in despicable ways. If envy is the motivating point of origin that leads to desiring and coveting, then it needs to be uprooted altogether.

This seems to be a tall order for human beings; jealousy is an impulsive, natural reaction. How can we avoid it?

The Peasant's Wife

The Torah's guidelines enable us to become more Godly people, to break free of the emotional limitations of being physical creatures. But how do we free ourselves from jealousy? *Sefer HaChinuch* (416) presents this question regarding the Torah's requirement to control our desires. Interestingly, he says that intelligent, honest people know that they are the masters of their emotions. In reality, however, the intensity of our desires makes us feel that these desires are often unmanageable.

If the *Sefer HaChinuch* considers it a basic assumption that emotions are controllable, why do we experience the opposite? What is the missing link here?

Let us examine the general nature of our desires. Is there a limit to that which arouses our jealousy? Consider the following parable: A simple peasant seeking a wife, due to his lowly status, has a small pool of potential candidates. Maybe he considers his neighbor's daughter, or the peasant girl down the road. This simple man would never yearn to marry the royal princess. Even if she is the most beautiful and desirable woman, he still wouldn't invest any emotional energy in longing for her. Why not? He doesn't consider the Princess to be a realistic option. Royalty doesn't marry commoners like him. (see Ibn Ezra, Exodus 20:13)

Our mindset is comparable to that of this man in the parable. We only long for things that we perceive as within the scope of personal possibility. Recognize this human phenomenon: Our desires remain within the boundaries of our self-perception and, therefore, place limitations on jealousy.

We only long for things that we perceive as within the scope of personal possibility.

Our desires are determined by our view of ourselves and the world. If this is true, then we do have ultimate control over our desires. Emotions might seem too powerful to subdue, but we can alter our intellectual framework. We can direct our feelings by manipulating our perception of ourselves. By being realistic about our strengths and weaknesses, we can change our thoughts and desires.

Custom Tool Box

How can we gain an accurate self-perspective? Let us look to the first commandment about believing in God. Introductions and conclusions often have a common theme or connection. Such is the case with the first commandment (I am Your God) and last commandment (You shall not covet). Deep belief in God includes an awareness that He is the Source of all creation, providing each individual being with exactly what it needs physically and spiritually. Therefore, to desire or covet what others have is antithetical to the first commandment.

Everything in an individual's possession is given to him in order to achieve his particular life purpose. Everyone has a God-given, custom-designed box of tools with which to do his particular job. Just as in practical life professions, for example, a chef has a box of kitchen utensils and a doctor has a box of medical supplies. Would a chef ever want a stethoscope? No, because it won't help him bake a cake. Would a doctor ever dream about owning an eggbeater? No, because it won't help him heal a patient's wound.

God gives us certain inborn talents, life circumstances, and physical possessions with which to fulfill our role in life. If there is something we lack, we must not need it. It would be unnecessary, and even counterproductive for achieving our unique potential, to have anything more than God gave us.

Having this perspective is not only important to us as individuals; these values influence those around us, especially the next generation. If our actions focus on materialism, then our children hear the underlying message and adopt that value. However, if our deeds are spiritually-oriented, then others will be influenced by our example.

Someone once shared with me how she handles jealousy between her children. She compares possessions to an eyeglasses prescription.

Prescriptions are customized to individual people. Would anyone ever insist that his eye doctor give him another person's prescription? Of course not! We realize that wearing someone else's glasses won't help us see and often blurs our vision. Since another person's glasses aren't going to help us see, there is no sense in wanting them. If someone in the family expresses desire for another's belongings, the parent tells him, "It's his prescription."

Emotional reactions to others' material possessions send powerful messages to our children. When our neighbors go on an expensive vacation, do we wish aloud that we could, too? The woman who serves on beautiful china plates—do we think about her, "Why don't I have plates like that?" We notice a new car in someone else's driveway. "Wow! Wouldn't it be amazing if I had one like that?" How do these responses affect other people, especially the young people who look at us as role models to emulate?

Treasured Possessions

On a personal note, once an appraiser came to assess the monetary value of our property for insurance purposes. He took a small scale out of his bag and said: "Okay, let's weigh your jewelry." So, I handed him the few inexpensive pieces that I own. He looked a bit disappointed and asked, "Is that all you have?" I replied, "Well, we do have a lot of books." He shook his head, "No, no. What about silver items?" I proceeded to show him a couple of menorahs. He asked, "What other silver things do you have?" I replied, "That's all the silver, but we have a lot of books." He frowned and asked, "Cameras?" We handed him our two cameras.

The exchange continued in this way. Whenever he asked for more, we would reply, "No, but we have a lot of books. Books are really important." After a while, the appraiser was frustrated with us and decided to look around our apartment himself. At the end of his survey, he commented, "You know, you have a lot of books!" I said, "Right! Books! That is important to us!"

I hope that my children gleaned two lessons from the incident. The first message is that books are worth acquiring. What we fill our homes with speaks volumes (!) about our priorities. I also hope they heard the assessor point out that we didn't own significant amounts of jewelry, silver or cameras. Our response was not a sigh or a frown, saying, "Wow—why don't we have more of those things?" If we had reacted with a hint of disappointment, the strong value placed on materialism would have been subtly conveyed to our children. The people around us, especially our children, observe all that we do. Our actions and reactions influence their thoughts and subsequently their actions.

We all have the ability to control our desires. The jealousy that leads us to desire has no place in our lives, because we each have exactly what we need. God provides each individual with the necessary customized tools to complete his unique mission. By elevating our perspective, we preserve this tenth commandment and transform ourselves. We grow one step closer to reaching the spiritual potential that was given exclusively to human beings.

Sources: Mishpatei HaShalom, Ta'am VaDa'as, Michtav Mei'Eliyahu

Shira Smiles is a highly sought-after international lecturer, a popular seminary teacher, and an experienced curriculum developer. She is well known for her unique teaching style, which seeks to bring understanding of Torah texts through analysis of relevant sources, while making the lessons learned from every verse relevant to her students' lives. Smiles teaches at Darchei Bina Seminary. In addition, she leads a number of women's study group classes in Beit Shemesh, Yerushalayim, and Modiin. Smiles also trains Torah teachers in special workshops all over the world.

Chapter 8

Balaam

THERE IS AN ICONIC American poem about overconfidence and missed opportunity. It is actually one of the best-known poems in American literature, although I am not sure how many high school students in the twenty-first century are familiar with it: "Casey at the Bat," which was first published in the *San Francisco Examiner* back in 1888. In brief, a baseball team from the fictional town of Mudville is losing by two runs in its last inning. Both the team and its fans, a crowd of five thousand, believe they can win if Casey, Mudville's star player, gets to bat. And, of course, he does! So sure is Casey of his abilities that he does not swing at the first two pitches, both called strikes. Let us pick up the poem at this point:

> The sneer is gone from Casey's lip, his teeth are clenched in hate,
>
> He pounds with cruel violence his bat upon the plate;
>
> And now the pitcher holds the ball, and now he lets it go,
>
> And now the air is shattered by the force of Casey's blow.
>
> Oh, somewhere in this favored land the sun is shining bright,
>
> The band is playing somewhere, and somewhere hearts are light;
>
> And somewhere men are laughing, and somewhere children shout,
>
> But there is no joy in Mudville—mighty Casey has struck out.[1]

Substitute Balaam for Casey and Moab and Midian for Mudville, and this poem serves as a metaphor for chapters 22 through 24 of the book of Numbers. These chapters attest to the overconfidence of Balaam, an overconfidence driven in part by the accolades he received from the people of

---

1. Thayer, "Casey at the Bat."

that generation: "For I know that he whom you bless is blessed indeed, and he whom you curse is cursed" (Numbers 22:6). The end of the narrative clearly depicts the opportunity he missed. Balaam, who envisioned wealth and even greater renown for cursing the Jewish people, is forced to admit his powerlessness in the face of God's opposition: "I could not of my own accord do anything good or bad contrary to the Lord's command. What the Lord says, that I must say" (Numbers 24:13).

All this raises several questions. First, who was Balaam and why was he so respected and honored by the nations of the world? Second, what was the source of Balaam's overconfidence? And lastly, what led him to miss the opportunity he so sought after?

In rabbinic literature, Balaam is said to be one of seven gentile prophets,[2] and he gradually rose to an exalted position among the non-Jews that was equal to that of Moses among the Jews (see Numbers Rabbah 20). These sources portray Balaam as initially being a mere interpreter of dreams. His abilities grew over time so that he became something akin to a sorcerer, and ultimately the spirit of prophecy descended upon him. The talmudic sages further ascribe to Balaam the gift of being able to ascertain the exact moment during which God is angry—a gift bestowed upon no other creature (see Babylonian Talmud, Berakhot 7a). Balaam is also included in the list of persons born circumcised, a list that includes Moses, as set forth in Avot de-Rabbi Natan.[3]

Through what merit did Balaam achieve this level of greatness? Louis Ginzberg, in his work *The Legends of the Jews*, addresses this question at length.

> In order that the heathens might not say, "Had we had a prophet like Moses, we should have received the Torah," God gave them Balaam as a prophet, who in no way was inferior to Moses either in wisdom or in the gift of prophecy. Moses was indeed the greatest prophet among the Israelites, but Balaam was his peer among the heathens. But although Moses excelled the heathen prophet in that God called him without any previous preparation, whereas the other could obtain Divine revelations only

---

2. The other six were Beor (Balaam's father), Job, and Job's four friends (see Babylonian Talmud, Bava Batra 15b).

3. Archaeological discoveries have added significant additional information about Balaam. For example, a 1967 expedition led by Professor Henk J. Franken of the University of Leiden at Deir Alla (a site that archaeologists believe to be biblical Succoth) uncovered traces of lettering on fragments of plaster. One fragment had written on it in bold letters the words: "the prophet, Balaam son of Beor." See Hoftijzer and van der Kooij, *Aramaic Texts*, 18 and Graves, "Bonus 38."

> through sacrifices, still Balaam had one advantage over the Israelite prophet. Moses had to pray to God "to shew him His ways," whereas Balaam was the man who could declare of himself that he "knew the knowledge of the Most High."[4]

Given all this, it is not surprising that Balak would come to Balaam in his time of need, as we see from the opening verses of chapter 22.

> Balak son of Zippor saw all that Israel had done to the Amorites. Moab was alarmed because that people was so numerous. Moab dreaded the Israelites, and Moab said to the elders of Midian, "Now this horde will lick clean all that is about us as an ox licks up the grass of the field." Balak son of Zippor, who was king of Moab at that time, sent messengers to Balaam son of Beor in Pethor, which is by the Euphrates, in the land of his kinsfolk, to invite him, saying, "There is a people that came out of Egypt; it hides the earth from view, and it is settled next to me. Come then, put a curse upon this people for me, since they are too numerous for me; perhaps I can thus defeat them and drive them out of the land. For I know that he whom you bless is blessed indeed, and he whom you curse is cursed" (Numbers 22:2–6).

What is less understandable is why Balaam so readily acceded to this request. Ginzberg's *Legends of the Jews* is harsh in its criticism of Balaam but gives no underlying rationale for his actions: "In spite of his high prophetic dignity, Balaam had never done anything good or kind, but through his evil tongue had almost destroyed all the world."[5] Rashi, however, begins to give us greater insight into Balaam's psyche. Undeterred by Balaam's refusal of his first request, Balak sends a second delegation to try to convince Balaam to come and curse the Jewish nation.[6] Balaam's response to these messengers is, at first glance, a bit odd:

> Balaam replied to Balak's officials, "Though Balak were to give me his house full of silver and gold, I could not do anything, big or little, contrary to the command of the Lord my God" (Numbers 22:18).

In his commentary on this verse, Rashi clarifies the intent of Balaam's response: "This tells us that he (Balaam) was avaricious and covetous of other peoples' wealth. He said: 'He ought to give me all his silver and gold, for,

---

4. Ginzberg, *Legends*, 76.
5. Ginzberg, *Legends*, 76.
6. Balaam refused Balak's first request not of his own accord but in response to God's specific instruction not to go with this delegation (Numbers 22:12).

behold, he would otherwise have to hire many armies to fight against them. Even then it is doubtful whether he would conquer or not conquer, but I would certainly conquer."

Balaam's greed is his defining character trait in this narrative, and we shall return to it shortly. There is, however, another question that must be addressed with regards to Balak's delegation. Balaam's greed may explain why he wished to undertake the mission of cursing the Jews, but why would he think he could actually curse them? A prophet as great as Balaam had to know that the Jews were God's chosen people.

What was Balaam thinking?

To try and resolve this question, let's consider Gd's verbal exchange with Balaam. When the first delegation arrives, God asks Balaam, "What do these people want of you?" (Numbers 22:9). An all-knowing and ever-present God of course knows what these people want of Balaam, so why put forth the question at all? The answer lies in the first question God poses to humankind shortly after Adam and Eve eat from the tree of knowledge of good and bad. Having eaten from it, having broken the one commandment given them by their Creator, the couple seeks to hide from God, who in turn asks a question to which He already knows the answer: "Where are you?" (Genesis 2:9). In his commentary on this question, Rashi spells out an important lesson about the hows and whys of rhetorical questions in the biblical text.

> He (God) knew where he (Adam) was, but He asked this in order to open up a conversation with him that he should not become confused in his reply if He were to pronounce punishment against him all of a sudden. Similarly, in the case of Cain, He said to him, "Where is Abel thy brother?" Similarly, with Balaam, "What do these people want of you?"—to open up a conversation with them.

Rashi is telling us that God poses rhetorical questions to individuals who have sinned or who are about to make poor decisions in order to give the individuals a chance to reflect on and to admit to their misdeeds. This is a lesson teens know all too well—namely, that it is better to fess up to a misdeed because lying about it only makes matters worse.

Returning to the exchange between God and Balaam regarding the purpose of Balak's delegation, Rashi explains in his commentary on Numbers 22:9 that "by putting this question, He (God) intended to delude him (Balaam). And indeed he (Balaam) thereupon said: 'It seems, then, that there are times when everything is not manifest to Him; His knowledge is not always alike. I will select a time when I can curse and when He will not observe it."

Let us compare these two narratives. God questions Adam rhetorically in the hope that he, Adam, will realize the magnitude of his sin and seek penetrance. Yet, with Balaam, God asks "to delude him." Why is this? It must be that God is aware of Balaam's true intentions, namely, to curse the Jewish people at a moment of divine wrath and thereby cause God Himself to destroy them. Yet, God, in the words of the talmudic sages, purposefully restrained His anger in order to baffle the wicked prophet and to save the nation from extermination (Babylonian Talmud, Berakhot 7a).

Balaam's greed and lust for wealth result in one of the most embarrassing scenes in the Bible. Balaam, the greatest prophet of the non-Jewish world, a man who knows the times of God's wrath and thinks himself capable of deceiving God, does not perceive an image of the divine that is clear as day to his donkey.

> But God was incensed at his going; so, an angel of the Lord placed himself in his way as an adversary. He was riding on his she-ass, with his two servants alongside, when the ass caught sight of the angel of the Lord standing in the way, with his drawn sword in his hand. The ass swerved from the road and went into the fields; and Balaam beat the ass to turn her back onto the road (Numbers 22:22–23).

Three times the donkey sees this angel, sword in hand, prepared to strike down Balaam. Three times she seeks to avoid the angel and save her master. But Balaam grows increasingly angry with each attempt, to the point of beating the ass with his stick (Numbers 22:27). It is here that God performs a great miracle and allows the donkey to speak: "What have I done to you that you have beaten me these three times?" (Numbers 22:28). Oblivious to this miracle, Balaam responds to the donkey: "You have made a mockery of me! If I had a sword with me, I would kill you" (Numbers 22:29). Rashi underscores how great is the fall of Balaam. Commenting on Balaam's longing for a sword, Rashi notes that:

> This utterance was a great shame for him in the sight of the Princes. This man was going for the purpose of slaying a whole nation by his mouth, and for this animal he required a weapon!

It is easy to think of Balaam's degradation and humiliation as a logical consequence of his greed. Consider the following mishnah from Avot 5:10:

> There are four types of people: One who says, "What is mine is yours, and what is yours is mine" is a boor. One who says,

"What is mine is mine, and what is yours is yours"—this is a median characteristic; others say that this is the character of a Sodomite. One who says, "What is mine is yours, and what is yours is yours" is a pious person. And one who says, "What is mine is mine, and what is yours is mine" is wicked.

Not unexpectedly, the last of the four, which most obviously reflects greed, is deemed wicked, as it should be. Yet the one whose attitude to wealth is "What is mine is mine and what is yours is yours" is seen as being a mediocre person, one seemingly not worthy of praise. While such a person is prepared to respect the property of another, he or she is not prepared to assist others or to even recognize a social obligation in view of the wealth in his or her possession. It is no wonder that the Mishnah calls this the mark of the people of Sodom. "The people of Sodom have been the archetype of an evil community deserving of destruction ever since Biblical times, primarily because of their selfish economic behavior."[7]

A similar sentiment is found in Ecclesiastes 5:9, which states that "One who loves money will never be satisfied with money." Qohelet Rabbah 1:13 comments on this verse and notes that: "One who has one hundred [of some currency] wants two hundred." In other words, greed is futile. It is a goal with no end. In this same vein, the Babylonian Talmud, Sotah 48b says that one who has bread in his basket or money in her pocket and asks, "what will I eat tomorrow," is lacking in faith. This means that wealth accumulation (which seems to be a definition of greed) demonstrates a lack of trust in God.

Yet there are sources that suggest that greed (and other attributes associated with the evil inclination such as sexual lust) may not in and other themselves be bad things.[8] Genesis Rabbah 9:7 makes this point explicitly:

> Rabbi Nahman said in Rabbi Samuel's name: "Behold, it was good" refers to the Good Desire; "And behold, it was very good" refers to the Evil Desire. (It only says "very good" after man was created with both the good and bad inclinations. In all other cases it only says "and God saw that it was good.") Can then the Evil Desire be very good? That would be extraordinary! But without the Evil Desire, however, no man would build a house, take a wife, and beget children. Thus said Solomon (Ecclesiastes

---

7. Tamari, *Challenge*.

8. In Judaism, the "evil inclination" or *yetzer hara*, refers to a person's innate inclination to do evil by violating the will of God. The term is drawn from the phrase "the imagination of the heart of man [is] evil" (Hebrew, *yetzer lev-ha-adam ra*), which occurs twice in the Hebrew Bible, at Genesis 6:5 and 8:21.

4:4): "Again, I considered all labor and all excelling in work, that it is a man's rivalry with his neighbor."

We see this same sentiment, that attributes such as greed and sexual desire, when properly channeled, are necessary for a functioning society also expressed in the Babylonian Talmud, Yoma 69b. So perhaps Balaam's downfall was not a product of his greed but was due to his excessive greed.

This is a nuanced point that high school students need to grasp. Many of the character traits we will consider in *Sefer BeMidbar* have both positive and negative attributes. The goal should thus be to find a "middle path," as was articulated more than eight hundred years ago by Rambam in his laws of character development.

> The upright path is the middle path of all the qualities known to man. This is the path which is equally distant from the two extremes, not being too close to either side. Therefore, the Sages instructed that a person measure his character traits, directing them in the middle path so he will be whole (Mishneh Torah, Hilkhot De'ot, chapter 1, law 4).

A last point to consider when preparing to teach the story of Balaam: This Jewish view that greed (or at least a little greed) may not be a bad thing reflects the outlook of modern psychologists. Dr. Neel Burton sums up this perspective rather well:

> Greed, though an imperfect force, is the only consistent human motivation, and produces preferable economic and social outcomes most of the time and under most conditions. Whereas altruism is a mature and refined capability, greed is a visceral and democratic impulse, and ideally suited to our dumbed down consumer culture. Altruism may attract our admiration, but it is greed that our society encourages and rewards and that delivers the goods and riches on which we have come to depend. Like it or not, our society mostly operates on greed and, without greed, would descend into poverty and chaos. Indeed, greed seems to be the driving force behind all successful societies, and modern political systems designed to check or eliminate it have invariably ended in the most abject failure.[9]

Perhaps, in the end, Balaam's talking donkey is the best metaphor for the goals of this unit. In other words, when we let greed get the better of us, we look and sound like talking asses.

---

9. Burton, "Is Greed Good?"

Sefer BeMidbar—Balaam
Sample Unit Plan

Unit	Primary Source(s)	Supplemental Reading(s)	Timeframe
Balaam	Numbers 22	Is Balaam Evil?	two–three weeks
	Rashi 22:4		
Middah:	Rashi 22:5		
Greed	Rashi 22:9	Is Greed Good?	
	Sforno 22:9		
	Rashi 22:11		
	Rashi 22:13		
	Ramban 22:13		
	Rashi 22:18		
	Rashi 22:20		
	Rashi 22:21		
	Rashi 22:29		
	Rashi 22:34		
	Rashi 22:35		

Essential Questions

1. Who was Balaam and why did Balak turn to him in his time of need?

2. What prompted Balaam to accept Balak's offer, even in the face of opposition from God?
3. In his conversations with the messengers and with God, is Balaam trying to be manipulative or deceitful or perhaps both?

Evaluating/Checking for Understanding

1. Daily discussions/student interactions

   Student questions and observations typically drive each day's discussion.

2. Occasional written reflections

   At the discretion of the teacher, a tool to foster further reflection on the unit's essential questions.

3. Character trait essay

   See appendix for assignment rubric.

4. Unit test

   Unit tests should, by definition, be crafted by individual teachers to meet the needs of their specific students. The Understanding by Design *framework created by Grant Wiggins and Jay McTighe is an excellent tool for the development of appropriate tests and assessments, as its emphasis on backward design forces teachers to consider in advance the assessment evidence needed to document and validate that the targeted learning goals have been achieved.*

Primary Source Texts

1. *BeMidbar* chapter 22: Read text and seek to identify problematic (what I call "red flag") words and phrases (with teacher's guidance, of course). These red flag words and phrases will likely vary from class to class depending on the sophistication and linguistic abilities of the students, coupled with the background and interests of the teacher.
2. *BeMidbar* chapters 23–24: Read English text so that students have overview of the entire narrative.
3. After reading these two additional chapters, return to chapter 22 and use commentaries A–M to shed light on this unit's essential questions.
4. Supplemental readings for each unit are intended to demonstrate that serious scholarship about and explanations of *Sefer BeMidbar* are not

limited to the classical medieval commentators but continue to our time. The supplemental readings for this unit include "Is Balaam Evil?" by Rav Alex Israel, which delves into the true nature of Balaam's character, and "Is Greed Good?" by Rabbi Gil Student, which provides an excellent overview of Jewish sources related to greed and how they apply to modern society.

Sefer BeMidbar—Balaam

Primary Texts

A. Rashi 22:4

"[And Moab said] to the elders of Midian"

But did not these (Moab and Midian) always hate one another, just as is stated (Genesis 36:35), "who had smitten Midian in the country of Moab," from which it is evident that Midian had come against Moab in war? But out of fear of Israel they now made peace between themselves (Midrash Tanhuma, Balak 3; cf. Babylonian Talmud, Sanhedrin 105a). And what induced Moab to take counsel of Midian? When they saw that Israel was victorious in a supernatural manner they said: the leader of these people grew up in Midian; let us ask them, what is his chief characteristic? They replied to them, "His power lies only in his mouth (in prayer)." Whereupon they said: "Then we must come against them with a man whose power lies in his mouth."

B. Rashi 22:4

"The land of the children of his people"

Of Balak's people, for he came from there, and this man (Balaam) had prophesied saying to him, "You are destined to be king."—And if you ask: Why did the Holy One blessed be He, let his Shechina rest upon so wicked a heathen, I reply that in order that the heathen peoples should have no excuse to say, "If we had prophets, we would have changed for the better," He raised up prophets for them. Yet they (these prophets) broke down the moral fence of the world, because at first they (the heathens) were fenced in against (they refrained from) immoral living, but this man (Balaam) counselled them to freely offer themselves to prostitution.

> "To call him"

The call was for him, for his benefit; for he (Balak) fixed for him (agreed to pay him) a large sum.

C. Rashi 22:9

> "Who are these men with thee?"

By putting this question He intended to delude him. And indeed he (Balaam) thereupon said: "It seems, then, that there are times when everything is not manifest to Him; His knowledge is not always alike. I will select a time when I can curse and when He will not observe it."

D. Sforno 22:9

> "Who are these men with thee?"

Who are these people with you on account of whom you went to the trouble to receive prophetic messages in order to know what to do for them? Have they really come to you to inquire about matters which will occur in the future and you want to know about the future in order to give them guidance? Or, have they stayed with you to enlist your help to pronounce curses over someone and you are now asking My permission to fulfill their request?

E. Rashi 22:11

> "And I will drive them out"

Meaning from the world; but Balak had said only (v. 6), "and I will drive them out from the land." I seek only to make them move away from me. Balaam, however, hated them even more than did Balak.

F. Rashi 22:13

> "To go with you"

But only with princes greater than you. This tells us that he was of a proud nature and he did not wish to divulge that he was under the control of the Omnipresent except in arrogant terms ("God will not permit me to go with you"). Consequently (v. 15), "Balak sent yet again [more princes, and more honorable than these]."

G. Ramban 22:13

"To go with you"

"But only with great princes." This teaches us that he was of a haughty spirit and did not want to tell [them] that he was under the control of God. Therefore [he spoke] in arrogant language. It was because of this that "Balak sent yet again princes." This is Rashi's language. But it is not correct, for Balaam's whole honor consisted of boasting and glorifying himself in the word of God. Moreover, he did not know that God would give him permission to go with other, greater princes. Rather, the meaning is that God did not want him to go at all. But Balak suspected that he was asking only in order to get a greater reward. Therefore he said to him, "When I first sent to invite you, why didn't you come to me? Am I really unable to reward you?" And for this reason, too, [the verse reads] "Then Balak sent other dignitaries, more numerous and distinguished than the first." [This was] to show him that he wanted him very much [to come], and he promised to give him as much wealth and riches as he would demand. But Balaam answered him that even for all his money, "I could not do anything contrary to the command of the Lord my God," for He is my God, and "I could not do anything, big or little" if I transgress His command, for [whatever I do] I do in His Name. Or perhaps [Balaam] is saying, "I could not do anything contrary to the command of the Lord my God," whether in a small matter or a great matter, for He is my God, and I am his servant.

H. Rashi 22:18

"Full of silver and gold"

This tells us that he was avaricious and covetous of other peoples' wealth. He said: He ought to give me all his silver and gold, for, behold, he would otherwise have to hire many armies to fight against them. Even then it is doubtful whether he would conquer or not conquer, but "I" would certainly conquer.

I. Rashi 22:20

"If [the men come] to call you"

If the call be for you, for your benefit, and you think to take a fee for it.

J. Rashi 22:21

"And he saddled his she-ass"

From here we may learn that the hatred one bears for a person makes one disregard the rule imposed upon him by his exalted position, for he, himself, not a servant, did the saddling. The Holy One, blessed be He, said: You wicked man! Their ancestor Abraham has already anticipated you in this, as it is said (Genesis 22:3), "And Abraham rose up early in the morning and saddled his ass."

K. Rashi 22:29

"I would there were a sword in my hand"

This utterance was a great shame for him in the sight of the Princes: this man was going for the purpose of slaying a whole nation by his mouth, and for this animal he required a weapon!

L. Rashi 22:34

"For I knew not"

This statement, too (cf. v. 29), was a disgrace for him, for in spite of himself he had to admit it—because he used to boast that he knew the will of the Most High (24:16) and now his own mouth bore testimony: "I knew not."

M. Rashi 22:35

"Go with the men"

On that road which a man is resolved to go, he is allowed to go (Babylonian Talmud, Makkot 10b).

Sefer BeMidbar—Balaam

Supplemental Reading

Is Balaam Evil?

—Rav Alex Israel

At first glance, this week's parasha looks like something out of Dungeons and Dragons: We have blessings and curses, talking donkeys, a frustrated demented king, and a traveling wizard whose curses repeatedly turn into blessings. Balaam the sorcerer and prophet is invited to curse the Children of Israel and it all goes rather wrong.

We would like to focus this week on one central question whose answer will radically affect our entire view of the parasha: is Balaam evil? Chazal (our Sages) refer to Balaam quite standardly as Bil'am Ha-rasha (the wicked). He is seen as greedy, egoistic, and a Jew hater. He attempts to subvert even God himself! Was he really such a villain?

The Positive View

A number of commentators, the Ramban (Rabbi Moshe ben Nachman, Spain, 1194–1274) at the top of the list, view Balaam in a remarkably positive light. They bring convincing proofs for their position from the text of the story itself. In fact, if you would stop reading now, pick up a Chumash and read the beginning of our parasha (Ch. 22 v. 2–20) you might begin to see what they mean.

Balaam's motto, a phrase which he repeats time after time throughout the parasha, seems to be:

> "Even if Balak gives me his house full of silver and gold, I cannot do anything, big or little, contrary to the word of the Lord my God" (See also 24:13)

and in another variation:

> "I can only repeat faithfully what the Lord puts in my mouth." (23:12 and see also 22:7, 13, 38; 23:26)

Balaam appears as a paradigm of obedience and submission to God. One can view almost the entire story from this vantage point. At every step, Balaam does nothing before he has consulted with God. When God tells him not to accompany Balak's ministers, he faithfully transmits God's message and refuses to go along with them. Only when God allows him to go, does he agree to their summons. Even when asked by King Balak himself, he gives no assurances. He simply repeats his motto that he is subject to the desires of God and that God is his sole controller.

Balaam comes over as a man of integrity. A good man.

This character appraisal of Balaam would appear to be accurate were it not for some strong contrary indications in the text. After Balaam forwards Balak's second request to God, God allows him to go. However no sooner had he left, we read how

> "God was incensed at his going and placed an angel of the Lord in his way as an adversary." (22:22)

In addition, there is the story of the angel with sword drawn coming apparently to stop Balaam fulfilling his evil plan.

The Ramban (22:22) does not see in these verses refutation of his overall view of Balaam:

> God's desire was to bless the people of Israel through the prophet of the gentiles. Balaam should have told Balak's ministers explicitly "I have been permitted by God to accompany you, but only on condition that I do not curse the people and that if God instructs me, I will bless them".... Now Balaam in his eagerness to go with them did not relate this message and said nothing at all. "When he rose in the morning, Balaam saddled his ass and departed with the Moabite dignitaries" (22:21) ... as if he desired to do their bidding. God was angry at his going because had he told them, they would not have asked him to go. In addition, there was the defamation of God in that his leaving, as if by God's consent, gave the impression that God had given permission to curse the people ...

The incident with the angel is to correct this fault in Balaam's attitude. The angel tells Balaam how he has distorted God's permit allowing him to go to Balak (See the Ramban's translation of pasuk 22)—he should have made his intentions clearly understood. Balaam repeatedly offers to return home, but God simply warns him a second time that he will say none other than that which God instructs him to say.

Balaam is still a good, God-fearing man; he merely made a mistake, which he was prepared to correct when it was pointed out to him (see 22:36).

Bil'am Ha-Rasha

Rashi (Rabbi Shlomo ben Yitzchak, France, 1040–1105) sees Balaam as a negative figure from the outset. We will review just a few of his comments in this vein.

After the first approach by Balak's people, God tells Balaam (22:12) "Do not go with them. You must not curse that people, for they are blessed." Rashi (quoting the Midrash Tanhuma) reads this as an exchange between Balaam and God: To the command of God, "Do not go with them," Balaam replies, "Then I will curse them from here!" "You must not curse that people," says God, to which Balaam answers, "then I will bless them." God says, "They are (already) blessed," as one says of the hornet: "not of your honey nor your sting."

Balaam replies to the Moabite messengers: (22:13) "The Lord will not let me go with you." Rashi, quoting the Tanhuma again, reads this phrase in an arrogant, self-centered tone:

> "The Lord will not let me go with YOU—but rather with ministers of a higher rank than you. We see from here his haughtiness. He didn't want to demonstrate that he was under the authority of God, but rather used a proud tone. Balak responded (22:15), 'Then Balak sent other dignitaries, more numerous and distinguished than the first.'"

Rashi here illustrates Balaam as egoistic, fortune seeking and proud.

Rashi also accuses Balaam of "an insatiable desire for wealth and excessive greed." When Balaam turns down Balak's offer with the words "Even if Balaam gives me his house full of silver and gold..." (22:18) Rashi reads between the lines noting Balaam's hidden agenda of wealth. Balaam realizes his market value if he could defeat the Israelites single-handedly and save Balak the cost of a war. He therefore suggests that an appropriate reward might be a house worth of gold and silver.

Rashi completes the picture of the evil Balaam with a note on the verse (22:21) "When he rose in the morning, Balaam saddled his ass and departed with the Moabite dignitaries." Why would the proud, honor-seeking Balaam do his own dirty work? Why would he saddle his own animal? Rashi comments:

> We learn from here that intense hatred can distort even ingrained character traits.... Here he saddled his ass personally.
>
> With the Moabite dignitaries: his heart and their hearts in unison.

There is one not insignificant question which threatens to challenge this view of Balaam. Why did God let Balaam go? Why did he not ban him from making the journey?

To this Rashi presents an answer that reflects our principle of free-will as well as the determination of Balaam (22:33):

> A person is lead in the way in which he desires to go.

God helps people to travel along the path of their desires. If Balaam wishes to curse the Israelites, so be it. Let him pay the cost of his crime at a later date. In the meantime, God lets him follow his heart's desire.

Understanding Rashi and the Ramban

When confronted with a difference of opinion of this type, we must ask ourselves how two Bible scholars could come to contrasting conclusions based on the same text. What is the textual basis of each opinion?

In a certain sense, the beginning of our parasha (Ch. 22) seems to give two separate stories of Balaam and it is the disparity between the two stories which gives rise to the ambiguity regarding the nature of Balaam's character.

Let us explain. The story can be split into two discreet sections. In essence, we see before us two 'stories':

The first about Balaam being approached with an offer from Balak and faithfully turning to God with each request, following His word at every turn.

The second story is that of Balaam and his ass. In this second story, the Moabite dignitaries seem to be nowhere in sight (See Ramban 22:33) and we witness Balaam in his confrontation with the angel who is apparently sent to stop him.

Interestingly enough, both stories conclude with almost an identical phrase; (Compare verse 20-21 with verse 35. There are some variations)

[sic] that "Go with the men but you will only repeat what I tell you. And Balaam went with the dignitaries of Moav/Balak."

The first 'story' seems to present a near perfect Balaam. He is God-fearing, loyal and obedient. When Balaam accompanies the Moabite emissaries, we know that it has full Divine approval. We have no reason to believe that God should be angry in any way

The second 'story,' however, sets a different scene. Its opening line is "God was incensed at his going" and it continues with the strange story of the talking donkey. The impression one draws from the story is definitely one of God's displeasure at Balaam.

This strange story is God's way of trying to get through to Balaam. What message is God sending him? God is expressing to Balaam the limits of human perception. Balaam cannot see that which his donkey sees. The human mind does not always see the Divine. Balaam has some thinking to do if he is to 'see' the truth. Maybe, in addition, God is illustrating to him that the power of speech is in the hands of God and not man. In the usual order of things donkeys cannot speak, humans can. But if God chooses, donkeys CAN speak and by the same logic, Balaam should realize that his speech is in God's hands. Important messages for a man on a mission to curse an entire nation.

These two 'stories' are the background information that we are told regarding Balaam. It would seem that the RAMBAN takes the first section of chapter 22 as his starting point. Balaam is basically good. He slips up. Honor and glory get in the way of his better side. God gets angry, Balaam apologizes, and we move on. And, in the final analysis, Balaam comes through. Balaam blesses the Jewish people rather than cursing them. He deviates not a letter from what God has told him to say.

Rashi however, seems to rely on the second story as the defining factor regarding Balaam. The first half of chapter 22 is read with the prior knowledge of the latter half. God is clearly angry with Balaam for going. Balaam never seems to get the message that God is displeased, maybe because he doesn't want to accept its implications.

Balaam acts like a child nagging his parent for something that the child wants contrary to his parent's better judgment. Balaam seems persistent in asking God repeatedly, and when he hears a positive response, jumps at the chance. He seems not to notice that God isn't exactly 'smiling' at him and that from an outsider's perspective, it would be clear that God would prefer that he stay at home.

It is in this light that Rashi interprets the entire first section of the chapter. Balaam is painted with foreboding colors.

Balaam's Second Attempt

If this were the only information at our disposal, it would be difficult to understand why Balaam is so widely perceived in a negative light. Both Rashi and the Ramban have logic and support behind their positions.

However, the story does not end with Balaam returning home (24:25). He reappears later in *Sefer BeMidbar* in two places.

The story of Balaam and Balak is followed immediately (Ch. 25) by an epidemic of promiscuity and idol worship in the camp of Israel. A plague ensues leaving 24,000 dead. The apparent perpetrators of the immorality are the Midianites—the same people who originally called on Balaam's services.

God says (25:7) "Assail the Midianites and defeat them for they assailed you by the trickery they practiced against you . . . ." Apparently, there is some element of underhand activity which has been deliberately planned to ensnare the Israelites in an orgy of idolatry and immorality.

Who is behind it all?

The children of Israel go to war against the Midianites (31:8–15)

> They killed Balaam ben Beor by the sword . . . . And Moses said "Why have you left the women alive? They are the very ones who, on BAALAM'S advice, induced the Israelites to trespass in the matter of Peor and the community of the Lord was struck by the plague."

It would appear that Baalam is the mastermind behind a scheme which caused serious damage to the fabric of the Israelite camp. The Talmud (Sanhedrin 106a) describes Balaam's thinking:

> Balaam said, "Their God despises promiscuity and they (the Israelites) enjoy fine cloth. Let me suggest a plan. Set up stalls selling fine cloth. Place an old woman at the door and a young prostitute inside." They set up the stalls . . . . When the Israelites came to the market, the old woman offered fine cloth at a high price, the younger girl offered it for less, time after time.

The Talmud continues as to how this familiarity was used to offer the Israelites wine, leading to sexual activity which after some time was conditioned on idol worship.

The Talmud continues:

> And they killed Balaam by the sword (31:8). [He had already gone home (24:25) so what was he doing there?]. He had returned to receive his payment for causing the plague of 24,000 dead amongst the Israelites.

In the light of this information, it is difficult not to see Balaam as a cunning, greedy and downright evil. He is a dangerous man. The Mishnah in Avot (5:23) states:

> He who has an evil eye, greed and haughtiness is following the hallmarks of the wicked Balaam.

Potential and Fulfillment

It would seem that we have reinforced Rashi's perspective. Rashi builds his opinion based on the wider context and looks at the totality of what we know about Balaam before making a judgment. He realizes that a mind which can devise and activate a plan to bring Israel into disfavor with its God must have a motivation. That motivation is one of three: pure wickedness, pride, or greed. God would not let Balaam curse the Jewish nation so Balaam found another way to cause harm.

But what of the Ramban? The Ramban, certainly, is truer to the language of the beginning of the parasha. How might he fit into the wider context?

Maybe we can offer the following thought. Balaam is a prophet. Indeed, Balaam is seen as the Gentile equivalent of Moses, the greatest of the prophets (Sifrei).

According to the Jewish tradition, prophecy comes only to those with perfected intellect and character. A controlled, ethical temper is a prerequisite for prophecy. The Ramban is unwilling to define Balaam as evil from the start because his gift of prophecy would indicate otherwise.

Indeed, Balak testifies to Balaam's exceptional power:

> "whom you bless is indeed blessed and who you curse is cursed" (22:6).

Only one other figure in the Bible is described by a similar epithet. It is Abraham. God tells Abraham

> "I will bless those who bless you and curse him that curses you" (Genesis 12:3)

However, with prophecy, as with any Divine given talent, comes responsibility. How does Balaam deal with the responsibility of being the greatest Gentile prophet? How does he actualize his spiritual potential?

Whereas Abraham uses his power to promote kindness, faith in God, honesty, and justice, Balaam promotes immorality and idolatry. Balaam abuses and wastes his spiritual potential to do good, by turning to evil. [In fact, the Talmud (Sanhedrin 106a) picks up on this point and notes that originally Balaam was a prop but later on is referred to as merely a sorcerer.]

A person is lead [sic] in the way in which he desires to go.

Every person, no matter what his or her background, can determine their life. We can choose good and we can choose bad. We can build or destroy. Only we decide. And God lets us be the way we want to be. Even the greatest past does not necessarily secure a great future.

Whether Balaam started off good or bad is of less relevance to us. What is important to us is that he goes down in history as Bil'am Ha-rasha—the wicked Balaam—because of the course of action that he chose. The questions that this parasha leaves us with relate to direction, potential and fulfillment. The man with the greatest potential seems to squander it.

This is a parasha where donkeys see more clearly than humans. God signals to Balaam what is right and Balaam is determined to close his eyes, going his own way. Maybe the lesson for us is to follow the clues that God leaves on our path and to let that pathway lead us towards God and goodness.

Rav Alex Israel teaches at Yeshivat Eretz Hatzvi and at the Pardes Institute of Jewish Studies where he serves as director of community education and the summer program. He is a popular lecturer at campuses and communities on three continents. In 2013, he published his first book: *I Kings: Torn in Two*, a commentary on *Sefer Melakhim*.

Sefer BeMidbar—Balaam

Supplemental Reading

Is Greed Good?

—Rabbi Gil Student

I. Self-Interest and Capitalism

The theoretical basis for Capitalism is self-interest, another term for greed. Those who devalue greed, who view the accumulation of wealth as a vice, necessarily see Capitalism as a system based on sin. It may currently be the best economic system but it is nevertheless a method for succeeding by strengthening one's evil inclination. The question remains whether greed is good according to Jewish sources.

Let us first note that the term "greed" often has a negative connotation, implying excessive desire for money. However, that is not what I mean here. When I use the word, I mean a desire that is not necessarily excessive nor unduly selfish. Most of us would consider it a natural desire. If you have a choice between receiving payment of $10 or $15 for the same task, a person influenced by what I am calling greed will choose the higher fee.

In a recent *First Things* article, Edward Skidelsky proposes two ways of evaluating the desire to accumulate wealth. Either it is "the root of evil and a sure path to corruption" or "a perfectly innocuous or even benign activity."[1] As a Christian thinker, he sides with the former view. This is not to say that he desires a return to a feudal system. He merely wishes government to

---

1. Edward Skidelsky, "The Emancipation of Avarice: What the Financial Crisis Reveals about Traditional and Modern Understandings of Economic Behavior," *First Things*, May 2011, https://www.firstthings.com/article/2011/05/the-emancipation-of-avarice.

use economic incentives to discourage greed, although without his giving examples I am at a loss to see how that is anything but a paradox. Maybe he means something like tax incentives for giving charity. Be that as it may, I'd like to explore the Jewish attitude toward the accumulation of wealth and where it falls in Skidelsky's dichotomy.

II. The Talmudic Sages

The Talmud certainly contains many statements denouncing physical desires. However, I am not certain that these can be applied to greed. Money may facilitate physical pleasures but its accumulation is not in itself a physical delight. Nor is jealousy the same as greed. The former means desiring what someone else has; the latter means desiring what one lacks. I cannot even think of a term in Hebrew for greed. Neither *ta'avah* nor *chemdah* seem to fit the bill.

The only relevant statement I could find in Talmud and Midrash amplifies the verse in Kohelet (Ecclesiastes 5:9): "One who loves money will never be satisfied with money." The Midrash Kohelet Rabbah (1:13) states: "One who has one hundred [of some currency] wants two hundred." In other words, greed is futile. It is a goal with no end.

Additionally, the Talmud (Sotah 48b) denounces as lacking faith someone who has bread in his basket—or money in his pocket—and asks what he will eat tomorrow. Wealth accumulation demonstrates a lack of trust in God. This statement also denounces greed for an indirect reason. Wealth accumulation for its own sake, rather than out of concern for the future, emerges unscathed.

This is further buttressed by the praise given to the wealthy, not just due to their charity but simply because of their wealth. R. Yehudah Ha-Nasi is lauded as exemplifying a combination of Torah and wealth (Gittin 59a). The wealth of three leaders of late–Second Temple Jerusalem are colorfully described with no hint of disapproval (Gittin 56a). In fact, the Talmud (Ta'anit 9a) even offers tithing as a sure-fire method of attaining riches and elsewhere (Hullin 105a) recommend best business practices that will generate wealth.

On the other hand, the Talmud (Avot 4:1) states that the truly rich person is one who is happy with his lot. And elsewhere (Avot 2:7) it points out that with more wealth come more worry. However, there are certainly multiple interpretive options for reconciling this contradictory data with none emerging as the clearly preferable understanding.

III. Medieval Scholars

Medieval philosophers and ethicists fall into a spectrum regarding asceticism. On one extreme, R. Avraham Ben Ha-Rambam (*Ha-Maspik Le-Ovdei Hashem, Histapkus*) adopts a radical asceticism. He even includes withdrawal from money as an appropriate behavior (p. 109 in Hebrew only edition):

> Contentment (*histapkus*) is one of the best traits and it means being happy with one's portion of this-worldly acquisitions and not being excited and anxious to add to them. This testifies to a lack of desire and minimal love for this-worldly pleasures, which bring man to great sins and diminish perfection.

On the other side, R. Yehudah Ha-Levi (Kuzari 2:50) allows for wealth accumulation if it does not detract from one's spiritual pursuits:

> Fasting is not an appropriate form of service for one whose physical desires and faculties are already weak and whose body is lean. Such a person would be better off taking care of his body. Nor is living in deprivation an appropriate type of service for one who is able to acquire luxury without too much effort, and whose wisdom and good deeds will not be compromised by his wealth. And certainly, if a person has a family to support, and his desire to make a living is therefore for the sake of Heaven, then for him monetary pursuit is healthy.[2]

According to R. Yehudah Ha-Levi, wealth accumulation is not just neutral but an acceptable goal as long as it is a low priority. You must place religious growth far ahead of earning beyond your basic financial needs.

According to R. Avraham Ben Ha-Rambam, if a transaction with one person can earn you enough for your family's needs but with another it can earn you double, you should opt for the smaller profit as a function of the ethical value of contentment. According to R. Yehudah Ha-Levi, you should opt for the higher profit since you expend no additional effort for it.

IV. Modern Thinkers

Asceticism reigned dominant among non-Chasidic thinkers in the 18th and 19th centuries. From what little I know about Chasidic thinkers, I believe that they differed on this point. Some advocated ascetic living and others

---

2. Yehudah HaLevi, *The Kuzari: In Defense of the Despised Faith*, translated by N. Daniel Korobkin (Nanuet, NY: Feldheim, 2009).

believed in embracing and sanctifying physical pleasures. R. Dov Katz, in his Tenu'as Ha-Mussar, describes how an influential Mussar thinker changed the non-Chasidic approach. R. Nosson Tzvi Finkel, the Alter of Slobodka, a leading pedagogue at the end of the 19th and beginning of the 20th centuries, believed that the changing times required emphasizing the non-ascetic approach to Judaism. His students became deans of leading yeshivas and, between them and the influence of Chasidism, not to mention the allure of luxury in our wealthy society, non-asceticism has dominated Orthodox Judaism over the past century.

This, perhaps, explains Dr. Meir Tamari's approach in his recent article "Jewish Ethics, the State and Economic Freedom." Quoting the Kuzari and not any dissenters, he writes: "Judaism does not see poverty as spiritual or desirable, nor the creation or increase of private individual wealth as evil or immoral."[3] Judaism only governs and provides an ethical framework for the accumulation of wealth, essentially sanctifying through divine legislation this otherwise mundane activity.

To summarize, there are different approaches to greed in Judaism. Everyone opposes excessive desire for money, even without using lying and other sins to earn it. Some denounce all attempts to acquire more than is necessary, while some approve of the accumulation of wealth if it does not detract from religious growth. This last view is, I believe, today's mainstream approach. Of course, this limited permission for wealth speaks of the ideal religio-ethical attitude to which many of us have not yet reached.

Rabbi Gil Student is the founder, publisher and editor-in-chief of Torah Musings, an online periodical focusing on multiple areas of interest, including textual studies in law, philosophy, and biblical commentary that are clear, interesting, and valuable to experienced students but understandable to those with limited Jewish education, as well as Jewish responses to news and dialogue among differing views within the Orthodox camp.

---

3. Meir Tamari, "Jewish Ethics, the State and Economic Freedom," in *The Oxford Handbook of Judaism and Economics*, edited by R. Aaron Levine (Oxford: Oxford University Press, 2010), 469.

Chapter 9

Phinehas

I MAGINE A HIGH SCHOOL history class of some sort. Perhaps it is an American history class. Perhaps contemporary world history. Then imagine the teacher giving her students a pop quiz consisting of a single question: "The formal definition of a zealot is a person who is fanatical and uncompromising in pursuit of their religious, political, or other ideals. With this as your benchmark, can you identify the zealot(s) in the list below?"

- Abraham Lincoln
- Susan B. Anthony
- David Ben-Gurion
- Martin Luther King, Jr.
- Osama bin Laden

How many students do you think would pass this quiz? Could you? Let's take a look at the teacher's grading rubric.

Abraham Lincoln: Against the advice of many of his top advisors and constituents, he plunged the nation into a bloody civil war to preserve the Union. In the midst of this war, he signed the Emancipation Proclamation, not as president, but as commander-in-chief of the army. Why such a radical move? He knew the order was unconstitutional per the ruling of the Supreme Court in the Dred Scott decision.[1] Yet he moved ahead. In the eyes

---

1. *Dred Scott v. Sandford*, also known simply as the Dred Scott case, held that "a negro, whose ancestors were imported into [the U.S.], and sold as slaves," whether enslaved or free, could not be an American citizen and therefore had no standing to sue in federal court. It further held that the federal government had no power to regulate slavery in the federal territories acquired after the creation of the United States. The last pillar of this decision ruled that "a negro of the African race was regarded . . . as an article of property, and held, and bought and sold as such, in every one of the thirteen colonies which united in the Declaration of Independence, and afterwards formed the Constitution of the United States." Among constitutional scholars, *Dred Scott v.*

of many, especially residents of the secessionist southern states, Lincoln was a zealot.

Susan B. Anthony: While she is best known for the pivotal role she played in the women's suffrage movement, consider some of the other causes she fought for in her lifetime. In 1837, at age sixteen, Anthony collected petitions against slavery as part of organized resistance to the newly established gag rule that prohibited antislavery petitions in the U.S. House of Representatives. She was a member of the Daughters of Temperance[2] and in 1849 gave her first public speech at one of its meetings. She was an active proponent of financial rights for women, and the campaign she helped lead finally achieved success in 1860 when the New York legislature passed an improved Married Women's Property Act that gave married women the right to own separate property, enter into contracts, and be joint guardian of their children. I think all would agree that Anthony meets the formal definition of a zealot.

David Ben-Gurion: In the prestate days, Ben-Gurion was executive head of the World Zionist Organization and went on to become the first prime minister of the newly established state of Israel. *Time* magazine famously ranked him as one of one hundred most influential people of the twentieth century. However, he could be extremely uncompromising, as demonstrated by the Altalena affair. In brief, a ship carrying arms purchased by a stand-alone militia, the Irgun, arrived in Israel in June 1948.[3] Ben-Gurion insisted that all weapons be handed over to the Israel Defence Forces (IDF). The Irgun members on the ship refused, and fighting broke out on a Tel Aviv beach. Ben-Gurion ordered the ship taken by force. Sixteen Irgun fighters and three IDF soldiers were killed in this battle. Another example: In 1960, when prominent American Jews expressed repugnance at Israel's kidnapping of the Nazi mass murderer Adolf Eichmann in order to bring him to trial in Jerusalem, Ben-Gurion reacted with rage: "[The] Judaism of Jews of the United States," he declared, "is losing all meaning and only a blind man can fail to see the day of its extinction."[4] Arabs throughout the world who

---

Sandford is widely considered the worst decision ever rendered by the Supreme Court. It has been cited in particular as the most egregious example in the court's history of wrongly imposing a judicial solution on a political problem.

2. The Daughters of Temperance focused not on outlawing alcohol but on strengthening liquor laws and drawing attention to the ill-effects of heavy drinking and drunkenness.

3. The main Jewish paramilitary organization during the British Mandate of Palestine was the Haganah which became the core of the IDF. The Irgun was an offshoot of the Haganah, and its members were absorbed into the IDF at the start of the 1948 Arab-Israeli war.

4. Gordis, "Why Many American Jews Are Becoming Indifferent or Even Hostile

were opposed to the Jewish state certainly viewed Ben-Gurion as a zealot, but it is equally certain that a sizable percentage of Israelis also saw their leader in this light.

Martin Luther King, Jr.: When asked about Dr. King, people typically refer to his "I Have A Dream" speech, a speech considered by some to be the finest political oration of the twentieth century,[5] or to him receiving the Nobel Peace Prize in 1964. Less well known is his "Letter from a Birmingham Jail."[6] It is difficult to read this text and not think "zealot." Take this excerpt as an example: "We have waited for more than 340 years for our constitutional and God given rights. The nations of Asia and Africa are moving with jetlike speed toward gaining political independence, but we still creep at horse and buggy pace toward gaining a cup of coffee at a lunch counter. Perhaps it is easy for those who have never felt the stinging darts of segregation to say, 'Wait.' But when you have seen vicious mobs lynch your mothers and fathers at will and drown your sisters and brothers at whim; when you have seen hate filled policemen curse, kick and even kill your black brothers and sisters; when you see the vast majority of your twenty million Negro brothers smothering in an airtight cage of poverty in the midst of an affluent society; when you suddenly find your tongue twisted and your speech stammering as you seek to explain to your six year old daughter why she can't go to the public amusement park that has just been advertised on television, and see tears welling up in her eyes when she is told that Funtown is closed to colored children, and see ominous clouds of inferiority beginning to form in her little mental sky, and see her beginning to distort her personality by developing an unconscious bitterness toward white people; when you have to concoct an answer for a five-year-old son who is asking: 'Daddy, why do white people treat colored people so mean?'; when you take a cross country drive and find it necessary to sleep night after night in the uncomfortable corners of your automobile because no motel will accept you; when you are humiliated day in and day out by nagging signs reading 'white' and 'colored'; when your first name becomes 'nigger,' your middle name becomes 'boy' (however old you are) and your last name becomes 'John,' and your wife and mother are never given the respected title 'Mrs.'; when you are harried by day and haunted by night by the fact that you are a Negro, living constantly at tiptoe stance, never quite knowing what to

---

to Israel."

5. According to data compiled by researchers at the University of Wisconsin–Madison and Texas A & M University, Dr. King's "I Have A Dream" speech was ranked first among the top one hundred American speeches of the twentieth century. See "Top 100 American Speeches."

6. King, "Letter."

expect next, and are plagued with inner fears and outer resentments; when you are forever fighting a degenerating sense of 'nobodiness'—then you will understand why we find it difficult to wait."

Osama bin Laden: As every student in this fictional class would know, he was the founder of al-Qaeda, the organization responsible for the September 11 attacks on the United States, along with numerous other mass-casualty attacks worldwide. He is the stereotypical zealot.

Regardless of how successful you were on this quiz, one thing should be evident. One person's zealot may well be another's hero, which makes the story of Phinehas (found in chapter 25 of *Sefer BeMidbar*) both troubling and very fitting for the teaching pedagogy I am proposing for the book of Numbers.

Let us begin by acknowledging the difficulties involved in any analysis of zealotry. It seems to me that zealotry is the grayest and most nuanced of the character traits we have studied so far. How so? Any discussion of zealotry has, by definition, two parts. First, is the person a zealot? Is he or she fanatical and uncompromising in his or her actions? Second, how are we to judge the action itself? Is it an objectively good outcome? An objectively bad outcome? Or does this assessment depend on the opinions of those doing the assessment? Moreover, does the passage of time give us a new and different perspective on the positive or negative aspects of this action?

To illustrate this conundrum, consider the first zealot in our quiz, Abraham Lincoln. There is little doubt that in his lifetime he was considered by many, supporters and foes alike, as a zealot, although most contemporary rankings of US presidents rate him as best of all time.[7] One of his acts of zealotry was the freeing of slaves. Before and during the Civil War, there were people who believed slavery to be morally reprehensible, while others saw the institution as necessary and normal.[8] In other words, judgments regarding slavery were very much dependent on those doing the judging. Today, however, very few individuals would defend the institution of slavery.

We can find similar examples for each zealot in our quiz except for Bin Laden, because none other than the most radicalized of his followers would

---

7. Wikipedia has compiled eighteen different surveys by scholars and political scientists that ranked U.S. presidents. Lincoln was ranked number one in ten of these eighteen surveys and was thus in the aggregate ranked number one. See "Historical Rankings."

8. As Robert E. Lee wrote to his wife in 1856: "The blacks are immeasurably better off here than in Africa, morally, physically, and socially. The painful discipline they are undergoing is necessary for their further instruction as a race, and will prepare them, I hope, for better things. How long their servitude may be necessary is known and ordered by a merciful Providence." See Robert E. Lee to Mary Anna Randolph Custis Lee, December 27, 1856, Lee Family Digital Archive.

see good in flying jet airliners into office towers and, as a consequence, causing the deaths of thousands of innocent people.

Turning to Phinehas, our first step is to determine whether or not he was a zealot.

After Balaam fails in his attempts to curse the Jewish people, he opts for a different approach to harm them. He convinces the leaders of Moab to prostitute their daughters in an attempt to lead the Jewish people to sin, and, sadly, this scheme works.

> While Israel was staying at Shittim, the people profaned themselves by whoring with the Moabite women, who invited the people to the sacrifices for their god. The people partook of them and worshiped that god. Thus, Israel attached itself to Baal-peor, and the Lord was incensed with Israel (Numbers 25:1–3).

God commands Moses to take the leaders of these activities and publicly impale them "before the Lord, so that the Lord's wrath may turn away from Israel" (Numbers 25:4). Before Moses can act on this command, one of the tribal leaders, Zimri, brings a Moabite princess, Cozbi, before Moses and the other leaders of the Jewish people. Zimri mocks and shows his distain towards Moses and his attempts to halt the sexual liaisons with the Moabite women by fornicating publicly with Cozbi then and there.[9] Moses and the other leaders are too shocked by the scene unfolding before them to act. Phinehas alone steps forward to defend the honor of Moses and of God Himself.

> When Pinchas, son of Eleazar son of Aaron the priest, saw this, he left the assembly and, taking a spear in his hand, he followed the Israelite into the chamber[10] and stabbed both of them, the Israelite and the woman, through the belly. Then the plague against the Israelites was checked (Numbers 25:7–8).

Any doubts the reader might have that Phinehas was motivated by zealotry are quickly dispelled by God's reaction to Phinehas's actions:

---

9. Various sources (see Rashi and Ibn Ezra in particular) maintain that Phinehas witnessed the sex act as it took place outside the chamber, whereas the verse here makes clear that he, Phinehas, slew Zimri and Cozbi in the chamber. Despite this, Ibn Ezra on verse 8 says that there are grounds to say that the slaying itself took place just outside the chamber.

10. As Rashi comments on verse 6: "They said to him: 'Moses, is this Midianite woman forbidden or permissible as a wife. If you say she is forbidden, then who made Jethro's daughter, a Midianite woman, permissible to you, etc.'" as is related there. (Sanhedrin 82a).

> The Lord spoke to Moses, saying, "Pinchas, son of Eleazar son of Aaron the priest, has turned back My wrath from the Israelites by his zealously avenging Me among them, so that I did not destroy the children of Israel because of My zeal" (Numbers 25:10–11).[11]

Having thus established that Phinehas was a zealot, we must in turn examine whether his contemporaries approved or disapproved of his actions, for this will help us decide if zealotry is a character trait the Torah is encouraging us to emulate or to avoid.

The talmudic sages acknowledge the boldness of Phinehas's actions and go so far as to say that the slaying of Zimri was legally correct, although they thought this was a ruling that should not be shared with the masses (Babylonian Talmud, Sanhedrin 82a, הבא לימלך אין מורין לו). Other opinions in the same section of the Talmud state that the leaders of that generation wished to excommunicate Phinehas for his act. In fact, according to this view, had Zimri turned on Phinehas and killed him, he would have deserved no punishment.

This uncertainty about how to interpret Phinehas's act is not limited to the talmudic sages. For instance, Rabbi Baruch Epstein, author of the commentary entitled *Torah Temimah*, concludes that zealotry is not to be encouraged and is not an ideal to be pursued. This is because a zealot, from a Jewish perspective, needs to be motivated by an unselfish, genuine desire to advance or defend the glory of God. Yet, in the end, who can tell what really is in the zealot's heart and mind? Is he defending God, or is he committing murder? It was this uncertainty that drove the desire of the talmudic sages to excommunicate Phinehas.

Rambam, too, is reluctant to unconditionally condone the actions of Phinehas. He holds that zealotry can be justified only if four conditions exist: the illicit intimacy is public knowledge, the killing occurs *in flagrante delicto* (in the act of fornication, especially illicit sex), there has been no prior authorization or discussion with authorities, and "the impunity of the criminal killing the zealot in self-defense" (Mishneh Torah, Hilkhot Esurai Be'ah 12:4).

For me, the best summary of Judaism's ambivalence towards zealotry was penned by Rabbi Jonathan Sacks:

> Why this moral ambivalence? The simplest answer is that the zealot is not acting within the normal parameters of the law.

---

11. There is not a consensus among the many translations of this verse for the word בְּקַנְאוֹ. All agree that this word describes the reason why Phinehas acts, but some translate it as "zealous" and others as "jealous."

> Zimri may have committed a sin that carried the death sentence, but Phinehas executed punishment without a trial.... There are extenuating circumstances in Jewish law in which either the king or the court may execute non-judicial punishment to secure social order. But Phinehas was neither a king nor acting as a representative of the court. He was acting on his own initiative, taking the law into his own hands. There are instances where this is justified and where the consequences of inaction would be catastrophic. But in general, we are not empowered to do so, since the result would be lawlessness and violence on a grand scale. More profoundly, the zealot is in effect taking the place of God. As Rashi says, commenting on the phrase, "Phinehas ... has turned My anger away from the Israelites by being zealous with My zeal," Phinehas "executed My vengeance and showed the anger I should have shown" (Rashi to Numbers 25:11). In general, we are commanded to "walk in God's ways" and imitate His attributes: "Just as He is merciful and compassionate, so you be merciful and compassionate." That is not, however, the case when it comes to executing punishment or vengeance. God who knows all may execute sentence without a trial, but we, being human, may not. There are forms of justice that are God's domain, not ours.[12]

This ambivalence notwithstanding, a number of commentators, including Rashi and Ramban, explain that Zimri, "the smitten man" (Numbers 25:14), was mentioned by name in this story to teach that Phinehas did not hesitate to kill him even though he was a tribal prince and there was a risk that his fellow tribesmen would seek to avenge his death. According to this school of thought, Phinehas is to be praised for having endangered himself in order to follow the dictates of his conscience. Nonetheless, it should be noted that zealotry in and of itself is not being celebrated. "Phinehas' act is not advocated for others. Rather, Phinehas' own greatness is on display. Phinehas endangered himself for the sake of the Torah and the Jewish people, proving that he had no other interest but avenging God's anger."[13]

Still, there was a price to pay. It is true, says the Kotzker Rebbe, that Phinehas's act was celebrated and his virtues praised, but he was nevertheless disqualified from being a leader of the Jewish people.[14] The Kotzker

---

12. Sacks, "Zealot."
13. Nachshoni, *Studies*, 1118.
14. Rabbi Menachem Mendel Morgensztern of Kotzk, better known as the Kotzker Rebbe, was a Hasidic rabbi and leader. He was a student of Reb Bunim of Peshischa and, upon the latter's death, attracted many of his followers. The Kotzker Rebbe was well known for his incisive and down-to-earth philosophies and sharp-witted sayings.

Rebbe further argues that, prior to killing Zimri, Moses thought that Phinehas would replace him as leader. However, once Moses saw the zealotry of Phinehas, he understood that Phinehas lacked the traits necessary to be a successful leader, even though Moses thought of Phinehas as holier than others. Moses understood better than anyone else that a leader must conduct himself with moderation and flexibility.

It may be that the story of Phinehas is not meant to celebrate zealotry, but it is a story about zealotry nonetheless. How are we to incorporate its lessons into our lives? How am I, as a teacher, to explain and expound it to students? Not surprisingly, we need only turn to the text itself for answers. When all is said and done, it is God Himself who validates the actions of Phinehas.

> Therefore, say, "I hereby give him My covenant of peace. It shall be for him and for his descendants after him [as] an eternal covenant of the Priesthood, because he was zealous for his God and atoned for the children of Israel" (Numbers 25:12–13).

Perhaps the best way to think about Phinehas is that this narrative should be interpreted as endorsing zealotry in a limited fashion. Phinehas does act in violation of the system and the normal mode of communal leadership, but he does so in the context of an ongoing plague in which 24,000 people have already died. And do not forget that that a public desecration of the divine was taking place. Bottom line, these were extraordinary circumstances, and, as such, they demanded extraordinary action.

This is a hard lesson for students to grasp. There are causes they are passionate about, some of them to the point of being zealots. They believe in their hearts and souls that they are doing the right thing, that they are doing good. Phinehas thought the same thing, but, without God's approval, who are we to say it was the correct course of action?

Phinehas teaches us that sometimes we must act before we think. However, his story also teaches us that there will inevitably be consequences to our actions when they are driven by zealotry. Sometimes, we just cannot be sure of what those consequences will be.

Sefer BeMidbar—Phinehas
Sample Unit Plan

Unit	Primary Source(s)	Supplemental Reading(s)	Timeframe
Phinehas	Numbers 25	The Rise of Phinehas	two–three weeks
	Rashi 25:1		
Middah:	Rashi 25:2		
Zealotry	Rashi 25:5	The Parameter of Phinehas's Zealotry	
	Rashi 25:6		
	Rashi 25:11		
	Rashi 25:12		
	Rashi 25:13		
	Rashi 25:14		
	Rashi 25:15		
	Sforno 25:1		
	Sforno 25:2		
	Sforno 25:12		
	Sforno 25:13		
	Sforno 25:14		

Essential Questions

1. Is zealotry permitted? If so, when and under what circumstances?
2. In the absence of approval by God (either before or after the fact), how are we to decide if and when to be religious zealots?
3. Are modern zealots such as Meir Kahane legitimate heirs to Phinehas and his defense of the Jewish people?

Evaluating/Checking for Understanding

1. Daily discussions/student interactions

    Student questions and observations typically drive each day's discussion.

2. Occasional written reflections

    At the discretion of the teacher, a tool to foster further reflection on the unit's essential questions.

3. Character trait essay

    See appendix for assignment rubric.

4. Unit test

    Unit tests should, by definition, be crafted by individual teachers to meet the needs of their specific students. The Understanding by Design *framework created by Grant Wiggins and Jay McTighe is an excellent tool for the development of appropriate tests and assessments, as its emphasis on backward design forces teachers to consider in advance the assessment evidence needed to document and validate that the targeted learning goals have been achieved.*

Primary Source Texts

1. *BeMidbar* chapter 25: Read text and seek to identify problematic (what I call "red flag") words and phrases (with teacher's guidance, of course). These red flag words and phrases will likely vary from class to class depending on the sophistication and linguistic abilities of the students, coupled with the background and interests of the teacher.
2. Discussions will focus on comparing and contrasting the approaches of Rashi and Sforno in their commentaries on this chapter, starting with an analysis of this chapter with Rashi's commentary (A–I) and then reexamining it in light of Sforno's commentary (J–O).

3. Supplemental readings for each unit are intended to demonstrate that serious scholarship about and explanations of *Sefer BeMidbar* are not limited to the classical medieval commentators but continue to our time. The supplemental readings for this unit include: "The Rise of Pinchas" by Rav Chanoch Waxman, "The Parameter of Pinchas' Zealotry" by Rabbi Zalman Baruch Melamed, and video clips on Meir Kahane (see links below) as a springboard for discussion of what a contemporary Jewish zealot looks like and how we should respond/react to him.

Resources on Meir Kahane

"Meir Kahane," Jewish Virtual Library, http://www.jewishvirtuallibrary.org/rabbi-meir-kahane.

"Rabbi Meir Kahane on the Jewish State," YouTube, https://www.youtube.com/watch?v=qDuWgmnDhLY.

"60 Minutes Rabbi MEIR KAHANE PART 1," YouTube, https://www.youtube.com/watch?v=ZXnyPkj54yo.

Sefer BeMidbar—Phinehas

Primary Texts

A. Rashi 25:1

"To commit whoredom with the daughters of Moab"

By the advice of Balaam,—as is related in the chapter חלק (Sanhedrin 106a).

B. Rashi 25:2

"And they prostrated themselves before their gods"

When anyone's passions overpowered him and he said to her, "Submit to me," she took out for him an image of Peor from her bosom, saying to him, "First prostrate yourself before this."

C. Rashi 25:5

"Kill everyone his men"

Each one of the judges of Israel killed two men (אנשיו is plural), and the judges of Israel were eighty-eight thousand in number, as it is related in Sanhedrin.

D. Rashi 25:6

"Before the eyes of Moses"

They said to him: "Moses, is this Midianite woman forbidden or permissible as a wife. If you say she is forbidden, then who made Jethro's daughter, a Midianite woman, permissible to you, etc." as is related there (Sanhedrin 82a).

"and they were weeping"

The law (decision on this matter) escaped him and therefore they all burst out into weeping (Sanhedrin 82a).—In the case of the Golden Calf Moses successfully resisted six hundred thousand men, as it is said (Exodus 32:20), "And he ground it to powder [and he made the children of Israel drink of it]," and here his hands were weak (he did not know what to do)?! But this was intentionally caused by God in order that Phineas might come and receive that which was meant for him.

E. Rashi 25:11

"Phinehas the son of Eleazar the son of Aaron the priest"

Because the tribes spoke disparagingly of him, saying, "Have you seen this grandson of Puti the father of whose mother used to fatten (פטם) calves for idolatrous sacrifices, and he has dared to slay a prince of one of Israel's tribes!," therefore Scripture comes and connects his genealogy with Aaron.

F. Rashi 25:12

"[I give to him] my covenant—peace"

This means: I give him my covenant that it should be to him as a covenant of peace; just like a man who shows gratitude and friendliness to one who has done him a kindness. So here, too, the Holy One, blessed be He, expressed to him His peaceful feelings towards him.

G. Rashi 25:13

"A covenant of an everlasting priesthood"

For although the priesthood had already been given to Aaron's descendants, it was given only to Aaron and his sons who had been anointed together with him and to their offspring whom they might beget after they had been anointed. But Phinehas who had been born prior to that and had not been anointed, had not as yet attained the status of priesthood until now. So, too, do we read in Zevahim 101b: Phinehas did not become a priest until he had slain Zimri.

"[He was zealous] for the sake of his God"

Just as (Numbers 11:29) "Are you zealous for My sake (לי)?" and (Zechariah 8:2) "I am zealous לציון," i.e., for Zion's sake.

H. Rashi 25:14

"And the name of the Israelite [who was smitten]"

Wherever it gives the genealogy of a good man in praise of him, it gives the genealogy of a bad man mentioned in the same story to disparage him.

I. Rashi 25:15

"And the name of the [Midianite] woman who was smitten etc."

This is stated to show you the hatred the Midianites bore to Israel—that they abandoned even a princess to prostitution in order to make Israel sin.

J. Sforno 25:1

"the people profaned themselves"

Originally, there had been no intention of committing idolatrous acts at all. All that the males had intended was to indulge their libido with the womenfolk who made themselves available. However, these people fell victim to precisely the warning of the Torah in Exodus 34:15-16 of what would happen if Jews would allow the Canaanites to remain in their country and conclude a covenant with them. They would be invited to their social gatherings resulting in their eating forbidden foods, and eventually intermarriage followed by lip service to their gods.

K. Sforno 25:2

"The people ate and worshipped their gods"

Thus is the way of the Evil Inclination, to go from wicked deed ("the people ate") to wicked deed ("and worshipped their gods").

L. Sforno 25:12

"My covenant of peace"

Peace with the angel of death. We have a similar meaning of this word "peace" in Job 25:20—"He makes peace in His lofty regions." Losses occur only as a result of confrontations by opposites. We find that as a result of this "peace, or armistice" with the angel of death Phinehas enjoyed an exceedingly long life on earth, more so than any other member of his generation. In fact, he was still serving as priest in the Tabernacle at Shiloh during the civil war between Benjamin and the other tribes. This occurred many years after the death of Joshua and the elders who were Joshua's assistants (Judges 20:28). Joshua 24:26 reports these elders as surviving Joshua for many years. If, as is indicated by the Talmud, Phinehas was still alive in the days of Jephthah (Judges 11:26), he must have been 300 years old by that time.

M. Sforno 25:13

"because he took impassioned action for his God"

Seeing he had had the courage to fight My fight, I have ennobled him, granting him "peace."

N. Sforno 25:14

"because he was zealous for his God"

Seeing he had had the courage to fight My fight, I have ennobled hi, granting him "peace."

"and atoned for the children of Israel"

Seeing that he did what he did in full view of his peers so that they would obtain expiation for not having protested Zimri's behavior, he proved himself fit to become a priest whose primary function it is to secure expiation for the sins of their Jewish brethren. As a priest he could continue in the role he had first adopted on this occasion.

O. Sforno 25:14

"The name of the Israelite who was killed"

Phinehas had endangered his own life by what he did in view of the high rank of his victim, one of the 12 princes of the people, as well as a princess from a neighboring country. [If not for this, the Torah might not have bothered to name the individuals concerned just as it did not name such sinners as the man gathering wood (Numbers 15:33) or the blasphemer (Leviticus 24:10).

Sefer BeMidbar—Phinehas

Supplemental Reading

The Rise of Phinehas

—Rav Chanoch Waxman

I

Parashat Phinehas opens with God declaring the reward of Phinehas. In a systematic fashion, God delineates both the rationale for the reward and the contents of the reward. The text of the Torah reads as follows:

> Phinehas the son of Eleazar, the son of Aaron the Priest, has turned my wrath away from the Children of Israel, in that he was vengeful for my sake (*be-kano et kinati*) amongst them, and I did not consume completely the Children of Israel with my vengeance (*be-kinati*). Therefore say, Behold, I give to him my covenant of peace. And he shall have it, and his descendants after him, the covenant of priesthood everlasting, because he was vengeful (*kinai*) for his God, and made atonement for the Children of Israel. (25:10–13)

Upon witnessing the brazen actions of the Israelite man, later identified as Zimri, a prince of the Simeonite tribe (25:14) and the Midianite women Cozbi, later identified as a princess of the Midianites (25:15), Phinehas took action. In response to Zimri's "bringing close" of the Midianite women in front of the "eyes of Moses" and "eyes of the entire congregation of Israel" (22:6), Phinehas arose from amidst the congregation, spear in hand. Following them into the tent they had entered, he impaled them both and the plague that had broken out amongst the people ceased (25:8). For his valor, and in merit having turned God's wrath from the people (25:11), God grants Phinehas his "covenant of peace" (25:12). Phinehas, a descendant of Aaron not previously numbered amongst the designated priests, is elevated to the priesthood (25:13).

As sketched here, the actions of Phinehas are heroic. By simple logic if a particular action is rewarded by God, it constitutes the right and just action. If such were not the case, God would not reward the action. Moreover, God himself describes the action of Phinehas as "turning his wrath" (25:11) away from the people and "achieving atonement" (25:13). Twenty-four thousand members of the Children of Israel had already died in the plague that resulted from the people engaging in harlotry with the daughters of Moab and Midian (25:1, 9, 15). If not for the initiative of Phinehas, and the atonement achieved by his actions, even more would have fallen.

Finally, the Torah describes Phinehas as being "vengeful" for his God (25:13). Phinehas acts on behalf of God. Again, certainly a good thing. In addition, the Torah depicts Phinehas as *be-kano et kinati*, translated above as no more than "being vengeful for my sake." Yet this is not precisely correct. The original language carries the connotation of "carrying out my vengeance." In a certain sense, Phinehas carries out the role of God. As such, there is no need for God to continue to consume the people with his vengeance, the ongoing plague. Phinehas plays the God-like role, the plague is rendered unnecessary, and the people are saved. In this light, Pinchas's bold action of vengeance constitutes a full-fledged act of *imitatio dei*, of emulating the ways of the divine, of walking in his ways. In point of fact, the second commandment refers to God as "a vengeful God (*el kana*)" (Exodus 20:5; Deuteronomy 5:9). Exodus 34:14 even goes so far as to claim that "the Lord's name is vengeance, he is a vengeful God." As such Phinehas's actions are not just heroic, just and for the sake of heaven. They even border on the divine.

This reading may generate a sense of discomfort. After all, is it not theologically problematic to attribute vengefulness to God? Likewise, is vengefulness a desirable trait and action, an integral part of the value matrix that comprises the ethical personality mandated by the Torah? Perhaps we should translate the stem k.n.a. used by the Torah in these varied contexts (Exodus 20:5; 34:14; Numbers 25:13) in a more moderate fashion. Perhaps it only carries connotations of jealousy, rage, zealousness and passion. Phinehas is passionate, zealous and jealous for God's sake. But does this really help matters?

Needless to say, in the time-honored tradition of philosophical exegesis of the Torah, we can engage in a bit of fancy footwork and claim that "the Torah speaks in the language of men," that the Torah's attribution of vengefulness, zealousness etc. to God does not really describe God himself or any emotional state of God. Rather these attributions simply describe his actions, in a language intelligible to the reader. While this may ease the theological difficulty, the issue of vengefulness as a desirable character trait remains in place. Phinehas is vengeful, Phinehas is zealous and Phinehas is violent. The Torah describes Phinehas as taking on a quasi-divine function, and for this action he is rewarded. Apparently, vengeance, zealousness and passion for God's sake are recommended traits and activities.

II

In commenting on the story of Phinehas, Jerusalem Talmud, Sanhedrin 9:7 makes the following striking claim:

> Phinehas acted against the will of the wise men. Rabbi Yuda ... said: They desired to excommunicate him. If not for the divine spirit that sprung upon him and said: And he shall have it, and his descendants after him, the covenant of priesthood everlasting ...

According to the Jerusalem Talmud, the action of Phinehas was perceived by the wise men, a Talmudic term for the rabbinic establishment, as inappropriate. As punishment for his brazenness, Phinehas was threatened with a form of excommunication. Only divine intervention and divine sanctioning of Pinchas's initiative prevented his punishment. On the simple level, this opinion of the Talmud may be seen as concerned with the proper functioning of the judicial system. The piece appears in Masechet Sanhedrin, a tractate whose overriding concern is with courts, the court system and proper modes of justice. Phinehas had just engaged in what we term in modern terminology an extrajudicial killing. While the Torah and Talmudic law specifies the requirement of witnesses and other judicial apparatus (see Deuteronomy 17:6 and Ibn Ezra 25:7), Phinehas acted as judge, jury and executioner.

Returning to the text provides some surprising support for R. Yuda's interpretation and helps reveal another dimension of meaning. Right before the "bringing forth" of the Midianite women by the Israelite man "in front of the eyes of the entire congregation (25:6), Moses had commanded the "Judges of Israel" to "kill, each one his men," all those who had "attached themselves to Baal Peor" (25:5). In other words, Moses had commanded the execution of justice by the judicial system upon those who had strayed after the foreign women and foreign god. It is in this context that Phinehas bypasses the slowly turning wheels of justice and performs his zealous elimination of Zimri and Cozbi. Moreover, the text specifies that the entire event occurs in a public context, in the language of the text "in front of the eyes of Moses and the eyes of the entire congregation" (25:6). From this perspective, the actions of Phinehas comprise not just a bypassing of the judicial system, an extrajudicial killing, but the very serious violation known in the Talmud as "teaching Halakha in front of one's teacher" (Babylonian Talmud, Berakhot 31b, Sanhedrin 17a). Proper rabbinic doctrine requires not just procedure, but also respect for hierarchy and authority. Phinehas rises in front of Moses his teacher, the ultimate religious and legal authority of the Children of Israel, and without waiting for word or approval from Moses carries out a different punishment than that mandated by Moses. While Moses, upon God's word, had commanded the judges to hang the sinners (see Rashi, Ibn Ezra 25:4, Ramban 25:5), Phinehas impales them (25:6–7). While this may seem a minor matter, Phinehas is not a judge, he does not receive the go ahead from the proper authority and his revolutionary action occurs in front of the entire community. In a certain sense, Phinehas's act is an act of subversion, a charismatic act that threatens the social structure, legal hierarchy and leadership structure of the Children of Israel. No wonder the Jerusalem Talmud states that "they desired to excommunicate him." No self-respecting court could do otherwise. While Phinehas's actions had clearly saved the day, no structure can tolerate subversion and revolution.

III

Reading the story of the straying at Shittim (25:1) and the rise of Phinehas as involving a tension between the leadership of Moses and the almost rebellious yet heroic action of Phinehas, brings us back to the issue of *kina*, the question of zealousness, passion and vengeance that we began with. In point of fact, Moses does not act with zealousness and passion at Shittim. He does not carry out God's vengeance. He simply operates the wheels of justice. As pointed out above, and highlighted by the Jerusalem Talmud, this is in marked contrast to Pinchas, the passionate avenging agent of the Lord.

But this is not the first time we have encountered a disconnect between Moses and *kina* or even an outright rejection of *kina* by Moses. Thirty-eight years previously, back in the wilderness of Paran, Moses had censured Joshua, another of the future leaders of Israel, for his *kina*. In the strange story of the prophecy of Eldad and Medad, the Torah recounts that unlike the seventy elders designated to share the burden of leadership with Moses, Eldad and Medad remained in the camp and prophesied while in the camp (11:26). While the Torah does not inform us as to the content of the prophecy, it does inform us as to Joshua's reaction. Upon hearing of their prophesying in the camp, Joshua urges Moses to "restrain them" (11:28). In less Biblical terminology, Joshua urges Moses to shut them up. As Ramban points out (11:28), regardless of the unmentioned content of the prophecy, the very act of prophesying in the camp, not under the leadership and spirit of the "father of all prophets," constitutes an undermining of the status of Moses. But while Joshua is zealous for Moses's sake and wants to restrain Eldad and Medad, it is Joshua that Moses wishes to restrain. Before stating his wish that all of Israel should be graced with prophecy and the divine spirit, Moses questions Joshua as to his *kina* for Moses's sake (11:29). Apparently, Moses has no need for *kina* and frowns upon it.

IV

This possible tension between Moses and the leadership of Moses on the one hand and the attribute of *kina* on the other is further strengthened by and an interesting overlap between the stories of Elijah recounted in Kings and the life of Moses.

When Jezebel, the wife of Ahab became aware of Elijah's slaughtering of 450 prophets of Baal after the showdown at Mount Carmel, Elijah was forced to flee to the desert (1 Kings 19:2–4). After prompting by an angel and a bit of food and water, the text reports that Elijah embarks on a journey of "forty days and forty nights" for which he will have no sustenance but that just consumed food and water. The journey culminates at "Horeb, the mountain of God" (19:8). This term and the desert setting constitute obvious echoes of God's first revelation to Moses. Moses had gone out to the "desert," eventually winding up at "Horeb, the mountain of God" (Exodus 3:1). Likewise, the imagery of "forty days and forty nights" sustained without food and water conjures up Moses's later experience at that very same place, usually known as Sinai. *Sefer Shmot* describes Moses's sojourn on the mountain in the aftermath of the Sin of the Golden Calf as lasting "forty days and forty nights." As part of this formula, the text specifies that during this time he neither ate bread nor drank water (Exodus 34:28), just like Elijah later on, in the desert, forty days and forty nights, without food or water, at Sinai. The point of this four-part parallel, of drawing the connection between Elijah and Moses, seems to be to set the scene for the upcoming conversation and divine theophany. Grasping this point requires some elaboration of the details of the story found in *Sefer Melakhim* [the book of Kings]. With this in mind, let us turn to some of the details.

The central part of the narrative of Elijah and Horeb begins with a conversation between God and Elijah.

Upon being asked by God, "What are you doing here Elijah?" Elijah responds as follows:

> I have been vengeful (*kano kinaiti*) for the Lord God of Hosts:
> for the Children of Israel have forsaken your covenant, thrown down your altars and slain your prophets with the sword....
> And they seek my life to take it. (19:10)

At this point, God conducts a little demonstration for Elijah. After commanding him to stand on the mountain "in front of the Lord," God informs Elijah that He will "pass by" (19:11). A great and mighty wind ensues, and then an awful noise, and then a fire. But God was not found in the wind, the noise or the fire. Rather, God was present only in the still small voice that followed the wind, noise and fire (19:12). Upon hearing the voice, Elijah exits the cave he was in and covers his face (19:13). Strangely enough, at this point God reiterates his original question. Once again, God questions Elijah with the exact same words. "What are you doing here Elijah?" whispers the divine voice (19:14). And once again Eliyahu knows why he has come to Sinai, why he has spent forty days and forty nights without food and water and even why God has passed by his face. Eliyahu repeats his previous response word for word.

> I have been vengeful (*kano kinaiti*) for the Lord God of Hosts:
> for the Children of Israel have forsaken your covenant, thrown down your altars and slain your prophets with the sword...
> And they seek my life to take it. (19:14)

All that has happened to Elijah has happened because of who he is. He is the righteous and zealous prophet of the Lord. He has acted with *kina* as he should and has been persecuted for his just and correct actions.

By repeating the identical words after the theophany in response to God's repeated question, Elijah telegraphs that from his perspective nothing has changed. God's sign, the sign of the still small voice, has had no effect on Elijah. His words after are the same as his words before. For we the readers, this indicates that Elijah has missed the point of the revelation. Whatever the point of bringing him to Sinai, whatever the point of the sign of the still small voice, Elijah has not gotten the point. Something else should have been heard. We may argue, that by no accident, following Elijah's response, God informs Elijah that he should anoint Elisha in his stead (19:16). God has no patience for prophets who fail to perceive. But what was it that Elijah missed? What was the sign of the still small voice?

The Moses imagery provides the key. In addition to the Moses symbolism that comprises the setting of the "sign of the still small voice," the entire story is peppered with thematic and linguistic elements drawn from Moses's experience on Sinai in the aftermath of the Sin of the Golden Calf. As pointed out previously, Elijah is instructed to stand on the mountain in front of the Lord (19:11). This constitutes a thematic, if not an exact linguistic parallel to the positioning of Moses. God tells him to "ascend the mountain" and stand/present himself in front of God on the mountain (Exodus 33:21; 34:2). Similarly, throughout the narratives, Moses and Elijah are both portrayed as located in protected rocky spaces, shielded from the brunt of the divine revelation. While Moses is in a niche in the rock (31:22), Elijah is in a cave (19:13). Finally, and most importantly, in both stories the revelation of God consists of Gods "passing by" or "passing over" the "face" of both Moses and Elijah (34:6; 19:13).

This brings us to the crucial point of contrast. Unlike Elijah, in his experience of the "passing by" of God, Moses perceives something new. He does not remain entrenched in previous paradigms or patterns. In fact, he perceives the famed attributes of mercy. Upon God's passing over, Moses proclaimed:

> The Lord, the Lord, a merciful God and gracious, slow to anger, abundant in kindness and truth. He stores up kindness for thousands of generations, and bears sin, iniquity and transgression and yet will not forgive completely. He visits the sins of the fathers upon the sons, the second, third and fourth generations. (34:6–7)

In his experience of the "passing by" of God, Moses perceives mercy, kindness, patience, slowness to anger and the like. In short, he perceives the attributes of God by which God now promises to lead the Children of Israel (see Exodus 33:12–13).

These merciful attributes, revealed as part of the process of the making of the second set of tablets and reconstitution of the covenant in the aftermath of the Sin of the Golden Calf (Exodus 34:1–10), constitute a radical change from the previous revelation of God's attributes found in the Torah. Previously, in the second commandment, God had described himself as:

> a vengeful God (*el kana*), visiting the sins of the fathers upon the sons, the second, third and fourth generations of those who hate me. Doing kindness for thousands of generations for those that love me and keep my commandments. (Exodus 20:5)

God identifies himself as primarily a vengeful God (*el kana*). After placing this terrifying attribute in the first position, the second commandment places the punishment of the children and future generations for the sins of the forefathers in the second position on the hierarchy of God's attributes. Both of these attributes correlate strongly with the notion of divine justice, or perhaps even something stricter. While the attribute of kindness and the consequent doing of kindness for future generations finally do make their appearance, this complex appears only at the end, in the third position of this three-part description. Moreover, the doing of kindness to future generations is limited by a very specific modifier. Apparently, God's kindness is confined to those who "love him" and keep his commandments. Justice, punishment and divine vengeance constitute the fates of sinners.

Let us return to the revelation to Moses in the aftermath of the Sin of the Golden Calf, or to adopt the terminology utilized previously, the perception of Moses in his experience of God's "passing by." The contrasts between the attributes of God listed in God's self-identification in the second commandment and the list of attributes revealed to Moses in the "passing by" revelation should be obvious. For starters, while the notion of God's visiting the sins of forefathers upon future generations also appears in the "passing by revelation," it has been bumped down to third position (34:7). In its place, the Torah places the previously third, and last, attribute of kindness, the doing of kindness for thousands of generations. To put this slightly differently, the second and third positions on the two lists have switched. While beforehand, in the second commandment (20:5), punishment was second and kindness was last, now, in Moses's revelation, kindness is second and punishment is last (34:7). Moreover, the kindness to future generations is no longer confined to those who love God and keep his commandments. It is unbounded and seems to encompass even the less deserving.

But this is only the minor part of the story. The true dramatic change occurs in the pole position of the hierarchy of God's attributes. While the second commandment had defined God as "a vengeful God" and placed this definition front and center, in the opening line of the list, this term is completely absent from the thirteen attributes. In its place, in "Moses's revelation," the aspects of God that Moses perceived when God "passed by," the Torah lists the primary attributes of mercy. As we should well remember, the text specifies in great detail what Moses calls out, what he perceives, upon God's passing by:

> The Lord, the Lord, a merciful God and gracious, slow to anger, abundant in kindness and truth . . . (34:6)

The difference between these attributes and the previous definition of "a vengeful God" could not be greater.

This brings us full circle to Elijah, Moses, and the intended revelatory and prophetic content of God's passing by. What was Elijah supposed to perceive in the sign of the still small voice? Why did God bring him to Sinai and place in him the position and place of Moses? Simply put, Elijah should have perceived what Moses perceived. Just as Moses perceived mercy, kindness and a complete absence of *kina*, the attribute of vengeance and zealousness in God's "passing by," so too Elijah should have perceived the same or similar divine attributes.

Arguably, the imagery of the sign may support this interpretation. As the text specifies, God was not present in the power of the wind, the noise, or the heat and flame of the fire. Rather, he was only present in the still small voice. But Elijah can only think, apprehend and speak about one thing. Upon being asked by God why he has come to Sinai, Elijah speaks again only of *kina* (1 Kings 19:13-14), the opposite of what Moses perceived, the opposite of the intended content and message of the revelation of God's "passing by."

To put this all together, God had attempted to educate Elijah in his ways, the ways of God revealed to Moses in the aftermath of the Sin of the Golden Calf. These are the modes by which God had promised to lead the people and the modes which a prophet and leader needs to apprehend, understand, emulate and bring to fruition. But Elijah only knows *kina*, the way of passion, zealousness, and fiery vengeance. He can no longer serve as prophet and leader and God informs him so.

But these ways, the mode of mercy, graciousness, and slowness to anger, the textual opposite of *kina* in *Sefer Shmot* are also the ways of Moses. After all, they are the attributes that Moses apprehended, in his experience of God's "passing by." They are the way in which God has promised to lead his people, the mode of providence a prophet and leader needs to apprehend, understand, emulate and bring to fruition. They are the attributes of Moses and Mosaic leadership. Once again, Moses and the attribute of *kina* do not mix.

V

Until this point, our analysis has focused on building a dual tension between Moses on the one hand and Phinehas on the other. While Moses operates the institutional leadership, Phinehas violates the normal judicial structure. While Moses, in his character and mode of leadership eschews the attribute of *kina*, the passion of zealotry and vengeance, Phinehas embodies these very attributes. But where does this leave us with our reading of the story of Shittim and the rise of Phinehas to prominence? Let us not lose sight of the point we began with. God heartily endorses Pinchas's actions in the plains of Moab. He rewards Phinehas with membership in the priesthood and describes Phinehas as acting for the sake of heaven and achieving atonement for the people of Israel (25:13). In the formulation of the text highlighted earlier, Phinehas's *kina* is in fact God's zealousness and vengeance.

Most probably, the parasha should be interpreted as endorsing *kina* in a limited fashion. In short, extraordinary circumstances demand extraordinary measures. While Phinehas does act in violation of the system and the normal mode of communal leadership, he acts in a context of an ongoing plague. Twenty-four thousand of the Children of Israel have already died. In front of the entire community of Israel and its collective leadership, at the Tent of Meeting itself, a place considered "in front of the Lord" Himself, Zimri now stands to add insult to injury. He "brings forth" a Midianite woman, with all the connotations of harlotry, idol worship and betrayal of God that she carries (25:1-2). They enter into a nearby tent for one purpose and one purpose only. At this moment of public desecration of the divine, Phinehas arises and acts for the sake of heaven. Extraordinary circumstances demand extraordinary action.

Alternatively, or perhaps even in parallel, the story can be interpreted in a slightly more radical fashion, as a story about violation of norms, the occasional need for revolutionary action and transition. Immediately after noting the action of Zimri in "bringing forth" the Midianite women in front of Moses and the entire community, the text states that "they were crying at the door of the Tent of Meeting." While some commentaries interpret the crying as referring to prayer (Ibn Ezra 25:6), most probably the crying reflects despair and even paralysis of Moses and the judges of Israel. (Ramban 25:5; Rashi 25:6). While the system has been put into play and may in fact be churning away, it does not really function. It cannot deal with the radical and revolutionary act of Zimri. Only a radical act, a revolutionary breaking of norms for the sake of heaven, can balance the radical and revolutionary act of Zimri. Only Phinehas and his *kina* for the sake of God can save the day. In this vein, Numbers Rabbah 20:24 states that Moses's "hands trembled" at Shittim so that Phinehas could come and take "that which was suited for him." Apparently, every leadership structure needs to be renewed upon occasion. Things need to be shaken up, and entrenched structures need to be shattered. They need to be built again with new blood, energy, verve and passion. Elevating Phinehas to the role of priest serves exactly this purpose. He becomes part of the system. In this light, the story of Shittim constitutes part of the theme of leadership transition prominent in the latter part of *Sefer BeMidbar*.

While both these readings are attractive, the Halakha seems to eschew them both. Instead, the Halakha seeks to limit the charismatic and revolutionary quality of Pinchas's actions. In doing so, it dissolves the tension between Moses and Phinehas we have carefully structured. Mishnah Sanhedrin 9:6 teaches regarding one who has intercourse with a non-Jewish woman—"the zealous *(kanai'n)* attack him." Phinehas's actions are in fact in perfect accord with the Halakha, i.e., the teachings of Moses. Rather than a revolutionary and extra-Halakhic act, Phinehas engages in no more than the letter of the law. He simply carries out the law. He is a *kanai*, a zealot, and the law demands that he stand up and kill Zimri.

The numerous midrashim paralleling this Mishnah, further emphasize this point. While Moses and his judges had forgotten the particular law in question and were busy debating whether Zimri was liable to the death penalty (Tanhuma Balak 21), Phinehas remembered the appropriate principle. In another version, Phinehas, upon remembering the appropriate law, reminds Moses of the rule that "our master has taught us" (Midrash Aggadah Numbers 25:2) before rising against Zimri. In other words, there is no tension between Moses and Phinehas. Phinehas is ever the loyal student, acting upon, and putting into place the rules of Torat Moses, the Torah of Moses.

VI

Before closing, let us try to bridge the gap between these variant interpretations. Quite possibly, Phinehas does act according to some given, previously existent criteria. At the same time, Phinehas's actions still possess a radical, and even anti-Moses quality. This requires some explanation. Once again, the story of Moses in the aftermath of the Sin of the Golden Calf should provide the key.

While not highlighted earlier, God does not completely retract his self-identification as "a vengeful God" in the revelation narrative that contains the thirteen attributes. Immediately after "passing by" Moses and revealing the attributes of mercy in all their contrast to the attributes of the second commandment, God informs Moses that he consents to renew his covenant with the Children of Israel (Exodus 34:10). As part of the list of commandments that comprises the contents of the renewed covenant, the Torah follows God's consent with the prohibition of contracting a counter covenant with the inhabitants of the land. This may lead to idol worship, and "you shall worship no other god, for the Lord's name is vengeance/jealousy (*kana shemo*), he is a vengeful/jealous God (*el kana*)" (34:14).

The context here is crucial. In elaborating upon the possible counter covenant that would arouse God's attribute of vengeance/jealousy, the Torah states the following:

> Lest you contract a covenant with the inhabitants/dwellers in the land and go astray (*zanu*) after their gods. And you will sacrifice to their gods, they will call to you, and you will eat from their sacrifices. And you will take of their daughters (*banot*) for your sons and their daughters will play the harlot (*ve'zanu*) for their gods. And your sons will stray/commit harlotry after their gods. (34:15–16)

The Torah here outlines a complex that might be termed double harlotry. Matters begin to go astray through involvement with the prior inhabitants of the land. The complex involves sacrifices to a foreign god, being called, eating, *zenut*, or harlotry, with foreign women and finally, *zenut*, a different form of harlotry, with foreign gods.

In this context, God stands in the role of the betrayed and consequently, jealous or vengeful husband. The people abandon their covenantal relationship with God for a foreign, and other, god. Realizing this point, should go a long way to explaining the use of the term *kina* as one of God's attributes. Parashat Sotah, the story of the women who has either committed adultery or whose husband possesses reason to think that she has betrayed him utilizes the stem k.n.a., the root of the term variously translated as "vengeful," "zealous" or "jealous," a full ten times (Numbers 5:14, 15, 18, 25, 29, 30). The Torah describes the betrayed husband as filled with "the spirit of vengeance/jealousy" (5:14, 30) and as *kinai et ishto*, jealous of his wife, or vengeful against his wife (5:14, 30). It is God's love and passion for Israel, their covenantal relationship and the problem of double betrayal with foreign women and foreign gods that is signaled by the use of this term to describe God. In this context, God's name is *kana*. He is the jealous and vengeful betrayed husband.

What we should realize is, that at Shittim, the Children of Israel engage in exactly the behavior predicted by God in the aftermath of the Sin of the Golden Calf. The narrative begins by specifying that the Children of Israel "dwelt" in Shittim and that the people began to stray/commit harlotry (*liznot*) after/with the daughters of Moab (25:1). This triple parallel of "dwellers/dwelt," "daughters" of a foreign people and "straying/harlotry" (*zenut*), is immediately followed by all of the other elements of the story in *Shmot*. The people are "called." There are "sacrifices" and the people "eat"

(25:2). And of course, the double straying/harlotry paradigm reaches its culmination with the people worshipping foreign gods, the people "bow to their gods" and "attach themselves" to Baal Peor (25:2). Not surprisingly, having been betrayed, and in response to the double harlotry of the people, God becomes angry (25:2), and is vengeful (25:11); a plague rages among the people (25:9).

From this perspective, Zimri's bringing forth of the Midianite women "to his brothers" in front of the eyes of Moses and the congregation comprises far more than just a brazen act of adultery. It is probably the predicted counter covenant of Exodus 34:15. In pointed contrast to God's already raging anger, Zimri proposes a treaty with the inhabitants of the land. It is in this context that Phinehas acts. He acts to sabotage the counter-covenant of Zimri. He acts on the basis of God's covenantal and covenant enforcing plague. His *kina* is in accord with God's *kina*. It is the passionate, zealous and jealous anger of the betrayed whose beloved has strayed. In other words, Phinehas acts in accord with a clear set of criteria, already set down by God in the aftermath of the Sin of the Golden Calf. He acts in accord with the divine wish already telegraphed in the plague and confirmed in its aftermath. While *kina* may have been limited by the revelation of the attributes of mercy, it still has its time and place.

To close the circle, we must return to Moses. Did Moses not remember the warning of God given in the aftermath of the Sin of the Golden Calf? Did he not recall the paradigm of double harlotry? Does Moses not realize that a leader is sometimes called to emulate the harsher side of God's leadership?

In fact, Moses himself had once acted the Pinchas/betrayed husband role. By no accident, God's definition of the double harlotry model is immediately followed by a warning against the fashioning of "molten gods" (34:16). This of course, is the term utilized by God to describe the Golden Calf (32:8). From God's perspective, the Sin of the Golden Calf constituted yet another example of "straying" and betrayal, another occasion for *kina*. Yet at that time, it was Moses who stood in the Phinehas/betrayed husband role. Upon receiving the go ahead from God (32:7) and after smashing the tablets, Moses grinds up the Golden Calf, places the powder in water and forces the Children of Israel to drink of the waters (32:20). This clearly parallels the drinking of "the bitter waters" forced upon the unfaithful wife by the betrayed and vengeful husband that comprises the centerpiece of the Sotah story (Numbers 5:17–24). Similarly, shortly after conducting this "ceremony," Moses summoned the Levites to battle and bid them pass through the camp "slaying each man his brother" (Exodus 32:27–28). Moses commanded a spontaneous act of violence. In sum, in the Sin of the

Golden Calf, Moses plays the Phinehas/betrayed husband role. He is full of vengeance and violence for God's sake.

To conclude, regarding the question of Moses's lack of *kina* and perhaps even inaction at Shittim, regarding the difference between Moses of *Sefer Shmot* and Moses of *Sefer BeMidbar*, we can never know or discern the exact dynamics that Moses has undergone. Much has passed between the second and fortieth years in the desert. We have not been with God for forty days and forty nights on the mountain, nor had God "pass by" while we stood upon the rock. We have not descended from the mountain our faces aglow with divine luminescence, or been subjected to forty years of leading the fractious and ever complaining Children of Israel. Suffice it to say that by the fortieth year of the desert journey, Moses's attachment to the people is not what it once was. They are rebels and in their constant rebellion doomed him to never entering the land (Deuteronomy 4:21). He is no longer their eternal leader, and a new generation of leaders is destined to lead the people over the Jordan. From this perspective, it is not surprising that at Shittim, Moses cannot or will not muster up the passion to play the role of the betrayed husband. While the leader must sometimes emulate one divine attribute and sometimes another, the attribute of *kina* and the passionate attachment it demands are no longer the role of Moses. This is left to Phinehas, to avenge the betrayal of God, to restore the covenant and to "take that which was suited for him" (Numbers Rabbah 20:24). While Phinehas acts according to the criteria of *Sefer Shmot* and his *kina* is justified, the narrative at Shittim is also about the transitions of *Sefer BeMidbar*, the change in leadership and the contrasts between Moses and Phinehas.

Rav Chanoch Waxman currently serves as a rav at Yeshivat Hamivtar. He has served as rabbi of the Albert Einstein Synagogue and has taught at Drisha Institute and at MaTan in Jerusalem. He is a featured speaker and writer for Yeshivat Har Etzion's Virtual Beit Midrash.

Sefer BeMidbar—Pinchas

Supplemental Reading

The Parameters of Pinchas' Zealotry

—Rabbi Zalman Baruch Melamed

Beyond Intellect and Emotion

Our portion opens with the Torah's praise for the "jealousy"—or more appropriately—"zealotry"—of Pinchas: "Phinehas the son of Eleazar the son of Aaron the Cohen turned back My anger from the Children of Israel; I am therefore awarding him with My Covenant of Peace." What's the meaning of this zealotry, what is its source, and why is Phinehas deserving of such an exceptional Divine reward?

One's intellect is the source of his moral character: and personality. Only after one appreciates that that which is good is truly good, does he begin to yearn for it—and as a result act towards achieving that end. Human intellect is beyond emotion; in fact, it actually guides and even directs emotion. An act of "jealousy" on behalf of God, however, does not stem from the intellect. Man possesses a quality even higher than the intellect: it exists on the subconscious level, in the depths of one's spirit; it constantly strives to reveal itself and to appear via the intellect and emotion. The role of intellect and emotion is to neutralize those factors that block the manifestation of zealotry. [This model is used by Rabbi Avraham Yitzchak Kook (of blessed memory) to explain the phenomenon of *emunah*, or faith. He stresses that *emunah* exists on a plane above and beyond intellect and emotion.]

It is from these depths that jealousy must spring; this jealousy—or zealotry—reveals itself once one puts aside all factors that inhibit the manifestation of his inner cleaving to the Creator of the Universe. This zealotry responds to any even slight manifestation of Hillul Hashem, or desecration of God's name. Zealotry that has its roots in an understanding of the Divine—inspires the "zealot" to reach a state of completion—or Sheleimut: "Behold, I am giving him My covenant of Peace (Shalom)."

In Tractate Sanhedrin, our Sages enumerate the deeds, which, if done by a Jew, warrant "Zealots smiting him." For example, "One who steals a vessel for use in the Temple . . . one who has relations with a Gentile woman . . ." and—even a Cohen who serves in the Temple while in a state of ritual impurity—are legitimately attacked and killed by zealots. The reason for Torah-sanctioned vigilance in these kinds of cases? The direct offense committed by the transgressor, who himself has stricken at the heart of the bond between the Children of Israel and the Holy One, blessed be He.

Our Sages explain that true zealotry may be defined as a situation in which the zealot does not inquire of a scholar how to act in the case at hand; in fact, should he make such an inquiry, a scholar would be bound not to instruct him to take action. Why? The very question as to how to respond indicates that the person has not internalized the level of zealotry required to permit his unilateral action. True zealotry flows naturally, from an inability of the person to tolerate the desecration of God's name. A well-known Torah dictum states that in situations of desecration to God's name, one does not allot honor even to a Rabbi.

A Dearth of Halakhot

The Shulchan Aruch, or Code of Jewish Law, does not detail the laws associated with Torah-approved zealotry. Author of the work "Chelkat Michokek" questions the reason for this omission. A possible approach to this question: it is inappropriate to write down such halakhot, since after all, the laws of zealotry—though they are compulsory—do not serve as the basis of actual halachic rulings. Thus, though Phinehas's zealotry is aptly discussed in the *Beit Midrash* (study hall)—it is inappropriate to engage in it in the framework of normative halachic codes.

Of Torah or Rabbinic Origin?

What is the source of the halakha that "zealots strike at offenders"? The great medieval sage, Rabbeinu Nissim ("Ran") maintains that it is a "Halacha L'Moshe M'Sinai"—namely, an oral tradition dating back to the giving of the Torah on Mount Sinai. His insistence that it is not rabbinic in origin stems from his view that the Sages do not have the power to initiate rabbinic death penalties outside of one-time emergency situations; they do not, says Ran; have the right to rule in this manner for generations to come.

A support for Ran's approach appears in the Midrash: Phinehas approaches Moses and says to him: "This is what you told us when you descended from atop Mount Sinai: 'One who has relations with a Gentile woman is justifiably attacked by zealots.'"

In his book of Responsa, the great rabbi known as "Radbaz" argues that the permissibility of unilateral acts of zealotry is rooted in rabbinic law. Ran's point doesn't faze Radbaz, since, according to the latter, the Sages did not rule that one should kill an offender outside of the framework of the law; rather, they ruled that one should not punish a zealot who takes unilateral action and kills an offender outside of the framework of the law.

Why? Our Sages understood that a person filled with love of Hashem to the point at which, out of zealotry, he kills another Jew guilty of desecrating God's name—is simply unable to conquer the holy emotions within him. It is thus improper to punish him.

Zimri's Right to Self-Defense

Our Sages, writing in the Talmudic tractate of Sanhedrin, maintain that if Zimri had turned on Phinehas and killed him, he (Zimri) would have been exempt from punishment. This statement seems to clash with another halakhic principle, namely, that one may kill a person whom he sees in pursuit of another person; here, it is permissible, and even a mitzvah, to kill the *rodef* (pursuer) since one "should not idly stand by the blood of his neighbor." Nevertheless, if the *rodef* turns around and kills the one who is trying to kill him, he (the *rodef*) is deserving of death. The obvious reason for this ruling: one who is on the verge of killing a *rodef* is about to fulfill a mitzvah; thus, the *rodef* himself has no permission to kill the one pursuing him.

How should we resolve the above principle with the rabbis' observation that, had Zimri killed Phinehas, Zimri would have been exempt from the death penalty? It must be that Phinehas, as the one who killed Zimri, was not fulfilling a mitzvah! For if killing Zimri were to have been a mitzvah, Zimri would not have had permission to defend himself.

A Lesson Learned

From this discussion, the Mishneh L'Melech on the Rambam, offers another observation: It is known that a relative of a manslaughter victim, may halakhically kill that man slaughterer should the latter leave his "city of refuge."

What would be the ruling if the (accidental) murderer turned around and killed the vengeful relative? Mishneh L'Melech maintains that the halakha in this instance may be learned from Zimri: It is not a positive mitzvah to kill one who committed manslaughter; the latter's punishment is exile to a city of refuge, and not death. However, the Torah understood the heart and mindset of the grieving relative, and ruled that it is improper to punish him for killing the person who killed his relative.

Since, then, the relative is not fulfilling a mitzvah in his killing of the murderer, he, the relative, is a *rodef*. Thus, the pursued murderer is permitted to defend himself by killing his "pursuer".

A zealous person such as Phinehas is a type of "blood avenger"—not on behalf of a dead relative—but on behalf of God. He is so identified with God that he is unable to suffer any affront, so to speak, to Hashem. This is why he stands up and acts out of his zeal. The fact that the zeal is not obligatory, but only permissible, does not detract from its value. Just the opposite is true: the value of this "jealousy" is so great, that it is impossible to mandate every person to reach his level . . .

Rabbi Zalman Baruch Melamed is the rosh yeshiva of the Beit El Yeshiva in Beit El, Israel.

Part Three

The Legal Positings of *Sefer BeMidbar*

Chapter 10

The Sotah

THERE IS A WELL-KNOWN talmudic tale in which a gentile approaches the great sage Shammai and asks him "to convert me on condition that you teach me the entire Torah while I am standing on one foot. Shammai, we are told, pushed him away with the builder's cubit in his hand. Undeterred, the gentile goes to the other great sage of that generation, Hillel, and makes the same request, to which Hillel responds, "that which is hateful to you do not do to another. That is the entire Torah, and the rest is its interpretation. Go study" (Shabbat 31a).

What are we to take away from this story?

Some see it as a reflection of the divergent personalities of these two sages, with Shammai portrayed as an old curmudgeon and Hillel as exceedingly kind with saint-like patience.[1] Another approach sees Shammai as

---

1. It should be noted that, in Pirqe Avot 1:15, Shammai says: "Receive [or greet] every person with a pleasant countenance," which stands in sharp distinction to any portrayal of him as an unpleasant curmudgeon. The same talmudic source (Shabbat 30b–31a) tells the story that best depicts Hillel's great patience: "There was an incident involving two people who wagered with each other and said: Anyone who will go and aggravate Hillel to the point that he reprimands him, will take four hundred zuz. One of them said: I will aggravate him. That day that he chose to bother Hillel was Shabbat eve, and Hillel was washing the hair on his head. He went and passed the entrance to Hillel's house and in a demeaning manner said: Who here is Hillel, who here is Hillel? Hillel wrapped himself in a dignified garment and went out to greet him. He said to him: My son, what do you seek? He said to him: I have a question to ask. Hillel said to him: Ask, my son, ask. The man asked him: Why are the heads of Babylonians oval? He was alluding to and attempting to insult Hillel, who was Babylonian. He said to him: My son, you have asked a significant question. The reason is because they do not have clever midwives. They do not know how to shape the child's head at birth. That man went and waited one hour and returned to look for Hillel, and said: Who here is Hillel, who here is Hillel? Again, Hillel wrapped himself and went out to greet him. Hillel said to him: My son, what do you seek? The man said to him: I have a question to ask. He said to him: Ask, my son, ask. The man asked: Why are the eyes of the residents of Tadmor bleary? Hillel said to him: My son, you have asked a significant question. The reason is because they live among the sands, and the sand gets into their eyes. Once

protecting the honor and dignity of Torah study, for he saw mockery, not sincerity, in the gentile's question. I think this is a reasonable way to understand the story, but, to me, it misses an important point. In dismissing the request of the gentile, Shammai made certain assumptions and judgments about him and his intentions. In the end, Shammai could not give this gentile the benefit of the doubt.[2]

The peril of being judgmental, about not giving someone the benefit of the doubt, is something that cannot be ignored or overlooked when employing a pedagogy based on imparting proper character traits to students. In our studies of *Sefer BeMidbar*, we have found that one could argue that it is easy to assume that Korah and Balaam are bad or evil people. They embody bad character traits, and it was ultimately their actions that revealed their true natures.[3] Yet jumping too quickly to such a conclusion goes against important core principles of Judaism, and, as we will see, doing so will color in an inappropriate manner one's understanding of the Sotah, that is, a woman suspected of adultery who must undergo an ordeal that will establish her guilt or innocence as detailed in the fifth chapter of Numbers.

---

again the man went, waited one hour, returned, and said: Who here is Hillel, who here is Hillel? Again, he, Hillel, wrapped himself and went out to greet him. He said to him: My son, what do you seek? He said to him: I have a question to ask. He said to him: Ask, my son, ask. The man asked: Why do Africans have wide feet? Hillel said to him: You have asked a significant question. The reason is because they live in marshlands, and their feet widened to enable them to walk through those swampy areas. That man said to him: I have many more questions to ask, but I am afraid lest you get angry. Hillel wrapped himself and sat before him, and he said to him: All of the questions that you have to ask, ask them. The man got angry and said to him: Are you Hillel whom they call the Nasi of Israel? He said to him: Yes. He said to him: If it is you, then may there not be many like you in Israel. Hillel said to him: My son, for what reason do you say this? The man said to him: Because I lost four hundred zuz because of you. Hillel said to him: Be vigilant of your spirit and avoid situations of this sort. Hillel is worthy of having you lose four hundred zuz and another four hundred zuz on his account, and Hillel will not get upset."

2. This gentile was one of three individuals who asked Shammai to convert them on seemingly ridiculous conditions. He rejected all three, whereas Hillel accepted each of them. The Talmud concludes its account of these three incidents as follows: "Eventually, the three converts gathered together in one place, and they said: Shammai's impatience sought to drive us from the world. Hillel's patience brought us beneath the wings of the Divine Presence."

3. Many people use the cliché "Love the sinner; hate the sin," which would seem appropriate when considering the misdeeds of certain individuals. There is no biblical source for this notion, although Christians believe that Jude 1:22–23 contains a similar idea: "Be merciful to those who doubt; save others by snatching them from the fire; to others show mercy, mixed with fear—hating even the clothing stained by corrupted flesh." According to this teaching, Christian faith should be characterized by mercy for the sinner and a healthy hatred of sin and its effects.

Judaism encourages its adherents to always give others the benefit of the doubt. The BabylonianTalmud, Shavuot 30a understands this to be a biblical commandment based on the verse "in righteousness you shall judge your neighbor" (Leviticus 19:15). The talmudic sages further explain that those who give others the benefit of the doubt will receive the same consideration from heaven (Shabbat 127b).

Many Jewish sources underscore the importance of not being judgmental and of giving others the benefit of the doubt. The one which I think best goes to the core of the issue has been ascribed to Rabbi Israel ben Eliezer, better known as the Baal Shem Tov, the founder of Hasidic Judaism. He taught: "When you see ill in your friend, it is your own ill that you are observing. Like a mirror that reflects nothing but what you place before it, so, too, what you see in your fellow reflects nothing but what you yourself possess."

The traditional understanding of the Sotah narrative, driven by the classical commentaries, can be harsh in its attitude toward and its condemnation of the woman accused of adultery. I believe that a careful reading of the text will show it to be akin to a mirror that reflects the shortcomings of her husband who was so quick to assume wrongdoing on her part.

Let us begin by examining the text.

> The Lord spoke to Moses, saying: "Speak to the Israelite people and say to them: If any man's wife has gone astray and broken faith with him in that a man has had carnal relations with her unbeknown to her husband, and she keeps secret the fact that she has defiled herself without being forced, and there is no witness against her—but a fit of jealousy comes over him and he is wrought up about the wife who has defiled herself; or if a fit of jealousy comes over one and he is wrought up about his wife although she has not defiled herself" (Numbers 5:11–14).

The harshness of commentaries on this narrative is not initially apparent. Rashi, for example, seems troubled that it first makes mention of the man and not the woman suspected of adultery. He argues that the story should have opened with "a woman who goes astray and acts treacherously ..." given that she was the source of the sin.[4] Because it opens with a reference to the husband, Rashi sees his actions as an underlying driver of the entire episode. Here is how he makes the connection.

> What is stated above, immediately before this section? "If you withhold the gifts due to the priest ..." By your life, you [the

---

4. See the supercommentary of the Siftei Hakamim on Rashi 5:12.

husband] will have to come to him [the priest] in order to bring him your faithless wife for the ordeal by the waters.[5]

Rashi also seems, at least initially, to seek some explanation for the woman's behavior, one that might lead the reader to view her more sympathetically.

> Our Rabbis have taught (Midrash Tanhuma, Naso 5): "Adulterers do never sin until a spirit of madness enters into them," as it written of her: "if she becomes mad." And so, too, of him [not the husband, but the adulterous man], Scripture writes: "Who so commits adultery with a woman lacks understanding." (Proverbs 6:32) (Rashi on 5:12).

An insanity defense. The modern reader would recognize and perhaps appreciate this. Yet Rashi is quick to discard this, as he continues in his commentary:

> But the plain sense of the verse is that "if she becomes mad" [כי תשטה] means: if she deviates from the path of modesty and thereby becomes suspect in his eyes. The word is similar to: "turn away [שְׂטֵה] from it, and pass by" (Proverbs 4:15); and to: "Let not your heart turn [יֵשְׂטְ] to her ways." (Proverbs 7:25) (Rashi on 5:12)

Sforno, in his comment on Numbers 5:14, finds further fault with the woman simply because "she disregarded her husband's warning and secluded herself with another man." So, too, Hizquni, who notes in his comment on Numbers 5:20 that

> The priest did not say to her: "if you have strayed," but he said to her that there was no question that she had strayed, the question was only to what extent she had strayed. She definitely deserved to have been shamed. Having caused her husband to suspect her, and having subsequently secreted herself with a man that her husband had specifically told her not to do, was disgraceful behavior, even if no intimacy had occurred.

Let us pause for a moment and reflect back upon the text itself. The husband here is jealous. (Dare we say, insanely jealous?) He has no proof. He suspects his wife is cheating on him. And text does not confirm this. It give this as one possibility ("he is wrought up about the wife who has defiled herself; or . . . he is wrought up about his wife although she has not defiled

---

5. The translation of the preceding verse is therefore: "A man who remains with his holy things, not giving them to the priest, they—the man and his wife—will become subject to him [require his services]." See Rashi on 5:12.

herself"). In order to clarify his suspicion and to ease his jealousy, he brings his wife to the priest in the tabernacle. His suspicion is tested there in a ceremony that causes the woman great humiliation and unpleasantness—even if she is innocent.

Aside from his jealousy, what prompts all this? The text is silent, but the talmudic sages in Sotah 3a are quick to fill in the gaps. Rabbi Ishmael asks why, in the case of this woman suspected of marital infidelity, the Torah chose to accept the testimony of a single witness. His question is prompted by the verse in Deuteronomy 19:15: "One witness shall not arise against a man for any sin or guilt that he may commit; according to two witnesses or according to three witnesses a matter shall stand." Thus, two witnesses provide conclusive proof of reality, but one witness typically does not. Rabbi Ishmael says that the the case of the Sotah was one in which the husband had legitimate reason to suspect his wife of immoral conduct (although the legitimate reason is not spelled out). The husband warned his wife not to be alone with the man who has aroused his suspicions. Yet, maintains Rabbi Ishmael, she ignored her husband's warnings a first time and was subsequently known to have been alone with the man in question once again after that warning.

This view is echoed in the classical medieval commentators and also in later commentaries, such as that penned by Rabbi Samson Raphael Hirsch in the mid-1800s. These commentaries minimize the wife's independence: "A wife is under the protection of her husband and owes him a duty. She is bound to respect his exclusive conjugal rights. She bears his name. She belongs to him."[6]

Without doubt, the talmudic sages and the commentators that followed were all products of their times. Many like to think that the walls of their houses of study (or even of the ghettos in which many of them subsequently lived) isolated these great scholars from the outside world. They did not. These scholars were not ignorant of or untouched by the movements, ideas, and common opinions of people in the times they lived. For them, it was axiomatic that a wife would unquestioningly obey her husband's demands, and merely being with a man her husband forbade her to associate with was cause enough for suspicion.

Today, many find this notion of the subservient wife, of a woman who belongs to her husband, offensive. We live in an era when young women in high school aspire to careers and leadership positions in many fields and look forward to relationships in which they and their spouses are equal in every sense and respect each other's wishes. Today, in a time of #MeToo,

---

6. Hirsch, *Pentateuch*, on 5:20.

woman are becoming ever more empowered and will not allow others to impose themselves on them.[7]

How then are we to teach the Sotah in a contemporary high school classroom?

According to a literal reading, it appears that the Sotah ceremony is forced upon the woman and that no one asks her opinion. From the outset, she seems to maintain that she bears no guilt, and she obviously has no wish to undergo such an unpleasant procedure simply because of the "jealous spirit" that has seized her husband.

Could it be that the entire narrative is the type of mirror the Baal Shem Tov had in mind when he warned us against being judgmental? Rabbi Elchanan Samet of Yeshivat Har Etzion seems to think so.

> The impression created by this [literal] reading is of a clearly one-sided position adopted by the Torah in favor of the husband, at the expense of the wife. The "jealous spirit" that overcomes the husband is the driving force behind the process described in the parasha, while the factual basis for his suspicion is quite flimsy. It is the husband himself who claims that his wife met privately with a man, and even if this is true, this does not mean that she was defiled. The entire process is based on the husband's claims, and it looks to us as though the parasha takes into consideration only his subjective view, while sacrificing the woman on the altar of his jealousy in order to ease it (or, alternatively, to justify it).[8]

Despite the parochial views of women on the part of the talmudic sages cited above, these same rabbis crafted legal parameters for the Sotah that are more balanced than a simple reading of the text might suggest, a balance that is mindful of the fact that there are two men involved in this tale: the suspected adulterer and the husband.

Regarding the former, while it is the accused woman who must actually drink the bitter waters, the waters affect her male partner in adultery identically. Just as the waters examine her, they also examine him (Babylonian Talmud, Sotah 27a).

---

7. "The power of #MeToo, though, is that it takes something that women had long kept quiet about and transforms it into a movement. Unlike many kinds of social-media activism, it isn't a call to action or the beginning of a campaign, culminating in a series of protests and speeches and events. It's simply an attempt to get people to understand the prevalence of sexual harassment and assault in society." See Gilbert, "Movement of #MeToo."

8. Samet, "Sota."

More fundamentally, the Torah awards the power of decision to the woman rather than to the man who must share her fate. She is not forced to drink the bitter waters at all. She can admit to adultery and accept a divorce. In fact, she does not have to admit to anything. She can simply refuse to drink the bitter waters. All she loses by doing so is her marriage settlement, merely a monetary loss. Thereafter, she is free to marry anyone she likes, even her lover if she were indeed involved in an adulterous affair.[9]

The situation of the man, the suspected adulterer, is far more tenuous. If she professes her innocence and insists on drinking the waters, he will gain nothing by admitting his guilt. As long as she decides to drink, if the water kills her, it will kill him, too (Sotah 28a). Thus, we see that Jewish law here treats both parties to adultery in precisely the same fashion. Whatever is a punishable offense for the female is the same for the male.

But what of the husband?

With him, things are a bit more complicated, because the Torah permits a man to marry several wives, while allowing a woman to be married only to one man.[10] Therefore, a man cannot be said to betray his wife, since he is permitted to marry other wives in addition to her. Logically, then, the Sotah narrative addresses only a husband's suspicion of his wife. Nevertheless, while there is no symmetry between a man and a woman in this sphere, the husband's claim of infidelity on the part of his wife does not free him from similar claims.[11] For this reason, the talmudic sages understood a husband's right to demand a test for his wife as being conditional upon his own moral record.

> "And the man shall be clean of sin, and that woman shall bear her iniquity" (Numbers 5:31)—when the man is clean of sin,

---

9. She can walk away from her husband and from the obligation to drink the bitter waters and "merely" suffer a monetary loss by doing so. Yet I must confess that I can write "merely" when it comes to her financial loss only because of my twenty-first century perspective. Today in the United States, we live in a culture in which women have legal and financial independence. This was not the case in ancient Israel. Women were typically dependent on men (their fathers or their husbands) both legally and economically. Leaving her husband and forfeiting her marriage settlement would have been devastating for a woman of those times. She would have been socially ostracized and left with no means to support herself. In the end, she may well have had the freedom to walk away from all this, but this freedom would have come with a high cost.

10. Rabbi Gershom ben Judah, best known as Rabbeinu Gershom, was a famous talmudist and halakhist who convened a synod around 1000 CE in which he instituted various laws and bans, including a prohibition of polygamy. This ban was accepted by Ashkenazi Jews. In modern times, Sefardi Jews have also given up the practice of polygamy.

11. Samet, "Sota."

then the waters test his wife. If the man is not clean of sin, the waters do not test his wife (Sotah 28a).

In Hilkhot Sotah 2:8, Rambam explains as follows: "If a man has ever had any illicit relations as an adult, then the waters that bring a curse will not test his wife.... As it is written, 'And the man shall be clean of sin, and that woman shall bear her iniquity': when the man is clean of sin, then the woman bears her iniquity." Rambam returns to this point later in his legal writings and expounds further:

> And all of these things apply only if the husband has never sinned himself (in this regard). But if he engaged in any illicit relations, then the waters do not test his wife, as we have explained. And if he did transgress and he makes his wife drink the water, this adds to his [previous] sin, for he causes God's Name to be blotted out in the water for no purpose, and he causes the waters of the Sotah to be cheapened, for his wife will tell others that she did engage in adultery and the water did not test her, and she will not know that it was her husband's deeds that caused this (Hilkhot Sotah 3:17–19).

While these legal positionings give us a more balanced and nuanced understanding of the Sotah narrative, they leave unanswered a fundamental question: Why a trial by ordeal? This is, after all, the only circumstance under which the Torah calls for a trial by ordeal.

Rabbi Samet believes that Ramban addresses this question. In his view, Ramban understands that the point of the ordeal is intended not to put at rest the mind of the husband who suspects his wife but to serve a broad, national purpose, namely, to cleanse the Jewish people from the suspicion of *mamzerut* (the status of children born of prohibited unions) "in order that they be worthy of God's presence dwelling among them."[12]

Ramban's explanation, however, fails to solve other difficulties concerning the uniqueness of this test, specifically, the need for a miracle in deciding a matter of law and the procedure involving the erasing of God's name. As Rabbi Samet observes:

> These two elements create the impression that making the Sotah drink the water is something that the Kohen is forced to do for lack of alternative. Indeed, in the Mishnah and Talmud, there is a noticeable trend towards avoiding this test wherever possible, either by means of having the woman confessing to her sin, or by her refusal to be tested—even without confessing. This

---

12. Samet, "Sota."

trend is incompatible with the explanation of Ramban that this miracle was performed "for Israel's glory, to make them a holy nation." To his view, it would seem that the more suspect women were tested, the greater the miracle and the greater the glory to the nation.[13]

Rabbi Samet goes on to resolve this difficulty with a beautiful insight. He posits that the need to decide the question of whether a woman suspected of adultery was actually defiled or not by means of a miracle has a simple explanation, one that involves the nature of the sin itself. Adultery is an act committed in secret, away from prying eyes. As such, it cannot typically be proven by witnesses. Without witnesses, it could not come before a court, and as a result, the sphere of adultery was almost completely removed from legal debate in biblical times. This leads Rabbi Samet to conclude:

> This has the effect of poisoning the relations of a couple where the husband suspects his wife, and has some basis for this suspicion, but he is unable—and will remain unable—to clarify the matter in the regular legal manner. The test initiated by the husband is meant to take the place of this legal discussion, which is almost always non-applicable. In this area where human law is helpless, and a dangerous rift may be caused in family relations, Divine law steps in as a replacement, thus healing the rift.[14]

There is an interesting yet depressing historical postscript to the Sotah story. Rabban Yochanan ben Zakai, who, according to tradition, lived from 30 BCE to 90 CE, was the leading scholar of his generation and is often thought of as "father of wisdom and the father of generations of scholars" because he ensured the continuation of Jewish scholarship after Jerusalem fell to Rome in 68 CE.[15] Yet, even while the Second Temple still stood, Rabbi Yochanan ben Zakai eliminated the Sotah ordeal entirely. "The Mishnah records that his motivation was the rampant frequency of male adultery, which made punishing the woman alone ludicrous. Tosefta Sotah, a collection of tannaitic statements rejected for inclusion in the Mishnah but often found in the Talmud, adds a more cynical reason: the adultery of the Sotah was performed in secret, in shame. By the time of the rabbis, adulterers were more brazen, seeing no reason to hide their deed. As a result, the use of a trial to ferret out adulterers was neither necessary nor a deterrent."[16]

13. Samet, "Sota."
14. Samet, "Sota."
15. Eisenberg, *Essential Figures*, 262.
16. Artson, "Sotah."

As an educator, I am not one to shy away from teaching difficult or complex material in a serious manner. Nevertheless, the story of the Sotah gives me pause. Over the years, I have taught classes of boys who were simply too immature or, worse still, just too sexist to handle this story. Too many of these young men would have said (or thought) things such as: "she asked for it" or "she had it coming." Such students truly need to grasp the lessons of the Sotah story, and I struggle to impart it to them using different materials and in different forums.

I have also taught classes of young women who were just too young for this material. Specifically, I would not teach it to girls in ninth or even tenth grade. However, there are some young women who cannot or will not go beyond a superficial reading of the narrative. They only see a story that is demeaning to women and are thus (understandably) unwilling to engage with the text through any other filter.

What I have laid out in this chapter is an approach I believe could work for either of these groups of students in the right circumstances and with the right teacher. It would certainly not be an easy instructional unit, but given the dangers of being overly judgmental, something we see far too often in our daily lives, it would be a most worthwhile learning experience.

Sefer BeMidbar—The Sotah
Sample Unit Plan

Unit	Primary Source(s)	Supplemental Reading(s)	Timeframe
The Sotah	Numbers 5	The Sotah (Samet)	two–three weeks
	Rashi 5:12		
Middah:	Siftei Hakhamim 5:12		
Being Non-Judgmental	Rashi 5:13	The Sotah (Weisz)	
	Sforno 5:13		
	Hizquni 5:13		
	Sforno 5:14		
	Sforno 5:15		
	Hizquni 5:20		
	Sforno 5:31		
	Hizquni 5:31		

Essential Questions

1. Why a trial by ordeal? What makes these circumstances so unique as to require heavenly intervention to adjudicate a legal matter?

2. Why does the Torah include a narrative that, at first glance, seems so demeaning to women?

3. Who is really being judged here?

Evaluating/Checking for Understanding

1. Daily discussions/student interactions

   Student questions and observations typically drive each day's discussion.

2. Occasional written reflections

   At the discretion of the teacher, a tool to foster further reflection on the unit's essential questions.

3. Character trait essay

   See appendix for assignment rubric.

4. Unit test

   Unit tests should, by definition, be crafted by individual teachers to meet the needs of their specific students. The Understanding by Design framework created by Grant Wiggins and Jay McTighe is an excellent tool for the development of appropriate tests and assessments, as its emphasis on backward design forces teachers to consider in advance the assessment evidence needed to document and validate that the targeted learning goals have been achieved.

Primary Source Texts

1. *BeMidbar* chapter 5: Read text and seek to identify problematic (what I call "red flag") words and phrases (with teacher's guidance, of course). These red flag words and phrases will likely vary from class to class depending on the sophistication and linguistic abilities of the students, coupled with the background and interests of the teacher. That said, some important examples of red flag words and phrases in this chapter appear in commentaries A–J.

2. Supplemental readings for each unit are intended to demonstrate that serious scholarship about and explanations of *Sefer BeMidbar* are not limited to the classical medieval commentators but continue to our time. The supplemental readings for this unit include: "The Sotah" by Rav Elchanan Samet and "The Sotah" by Rabbi Nosson Weisz. Both articles help clarify the role of the husband in this ordeal, especially the problems with him rushing to judgement of his wife. These articles are important tools for teaching the problems with being quick to judge others.

Sefer BeMidbar—The Sotah

Primary Texts

A. Rashi 5:12

"If any man's wife go aside [and act deceitfully against him]"

What is stated above, immediately before this section? "If you withhold the gifts due to the priest" (cf. Rashi on v. 10): by your life, you will have to come to him in order to bring him your faithless wife for the ordeal by the waters (Berakhot 63a). (The translation therefore is: "A man who remains with his holy things, not giving them to the priest, they—the man and his wife—will become subject to him [require his services])."

"Any man" [literally "a man, a man"]

The double expression "a man, a man" is employed to teach you that she (the faithless wife) deals treacherously in two respects—against Him above Who bears the appellation of "Man," as in the text "[the Lord is] a Man of the war" (Exodus 15:3), and against her husband here below.

"Should any man's wife go astray"

Our Rabbis have taught (Midrash Tanhuma, Naso 5): "Adulterers do never sin until a spirit of madness enters into them," as it written, of her כי תשטה "if she becomes mad" (taking תִשְׂטֶה in the sense of תִשְׁטֶה, i.e., to become a שׁוֹטֶה, and so, too, of him Scripture writes (Proverbs 6:32), "Who so commits adultery with a woman lacks understanding."—But the plain sense of the verse is that כי תשטה means: if she deviates from the path of modesty and thereby becomes suspect in his eyes. The word is similar to (Proverbs 4:15), "turn away (שְׂטֵה) from it, and pass by" and to (Proverbs 7:25) "Let not your heart turn (יֵשְׂטְ) to her ways."

"And she acts unfaithfully against him"

Wherein consists this infidelity? "That a man lie with her."

B. Siftei Hakhamim (on Rashi's first comment on 5:12)

What is written [immediately] above this subject? Normally Rashi only makes inferences from juxtapositions when matters are not written in their normal place, because then they were certainly written so for one to make an inference. Nonetheless, since there is no comparison between the laws of marriage and those of terumah and sanctified property, it is certain that they were only juxtaposed in order for one to make an inference. (*Gur Aryeh*) explains that [Rashi's inference] is not from the juxtaposition of the passages, because if this were so he should have said "why was the Parasha of the Sotah juxtaposed to that of sacred property," as is his normal style. Rather, Rashi was answering the question: The Parasha should not have begun with the man, rather with the woman—saying "a woman who goes astray and acts treacherously . . ." given that she was the source of the sin. Therefore he explains "what is written above . . ." meaning that *he* was the source of the sin and "any man" refers to the passage above. See there. (*Nachalat Yaakov*) The matter is puzzling—"Tuviah sinned and Zeigud was punished?" So too here—the husband sinned because he withheld the gifts to the kohanim and the woman was disgraced such that she had to come before the kohen! All the more so if she literally became defiled, it is difficult to understand how the sin of the husband could cause the sin of the wife. Rather, this is the correct explanation: The woman certainly has sins of her own and her sins caused the sin of promiscuity. Nonetheless if it were not for the combination of the sin of the husband with her sin of promiscuity, her sin would certainly have caused it to become publicized without the warning and seclusion. Thus the Beit Din would have killed her without causing disgrace to the husband, obliging him to bring her before the kohen and cause her to drink in order for her to die through the lethal waters. Instead, the combination with the sin of the husband caused there to be witnesses to the seclusion rather than witnesses to the defilement, and he had to bring her to the kohen in order to cause her to drink. Likewise, if she were to come away exonerated from the charge of promiscuity, had it not been for the combination with the husband's sin, the sin of the wife would have led to a simple rumor, without witnesses to her seclusion. Alternatively, there would have been only one witness to her defilement or she would have said that she would not drink—and in all of these cases one would not cause her to drink. Rather, here the combination with the sin of the husband caused him to have to bring her to the kohen in order to cause her to drink. (*Gur*

Aryeh) [One may ask:] It appears that this is not specific to the case of a Sotah, because had he been a zav or metzora he would also have needed a kohen, given that they too require a kohen. For if one did not say so, why should Sotah be different? One may answer that the cases of a zav or metzora are different. If he wanted to be a sinner and not bring an atonement, who would know? Thus he would not necessarily need a kohen. However with a Sotah, even a sinner would not wish his wife to be promiscuous, since it is the nature of people for this to be detestable, as the Torah writes "and he was jealous." And since he was jealous, he would certainly bring her before the kohen. When one appreciates this matter further, one will see that it is measure for measure. Since he did not wish to give the gifts to the kohen, asking why he should give his money to the kohen, the Torah said "By your life you will need him." You shall know the greatness of the kohen—that he is the intermediary between Hashem and Yisrael, making peace between them through the offerings. Yisrael are called Hashem's wife as it writes, "If you do not know, most beautiful of women" (Song of Songs 1:8) and in many other places where they are termed a wife. Therefore this man will now require a kohen to whom he will bring the Sotah, in order that he can also make peace between him and his wife. She strayed from him and the kohen would make peace between them. Surely this is exactly the same as when a kohen makes peace between Yisrael and their Father in Heaven, causing the Divine Presence to rest in the world. Similarly Rashi explains in Parashat Masei (Numbers 35:25) that Hashem is called a husband to Yisrael (see *Gur Aryeh* there). This man was one of them but he did not wish to recognize the greatness of the kohen, therefore he had to bring the Sotah to the kohen in order to make peace between himself and his wife.

C. Rashi 5:13

"[And a man lie] with her carnally"

This implies: that only her sexual intercourse with another man makes her unfit for continuing in marital relation with her husband, but the fact that her sister had sexual intercourse with him does not make her unfit for such (Yevamot 95a) [as was once the case with two sisters who greatly resembled each other (Tanhuma 5:2:6)].

"And it be hid from the eyes of her husband"

Since it speaks of the eyes of the husband, it excludes the case of a blind man (i.e., a blind man cannot subject his wife to the ordeal). On the other hand, it states: "if it be concealed from his eyes"; it follows therefore that if he sees her improper conduct and willfully closes his eyes to it the waters cannot try her (i.e., she cannot be subjected to the ordeal).

D. Sforno 5:13

"And another man has lain with her"

It is characteristic of the evil urge to cause the sinner to proceed from a relatively mild sin to ever more serious sins.

"And it be hid from the eyes of her husband"

Even though there had been indications of mistrust, jealousy, etc., her latest indiscretion remained hidden from the eyes of her husband. It is as if his eyes had been too weak to see what was going on. Had her husband been aware of her infidelity, the waters would not even have the power to bring this to light. Our sages have made this quite clear.

E. Hizquni 5:13

"And there was no witness against her"

Rashi comments on this phrase that we must contrast it with what the law would be if there had been a witness testifying against her. Even the testimony of a single witness would be enough not to let her drink the potentially disastrous waters. The line also means that whereas we do not have a witness that she had carnal relations with a man not her husband, we do have witnesses that she had hidden herself, so that she could have committed that sin easily. The grammatical construction here is similar to Leviticus 24:14: "they will (all) stone him"; the extra word אותו instead of the pronoun ending, i.e. ורגמוהו, teaches that he will be stoned naked, his clothing will not be stoned. Here, the word אותה means the reverse, i.e. while she was clothed (Talmud Sanhedrin, folio 45). There are numerous examples of such constructions in the Torah and the reason why extra letters were used to teach us certain halakhot, legal rulings. The word "even," in Rashi's commentary here, is clearly a printer's error. The Talmud in tractate Sotah, folio 3 has Rabbi Yishmael raise the question why in the case of this woman suspected of marital infidelity, the Torah chose to accept the testimony of a single witness at all? In answer it is suggested that there is some logic for such a procedure. This was a case where the husband had legitimate reason to suspect his wife of immoral conduct, and he had warned her not be alone with the person whom he suspects her of being too friendly with. His suspicions had been aroused because she had already once contravened his warnings and had been known to have been alone with the man in question after that warning. Moreover we have a statement in the Talmud tractate Ketubbot, folio 9, according to which: a woman (wife) is not forbidden for a husband to continue to have marital relations with on the basis of the testimony of a single witness, until we have two valid witnesses that can accuse her of having been unfaithful to her husband, and her husband had already been jealous of her and she had subsequently secluded herself with the man against whom her husband had warned her not to seclude herself. In commenting on this statement in the Talmud, Rashi writes that the Talmud cites an example when there was no witness at all that accused her of having had carnal relations, but that there had been witnesses to the husband expressing his jealousy, and her secreting herself with the man in question nonetheless. If however, there was one witness accusing her of additional seclusion, after all this, such a witness is sufficient. He bases himself on the words "against her" in our verse. In Rashi's opinion that word refers to testimony of carnal union [although there had not been two witnesses]. We read the line as if it had said; "there were no two witnesses against her but only one." In other words, the extent of the value of this one witness is for the accused woman not to have to drink the bitter waters in order to prove her innocence and the consequences if she had lied.

F. Sforno 5:14

"And she had not become defiled at all"

Nonetheless she disregarded her husband's warning and secluded herself with another man.

G. Sforno 5:15

"Then the man shall bring his wife"

In spite of this (i.e., she disregarded her husband's warning and secluded herself with another man), we do not say that seeing that her husband had sat by silently while his wife had behaved unchastely, accusing her in his heart without saying a word, that this is proof of the husband's bad attitude and we should therefore ignore his jealousy seeing he had allowed matters to get to the point where she had slept with another man; neither do we ignore his jealousy if she had not given him cause as something not worth paying attention to. We still subject her to the destruction (erasing) of the name of God (in the procedure the Torah will presently describe) in order to reveal the truth.

H. Hizquni 5:20

"But since you have strayed, etc."

The priest did not say to her: "if you have strayed," but he said to her that there was no question that she had strayed, the question was only to what extent she had strayed. She definitely deserved to have been shamed. Having caused her husband to suspect her, and having subsequently secreted herself with a man that her husband had specifically told her not to do, was disgraceful behavior, even if no intimacy had occurred

I. Sforno 5:31

"The man shall be absolved of iniquity"

Even though he had suspected his wife's fidelity. The reason is that by her conduct she had given him just cause for such suspicions. Had she not ignored his warnings things would not have come to such a pass. We have our sages in Shabbat 56 on record that David did not accept badmouthing which was designed to make Mephiboshet appear as having been disloyal to him. He rather based himself on visual evidence. [Note: this was Shmuel's interpretation in the Talmud in Shabbat of what had occurred. Rav disagrees with his assessment.]

"And the woman shall bear her iniquity"

That if she had been guilty of adultery she would die, and if not, her public embarrassment at undergoing the procedure as a punishment for having had the effrontery to ignore her husband's warning would be her punishment.

J. Hizquni 5:31

"Her iniquity"

The meaning of the word "iniquity" here is the same as the same word in 1 Samuel 28:10: "if in this matter you would become guilty of something, etc.";

King Saul absolves the witch of Endor in advance of her complying with his request. Once the moral standards of the Jewish people had declined so that the incidence of infidelity, adultery, was no longer a rare event, the practice of subjecting women accused of such to Divine intervention in order drink the bitter waters to clear her name was discontinued. This discontinuation was based on when the prophet Hosea (4:14) wrote (quoting God), "I will not punish your daughters for engaging in adultery." The Aramaic Translation ("the Targum") on this line translates the words "I will not punish," as if the prophet had said: "I will not examine if the accusation is justified" (by letting My Holy Name be dissolved in water).

Sefer BeMidbar—The Sotah
Supplemental Reading

The Sotah: (*BeMidbar* Perek 5:11–31)

—Rav Elchanan Samet

A. Unique Examination with Miraculous Results

> (27) And [the Kohen] shall make her drink the water, and it shall be that if she became defiled and betrayed her husband, then the water that brings a curse shall enter her and become bitter, and her stomach will swell and her thigh will fall away, and the woman shall become a curse among her people.
>
> (28) And if the woman was not defiled and she is pure, then she shall be free, and she shall conceive seed.

The Ramban notes the uniqueness of the examination of the woman with water—a procedure unlike any other in the Torah:

> And behold, nowhere in the laws of the Torah is there something that depends on a miracle except for this matter, which is a fixed wonder and miracle that is performed for Israel.

This law is unique in several respects. Firstly, the miracles in the Torah are generally performed for a great and public need: to verify the authenticity of a prophet, to bring salvation or punishment to a group—or to an individual of importance to a group. Nowhere in the Torah are miracles performed for individuals in a family situation, as in our parasha. But here we have a "FIXED wonder and miracle that is performed for Israel."

Secondly, the sphere in which the miracle takes place is altogether a legal one. The question of whether a woman has betrayed her husband is one with halakhic ramifications in several spheres. If the woman indeed committed adultery, and did so before witnesses and in the necessary circumstances, then she and the man involved must receive the death penalty (Leviticus 20:10). Furthermore, a woman who has betrayed her husband, even in the absence of witnesses, is forbidden to him thereafter and he must divorce her, but she is also then forbidden to the man with whom she committed adultery. Additionally, a woman who has committed adultery loses her right to her ketubah.

The problem arises in the case of a woman who is suspected of committing adultery—in circumstances that lend substance to this suspicion. What is to be done with the woman in each of the spheres described above? Is this not a question that should be clarified and ruled by a court?

The Sages (Bava Metzi'a 59b) declare that "the Torah is not in heaven." As Rabbi Yirmiya explains, "Since the Torah was given at Mt. Sinai, we pay no attention to heavenly voices [in legal matters], for God already wrote in the Torah, given at Mt. Sinai, 'You shall follow the majority' [of sages]."

Admittedly, the doubt that arises in our parasha surrounds not the proper halakhic ruling, but rather the facts of the case themselves—was the woman defiled or not? However, ultimately the question is one that boils down to a legal ruling, and here, instead of the court passing a ruling, as it would in any other legal matter, the question is decided by means of a miracle, with the involvement of a Kohen.

Thirdly, in verse 23 the Kohen is commanded to "write these curses in a book and shall erase them with the bitter water" and the Mishnah (Sotah 2:3) determines that the words to be erased include God's Name. Yet in Deuteronomy (12:2–4), as interpreted by the Sifri, we learn that there is a prohibition against erasing God's Name. Thus, the command to the Kohen to erase the curses that he has written—including God's Name—contradicts a prohibition in the Torah.

We may therefore summarize the problems that arise from this law of examining the Sotah with water as follows: THE VERY NEED FOR A FIXED MIRACLE in a private family matter, THE SPHERE IN WHICH THE MIRACLE TAKES PLACE—the clarification of a halakhic matter, and THE WAY IN WHICH THE MIRACLE IS PERFORMED—through an act that is prohibited. Each of these elements defines the uniqueness of this law.

B. The Ordeal

Although "nowhere in THE LAWS OF THE TORAH is there something that depends on a miracle except for this matter," among the laws of the nations it was quite common for various legal matters to be clarified through non-rational and supernatural means. The special term used by anthropologists for such clarifications is "ordeal." Prof. Yaakov Licht z"l, in his article "Examination of the Sotah by Ordeal" (Mechkarim ba-Mikra, 5747 [Hebrew]), reviews the customs of ordeal among the various cultures from antiquity until our times as background to his discussion of the examination of the Sotah.

The purpose of the ordeal is to clarify whether a person suspected of a crime is guilty or not. This is accomplished by means of a supernatural sign that involves the body of the subject. The most common form of ordeal was an examination using hot iron: the suspect would hold an iron pole upon his hands, or would tread on it barefoot. In the instructions for performing the ordeal it was set down how the burn should be dressed and how it should be examined after a few days: if the burn had begun to heal nicely, the suspect was declared innocent. Licht writes:

> In one respect, the test of the Sotah differs from most of the ordeals that I found in historical testimonies . . .: the suspect is not tested with something that would usually cause harm, but rather by drinking water containing a little dust and ink . . . without poison in it. This is a type of ordeal in which something that is not harmful by nature comes to cause harm, to prove the subject's guilt . . . No harm will come to a woman suspected of adultery who is not guilty . . . because according to nature there is no danger present here from the start.

This difference is of great significance; it differentiates between the test of the Sotah with water and most of the ordeals practiced by other nations—in terms of the reliability of the examination, as well as in human and religious terms.

a. An ordeal by something that causes harm, such as a red-hot iron, creates real (and justified) fear in the heart of the subject, perhaps causing him to confess to a deed even if he is not guilty of it—just to save himself from having to undergo the cruel examination.

b. The ordeal by something harmful generally harms everyone who is subjected to it, and the determination of guilt depends on the degree of harm or the subject's success in recovering from the damage quickly.

Thus there is no clear and unequivocal distinction between a subject who is guilty and one who is innocent.

c. The ordeal physically harms even a suspect who is innocent, even if the examiner declares the subject's innocence.

d. The "miraculous" element of the ordeal has a partially rational explanation.

In contrast to the above, the test of the Sotah by water is not located in the blurred midway between miracle and nature. The water by means of which the woman is tested, containing a tiny amount of dust and some blotted ink, does not by nature have the power to determine her guilt. When this test reveals the guilt of the woman, there is a dramatic and clearly miraculous demonstration of Divine involvement that has no rational explanation, and it is completely independent of any interpretation by the Kohen.

Despite these fundamental differences, Licht rightly asserts that "the test of the Sotah is the only explicit 'ordeal' in the Torah," and he lists the characteristics of the test that indicate its definition as an ordeal:

> Firstly, we have here the main marker [of an ordeal]: the request for an impressive sign from God. Secondly, there are several characteristic signs: the absence of witnesses and proof is emphasized in the text (verse 13); the test determines only the question of fact . . .; the test is complex, requiring symbols that are part of the Temple service, actions that are calculated to influence the emotions of the subject, and impressive statements by the Kohen. All of these are common among the regular ordeals of various cultures. Even the oath that the woman must take falls into this category . . . for the ordeal is fundamentally connected to the oath, and an oath is always present in an ordeal.

Licht's work allows us to reformulate the second question posed in the previous section. It is possible that the Sages' opposition to halakhic rulings being based upon heavenly signs was their reaction to the custom of ordeals that was prevalent in the legal systems of many other nations. In other words, a miracle does not constitute proof in a legal debate. The law of testing the Sotah is unique in its very similarity to the "ordeal" practiced by other nations (despite all the fundamental differences), and this is an additional wonder on top of all the others mentioned previously.

C. Ramban's Explanation for the Uniqueness of This Law

A mitzvah so exceptional and surprising requires some explanation. The Ramban addresses principally the first question presented in section a. above, concerning the very need for a miracle to decide a private, family question. According to his explanation, the point of the miracle is not to put at rest the mind of the husband who suspects his wife, nor any other limited family purpose, but rather a broad, national one: "To cleanse Israel from [the suspicion of] *mamzerut* (the status of children born of prohibited unions), IN ORDER THAT THEY BE WORTHY OF THE SHEKHINA DWELLING AMONG THEM." He brings proof of a hint at the broader national context of this miracle from the Mishnah: "When the number of those who engaged in adultery increased, the [practice involving the] bitter waters ceased." When adultery became widespread, the merit of the nation of Israel was diminished, and they were no longer worthy of having such a great miracle performed for them.

The Ramban's explanation, however, fails to solve the other difficulties concerning the uniqueness of this test: the need for a miracle in deciding a matter of Torah law, and the procedure involving the erasing of God's Name. These two elements create the impression that making the Sotah drink the water is something that the Kohen is forced to do, for lack of alternative. Indeed, in the Mishnah and Talmud there is a noticeable trend towards avoiding this test wherever possible, either by means of having the woman confessing to her sin, or by her refusal to be tested - even without confessing (we shall discuss this option below). This trend is incompatible with the explanation of the Ramban that this miracle was performed "for Israel's glory, to make them a holy nation." To his view, it would seem that the more suspect women were tested, the greater the miracle and the greater the glory to the nation.

The uniqueness of the test of the Sotah can be explained in a positive way—as a great and unique merit attached to the nation of Israel, as the Ramban understood it. It can also be understood in a negative way—as a concession by the Torah for unusual actions and procedures to be undertaken because of various special circumstances. The questions presented above would seem to point in the latter direction.

D. Helplessness of Human Law in Dealing with Adultery

The need to decide by means of a miracle the question of whether a woman suspected of adultery was actually defiled or not, has a simple explanation: the sin of adultery, by nature, is not usually able to be proven by witnesses.

It is committed in secret, and therefore it is extremely rare that such a case would come before a court. As a result, the sphere of adultery is almost completely removed from legal debate. This has the effect of poisoning the relations of a couple where the husband suspects his wife, and has some basis for this suspicion, but he is unable—and will remain unable—to clarify the matter in the regular legal manner.

The test initiated by the husband is meant to take the place of this legal discussion, which is almost always non-applicable. In this area where human law is helpless, and a dangerous rift may be caused in family relations, Divine law steps in as a replacement, thus healing the rift.

E. Laws of the Sotah according to Chazal

The parasha of the Sotah is one of the parashot of the Torah where a noticeable discrepancy exists between the impression created by a "simple reading" and the perception of Chazal—the halakhic perception, as molded in the Mishnah, the Talmud and ultimately the final and binding halakhic ruling.

The "simple reading" would suggest that the parasha presents a woman who has met privately with a man, and her husband suspects that she was defiled through that encounter, but he has no proof, nor are there any witnesses who can testify. The husband is seized by a "spirit of jealousy," and in order to clarify his suspicion and to ease his jealousy he brings his wife to the Kohen in the *Mishkan*. His suspicion is tested there in a ceremony that causes the woman great humiliation and unpleasantness—even if she is innocent. According to a literal reading, it appears that this ceremony is forced upon the woman, and no one asks her opinion. It seems that from the outset she maintains that she bears no guilt, and she obviously has no wish to undergo such an unpleasant procedure simply because of the "jealous spirit" that has seized her husband.

The impression created by this reading is of a clearly one-sided position adopted by the Torah in favor of the husband, at the expense of the wife. The "jealous spirit" that overcomes the husband is the driving force behind the process described in the parasha, while the factual basis for his suspicion is quite flimsy. It is the husband himself who claims that his wife met privately with a man, and even if this is true, this does not mean that she was defiled. The entire process is based on the husband's claims, and it looks to us as though the parasha takes into consideration only his subjective view, while sacrificing the woman on the altar of his jealousy in order to ease it (or, alternatively, to justify it).

Before presenting the halakhic perception of our parasha, it should be remembered that the Torah permits a man to marry several wives, while allowing a woman to be married only to one man. Therefore, a man does not "betray" his wife, since he is permitted to marry other wives in addition to her, and for this reason the parasha addresses only a husband's suspicion of his wife. But while there is no symmetry between a man and a woman in this sphere, the husband's claim of infidelity on the part of his wife does not free him from similar claims. The closing verse of our parasha served Chazal as the basis to make the husband's right to demand a test for his wife conditional upon his own moral record. We find in a beraita (Sotah 28a):

> "And the man shall be clean of sin, and that woman shall bear her iniquity" (verse 31)—when the man is clean of sin, then the waters test his wife. If the man is not clean of sin, the waters do not test his wife.

The Rambam explains (Hilkhot Sotah 2:8):

> If a man HAS EVER HAD ANY ILLICIT RELATIONS as an adult, then the waters that bring a curse will not test his wife ... As it is written, "And the man shall be clean of sin, and that woman shall bear her iniquity": when the man is clean of sin, then the woman bears her iniquity.

The Rambam returns to this point later (3:17–19):

> And all of these things apply only if the husband has never sinned himself (in this regard). But if he engaged in any illicit relations, then the waters do not test his wife, as we have explained. And if he did transgress and he makes his wife drink the water, this adds to his [previous] sin, for he causes God's Name to be blotted out in the water for no purpose, and he causes the waters of the Sotah to be cheapened, for his wife will tell others that she did engage in adultery and the water did not test her, and she will not know that it was her husband's deeds that caused this. FOR THIS REASON, WHEN THE NUMBER OF THOSE WHO ENGAGED OPENLY IN ADULTERY DURING THE SECOND TEMPLE PERIOD INCREASED, THE SANHEDRIN CANCELLED THE PRACTICE OF THE BITTER WATER....

Another claim that requires addressing is that the woman who is cursed by the water and is revealed as having been defiled, did not sin alone: she had a partner in crime. As we know, a man and a woman are equal when it comes to punishment for forbidden sexual relations, as is stated explicitly in our case (Leviticus 20:10), "man who commits adultery with a married woman ... the adulterer and the adulteress shall surely die." Why, then, does the parasha of Sotah deal only with the woman, while her partner in crime seems to suffer no consequences at all?

The Halakha nullifies this lack of symmetry. Mishnah Sotah (5:1) teaches: "Just as the water tests her, so does it test him." The Gemara (28a) brings various derivations for this law, explaining that the bitter waters will affect him, too, no matter where he may be.

Having presented the above introduction, we may now look at the Halakha's approach to the topic of Sotah in general terms. Firstly, it must be pointed out that according to Halakha, the man's demand that his wife be tested is approved only against a clearly defined legal background; under no circumstances is such a claim addressed when his jealousy has no evidentiary support. The main exegetical innovation of the Halakha in our parasha concerns verse 14:

> And he is overcome with a spirit of jealousy, and he is jealous for his wife ....

This "spirit of jealousy" is not a description of a feeling that suddenly attacks the husband AFTER his wife has secluded herself with another man, but rather a description of an act with legal significance, which is performed PRIOR to her secluding herself with him. Rashi interprets the verse as follows:

> "And he is overcome"—prior to the seclusion, "with a spirit of jealousy, and he is jealous ..."—our Sages explained: this is an expression of warning, [with the husband] telling the wife: Do not seclude yourself with so-and-so.

What causes the husband to warn his wife in this way? It may be his suspicion of the man involved, or of the relationship between his wife and that man, or rumors and murmurings among his neighbors. In any event, this warning must be given in front of two witnesses, as the Rambam rules at the beginning of Hilkhot Sotah, on the basis of the first Mishnah in Sotah:

> The jealousy about which the Torah speaks—"and he is jealous for his wife"—means that he tells her, before witnesses: Do not seclude yourself with so-and-so.

Rashi explains the continuation of verse 14 as follows:

> "And she was defiled, or he was overcome ... and she was not defiled"—in other words, he warned her and she subsequently

acted against his warning, and it is not known whether she was defiled or not.

In other words, the "seclusion" that was discussed in verse 13 occurs only AFTER his official warning to her before witnesses, and only if she secludes herself with the specific man her husband mentioned.

What halakhic situation is created by this jealousy and this seclusion? We are no longer dealing with an incidental encounter between the woman and a man other than her husband, which gives rise to the latter's jealousy. Rather, this is a seclusion with a man who is already suspected by the husband with regard to his wife. The suspicion was strong enough that the husband already warned his wife, in front of two witnesses, not to seclude herself with that man. The woman acted against this stern warning and did indeed seclude herself with the man concerned, for a period of time that would make it possible for her to have been defiled.

It is no wonder that under these circumstances, the husband's suspicion of his wife is formulated almost as a certainty (verses 12–13):

> A man, if his wife acts foolishly and betrays him ... and a man lies with her and gives seed, and the matter is hidden from her husband for she was secluded, and she was defiled but there is no witness....

But this is the question that the rest of the parasha goes on to examine: whether the situation described in these verses actually took place. Why, then, is the suspicion described here as a certainty? The answer is that the circumstances of this seclusion are so serious that it is not unreasonable to assume that the event did take place.

The halakhic result of all this is, as the Rambam rules:

> If she was secluded with him for long enough to become defiled ... THEN SHE IS FORBIDDEN TO HER HUSBAND UNTIL SUCH TIME AS SHE DRINKS THE BITTER WATER AND THE MATTER IS CLARIFIED. And at a time when the water of the Sotah is no longer in use—she is forbidden to him forever, and she leaves [the marriage] without her ketubah.

Let us now return to the "simple reading" and ask: what happens if a woman secluded herself with a man and remained there for long enough to become defiled, without her husband's jealousy first being aroused? Thus rules the Rambam (1:4–5):

> If there was no prior jealousy, and two witnesses come and testify that she secluded herself with a man and remained there

long enough to become defiled, SHE IS NOT FORBIDDEN TO HER HUSBAND, NOR DOES SHE DRINK [the water].

Moreover:

> If the husband said to her, before two witnesses, "Do not speak to so-and-so" (but did not say "Do not seclude yourself")—this is not defined as jealousy [for the purposes of this law]. And then, even if she secludes herself with that man, and there were witnesses, and she remained long enough to become defiled—she is not forbidden to her husband, and she does not drink for this type of jealousy.

It should be clarified here that the words, "She does not drink," mean that the husband cannot bring her to the Kohen, and the Kohen may not make her drink. This instance is not what the parasha of Sotah is discussing!

Let us now examine the event to which the halakha refers in the parasha of Sotah. A couple has arrived at such a crisis in their relationship that they are unable to continue living together. What are the possibilities that are open to them, from the point of view of Halakha? The husband may, of course, decide that he no longer wishes to be married, and may divorce her (with payment of the wife's ketubah, if he is not prepared to clarify his suspicions through the test of the water). The wife, likewise, may decide that she is not prepared to be tested, and thus brings the marriage to an end, as Rambam rules (2:1):

> A woman whose husband was jealous for her and she secluded herself—she is not forced to drink. If she confesses and declares, "Yes, I was defiled," she goes out without her ketubah, and is forbidden to her husband forever, and does not drink. [But she and the adulterer are not put to death because there are no witnesses to the actual sin.]
>
> Likewise IF SHE SAYS, "I AM NOT DEFILED, AND I SHALL NOT DRINK," SHE IS NOT FORCED TO DRINK, and she goes out without her ketubah [since her husband is ready to remain with her if she agrees to the test].
>
> And likewise if the husband says, "do not wish for her to drink"... then she does not drink; she receives her ketubah and leaves, and she is forbidden to him forever.

But what if both of them—the husband and the wife—wish to continue living together, and to repair their relationship? The Torah allows for such a possibility: a test through the waters of the Sotah. Only on the basis of this test can the woman once again be permitted to her husband, if she is found to be innocent, and the family has a chance of being rehabilitated.

This test, then, is performed only upon the joint wish of both the husband and wife; each of them may prevent the performance of the test if he or she does not want it. This reality is far from the impression created by the literal reading, according to which the husband forces the test on his wife against her wishes. According to Halakha, however, only if she is prepared to undergo this procedure of her own free will is it carried out. The woman will be willing to do so out of her desire to continue living with her husband, and out of the knowledge that she was not defiled.

Can the woman change her mind once the process has already begun? Not only is she able to change her mind, but she is even encouraged to do so. The encouragement is, admittedly, mostly towards her confessing to having been defiled, but even if she simply declares, "I shall not drink," without confessing, she is allowed to stop the process (Rambam 3:2).

Once she has declared, "I shall not drink," is she entitled to change her mind and to request the continuation of the process? Rambam rules (4:3):

> A Sotah who says, "I shall not drink" out of fear and intimidation, may change her mind and say, "I shall drink."

However, there is a limit, after which the woman can no longer turn back, unless she admits that she was defiled:

> If she says, "I shall not drink," before the scroll [with the curses] is blotted out, then the scroll is put away ... and her mincha offering is sprinkled over the ashes of the altar. But if she says, "I shall not drink," after the scroll has already been blotted out, she is forced to drink the water, and is threatened that she must drink, and she is told: "My daughter, if it is clear to you that you are pure, then stand still and drink and do not fear" ... If she says, "I am impure," then although the scroll is already blotted out, the water is poured out, since it contains no sanctity, and her mincha offering is sprinkled over the ashes. (Rambam 4:4–6)

What, then, is the meaning of the expression, "She is forced to drink the water"? Is it because the scroll has already been blotted out and we do not wish for this blotting of God's Name to be for no purpose? From Rashi's interpretation of the beraita that serves as the source for this law of the Rambam (Sotah 7b), we learn a different reason:

> After [the scroll] is blotted out, they tell her words of comfort, to drink if she is innocent, IN ORDER TO MAKE HER PERMISSIBLE TO HER HUSBAND, in order that she will not fear

the water and say, "I am defiled" if she is actually pure, thereby disgracing herself and her children.

In other words, we assume that the woman has changed her mind at this stage out of fear of the water in which the words of the curses have been blotted out, and not because she is truly defiled. For this reason she is made to drink against her will—for her own good, in order to make her permissible to her husband, and to prevent rumors from spreading about her. And now, after the woman has drunk:

> If she is pure, she leaves and goes, AND SHE IS PERMITTED TO HER HUSBAND ... A Sotah who drank and is [found to be] innocent, is strengthened, and her face shines, and if she had any illness—it leaves her, and she is able to become pregnant and bears a son ... (Rambam 3:16, 22)

F. "Great Is the Value of Peace between Husband and Wife"

Chazal's perception of the parasha of Sotah, as described above in general terms, resolved—to their view—one of the great questions surrounding this parasha, which was particularly difficult for them: the blotting out of God's Name in the scroll. We read in the Gemara (Hullin 141a):

> Mar said: GREAT IS THE VALUE OF PEACE BETWEEN HUSBAND AND WIFE, for the Torah says: the Name of the Holy One, written in holiness, is blotted out in the water!

We may perhaps broaden this statement and thereby answer our other questions. "Great is the value of peace between husband and wife"—this explains why a miracle is required here, and why we use this miracle in a halakhic context. In order to understand this great need, we must return to the background of the test of the Sotah: a man and his wife encounter a tragic crisis that threatens the continuation of their marriage. They wish to continue living together peacefully, but this is impossible, both because of the husband's grave suspicion that his wife has betrayed him, and because this very suspicion makes the woman forbidden to him until the matter is clarified.

How, then, is this marriage to be saved? In the very difficult situation in which the couple finds itself—after the woman has secluded herself with a man concerning whom her husband has previously warned her, before witnesses, not to seclude herself—the woman's declaration of her innocence is not sufficient. Neither her husband nor the court can accept this claim against the heavy suspicion that rests on the woman, and even a regular oath will not suffice. In order to make her permissible to her husband and to allow her to return to him, a factual test is required that no human legal system can provide. This test is what will make the woman's oath as to her innocence altogether reliable.

Against this background, we can understand why the Torah goes out of its way in offering the woman and her husband a test that is based on a miracle. Only this procedure can, in these circumstances, allow for faith to be entrusted once again, for the woman to return to her husband, and for their "shalom bayit" to be restored.

Rav Elchanan Samet is a lecturer at Herzog College and is affiliated with Yeshivat Har Etzion. He has published three series of commentaries on the Torah as well as a number of other books on Bible and Rambam.

Sefer BeMidbar—The Sotah

Supplemental Reading

The Sotah

—Rabbi Noson Weisz

One of the laws discussed in Parshat Naso is known as the law of the Sotah, which describes how a Jewish court is meant to deal with an adulterous woman. (Numbers 5:12–31)

If a woman is accused of adultery by her husband, and there are serious grounds for suspicion, she is given a choice: accept a divorce or stand up to a strange test. The test, if she opts for it, requires her to drink "bitter waters" into which the name of God had been dissolved. If she is guilty, she dies instantaneously.

If we could hold a contest to determine the most misunderstood commandment in the Torah, then the law of the Sotah would have to be declared the hands-down winner.

The chief problem lies in the mistaken idea that this law is meant to put down women. But this is far from the case. As in everything else, the truth is in the details.

First let's set the record straight as to the facts:

Setting the Record Straight

While it is the accused woman who must actually drink the bitter waters, the waters affect her male partner in adultery identically. Just as the waters examine her, they also examine him. (Talmud, Sotah 27b)

What is more, the Torah awards the power of decision to the woman rather than to the man who must share her fate. She is not forced to drink the bitter waters at all. She can admit to adultery and accept a divorce. The truth is she doesn't even have to admit to anything. She just has to refuse to drink the bitter waters on any grounds at all. She can say she has too much anxiety; she can say she would rather lose money than cause the holy name of God to be rubbed out; she can say she can't live with such a suspicious husband anyway etc. All she loses if she chooses not to drink is her *ketubah*, her marriage settlement, merely a monetary loss. She is free to marry anyone, and walk away from the entire mess totally unencumbered.

The man, on the other hand, is at her mercy. If she professes her innocence and insists on drinking the waters it will avail him naught to admit to his guilt. As long as she decides to drink, if the water kills her, it will kill him too.

In general Jewish law treats both parties to adultery in precisely the same fashion. Whatever is a punishable offense for the female is the same for the male.

God's Cooperation

Nachmanides points out that of all the 613 commandments, it is only the Sotah law that requires God's specific co-operation to make it work. The bitter waters can only be effective miraculously. The Torah assures guilty adulterers that their horrible deaths will follow the drinking of the waters instantaneously, and it promises the innocent woman who was wrongfully accused and elected to go through the humiliating Sotah experience to demonstrate her innocence that she will conceive a child even if she is barren.

In fact, the Talmud says that Chana, the prophet Samuel's mother, and a prophetess in her own right, who was barren, threatened God that if He would not help her to conceive through her prayers she would make herself into a Sotah and force Him into helping her anyway. (Berakhot 31b)

The Sotah law is also the only commandment whose fulfillment requires the erasure of God's name, an act that is ordinarily forbidden and punishable by the administration of lashes. The commentators all explain that the stakes involved in Jewish family purity and the preservation of marital trust that serves as its foundation are so high, that God is willing to tolerate the erasure of His own name, as well as to depart from His ordinary policy of conducting the world according to the rules of nature in order to restore domestic trust and marital peace.

Thus, anyone who is skeptical about the existence of God or about the fact that He intervenes in human lives can safely assume that the entire Sotah story as it is described in the Talmud never happened at all. On the other hand, anyone who accepts the truth of Torah as interpreted by the sages cannot fail to be moved by God's obvious concern for the sanctity of a Jewish marriage.

Every miracle is an outright violation of the Divine policy to remain hidden behind natural phenomena and stay out of man's way, so as not to disturb the unhampered exercise of free will. Yet, whereas the holiest rabbis or the greatest tragedies cannot persuade God to alter this policy of concealment, every Jewish Sotah had the power to force God to come right out into the open.

The Sotah law is the diametric opposite of discrimination against the Jewish woman. It emphasizes her supremacy in the all-important area of family purity. When it comes to these issues the Jewish male is a mere appendage.

> While studying at the famed yeshivas of Chaim Berlin, Lakewood, and the Mir in Jerusalem, **Rabbi Noson Weisz** also received a degree in microbiology from the University of Toronto, a MA in political science at the New School for Social Research, and his LLB from the University of Toronto. Rabbi Weisz is currently a senior lecturer at Yeshiva Aish HaTorah in Jerusalem.

Chapter 11

The Nazirite

IN THE 1970S AND 1980S, Billy Joel was a dominant force in the music industry. During those years, he won five Grammys, including album of the year for 52nd *Street* and song of the year and record of the year for "Just the Way You Are." Joel was inducted into the Rock and Roll Hall of Fame in 1999, and, as recently as 2017, was still doing live performances every month in New York's Madison Square Garden to sold-out audiences.

Yes, I am a fan, and one of my favorite songs of his is entitled "I Go To Extremes."[1] In the chorus of the song, the singer repeatedly states that he does not know "why I go to extremes." For Joel, at least in this song, "too high or too low, there ain't no in-betweens." No middle ground. It's all or nothing. Or, said differently perhaps, it's my way or the highway. When thinking about *Sefer BeMidbar*, especially the narrative of the Nazirite, I am often reminded of this song. Without doubt, the Nazirite does go to extremes, but how so? Let's take a look at the pertinent section of chapter 6 in the book of Numbers.

> The Lord spoke to Moses, saying: Speak to the Israelites and say to them: If anyone, man or woman, explicitly utters a Nazirite's vow, to set himself apart for the Lord, he shall abstain from wine and any other intoxicant; he shall not drink vinegar of wine or of any other intoxicant, neither shall he drink anything in which grapes have been steeped, nor eat grapes fresh or dried. Throughout his term as Nazirite, he may not eat anything that is obtained from the grapevine, even seeds or skin. Throughout the term of his vow as Nazirite, no razor shall touch his head; it shall remain consecrated until the completion of his term as Nazirite of the Lord, the hair of his head being left to grow untrimmed. Throughout the term that he has set apart for the

---

1. This song, which describes the ups and downs of the singer's life, was released in 1989 on *Storm Front*, which was the eleventh studio album by Joel.

Lord, he shall not go in where there is a dead person. Even if his father or mother, or his brother or sister, should die, he must not defile himself for them, since hair set apart for his God is upon his head: throughout his term as Nazirite he is consecrated to the Lord (Numbers 6:1–8).

Not eating grapes or drinking wine does not seem so extreme or radical, nor does avoiding haircuts. Yet it is hard not so see extremism in one who sets himself (or herself) apart from the community, because being part of the community is a core Jewish value, as Hillel famously taught: "Do not separate yourself from the community" (Avot 2:5).

From a Jewish perspective, how does community involvement manifest itself? Rabbi Yisrael Lipschutz enumerates five aspects of communal identification, three of which reflect fairly obvious points.[2] "The three include not deviating from communal customs, empathizing with their pain even if you personally escaped some widespread communal suffering, and not turning to God with individual requests, but instead beseeching God with supplication for all those in similar need."[3] Interestingly, Rabbi Lipschutz goes on to describe a meeting to plan a communal project. Maybe it is to promote Torah study, prayer, charity, or some other collective need—the details are unimportant. What matters is one's sense of community, for, in Rabbi Lipschutz's view, a person should not say "Let the community decide whatever it wants, and I will be content either way," but one should add their voice to the discussion and participate in this communal conversation. Why? Does not agreeing to go along with whatever the community decides indicate flexibility and selflessness? Apparently not, since "it can also reveal a negative desire to avoid involvement and a failure to contribute to communal discourse. Not taking a stand may not come from a place of easy accommodation, but from apathy towards communal concerns."[4]

The question the talmudic sages and later commentators on the Torah wrestle with is whether the extremism of the Nazirite (clearly his or her defining character trait) is a positive or negative attribute—an odd question given the sages' view on the importance of community. The key phrase from the Nazirite narrative that drives their deliberations is the one that speaks of a person setting "himself apart for the Lord." In their efforts to evaluate that actions of the Nazirite, these rabbis looked not only to the laws of the

---

2. Rabbi Israel Lipschutz, who lived from 1782 to 1860, served as rabbi of two important German communities, Dessau and then Danzig. He was the author of *Tiferet Yisrael*, a well-known commentary on the Mishnah.

3. Quoted in Leff, "Do Not Separate Yourself."

4. Leff, "Do Not Separate Yourself."

Nazirite in *Sefer BeMidbar* but also to individuals whom history records as having been Nazirites.

The best-known Nazirite in the Bible, Samson, ironically never took this upon himself, as we see in chapter 13 of Judges.

> The Israelites again did what was offensive to the Lord, and the Lord delivered them into the hands of the Philistines for forty years. There was a certain man from Zorah, of the stock of Dan, whose name was Manoah. His wife was barren and had borne no children. An angel of the Lord appeared to the woman and said to her, "You are barren and have borne no children; but you shall conceive and bear a son. Now be careful not to drink wine or other intoxicant, or to eat anything unclean. For you are going to conceive and bear a son; let no razor touch his head, for the boy is to be a Nazirite to God from the womb on. He shall be the first to deliver Israel from the Philistines" (Judges 13:1–5).

Samson is the last of the judges mentioned in the book bearing this same name. In addition to being a Nazirite, he was given immense strength by the Lord to aid him against his enemies and allow him to perform remarkable (some would say superhuman) feats, including slaying a lion with his bare hands and massacring an entire army of Philistines using only the jawbone of an ass. As even the most casual student of the Bible knows, Samson was betrayed by his lover, Delilah, who had his hair cut while he was sleeping and then turned him over to his Philistine enemies. His eyes gouged out and forced to grind grain in a mill at Gaza, Samson prays to God to restore his strength. He does, and Samson dies a martyr's death when he tears down the columns of a pagan temple, thereby killing all his Philistine enemies.

While better known, Samson may not be the only important biblical figure who was a Nazirite. The last mishnah of tractate Nazir (chapter 9, mishnah 5) deals with the question of whether Samuel, the biblical prophet, was a Nazirite. Rabbi Nehorai argues that he was, based on the verse, "And no razor [*morah*] shall come upon his head" (1 Samuel 1:11). Rabbi Nehorai points out that the Bible uses the same word in reference to Samson when it states: "let no razor [*morah*] touch his head" (Judges 13:5). To him, this demonstrates that just as one (Samson) was a Nazirite, so, too, was the other (Samuel).

Rabbi Yose disagrees, maintaining that *morah* does not mean "razor" in the case of Samuel but refers to fear of flesh and blood. This would mean that the previously cited verse does not read, "and no razor [*morah*] shall come upon his head," but rather "and no fear [*morah*] shall come upon his head." In response, Rabbi Nehorai notes that with regards to Samuel the verse says, "How can I [Samuel] go? If Saul will hear it he will kill me" (1 Samuel 16:2). To Rabbi Nehorai, this shows that Samuel was indeed afraid of flesh and blood.

How are we to understand this mishnah? As we have often done, we need to look very carefully at the biblical verses themselves.

When Samuel's mother Hannah prays to God to give her a child, she promises that if she does have a male child, no "*morah* shall ever touch his head." The obvious contextual meaning seems clear. When Samson's mother was promised that she would have a child, she was commanded that "no razor shall touch his head." Similarly, when told she would bear a son, Hannah promises that "no razor shall touch his head." Just as one is a Nazirite, so, too, is the other. This is Rabbi Nehorai's argument.

However, unlike Samson's mother, Hannah does not promise to impose the other two Nazirite prohibitions upon her son: the prohibition against becoming defiled through contact with the dead and the prohibition against consuming (eating or drinking) anything from the vine. Moreover, Samuel is never subsequently referred to as a Nazirite, nor does he seem to act as one. Therefore, Rabbi Yose interprets the Hebrew word *morah* to refer to fear. Hannah does not declare Samuel to be a Nazirite. She merely promises that he will not be afraid of anyone.

Here, then, is the crux of the dispute. While the word *morah* can mean "fear," the simple meaning of the word in the verses we have considered seems to be "razor." Rabbi Yose interprets it to mean "fear" because there is no textual evidence that Samuel was a Nazirite. Rabbi Nehorai rejects this position by pointing out that it simply does not fit with the facts of Samuel's life. Samuel did fear Saul, as the text attests. Therefore, the word *morah* must mean "razor," and Samuel must have actually been a Nazirite.

This dispute continues through later sources. For example, a fragmentary scroll found among the Dead Sea Scrolls at Qumran has a version of 1 Samuel 1:22 that reads "he will be a Nazirite for good, for all his life" instead of the traditional reading: "[For when he has appeared before the Lord], he must remain there for good." In the Wisdom of Ben Sira, a second century BCE text, we find a reference to Samuel, a prophetic Nazirite (46:3). The Septuagint, the third century BCE translation of the Bible into Greek, adds to verse 11 "and he shall not drink wine or strong drink." Josephus, too, states that Samuel did not drink wine. All of this highlights the strong trend in Second Temple Judaism to view Samuel as a Nazirite."[5]

This trend is consistent with research on Nazirite vows and practices. Scholars have noted that the Nazirite phenomenon was widespread in the

---

5. Kulp, "Nazir."

Second Temple period. Some maintain that "there is no sense in limiting its proliferation to the last generation immediately preceding the destruction of the Temple simply for lack of information, as Büchler does. The Talmud testifies to the inclination of the 'first Hasids' to maintain it. Nazirites gathered in Judas Maccadaeus' camp during times of stress and rebellion, as described by 1 Maccabees (III 49). From the time of Yose ben Yoezer up to that of Simeon ben Shatah, the yearning for sanctification did not stop, and bands of Nazirites, as in the quoted legend, were doubtless a common occurrence."[6]

There is one last Nazirite of historical note worth mentioning: Queen Helena of Adiabene, who is discussed in the third chapter of the talmudic tractate Nazir. The queen vowed that if her son returned safely from war, she would lead the life of a Nazirite for seven years. Her story confirms the statement of Josephus in *Jewish War* 2:313 that it was the custom for someone in trouble or danger to undertake a Nazirite vow.

Let us now circle back to our initial question about the merits of being a Nazarite. Just because something exists or is prevalent does not necessarily mean it is a good thing. (There are so many examples one can bring to illustrate this point that I leave it to the reader to come up with his or her own.) This is particularly true when it comes to the Nazirite, and the debate of the virtues (or lack thereof) of being a Nazirite stems from the fact that he or she must bring a sin offering at the conclusion of his/her Nazirism.[7]

Those who view Nazirism as a virtue find support for their position in the Nazirite story itself. These proponents ask, why do the narratives of the Nazirite and the Sotah interrupt the story of the consecration of the Levites set forth in *Sefer BeMidbar*? Specifically, chapters 3 and 4 discuss the selection of the Levites and their functions. Suddenly, this storyline is interrupted by the Sotah (chapter 5) and the Nazirite (chapter 6), only to return to the Levites in chapters 7 and 8, which deal with the dedication of the tabernacle and the sanctification of the priests and Levites for their service.

Those who regard Nazirism positively maintain that the Torah seeks to emphasize that it is possible for any man or woman in Israel on his or her own to reach an elevated level of sanctity, as compared to the priests and Levites, who were chosen and sanctified because of their inherent qualities.[8]

---

6. Joshua, *Studies*, 148.

7. See Numbers 6:14 which states: "As his offering to the Lord, he shall present: one male lamb in its first year, without blemish, for a burnt offering; one ewe lamb in its first year, without blemish, for a *sin offering*; one ram without blemish for an offering of well-being."

8. Bazak, "Why Are the Laws of the Nazir and the Sota Juxtaposed?"

The parallels cited below between the Nazirite and priest underscore this viewpoint:

- Concerning the priests, the Torah tells us: "They shall be holy to their God" (Leviticus 21:6); and concerning the Nazirite, the Torah states: "He is holy to God" (Numbers 6:8).
- Regarding their service in the tabernacle, the priests are commanded: "You shall not drink wine or strong drink" (Leviticus 10:9). So, too, the Nazirite: "He shall abstain from wine and strong drink" (Numbers 6:3).
- Both the priest and the Nazirite are forbidden from becoming ritually impure through contact with a corpse.

There is, however, a problem with this last point of comparison. The sanctity of the priests is directly connected to the special commandments they must observe when serving in the tabernacle,[9] whereas this specific type of sanctity does not apply to a Nazirite, because he does not perform any service in the tabernacle whatsoever. For this reason, "the sanctity of the Nazir resembles more closely the sanctity of the Kohen Gadol [High Priest]. In contrast to the regular kohanim [priests], whose sanctity is dependent upon and arises from their service in the Temple [or, as was the case in the wilderness, the tabernacle], the sanctity of the Kohen Gadol arises from the very fact that he is anointed with the anointing oil."[10]

The mishnah in tractate Nazir makes this same comparison but in a more forceful manner and then presents a spirited debate over who has a higher level of sanctity, the high priest or the Nazirite.

> A Kohen Gadol [high priest] and a Nazirite do not render themselves ritually impure for their relatives, but they may become impure for a *met mitzva* [a person who has died and who has no one else to tend to burial arrangements]. Suppose that [the high priest and a Nazirite] were walking on the road, and they see an unidentified corpse. Rebbi Eliezer says, "Let the Kohen Gadol defile himself, but not the Nazirite," but the Sages say, "Let the Nazirite defile himself, but not the Kohen Gadol." Rebbi Eliezer said to them: "Let the Kohen defile himself, for he does not bring a [guilt] offering for becoming impure, rather than the Nazirite, for he is obligated to bring a [guilt] offering." They

---

9. See Leviticus 21:6–8: "They shall be holy to their God and they shall not defile the name of their God, for the offerings to God by fire—the bread of their God—they offer up, and they shall be holy ... and you shall sanctify him for he offers the bread of your God; he shall be holy to you."

10. Bazak, "Why Are the Laws of the Nazir and the Sota Juxtaposed?"

answered him: "Let the Nazirite defile himself, for his sanctity is not an eternal sanctity, rather than the Kohen Gadol, whose sanctity is an eternal sanctity" (Nazir 7:4).

In sum, those who are pro-Nazirite see a powerful lesson being transmitted by the Nazirite commandments, namely, that a regular Israelite can achieve the highest level of sanctity. This sanctity may well be of temporary duration, but it is nonetheless an elevated level that matches that of the high priest.

A number of commentators on this biblical narrative are equally positive about the virtues of being a Nazirite. Sforno, for example, comments on Numbers 6:2 that a Nazirite "will separate himself from all the vanities and physical pleasures in life in order to devote himself exclusively to the service of the Lord, to study His Torah and practice walking in His ways." Hizquni comments on the same verse that the laws of the Nazirite come to teach "a valuable lesson in how to preserve one's sin-free status." Arguably the strongest defense of Nazirism found among the classical commentators is offered by Ramban:

> The reason why a Nazirite must bring a sin-offering "when the days of his Nazirism are fulfilled" has not been explained. In accordance with the plain meaning of the text, [it is because] this man sins against his soul on the day of completion of his Nazirism. Until now, he was separated in sanctity and the service of God, and he should therefore have remained separated forever, continuing all his life consecrated and sanctified to his God, as it is said: "And I raised up of your sons for prophets, and of your young men for Nazirites" [Amos 2:11]. There the text compares the Nazirite to a prophet, and it is further written: "All the days of his Nazirism he is holy unto the Eternal" [Amos 2:8]. Thus [when he completes his Nazirism and returns to his normal life], he requires atonement, since he goes back to be defiled by material desires of the world (Ramban on Numbers 6:11).

There is a logic to Ramban's perspective, but it is rejected by a number of talmudic sages. Nazirism is a form of asceticism, and the rabbinic attitude toward asceticism is best summed up by Eleazar ha-Kappar, who holds that the Nazirite is "a sinner by reason of the soul" (Numbers 6:11) because he denied himself wine: "If then one who denies himself wine only is termed a sinner, how much so then one who is an ascetic in all things!" (Nazir 19a). Support for this notion is also found in the Jerusalem Talmud, Qiddushin 4:12, where the mishnah states: "Man is destined to be called to account for everything (permitted) he saw (and desired) but did not partake of."

Even the structure of the Talmud itself can be seen as a clear but subtle condemnation of the Nazirite. The Talmud in Sotah 2b connects the alleged transgression of the accused woman to wine when it argues that anyone who sees a Sotah in her disgrace should abstain from wine (presumably going so far as to take the Nazirite vows). Not surprisingly, tractate Nazir is ultimately placed in the section of the Talmud that deals with the laws of women. It immediately precedes tractate Sotah, which is about a woman suspected by her husband of having been unfaithful, and is followed by tractate Gittin, which discusses divorce. It seems a fair assumption that the talmudic sages saw all three (adultery, Nazirism, and divorce) as worthy of condemnation.

Pushback against Nazirism is also found in several biblical commentaries and other rabbinic sources. For instance, Kli Yakar, while conceding that there are people who strive to add holiness to themselves by practicing restraint, argues in his commentary on Numbers 6:11 that such individuals may nonetheless be considered to have sinned. In the eyes of Kli Yakar, the act of separating oneself from the rest of humanity is wrong, a view that reflects Hillel's emphasis on the importance of community cited at the beginning of this chapter.

The midrash is even more critical, holding that the Nazirite "has sinned through his soul, since his evil inclination overtook him, such that he had to abstain from wine" (Solomon Astruc, *Midreshei Ha-Torah*).

Rambam is also critical of the Nazirite and sees the very act of becoming a Nazirite as a sin. As he writes in his introduction to Pirqe Avot:

> Our Torah, about which King David stated, "The Torah of the Lord is perfect . . . making wise the simple" [Psalm 19:7], advocates no mortification. Its intention was that man should follow nature, taking the middle road. He should eat his fill in moderation, drink in moderation. He should dwell amidst society in uprightness and faith and not in the deserts and mountains. He should not wear wool and hair nor afflict his body. On the contrary, the Torah explicitly warned us regarding the Nazirite.

And what are we to make of Ramban's explanation of the sin offering brought by the Nazirite, that his sin lies with ending his Nazirism and not undertaking it? Rabbi Samson Raphael Hirsch acknowledges that the Nazirite hopes to "spiritually and morally ennoble himself," but he observes that while "there has been no actual sin or misbehavior against the social life of the community, the vow of the Nazirite would appear in itself as an unsociable arrogance."[11] And for this he must bring a sin offering.

---

11. See Hirsch, *Pentateuch*, on Numbers 6:12.

During the 1964 presidential campaign, Barry Goldwater, a five-term United States senator from Arizona and the Republican Party's nominee for president, said: "I would remind you that extremism in the defense of liberty is no vice. And let me remind you also that moderation in the pursuit of justice is no virtue."[12] There is a certain truth to his words, and the account of the Nazirite underscores this. There is a kind of bifurcation to this narrative. The Nazirite may be seeking to improve and elevate himself, but at what cost? I think Toldot Yitzhak on Numbers 6:11 sums it up best:

> We may answer that on the one hand, he is holy, while on the other hand, he is a sinner. In terms of his soul, he his holy—for the soul is made more perfect through separation from the desires of this world, but the perfection of the body lies in not being separated from the desires of this world to an extreme, but rather by living in moderation: eating and drinking, consuming meat, and imbibing wine as proper for the body's wellbeing. Thus, in terms of the soul, the Nazirite is called "holy," while in terms of the body, he is called a sinner.

There is a last thought about the Nazirite worth sharing with teens as they reflect on extremism and the impact it can have on their lives. It is noteworthy that the Torah does not suggest an appropriate period for the length of a Nazirite's vow. This is easily understood if one remembers that Nazirism is a process of personal abstinence, undertaken to temper one's desires and to achieve a more moderate lifestyle. Consequently, the appropriate period for this vow is subjective and will differ from person to person. Some may be able to achieve the desired level of moderation after a month-long period of abstinence. Others may require a period of abstinence extending for months or even years. So how does the Nazirite determine the appropriate period for this vow of abstinence? "He must evaluate himself on a completely objective basis and determine the intensity of his tendency of overindulgence. Once he makes an honest judgment of himself, he can determine the appropriate length of time that he must engage in abstinence in order to overcome his tendency. In other words, the person contemplating a Nazirite vow must engage in a process of personal introspection in which he is both the subject and object of the investigation."[13]

This is, I think, the enduring lesson teachers should seek to impart to their students when studying the Nazirite narrative. The time and place for extremism, the depth and duration it should be followed, cannot be easily

---

12. Goldwater, "Goldwater's 1964 Acceptance Speech." Goldwater was labeled an extremist for this remark and was defeated overwhelmingly in the 1964 election.

13. Fox, "Lessons."

determined. It may work for some and in the end be praiseworthy. Yet it may well backfire for others and result in misguided or even sinful activities.

Is it thus any wonder that God only set forth these commandments in the book of Numbers?

Sefer BeMidbar—The Nazirite
Sample Unit Plan

Unit	Primary Source(s)	Supplemental Reading(s)	Timeframe
The Nazirite	Numbers 6	Why are the Laws of the Nazirite and the Sotah Juxtaposed?	two–three weeks
	Rashi 6:1		
Middah:	Sforno 6:1		
Extremism	Rashi 6:11		
	Hizquni 6:11		
	Mishnah Nazir 7:4	Lessons from the Nazirite	
	Rambam 6:11		
	Toldot Yizchak 6:1		

Essential Questions

1. What would motivate a person to become a Nazirite?
2. How are we to reconcile a Nazirite separating himself from the community with the talmudic view of the importance of community?
3. Why is the Nazirite commanded to bring a sin offering at the conclusion of his Nazirism? Did he not specifically vow "to set himself apart for the Lord"?

Evaluating/Checking for Understanding

1. Daily discussions/student interactions

   Student questions and observations typically drive each day's discussion.

2. Occasional written reflections

   At the discretion of the teacher, a tool to foster further reflection on the unit's essential questions.

3. Character trait essay

   See appendix for assignment rubric.

4. Unit test

   Unit tests should, by definition, be crafted by individual teachers to meet the needs of their specific students. The Understanding by Design *framework created by Grant Wiggins and Jay McTighe is an excellent tool for the development of appropriate tests and assessments, as its emphasis on backward design forces teachers to consider in advance the assessment evidence needed to document and validate that the targeted learning goals have been achieved.*

Primary Source Texts

1. *BeMidbar* chapter 6: Read text and seek to identify problematic (what I call "red flag") words and phrases (with teacher's guidance, of course). These red flag words and phrases will likely vary from class to class depending on the sophistication and linguistic abilities of the students, coupled with the background and interests of the teacher. That said, some important examples of red flag words and phrases in this chapter appear in commentaries A–G.

2. Supplemental readings for each unit are intended to demonstrate that serious scholarship about and explanations of *Sefer BeMidbar* are not limited to the classical medieval commentators but continue to our time. The supplemental readings for this unit include: "Why Are the Laws of the Nazirite and the Sotah Juxtaposed?" by Rav Amnon Bazak, an article that focuses on the extent to which the accused woman is in control of her fate, and "Lessons from the Nazirite" by Rabbi Bernie Fox, an article that discusses moderation and the purpose of the Nazirite's vow.

Sefer BeMidbar—The Nazirite

Primary Texts

A. Rashi 6:1

"If he clearly utters"

Why is the section dealing with the Nazarite placed in juxtaposition to the section dealing with the Sotah? To tell you that he who has once seen a Sotah in her disgrace should abstain from wine, because it may lead to adultery.

B. Sforno 6:1

"To set himself apart for the Lord:

To separate himself from all the pleasures in order to devote himself exclusively to the service of the Lord, to study His Torah and practice walking in His ways.

C. Rashi 6:11

"For that he hath sinned by the dead"

That is, that he has not been on his guard against defilement by a corpse. [But] R. Eleazer ha-Kappar said: "his sin consists in that he has afflicted himself by abstaining from the enjoyment of wine."

D. Hizquni 6:11

"For that he hath sinned by the dead"

He should have made sure that the building he entered did not contain a corpse. The Torah had specifically warned him not to enter such a building in verse 6 of our chapter.

E. Mishnah Nazir 7:4

A Kohen Gadol [high priest] and a Nazirite do not render themselves ritually impure for their relatives, but they may become impure for a *met mitzva* [a person who has died and who has no one else to tend to burial arrangements]. Suppose that [the high priest and a Nazirite] were walking on the road, and they see an unidentified corpse. Rebbi Eliezer says, "Let the Kohen Gadol defile himself, but not the Nazirite," but the Sages say, "Let the Nazirite defile himself, but not the Kohen Gadol." Rebbi Eliezer said to them: "Let the Kohen defile himself, for he does not bring a [guilt] offering for becoming impure, rather than the Nazirite, for he is obligated to bring a [guilt] offering." They answered him: "Let the Nazirite defile himself, for his sanctity is not an eternal sanctity, rather than the Kohen Gadol, whose sanctity is an eternal sanctity."

F. Ramban 6:11

"The priest shall offer one as a sin offering"

The reason why a Nazirite must bring a sin-offering "when the days of his Nazirism are fulfilled" has not been explained. In accordance with the plain meaning of the text, [it is because] this man sins against his soul on the day of completion of his Nazirism. Until now, he was separated in sanctity and the service of God, and he should therefore have remained separated forever, continuing all his life consecrated and sanctified to his God, as it is said: "And I raised up of your sons for prophets, and of your young men for Nazirites" (Amos 2:11). There the text compares the Nazirite to a prophet, and it is further written: "All the days of his Nazirism he is holy unto the Eternal" (Amos 2:8). Thus [when he completes his Nazirism and returns to his normal life], he requires atonement, since he goes back to be defiled by material desires of the world.

G. Toledot Yizhak 6:11

"The priest shall offer one as a sin offering"

We may answer that on the one hand, he is holy, while on the other hand, he is a sinner. In terms of his soul, he his holy—for the soul is made more perfect through separation from the desires of this world, but the perfection of the body lies in not being separated from the desires of this world to an extreme, but rather by living in moderation: eating and drinking, consuming meat, and imbibing wine as proper for the body's wellbeing. Thus, in terms of the soul, the Nazirite is called "holy," while in terms of the body, he is called a sinner.

Sefer BeMidbar—The Nazirite
Supplemental Reading

Why Are the Laws of the Nazirite and the Sotah Juxtaposed?

—Rav Amnon Bazak

A. Introduction

IN RESPONSE TO THE question in the title above, the Gemara (Sotah 2a) answers: "To teach you that anyone who sees the Sotah (suspected adulteress) in her disgrace will vow to abstain from wine [as does the Nazirite]." This conveys an educational message as to the serious damage that can result from excessive consumption of alcohol. Indeed, the connection between wine and prohibited sexual relationships appears many times in Tanakh— from the somewhat opaque story of Noach's inebriation, via Lot and his daughters, up to warnings by the prophets about wine, such as "Prostitution and wine and new wine take away the heart" (Hosea 4:11). However, the literal text seems to indicate another reason for the juxtaposition of the two subjects.

B. "He Shall Grow the Hair of His Head Wild"

First we must ask, why are the parashot of the Nazirite and the Sotah placed together with issues pertaining to the consecration of the Levites? Chapters 3–4 discuss the selection of the Levites and their functions, chapters 7–8 deal with the dedication of the *Mishkan* and the sanctification of the

Kohanim and Levites for their service. Why, in the middle of this process, do the Sotah (chapter 5) and Nazir (chapter 6) suddenly appear?

It seems that the Torah seeks to emphasize that, although the Levites were chosen because of their inherent qualities, it is still possible for any man or woman in Israel to reach an elevated level of sanctity. We may point to several parallels between the Nazirite and the Kohanim:

1. Concerning the Kohanim we are told, "They shall be holy to their God" (Leviticus 21:6), and concerning the Nazirite—"He is holy to God" (6:8).
2. During his service the Kohen is commanded, "You shall not drink wine or strong drink" (Leviticus 10:9), just as the Nazirite is commanded, "He shall abstain from wine and strong drink" (6:3).
3. Both the Kohen and the Nazirite are forbidden from becoming ritually impure through contact with a corpse.

However, this last point of comparison raises a difficulty. The sanctity of the kohanim, resulting in special mitzvot that they must observe, arises from their service in the Temple, as explained in parashat Emor:

> They shall be holy to their God and they shall not defile the name of their God, for the offerings to God by fire—the bread of their God—they offer up, and they shall be holy ... and you shall sanctify him for he offers the bread of your God; he shall be holy to you ... (Leviticus 21:6-8)

Clearly, this sanctity cannot be attributed to a Nazirite, since he does not perform service in the Temple.

Thus, it would seem that the sanctity of the Nazirite resembles more closely the sanctity of the Kohen Gadol. In contrast to the regular kohanim, whose sanctity is dependent upon and arises from their service in the Temple, the sanctity of the Kohen Gadol arises from the very fact that he is anointed with the anointing oil:

> The one who is Kohen Gadol from among his brethren, who shall have the anointing oil poured over his head and who is consecrated to wear the holy garments ... He shall not go in to any dead body, nor shall he render himself impure for his father or for his mother ... He shall not desecrate the Temple of his God, for the crown (*nezer*) of the anointing oil of his God is upon him; I am God. (Leviticus 21:10-12)

It should be noted that aside from the "crown" (*nezer*) mentioned here—the oil with which the Kohen Gadol is anointed once in his life—there is also another *nezer* that is placed upon the Kohen Gadol's head throughout his life—the *tzitz*. The Torah commands the two types of *nezer* in juxtaposition:

> You shall place the turban upon his head and you shall place the holy NEZER upon the turban. And you shall take the ANOINTING OIL and pour it over his head, and anoint him. (Exodus 29:6–7)

It is the crown of oil and the crown of the *tzitz*, more than anything else, that express the unique sanctity of the Kohen Gadol.

All of this is very similar to what we are told concerning the Nazirite:

> He shall not be rendered impure for his father or his mother or his brother or his sister, if they should die, for the crown (*nezer*) of God is upon his head. All the days that he is a Nazirite he is holy to God. (Numbers 6:6–7)

What is the *nezer* that is referred to here? From the verses it would appear that it is the Nazirite's long hair that represents his crown: "All the days of his Nazirite vow, no razor shall pass over his head; until the days of his being a Nazirite to God are fulfilled he shall be holy, he shall grow his hair wild (long)" (Numbers 6:5). Both the Nazirite and the Kohen Gadol are forbidden to render themselves ritually impure through contact with a corpse—even for the purposes of tending to their own close relatives—for God's CROWN (*nezer*) is upon their heads. A person who undertakes the obligations of a Nazirite can sanctify himself through growing his hair long, and this sanctity obligates him to avoid ritual impurity and to abstain from wine.

However, there is a clear difference between the sanctity of the Kohen Gadol and that of the Nazirite. While the natural sanctity of the Kohen Gadol obligates him to refrain from growing his hair (Leviticus 21:10), the Nazirite—whose (temporary) sanctity is based on choice—is commanded precisely the opposite: "He shall grow his hair long" (6:5). The sanctity of the Kohen Gadol is not connected to his hair. On the contrary—it is possible that the prohibition against growing his hair, even during a period of mourning, is aimed at preventing any effacement of the *tzitz*, or of the impression left by his anointment with oil, both of which symbolize his sanctity. The sanctity of the Nazirite, in contrast, finds expression in God's crown that is upon his head—i.e. his hair, and the moment that his period of being a Nazir is over, he must shave his head. Indeed, the most famous of all nezirim—Shimshon—testifies as follows:

> No razor has touched my head, for I am a Nazir to God from my mother's womb. If my hair was to be shaven then I would lose my strength and become weak, and I would be like any other person. (Judges 16:17)

In light of the above, we can understand the single prohibition addressed to kohanim that does not apply to the Nazirite—that of marrying a widow, divorcee, etc. This prohibition pertains, by definition, to an extended period, and hence it does not apply to a Nazirite, whose period of special sanctity is only temporary.

The juxtaposition of the parasha of the Nazirite to that of the sanctification of the Kohanim and Levites therefore comes to teach us that although the tribe of Levi has a special quality of sanctity from birth, a regular Israelite can achieve the highest level of sanctity, through becoming a Nazirite. This sanctity will, admittedly, be of temporary duration, but it is truly an elevated level, matching that of the Kohen Gadol.

Let us now clarify the significance of the juxtaposition of parashat Sotah to this broad context.

C. "And He Shall Loosen Woman's Hair"

The connection between the parasha of the Nazirite and that of the Sotah is clear.

1. Both open with a similar introduction: "And God spoke to Moses saying, Speak to the Israelites and say to them: A man whose wife has gone astray . . ." (5:11–12); "And God spoke to Moses saying, Speak to the Israelites and say to them: A man or woman who makes a special vow of a Nazirite . . ." (6:1–2)

2. Both also conclude with the same formulation: "This is the teaching of jealousy, when a woman strays . . ." (5:29); "This is the teaching of the Nazirite, who vows . . ." (6:21).

3. In both instances, the kohen plays a central role, inter alia fulfilling the mitzva of the wave offering: "And he shall wave the mincha offering before God" (5:25); "And the Kohen shall wave them for a wave offering before God" (6:20).

However, this similarity only serves to sharpen the very acute difference between the Nazirite and the Sotah. We discussed the sanctity of the

Kohanim, addressed in Leviticus 21. This chapter follows immediately after chapter 20, which lists the forbidden sexual relationships. There, too, there is an inverse connection between the two juxtaposed chapters, for they present the two extremes: chapter 21 describes the loftiest levels of human sanctity, while the prohibitions of *arayot* represent the greatest possible affront to sanctity. The essence of the Torah's teaching in this sphere is the obligation of the Israelites to be holy. The parasha of *arayot* begins with the warning, "You shall sanctify yourselves and be holy, for I am the Lord your God" (Leviticus 20:7). The first on the list of prohibited relations, following mention of one who curses his father or mother, is: "If a man commits adultery with a married woman, he commits adultery with his neighbor's wife—the adulterer and the adulteress shall surely die" (Leviticus 20:8). At the end of the list, the Torah stresses once again, "You shall be holy to Me, for I, God, am holy, and I have distinguished you from the nations to be Mine" (verse 26).

It is difficult, then, to ignore the connection between chapters 20–21 in *Vayikra* and chapters 5–6 in *BeMidbar*. In *BeMidbar*, too, we find that the chapter expressing the most severe affront to sanctity appears first: adultery between a married woman and another man. The affront to sanctity is expressed, inter alia, in the fact that the punishment of the Sotah comes about through "holy waters" (5:17). This is measure for measure: the holy waters harm a person who caused harm to the sanctity of the Israelites. But immediately thereafter we find chapter 6, expressing the other side: man's ability to achieve exceptionally elevated levels of sanctity.

This contrast between the Nazirite and the Sotah is given a prominent place in the parasha. While the Nazirite is obligated to let his hair grow long and wild (*gadal pera' se'ar rosho*), when it comes to the Sotah it is specifically the Kohen who is commanded, "He shall loosen the woman's hair" (*para' rosh ha-isha*). The Nazirite grows his hair long of his own accord, and this symbolizes his special status; the Sotah has her hair loosened by the Kohen, expressing degradation and disgrace.

Indeed, the Tanakh relates to hair in two ways. On the one hand, we know of some biblical figures whose special character was symbolized by their hair—including the prophet Samuel who, like a Nazirite, was "devoted to God for all the days of his life, and a razor shall not touch his head" (1 Samuel 1:11); likewise the prophet Elijah, who was called a "hairy man" (2 Kings 1:8). Absalom, son of David, was not a positive character in terms of morality, but his special beauty also stood out in his hair (2 Samuel 14:25–26—"No one was as beautiful as Absalom in all of Israel; of great praise—from his feet to his head there was no blemish in him. And when he shaved his head—it was after a long time that he shaved, for it was heavy upon him and so he shaved—he weighed the hair of his head: two hundred shekalim of the king's weights").

On the other hand, letting hair grow long and wild expresses degradation or mourning. An example of this is to be found concerning the *metzora*—"His hair shall grow long and he shall cover his upper lip, and he shall call out, 'Impure, impure!'" (Leviticus 13:45). Likewise a mourner—as we learn from the prohibition to the Kohen Gadol: "He shall not grow his hair."

Thus, we learn that the sanctity of kohanim is natural, stemming from birth, and they must not grow their hair long. The status of the Israelites, on the other hand, is determined in accordance with their actions. If they so wish, they may attain the pinnacle of sanctity, which is expressed externally through growing their hair long; an affront to sanctity, on the other hand, leads to loosening ("making wild") of the hair by others.

Rav Amnon Bazak is a *Shiur Bet Ram* at Yeshivat Har Etzion and teaches Bible and oral law at the Herzog College and at the Women" Beit Midrash in Migdal Oz. He completed his *hesder* army service in the military rabbinate and was later ordained as a rabbi and received his BEd degree at Herzog College for Teacher Training. Rav Bazak has authored several books on Bible study.

Sefer BeMidbar—The Nazirite

Supplemental Reading

Lessons from the Nazirite

—Rabbi Bernie Fox

> *And this is the law of the Nazirite, when the days of his Nazirite vow are fulfilled: He shall bring himself to the door of the Ohel Mo'ed. (Sefer BeMidbar 6:13)*

1. The Laws of the Nazirite

Parshat Naso describes the mitzvah of the Nazir—the Nazirite. The Nazirite is a person who takes a vow to separate oneself from material pleasures. The Nazirite may not drink wine or cut his hair. The Nazirite is also prohibited in defilement through contact with a dead body. The purpose of this removal from material affairs is to encourage greater devotion to Hashem and the Torah. The Torah does not specify the period for which a person must commit oneself to being a Nazir. In practice, the period of time is discretionary. A person may vow to be a Nazirite for a year or for a number of years. However, thirty days is the minimum period for which a person may vow to be a Nazirite. If a person vows to be a Nazirite and does not specify the period for which the vow will be in-force, then it remains in-force for thirty days.

Upon completion of the period of the vow, the Nazirite performs a series of activities in the Temple. These include shaving off the long hair that he has grown during the period of the vow and bringing a number of sacrifices.

2. The Nazirite Brings Himself to the Tabernacle

In the above passage, the Torah explains that on the day that the Nazirite completes his vow "he brings himself to the Ohel Mo'ed"—the Tabernacle and initiates the process described above. This translation of the passage is suggested by Rashi. However, Rashi acknowledges that this translation is not literal. The literal translation of the passage is the "he brings him" [Rashi on Numbers 6:13]. Onkelos actually suggests this literal translation.

The problem with the literal translation is obvious. Who are the "he" and the "him" in the passage? Presumably the "him" brought to the Tabernacle is the Nazirite. But who is the "he" who brings the Nazir to the Tabernacle? Because of this difficulty Rashi suggests that the passage must be translated less rigorously and that it actually means that the Nazirite brings himself.

Of course, Rashi's innovative translation does not completely solve the problem presented by the passage. The passage remains difficult to understand. Why did the Torah not express itself more simply and leave out the transitive "brings" and in its place use the intransitive "comes"? The Torah could have said that upon completing his vow, the Nazirite comes to the Ohel Mo'ed! By expressing itself in this straight-forward manner the Torah would have averted the need to translate the passage in a less than literal manner.

Rav Meir Simcha of Devinsk—Meshech Chachmah offers an important answer to this question. Before considering his explanation of the passage, more information about the mitzvah of Nazirite is needed.

3. Moderation and the Purpose of the Nazirite's Vow

Maimonides explains the Torah is designed to help us achieve moderation in all of our attitudes. But what constitutes moderation? The term "moderation" assumes that the moderate attitude is balanced between extremes. In other words, every proper attitude occupies a midpoint along a continuum of possible attitudes. An example helps illustrate Maimonides' position. A person who has a moderate attitude toward personal wealth is able to use his wealth in order to secure a meaningful improvement in his condition. This attitude is balanced between the extreme attitudes demonstrated by the spendthrift and those of the miserly person. The miser cannot part with his wealth even when circumstances dictate that the expenditure is worthwhile. The spendthrift expends his wealth with abandon, unable to consider the true value of the items he purchases. According to Maimonides, we should strive to conduct ourselves in a manner that is balanced between the two extremes. A person should not be a spendthrift. Neither should one be stingy.

Similarly, we are not permitted to act cowardly. We also may not endanger ourselves unnecessarily. Instead, our attitude toward risk should reflect moderation. We should be willing and able to subject ourselves to a reasonable risk if the circumstances so demand. The same pattern applies to all behaviors and attitudes. We must seek the middle road.

Inevitably, we all have attitudes that are not moderate but instead somewhat extreme. Some of us may be overly shy. Others may be egotistical. How does one correct a flaw? Maimonides explains that the Torah suggests that we temporarily force ourselves to adopt the behavior and attitude of the opposite extreme. The stingy person practices being a spendthrift. The glutton adopts a very restricted diet. With time, this practice will enable the person to break the original attachment. One will be able to adopt the moderate behavior and attitude required by the Torah.

Maimonides explains that the mitzvah of the Nazirite should be understood in this context. The Nazirite is a person who was overly attached to material pleasures. The Nazirite makes a vow to adopt the behavior associated with the opposite extreme. He embraces self-denial for a period of time. The ultimate goal is to free the personality from inordinate attachment to material pleasures. This will allow him to ultimately achieve an attitude of moderation.

However, the Torah does not want us to mistakenly view the Nazirite's behavior of self-denial as an ideal. We must recognize that the Nazirite's vow is intended as a corrective measure for an extreme attitude and behavior. [Rambam on the Mishnah, introduction to Pirqe Avot, chapter 4.]

4. The Discretionary Period of the Nazirite's Vow

Meshech Chachmah comments that it is notable that the Torah does not suggest an appropriate period for the length of the Nazirite's vow. However, this is completely understandable based upon the interpretation of the mitzvah presented by Maimonides. The Nazirite is undertaking a process of personal abstinence, in order to temper his desires and to achieve a more moderate lifestyle. The appropriate period for this vow is subjective and will differ from person to person. One individual may be able to achieve the moderation he seeks after a month-long period of abstinence. Another person may require a period of abstinence extending for a month or even years. How does the Nazirite determine the appropriate period for his vow of abstinence? He must evaluate himself on a completely objective basis and determine the intensity of his tendency of overindulgence. Once he makes an honest judgment of himself, he can determine the appropriate length of time that he must engage in abstinence in order to overcome his tendency. In other words, the person contemplating a Nazirite vow must engage in a process of personal introspection in which he is both the subject and object of the investigation. He is the subject who conducts the investigation and he is also the object of the introspection.

5. Honest and Rigorous Introspection

How does one engage in objective introspection? Meshech Chachmah continues and explains this process. It requires that the person look upon himself with the same critical attitude that he typically adopts when analyzing the behaviors of peers and neighbors. Generally, we have no difficulty in identifying the flaws, wrongdoings, and failings of others. However, this critical capacity fails us when we consider our own behaviors and attitudes. The person considering the vow of a Nazirite must subject himself to the same critical scrutiny that he more easily applies to others. This is the meaning of being both the subject and object of the investigation.

On the basis of this observation, Meshech Chachmah explains the strange expression employed by the Torah in the above passage. The Nazirite brings him or himself to the Tabernacle. This strange phrasing beautifully captures the introspective aspect of the Nazirite. He, alone, determines the length of his vow and when he will come to the Tabernacle to complete his duties and obligation as a Nazirite. He makes this determination based upon objective introspection. He treats himself not as "me" but as him. He—the Nazirite who has evaluated his flaws and embarked upon a path of personal improvement—brings him—the person whom he objectively evaluated—to the Tabernacle. [Rav Meir Simcha of Devinsk, Meshech Chachmah on Numbers 6:13.]

6. Applications of the Lesson of the Nazirite

Of course, to understand Meshech Chachmah's comments as relevant only to the Nazirite is to miss his point. Each of us should constantly strive to improve ourselves. Meshech Chachmah is suggesting that this process is best executed through being as critical and ruthless with ourselves as we are with others. A corollary to this insight is that by engaging in this process of introspection and recognizing our own shortcomings, hopefully, we will become more forgiving of others and their failings.

Rabbi Bernie Fox has served on the faculty of Northwest Yeshiva High School since 1980. He was appointed head of school in 1986. Rabbi Fox is a member of the first *semicha* class of Yeshiva Bnai Torah of Far Rockaway and earned Masters of Business Administration Degree from Long Island University, Brooklyn.

Chapter 12

The Daughters of Zelophehad

ENCOMPASSING ALL OF SEVEN verses, the story of the daughters of Zelophehad (which we find in chapter 27 of *Sefer BeMidbar*) is the shortest of the narratives we will examine in this book.

> The daughters of Zelophehad, of Manassite family—son of Hepher son of Gilead son of Machir son of Manasseh son of Joseph—came forward. The names of the daughters were Mahlah, Noah, Hoglah, Milcah, and Tirzah. They stood before Moses, Eleazar the priest, the chieftains, and the whole assembly, at the entrance of the Tent of Meeting, and they said: "Our father died in the wilderness. He was not one of the faction, Korah's faction, which banded together against the Lord, but died for his own sin; and he has left no sons. Let not our father's name be lost to his clan just because he had no son! Give us a holding among our father's kinsmen!" Moses brought their case before the Lord. And the Lord said to Moses: "The plea of Zelophehad's daughters is just: you should give them a hereditary holding among their father's kinsmen; transfer their father's share to them (Numbers 27:1–7).

As I hope to demonstrate, there is much we can learn from the story of these five women, not the least the key elements pertaining to inheritance laws. Let us start there.

These women approach Moses with a seemingly straightforward question. How does the law deal with a case such as ours, when a man dies with only daughters and no sons? Surely Moses, the man who spent forty days and nights on Mount Sinai learning the law from God Himself, would know how to resolve this issue. Yet Moses is at a loss as to what to do. Rashi offers two possibilities for this lapse.

According to Rashi's first explanation, "the law on this subject escaped him." Why? Because in this view, found in Sanhedrin 8a, Moses is being punished for having set himself up as the supreme judge by saying, "And the cause that is too hard for you, you shall bring to me" (Rashi on Numbers 27:5). This explanation, however, seems at odds with the Torah's description of Moses as the humblest of all men (Numbers 12:3). Hence, Rashi offers a second explanation, as he often does when not fully satisfied with his first. Per this second explanation, the inheritance laws that flow from the request of the daughters of Zelophehad should have been written by Moses, as was the case with most laws in the Torah. In other words, these laws should have been taught to the people by Moses without need of some incident that made their promulgation necessary. What, then, is different in this case? Quite simply, it was the greatness of the daughters of Zelophehad. Their merit and standing was so high that God determined that these laws should be, as it were, written through them.

What is the source of their great merit? One need only look to the first verse of their story. They are introduced in the opening verse of chapter 27 in an unusual manner: "The daughters of Zelophehad, of the family of Manasseh—son of Hepher, son of Gilead, son of Machir, son of Manasseh, son of Joseph—came forward. The names of the daughters were Mahlah, Noa, Hoglah, Milcah, and Tirzah" (Numbers 27:1). Rashi immediately questions the need to trace the lineage of these woman all the way back to Joseph. His explanation of this point highlights the great righteousness of the five sisters:

> [This tracing of their lineage back to Joseph teaches] that they were righteous all of them [every one of the family members here mentioned in the pedigree], for in every case where a person's doings and his ancestors' doings are nowhere plainly described and Scripture somewhere enters into the details of the pedigree in respect to one of them, tracing his genealogy back to someone worthy of praise, it is evident that the person in question is himself a righteous man and a son of a righteous father. But if it gives his genealogy in connection with something deserving of reprobation as, for example, "Ishmael the son of Nethaniah the son of Elishamah came . . . and smote Gedaliah" (2 Kings 25:25), then it is quite certain that all who are mentioned in connection with him were wicked people.

Rashi's opening commentary on the first verse in this chapter also underscores the women's connection to and longing for the land promised to their forefathers:

> It is to suggest the following idea to you: Just as Joseph held the Promised Land dear, as it is said, "And ye shall bring my

bones up [to Palestine] from hence" (Genesis 50:25), so, too, his daughters held the land dear, as it is said, "Give us an inheritance" (Numbers 27:4).

What compels Rashi to link the daughters' lineage to the land of Canaan? Said differently, why should their seeking a portion of the land indicate that they loved it? Perhaps they loved only themselves and wished an inheritance.[1]

The commentators offer a variety of rationales in response to such questions.[2] For example, Kli Yakar states that the general intention of the sages was to compliment all women. How so? We know from the conclusion of the Torah that not a single man above the age of twenty at the time of the incident with the spies (other than Joshua and Caleb) entered the promised land, whereas the women of this generation were not subject to this harsh decree: "None of the men who have seen My Presence and the signs that I have performed in Egypt and in the wilderness, and who have tried Me these many times and have disobeyed Me, shall see the land that I promised on oath to their fathers; none of those who spurn Me shall see it" (Numbers 14:22–23). The women thus deserved to inherit a portion in the land in a way men did not.

While interesting, the explanation of Kli Yakar is *not* based on the plain meaning of the text. In contrast, the commentary *Ha'amek Davar*, written by Rabbi Naftali Zvi Yehuda Berlin, proves from the text itself that these five women loved the land.[3] He notes that the text emphasizes that these women sought an inheritance "among their father's brethren" (Numbers 27:4), that is, in the territory to the west of the Jordan River, which had not yet been conquered rather than in the land of "their grandfather's portion," that is, the land to the east of the Jordan River, which had already been conquered. We must remember that half of their tribe, the tribe of Manasseh, chose portions in this already conquered territory, whereas the daughters of Zelophehad preferred to remain with the half of Manasseh that crossed the Jordan River. For Rabbi Berlin, this proves that these women truly loved the land of Israel and were not interested in the mere acquisition of land.

The point raised by Rabbi Berlin underscores the following. To fully understand the depths of the connection of the daughters of Zelophehad

---

1. Prior to their inquiry and the clarification of the matter, the established law was that only male descendants could inherent their fathers' portions.

2. The summary of sources cited below is culled from the essay on Zelophehad's daughters in Nachshoni, *Studies*.

3. Naftali Zvi Yehuda Berlin, otherwise known by the acronym Netziv, lived from 1816 to 1893 in both Russia and Poland. He served as dean of the Volozhin Yeshiva and authored several works of rabbinic literature in Lithuania.

to the Holy Land, one must contextualize their longing via a comparison to the actions of the tribes of Gad and Reuben as the Jewish People prepared themselves for the conquest of Canaan.

Chapter 32 of Numbers opens with a surprising, if not shocking, request from the tribes of Gad and Reuben:

> The Reubenites and the Gadites owned cattle in very great numbers. Noting that the lands of Jazer and Gilead were a region suitable for cattle, the Gadites and the Reubenites came to Moses, Eleazar the priest, and the chieftains of the community, and said: "Ataroth, Dibon, Jazer, Nimrah, Heshbon, Elealeh, Sebam, Nebo, and Beon—the land that the Lord has conquered for the community of Israel is cattle country, and your servants have cattle. It would be a favor to us if this land were given to your servants as a holding; do not move us across the Jordan" (Numbers 32:1–5).

Choose your adjective: outraged, incensed, aghast. What is clear is that Moses is not at all pleased by this request: "Are your brothers to go to war while you stay here? Why will you turn the minds of the Israelites from crossing into the land that the Lord has given them?" (Numbers 32:6–7).

The classical commentators, most notably Ramban, try to make sense of this request and find some positive underpinnings to it. Ramban argues in his commentary on the first two verses of this chapter that:

> Moses suspected that they [the tribes of Gad and Reuben] were only suggesting this because they were afraid of the people in the land of Canaan, concerning whom the Spies had said, "We are not able to go up against the people, for they are stronger than we." Therefore, he told them that they did not trust in God, just like their fathers and therefore He would again punish them like their fathers, by "leaving them in the wilderness" (Numbers 32:15). Therefore they answered him: "Far be it from us to fear them! For we shall pass over armed for battle, and we shall be the most eager and the first among the people to fight against the enemies of the Eternal, for they are bread for us" (Numbers 14:9).

Ramban further contends that there is an element of selflessness in Gad and Reuben's request. They point out to Moses that they have more cattle than the other tribes. By requesting (not demanding!) an inheritance on the east bank the Jordan River, they would thus ensure that the portions allotted to the other tribes in the territory to the west of the Jordan River would be larger. Alternatively, Gad and Reuben say that they will cross over together with the other tribes but will ultimately return to the land to the east of the Jordan River. This is, they suggest, territory that the other tribes do not desire and that is more suitable for them (and more desirable) because of the large number of cattle they possess (see Ramban on Numbers 32:19).

Were we to end our analysis of the daughters of Zelophehad here, we would have another proof of our basic contention, that *Sefer BeMidbar* uses narratives focused on individuals to teach important lessons about character development and about certain important halakhic and legal matters. Unlike the other narratives we have studied to this point in *Sefer BeMidbar*, however, the story of the daughters of Zelophehad is not centered on character traits such as greed, jealousy, or zealotry. Rather, theirs is a tale of devotion to family, to nation, and to homeland. In other words, their storyline is about a mindset and a life philosophy.

Mindset and philosophy. These are key concepts in defining what any Jewish day school environment is about. Indeed, every day school has a vision of what it hopes to be and achieve, typically accompanied by a mission statement that formally summarizes its aims and values. For instance, the school at which I work defines itself in its mission statement as "a college preparatory, coeducational, early childhood–twelfth grade, independent Jewish day school, guided by Modern Orthodox values and principles." Yet, if you were to ask most of our students and many of our teachers how we define "Modern Orthodox values and principles," they would be at a loss. And I do not believe that this is unique to our school.

For me, the story of the daughters of Zelophehad offers an important, twofold teaching opportunity. First, it encompasses a unit on strong women, brave women, who help shape the future of the Jewish people as they stand poised to enter the promised land. Including this in any curriculum for a Bible class would, I hope, be a given, especially in light of the issues we touched upon earlier in our discussions of the Sotah narrative and its resonance in the #MeToo era we now live in.

Second, in schools such as mine, the story of these five women can be a mission-aligned unit that will allow students to learn more about what their school represents and aspires to be. Of course, it is difficult to craft a mission-aligned curriculum if one does not fully understand or cannot correctly articulate the philosophies that define one's school or religious institution. Hence, before beginning a detailed analysis of the text of chapter 27, we should first delve into the philosophical undercurrents of Orthodox Judaism in America today.

In the Orthodox world I inhabit, there are important nuances and philosophical differences between those on the left of this religious spectrum (usually referred to as "Modern Orthodox") and those to the right (referred to in America as "Black Hat" Jews).[4] One's view on these philosophical points will inevitably shape and color any discussion of the daughters of Zelophehad.

Broadly speaking, there are three areas in which those on the left of the Orthodox spectrum differ from those on the right. The first focuses on the value of secular knowledge and education. At first glance, this seems a bit odd. Why would one not value secular knowledge and education? As Rabbi Norman Lamm, the one-time chancellor of Yeshiva University, notes: "Often, numbers of Jews, overwhelmed by the majority culture and unwilling or unable to remain confidently independent as a cognitive and religious minority, have assimilated into the host culture; they and their descendants have been lost forever to Jewish posterity. This painful phenomenon has occurred from Biblical times onward."[5] Indeed, Jews of European descent (who comprise the vast majority of American Jewry) historically had little to do with secular learning. For centuries in Europe, the curriculum of Jewish schools (as well as the research of scholars) was overwhelmingly confined to the Talmud and legal codes. Even biblical studies and Hebrew language studies received precious little attention. "Secular wisdom usually did not come into consideration at all, and if it did, it was spurned."[6]

Yet, as Rabbi Lamm explains, modernity presents challenges to Jews and their faith in new and increasingly demanding ways. In turn, these challenges in the eyes of many underscore the need for Jews living in the twenty-first century to have strong foundations in both Jewish learning and modern, secular culture. Proponents of this approach use the term *Torah Umadda*, which, in the words of Rabbi Lamm, "denotes the synergistic interrelation of religious study and secular or profane knowledge. The belief implied in this locution is that the interaction between the two yields constructive results."[7]

The second philosophical divide between the Jewish Orthodox worlds centers on the modern state of Israel, and an understanding of this issue requires us to examine a more ancient debate, namely, how the Third Temple will be rebuilt in the messianic era.[8] There are two schools of thought on this

---

4. I prefer this term to "Haredi" or "Ultra-Orthodox," two terms that are frequently used in the mainstream media, but that have a pejorative sense based on the politics of Israeli society.

5. Lamm, *Torah Umadda*, 5.

6. Lamm, *Torah Umadda*, 40.

7. Lamm, *Torah Umadda*, 6.

8. As most readers probably know, there were two temples erected by the Jews on Mount Moriah in Jerusalem. The first, built by Solomon (1 Kings 6), stood for 410 years and was destroyed by the armies of Babylonia at the command of King Nebuchadnezzar

issue among Jewish scholars. The first is championed by Rashi, who maintains that the Third Temple has already been built by the hands of God and is waiting in heaven for God to allow it to descend to the Temple Mount in Jerusalem.[9] In contradistinction to Rashi's view stands that of Rambam. In the *Mishneh Torah*, in the section devoted to the laws involving the rebuilding of the temple (a section called "the laws of Beit Habechirah"), Rambam states that the Third Temple will be built by the Jewish people themselves, and he goes on to provide the exact measurements and dimensions to be used in building this edifice.

Applying this debate to Zionism in general and the establishment of the State of Israel in particular, those who ascribe to Rashi's perspective on the building of the Third Temple see the modern state as an act that goes against the will of God. Instead of actively working to establish and build a Jewish homeland, proponents of this viewpoint maintain that the Jewish people should have patiently waited for God Himself to lower the completed temple onto His holy mountain in Jerusalem.[10] Today, this opposition expresses itself in certain Black Hat synagogues whose members will not recite the prayer for Israel composed in 1948 by the Sephardi and Ashkenazi chief rabbis of the newly formed State of Israel. Why? Because the prayer opens with the line referring to the messianic redemption, "Our Father who is in heaven, Protector and Redeemer of Israel, bless the State of Israel, *the dawn of our deliverance*."

And what of those Orthodox Jews at the other end of the spectrum? Modern Orthodoxy embraces the modern State of Israel and sees theological significance in its founding.[11] This is not to say that the Modern Or-

---

in the year 586 BCE. Seventy years later, Jews were allowed to return to the Holy Land and begin reconstruction of a second temple under the auspices of Ezra and Nehemiah (Ezra 1:1—6:22). The Second Temple stood for 420 years and was destroyed by the Roman armies under the command of Titus in the year 68 CE.

9. See Rashi's commentary to the talmudic tractates of Rosh Hashanah (30a) and Sukkah (41a). Others who agree with Rashi's understanding include Tosafot (Sukkah 41a and Shevuot 15b), Tosafot HaRosh (Sukkah 41a), Ritva (Sukkah 41a), and Rabbeinu Avrohom Min HaHar (Sukkah 41a).

10. This is not a theoretical argument. One group in particular, the Neturei Karta, which dates back to 1938, opposes Zionism and calls for a dismantling of the State of Israel in the belief that Jews are forbidden to have their own state until the coming of the Jewish messiah.

11. The debate among Modern Orthodox scholars is not whether the establishment of the state is part of the messianic process but what point of the process it represents. Is it a beginning? A hint of a beginning? Something further along? For an insightful analysis of this issue, see Soloveitchik, *Kol Dodi Dofek*. Given first as an address at Yeshiva University in New York on the occasion of Israel's Independence (Yom Ha'atzmaut 1956), *Kol Dodi Dofek* discusses God and the Holocaust, the importance of

thodox community is oblivious to the many social, political, and religious issues that exist in Israel. Rather, this community recognizes that reaching the time of the messiah and the rebuilding of the temple is a process, and the founding of Israel is part and parcel of that process. As Rabbi Aharon Lichtenstein so aptly put it: "The truth is that there is great pain in pondering the State of Israel, because the disappointment is so great. Many say sincerely that that this is not the child for whom we prayed. But would we be better off without the child altogether? Would we be better off barren? No! We must raise families, in the national sense, with the visage of Jacob-Israel emblazoned upon their foreheads."[12]

The third aspect of the philosophical disagreement between the left and the right in the Orthodox world involves the role of women in Judaism. The discussion here is very broad and encompasses a number of topics, from the question of whether Jewish education for women should differ from that of men to the question of what communal leadership roles, including that of rabbi, should be open to women in modern times. In the context of the daughters of Zelophehad, the question of leadership is most germane.

In more traditional, right-leaning communities, the expectation is that women will not be in positions of public leadership. The underpinning for this perspective is found in the verse from the book of Psalms: "All the honor of the king's daughter is within" (Psalm 45:14). The talmudic rabbis saw in this verse a basis for the differing natures of men and women. In their opinion, men belonged in the marketplace whereas women were needed at home. Indeed, by talmudic times, the exclusion of women from the public domain was taken for granted.[13] For example, the midrash in Sifre Deuteronomy, Pisqa 157, in analyzing Deuteronomy 17:15—"Be sure to set as king over yourself one of your own people"—opines that "a king, but not a queen .... A man may be appointed leader of a community, but not a woman."

Not surprisingly, family was highly valued in talmudic times, but much of communal life and most of ritual observance was (and remains) divided by gender. Men led the prayers, codified legal decisions, controlled the community chest, and dealt with the outside world. This impacted

---

the modern State of Israel, and the role of Zionism in American Orthodoxy. *Kol Dodi Dofek* has become a classic text of religious Zionist philosophy.

12. Sabato, *Seeking His Presence*, 223. Rabbi Aharon Lichtenstein received his advanced training and rabbinic ordination at Yeshiva University from his primary mentor and father-in-law, Rabbi Joseph B. Soloveitchik. In addition to his yeshiva studies, Rabbi Lichtenstein completed a PhD in English literature at Harvard University. From 1971 until his death in 2015, he was rosh yeshiva of Yeshivat Har Etzion in Alon Shvut, Israel.

13. Wegner, "Women," 84.

women's sphere of influence, which tended to be limited to the private domain. As a result, women were discouraged (and still are in some communities today) from pursuing higher education or religious pursuits, primarily because of the fear that women who engage in such pursuits might neglect their primary duties as wives and mothers. This worldview can be summarized as follows:

> A woman's primary concern must be the religious well-being of her family. The religious life of a woman is part of Jewish life and indispensable for Jewish survival. If a career is a primary dedication, the pursuit of a career is inconsistent with the ideals of Jewish womanhood. If, on the other hand, it is understood that a career is only a secondary consideration and remains subservient to the primary dedication of building a Jewish home, then considerations that enter into a specific career decision are similar to those that may determine a man's choice.[14]

In contrast, the Modern Orthodox world takes a more expansive view on the leadership positions woman can and arguably should hold, a stand that seems in accordance with the rich biblical tradition on the leadership roles played by women. Start with the matriarch Sarah, about whom our rabbis have stated that her level of prophecy exceeded that of Abraham (see Rashi on Genesis 21:12), and continue on to Miriam, Deborah, and Hannah, who established song and prayer in Israel, and the wife of Manoah and the Shunamite woman, who were closer to the knowledge of God and to prophecy—moreso than their husbands, as the biblical text testifies (see Judges 13:8–11 and especially 22–23, and 2 Kings 4:8–10, and especially 22–23). There was also Queen Shlomtzion, who, according to the talmudic sages, was more worthy of the Hasmonean throne than her husband (Kiddushin 66a, Sotah 22b).

Modern Orthodox communities generally acknowledge that dramatic changes have been taking place in the lives of ritually observant Jews over the last fifty years. As Rabbi Michael Broyde noted not so long ago: "By and large we live in a society where many women are studying Torah intensively and participating extensively in a plethora of professional capacities, including many different roles in Jewish communal life: Women teach our children, found and run our schools, counsel troubled adults, run social service agencies, lecture on Torah topics and texts, and serve as outreach professionals."[15]

---

14. Meiselman, *Jewish Woman*, 169.
15. Broyde, "Orthodox Women Clergy?"

While debate still rages within the Modern Orthodox community regarding the question of the ordination of women, there is general consensus that women in communal leadership positions such as synagogue presidents and heads of schools has been a positive development. For instance, even the influential Orthodox Union, which remains adamantly opposed to the ordination of women, issued a statement in early 2017 in which it strongly encouraged its member synagogues to employ women in other, non-rabbinical types of leadership positions.[16] Its statement specifically endorsed the notion that women can and should teach Torah, including on advanced and sophisticated levels. This statement also encouraged women to lecture on Torah topics and share Torah insights; to assume communally significant roles in pastoral counseling, in community outreach to the religiously affiliated and unaffiliated, as well as in youth programming; and to advise on issues of family purity in conjunction with local rabbinic authorities, when a community's local rabbinic and lay leaders deem that step to be appropriate.

By this point, it should be clear that one's understanding of the philosophical issues that divide the left from the right in the Orthodox world will inevitably impact how one teaches the narrative of the daughters of Zelophehad in a Jewish setting. Do we see their actions as a template for women in leadership roles for future generations, or do we explain their story as something unique to their time and circumstances? Do we hear the yearnings of future Zionists in their longing for an inheritance in the promised land, or do we teach this unit through a filter of *Eretz Yisrael*, the land of Israel, and not *Medinat Yisrael*, the modern State of Israel? The left and the right of the Orthodox spectrum would answer each of these questions quite differently.

I can imagine a similar debate taking place in the planning of church Bible study groups, and I suspect that some classes, especially those held in evangelical congregations, would mirror the Orthodox left when it comes to the daughters of Zelophehad. Here's why.

At its core, their story is about their love for the land of Israel, and American Christians of various denominations have long been enamored of the Jewish return to Zion. Belief in the historical accuracy of the biblical

---

16. The Union of Orthodox Jewish Congregations of America, more popularly known as the Orthodox Union (OU), is one of the oldest and largest Orthodox Jewish organizations in the United States. Its member synagogues and their rabbis typically identify themselves with Modern Orthodox Judaism. The OU is best known for its kosher certification service. However, it also supports a network of youth programs, Jewish and religious Zionist advocacy initiative, programs for the disabled, and localized religious study programs. The full text of the statement can be found on the OU website: www.ou.org/assets/OU-Statement.pdf.

narratives influenced public opinion and helped make the case for a Jewish state. But in the first two decades of Israeli history, the ties between Israeli and American Jews and fundamentalist Christians were few.[17] Israel's remarkable (some would say miraculous) victory in the Six-Day War of 1967 changed the dynamics of this relationship. As Israeli journalist Gershom Gorenberg noted: "The Six-Day War did more than create a new political and military map in the Middle East. It also changed the mythic map, in a piece of the world where myths have always bent reality."[18]

The daughters of Zelophehad are no myth, and their devotion to family and to homeland are powerful models for individuals of all faiths. In the end, there is much the story of the daughters of Zelophehad has to teach the typical teen. Admittedly, the life philosophy I see reflected in the actions of these women resonates with my Modern Orthodox orientation. The commitment I see in the daughters of Zelophehad to building and being part of the establishment of a Jewish homeland in the promised land echoes the dreams and visions of individuals from Theodor Herzl to the brave souls in the modern state who daily work to keep the Zionist ideal alive. Their willingness to step forward and question the status quo, to be leaders, and to push Moses to inquire of God how to handle their situation reminds me of the remarkable women in my school, in my community, and, most importantly, in my family and of how grateful I am to be associated with them.

Is this Modern Orthodox slant the only way to teach the tale of the daughters of Zelophehad in a Jewish day school setting? Surely not, but in my eyes, it is the one that most affords them the honor and respect they deserve.

Think about it. These women saw things in life bigger than themselves, things like preserving the memory and legacy of their father and establishing for their families and for future generations a binding connection to the land of Israel. They were willing to take a stand and demand of their leader, Moses, that he reconsider their circumstances and grant them an inheritance in the land. This took courage on their part to stand up for their beliefs and to risk rejection or being ostracized.

Can you think of lessons more important than these to teach high school students? I can't.

---

17. Goldman, *Zeal*, 270.
18. Goldman, *Zeal*, 271.

Sefer BeMidbar—The Daughters of Zelophehad

Sample Unit Plan

Unit	Primary Source(s)	Supplemental Reading(s)	Timeframe
Reubenites	Numbers 32	Reviving Religious Zionism	two–three weeks
Gadites	Ramban 32:2		
	Ramban 32:19		
	Ramban 32:1–32		
	Ramban 32:22		
Daughters of Zelophehad	Numbers 27	The Daughters of Zelophehad: Legitimate Feminist Claims	
	Rashi 27:1		
	Rashi 27:3		
Middah:	Sforno 27:3		
Zionistic	Rashi 27:4		
	Rashi 27.5		

Essential Questions

1. Is the request of the Reubenites and Gadites reasonable or selfish? How does the timing of their request color our view of it?

2. Was Moses's response to their request appropriate?
3. Is the request of the daughters of Zelophehad reasonable or selfish?
4. Can we compare these two requests? Should we?

Evaluating/Checking for Understanding

1. Daily discussions/student interactions

   Student questions and observations typically drive each day's discussion.

2. Occasional written reflections

   At the discretion of the teacher, a tool to foster further reflection on the unit's essential questions.

3. Character trait essay

   See appendix for assignment rubric.

4. Unit test

   Unit tests should, by definition, be crafted by individual teachers to meet the needs of their specific students. The <u>Understanding by Design</u> framework created by Grant Wiggins and Jay McTighe is an excellent tool for the development of appropriate tests and assessments, as its emphasis on backward design forces teachers to consider in advance the assessment evidence needed to document and validate that the targeted learning goals have been achieved.

Primary Source Texts

1. Read articles on state of religious Zionism ("Reviving Religious Zionism" by Daniel Shoag, which follows this unit plan and "Is Religious Zionism in Crisis?" by Rabbi Yaakov Filber, which can be found online via a Google search) in order to understand what it is and how it has evolved since the creation of the modern State of Israel. A summary chart of the spectrum of views on religious Zionism also follows this unit plan.

2. *BeMidbar* chapter 32: Read text and seek to identify problematic (what I call "red flag") words and phrases (with teacher's guidance, of course). These red flag words and phrases will likely vary from class to class depending on the sophistication and linguistic abilities of the students, coupled with the background and interests of the teacher.

That said, some important examples of red flag words and phrases in this chapter appear in commentaries A–D.

3. *BeMidbar* chapter 27: Read text and seek to identify problematic (red flag) words and phrases (with teacher's guidance, of course). These red flag words and phrases will likely vary from class to class depending on the sophistication and linguistic abilities of the students, coupled with the background and interests of the teacher. That said, some important examples of red flag words and phrases in this chapter appear in commentaries E–I.

4. Supplemental readings for each unit are intended to demonstrate that serious scholarship about and explanations of *Sefer BeMidbar* are not limited to the classical medieval commentators but continue to our time. The titles of supplemental readings for this unit speak for themselves: "Loving the Land of Israel" and "The Daughters of Zelophehad: Legitimate Feminist Claims," both by Rabbi Ephraim Z. Buchwald.

Sefer BeMidbar—The Daughters of Zelophehad

Primary Texts

A. Ramban 32:1–2

"And the children of Gad and the children of Reuben came and spoke to Moses"

In the preceding verse Scripture mentioned the children of Reuben first, "Now the children of Reuben and the children of Gad had a very great multitude of cattle," as is the correct way, for he [Reuben] was the firstborn and he was the son of the principal wife [i.e., Leah, whereas Gad was the son of Leah's handmaid, Zilpah]. Similarly, when Scripture also tells of this event it says, "And unto the Reubenites and unto the Gadites I gave . . ." However, in the whole of this section He mentions the children of Gad first, because it was they who suggested this idea, and it was they who first spoke to Moses about this inheritance; and they were also stronger than the children of Reuben, as it is said "and he [the Gadites] tear the arm, yea, the crown of the head," and therefore they were not afraid of living alone among the inhabitants of the land. Now Moses suspected that they were only suggesting this because they were afraid of the people in the land of Canaan, concerning whom the Spies had said, "We are not able to go up against the people, for they are stronger than we." Therefore, he told them that they did not trust in God, just like their fathers and therefore He would again punish them like their fathers, by "leaving them in the wilderness" (verse 15). Therefore they answered him: "Far be it from us to fear them! For we shall pass over armed for battle, and we shall be the most eager and the first among the people to fight against the enemies of the Eternal, for they are bread for us" (14:9).

B. Ramban 32:19

"For our inheritance has come to us"

"We have already received it on the eastern side [of the Jordan]." This is Rashi's language. But it would not be correct for them to speak in this manner in front of Moses, saying, "we have already received it," for it was not up to them, but on his will that the matter depended, and they did not receive it until he decided to give it to them. Instead, they said to Moses: "for you do not have to give us an inheritance with them, thereby making their inheritance in the good Land smaller, for an inheritance which is suitable for us has come to us, since it is a land fit for cattle, and we have more cattle than the other tribes." This they said in the nature of a request, not by way of contention. Or perhaps they said, "For we will not inherit with them, because even if you do not want to give us the land now, we will cross over together with them, we and all that we have, but we will not inherit with them, for we will return to this land which is the inheritance that is suitable for us, and which we want, and which none of the other tribes want at all."

C. Ramban 32:19

"And the children of Gad and the children of Reuben answered saying . . . we will pass over armed"

They said to Moses, "Our lord need not command us with a double condition [see verses 29–30]. Far be it from your servants to transgress that which my lord commands! For [your words] are the words of God, and we will not transgress His commandment!" And this is the meaning of the expression "as the Eternal has said," for at the beginning they had said that they would do "as my lord commanded" (verse 25).

D. Ramban 32:32

"And half the tribe of Menashe the son of Yosef"

At the beginning the tribe of Manasseh did not come to Moses, but when Moses apportioned the land to the two tribes, he saw that the land was larger than they required, and therefore he asked for people who were prepared to take their inheritance with them. And there were people of the tribe of Menashe who wanted that land—perhaps they were owners of cattle—and therefore he gave them their portion.

Now the meaning of ולחצי is "unto one part" of them. Similarly, "Then were the people of Israel divided *lacheitzi* (into two parts): *chatzi* (part of) the people followed Tibni the son of Ginat, to make him king, *v'hachatzi* (and the other part) followed Omri." (1 Kings 16:21) And the explanation is: The children of Manasseh consisted of eight paternal families as is written in the section dealing with the census, and the families of the Machirities and of the Gileadites took their inheritance in this land because they were men of valor and they conquered it for themselves, and Moses gave them a large part of it. The six families, however, crossed over the Jordan, as it is written in the book of Joshua, "And the lot was for the rest of the children of Manasseh according to their families; for the children of Abiezer, and for the children of Helek, and for the children of Asriel, and for the children of Shechem, and for the children of Hepher, and for the children of Shemidah." And this is the meaning of what is written there, "And there fell ten parts to Manasseh, beside the land of Gilead and Bashan, which is beyond the Jordan."

E. Rashi 27:1

"Of the families of Menashe, the son of Joseph"

Why is this stated? Has it not already been said son of Manasseh, and consequently we know that they belonged to the family of Manasseh the son of Joseph?! But it is to suggest the following idea to you: Just as Joseph held the Promised Land dear, as it is said (Genesis 50:25), "And ye shall bring my bones up (to Palestine) from hence," so, too, his daughters held the Land dear, as it is said (v. 4), "Give us an inheritance"; and further to teach you that they were righteous all of them (everyone here mentioned in the pedigree), for in every case where a person's doings and his ancestors' doings are nowhere plainly described and Scripture somewhere enters into the details of the pedigree in respect to one of them, tracing his genealogy back to someone worthy of praise, it is evident that the person in question is himself a righteous man and a son of a righteous father. But if it gives his genealogy in connection with something deserving of reprobation,—as, for example (2 Kings 25:25), "Ishmael the son of Nethanian the son of Elishama came ... and smote Gedaliah," then it is quite certain that all who are mentioned in connection with him were wicked people.

F. Rashi 27:3

"And he was not [. . . in the congregation of Korah]"

Because they intended to state that HE DIED IN HIS OWN SIN they felt compelled to say he had taken no part in the sin of those who murmured, nor had he been in the congregation of Korah who incited the people against the Holy One, blessed be He (cf. Sifre Numbers 133:3 and Babylonian Talmud, Bava Batra 118b), but he had died through his own sin only, and had not made others to sin with him (Sifre Numbers 133:3).—As regards what this sin was, R. Akiva said that he was the man who gathered sticks on the Sabbath day (Numbers 15:32); R. Simeon said that he was one of those who presumed to disobey God's command (Numbers 14:44).

G. Sforno 27:3

"He was not one [of the faction, Korah's faction]"

He was not a member of the rebellious people who had made common cause with Korah. Those people had been banished by Moses, i.e., disinherited by him, deprived not only of potential property but even of all their actual belongings, as we have been told in Numbers 16:26. The words כל הרכוש in verse 32 of that chapter make clear that they had forfeited all claims to anything.

"But he died for his own sin"

He died on account his personal sin, something that did not involve the claims of his heirs to his estate. [The daughters did not mean to malign their father by saying this; rather, they meant to say that their father had completely atoned for his sin by his premature judicial execution.]

H. Rashi 27:4

"Why should the name of our father be done away"

We stand in the place of male children, and if you say that females are not regarded as issue in respect to inheritance, then our mother should marry her deceased husband's brother.

I. Rashi 27:5

"And Moses brought their cause [before the Lord]"

The law on this subject escaped him (Sanhedrin 8a). Here he received punishment because he had assumed a "crown" (he had set himself up as the supreme judge) by saying (Deuteronomy 1:17), "And the cause that is too hard for you ye shall bring to me." Another explanation: This chapter ought to have been written by Moses (i.e., like most laws in the Torah it should have been spoken to the people by Moses without his having waited until some incident made its promulgation necessary), but for the fact that the daughters of Zelophehad had so much merit, it was therefore written through them (it was their complaint which gave occasion for stating it) (Bava Batra 119a and Sanhedrin 8a).

Sefer BeMidbar—The Daughters of Zelophehad

Supplemental Reading

Reviving Religious Zionism

—Daniel Shoag

Today the term Zionism is oversimplified. Having once stood for a range of sophisticated and nuanced ideologies, it has taken on a popular meaning of blanket support for the Jewish State. Yet, with Zionism today facing intellectual assault, Zionists must clearly define their beliefs to defend them more effectively. This article will focus on a particular brand of Zionism—Religious Zionism—the ideology of those who support Jewish autonomy on religious grounds.

Arguably a rather large percentage of American Jews may be called religious Zionists. Many, if not most Jewish congregations in America pray for the State of Israel and refer to it as *Reishit Shmichat Geulateinu* or the "beginning of our redemption." This prayer, as well as others, reflect the view that the Jewish State has value not only culturally or politically, but religiously as well. The religious interpretation of Jewish sovereignty is also unmistakably evident in the focus on the State of Israel in sermons and synagogue activities and in the religiously oriented celebrations of Yom Ha'atzmaut (Independence Day) and Yom Hazikaron (Memorial Day).

The religious approach to Zionism, however, has a number of powerful critics. One of the most eloquent and passionate critics of the view that the State of Israel has religious importance is the late Professor Yeshayhu Leibowitz of Hebrew University. An ardent Zionist, Leibowitz nonetheless believes that "the State of Israel of our day has no religious significance," and he powerfully criticizes the existing lines of Zionist thought that attributed significance to the Jewish nation-state.

In this essay I will outline some of the existing major lines of Religious Zionist thought, summarize Leibowitz's critique of these positions, and then propose a possible fruitful new direction for Religious Zionism.

Religious Significance

Much of American Jewry relates to the modern Jewish nation state as something "holy." Conditioned as Americans are to view religion and state as inherently separate domains, it may seem strange for American Jewry to view the Israeli Knesset (parliament) as a religiously important body. Yet this is the only possible interpretation one could give to the prayers and verses found in the prayer books of most Reform, Conservative and Orthodox Jews across the country.

This significance is different too from the more general idea that the Land of Israel itself is holy, a long established Jewish tradition. There are numerous commandments pertaining to the land, but these commandments give significance to a geographic area, not a political body. Many American Jews consider not only the land religiously important but the political Jewish nation-state which governs the land religiously important as well.

Rabbi Kook

One of the best-known and most explicitly religious interpretations of Zionism was expressed, perhaps most famously, by Rabbi Avraham Yitzhak Hacohen Kook. Kook, the first chief Rabbi of the pre-state Jewish settlement in Israel known as the Yishuv, was well known for his tireless efforts to bring together Israel's secular and religious communities. Kook was also, however, an unabashed messianist who saw within the Zionist movement the redemption promised by the prophecies. Kook's Hegelian thought premises that the end of history or redemption would follow the synthesis of secular Zionism and traditional Judaism. Kook believed that the great upheavals he saw in the world around him during World War I were the chaos which the prophecies predicted would precede the Messiah. Kook writes, "The time of the songbird has come ... The present world war [WWI] is filled with deep, awesome, colossal expectations, combined with all of the vicissitudes of the times, which point to the Revealed End with the settlement of Eretz Yisrael."[1] Zionism and the future State of Israel were religiously significant

---

1. David Samson and Tzvi Fishman, eds., *The Teachings of HaRav Avraham*

for Kook, then, because they represented the manifest hand of God in history. To Kook, the State of Israel represented the herald of the Messiah, the beginning of redemption, and the work of the Lord.

Rabbi Kook's son and successor, Rabbi Tzvi Yehuda ha-Cohen Kook, carried his father's idea even farther in advocating that Israeli military and political decisions be made on the basis of the impending messianic age. In the words of Rabbi Ya'akov Ariel, the chief Rabbi of Ramat Gan, "Rabbi Tzvi Yehudah's greatness lay in his translation of the broad, deep teachings of his father into the language [of] action."[2] The political ideology formulated by Rabbi Tzvi Yehudah and his contemporaries at the Merkaz HaRav Yeshiva was unique in its stress on maintaining the entire land of Israel, including the territories conquered in the Six Day War in 1967. "The State of Israel is divine . . . Not only can/must there be no retreat from [a single] kilometer of the Land of Israel, God forbid, but on the contrary, we shall conquer and liberate more and more."[3] It is this ideology, created by the latter Rabbi Kook and premised on the new idea of messianic determinism, which spurred what today has become one of the most prominent faces of Religious Zionism, the settlement movement of Gush Emunim.

Leibowitz's Criticism of Kook

This view of the religious significance of the state of Israel has been the subject of fierce and perhaps mortal criticism from Yeshayahu Leibowitz, a noted ethicist and professor at the Hebrew University in Jerusalem.

While professing great respect for the personality of Rabbi Kook himself, Leibowitz attacks the sage's claim that the state of Israel represents the hand of God in history by simply pointing out that there has been no direct sign from God backing that claim. He argues, "All of us, therefore, having no insight into the designs of Providence, must exercise utmost caution before proclaiming events of the nature of military victory or national political deliverance as the 'dawn of redemption' or 'the sprouting of our redemption.'"[4]

While many claims that the Jewish State's successes are indeed a direct sign from God, Leibowitz points out that the Bible is rife with tales of great national victories won by men whom our tradition has nonetheless

---

Yitzhak HaCohen Kook War and Peace (Jerusalem: Torat Eretz Yisrael, 1996), 36.

2. Aviezer Ravitsky, *Messianism, Zionism and Jewish Religious Radicalism* (Chicago: University of Chicago Press, 1996), 123.

3. Ravitsky, *Messianism*, 132.

4. Yeshayahu Leibowitz, "Redemption and the Dawn of Redemption" (1971), in *Judaism, Human Values, and the Jewish State* (Cambridge, MA: Harvard, 1992), 123.

considered wicked. For example, though King Jeroboam "restored the border of Israel from the entering of Hamath to the sea of Arabah" and "recovered Damascus . . . which had belonged to Judah in Israel," he was still said to do "that which was evil in the sight of God" (2 Kings 14:23–25).[5] In fact, the prophet Amos even curses Israel for the actions of Jeroboam, saying, "Yarov'am shall die by the sword and Israel shall surely be led captive out of their own land" (Amos 8:11).[6]

Having thus established that military and political victories are not, in themselves, sufficient proof of God's work, Leibowitz then argues that "since the establishment of the state of Israel was not inspired by the Torah, nor undertaken for the sake of Torah, religiously speaking, its existence is a matter of indifference."[7] Taking this thought a step further, Leibowitz writes that "Zionism as an aspiration to political-national independence is a legitimate Jewish aspiration . . . but it must not be given a religious aura."

"The category of holiness is inapplicable to the state," Leibowitz writes. "Only God is holy and only His imperatives absolute."[8] To Leibowitz, in short, "the State of Israel of our day has no religious significance."

David Hartman's Response to Yeshayahu Leibowitz

Leibowitz, in his attack on the idea of a "holy" state, does allow the possibility that a historical event, such as the creation of Israel, could have religious impact by providing opportunities for furthering Jewish practice. "In Judaism," he writes, "each historical situation, every historical vicissitude and change, and even the historical process as a whole are treated not from the point of view of a specific religious-historical conception, but from the perspective of the religious interest."[9] Leibowitz believes that this doctrine of "religious opportunism" accounts for the differing political messages of the prophets, for each conveyed "only the absolute demand to serve God" while their attitude toward history "change[d] according to the changing

---

5. Translation from Noson Scherman, ed., *The Stone Edition Tanach* (Brooklyn, NY: ArtScroll, 1996).

6. Translation from Scherman, *Stone Edition Tanach*.

7. Yeshayahu Leibowitz, "The Religious Significance of the State" (1975), in *Judaism, Human Values, and the Jewish State* (Cambridge, MA: Harvard, 1992), 214.

8. Yeshayahu Leibowitz, "The Significance of Redemption" (1977), in *Judaism, Human Values, and the Jewish State* (Cambridge, MA: Harvard, 1992), 106.

9. Yeshayahu Leibowitz, "Ahistorical Thinkers in Judaism" (1980), in in *Judaism, Human Values, and the Jewish State* (Cambridge, MA: Harvard, 1992), 96.

implications of the historic situations for the observance of the Torah and the Mitzvoth."[10]

Picking up on Leibowitz's caveat, Rabbi David Hartman makes a vision of a Jewish state central to his religious perspective. Hartman sees the role of the state of Israel as the expansion of Jewish responsibility and involvement in the world, a concept central to his "covenantal" theology that emphasizes the activist aspects of man's relationship with God. "By infusing Torah with the original Zionist passion for Jewish responsibility, we can renew the Sinai covenant once again in the conditions of modern Israel."[11]

Yet, in spite of the ease with which the Jewish state fits in to Hartman's broader theology, he is admittedly dependent on the loophole which Leibowitz himself provides. "One can religiously embrace modern Israel not through a judgment about God's actions in history but through an understanding of the centrality of Israel for the fullest actualization of the world of mitzvoth,"[12] he writes. Ultimately, it is this dependency which undermines Hartman's approach. Leibowitz, well aware of his own qualification, still does not find the Jewish nation-state holy, despite its obvious benefit to "religious interests" because Judaism designates the ends as religiously important, not the means. In other words, while Leibowitz believes Israel might have a religious impact, he does not believe it held religious significance. To him, it is the religious equivalent of a pious Jew winning the lottery—it enables religious practice but is not meaningful in and of itself. Hartman, who wishes to set up the State of Israel as religiously important, never manages to overcome the difficulty hidden in Leibowitz's loophole. Thus, while Hartman speaks powerfully about Israel's role in expanding Jewish activism, he never manages to establish a stable base on which to ground his theory of religious Zionism.

The Rav: Rabbi Joseph Dov Soloveitchik's Halakhic Option

Rabbi Joseph Dov Soloveitchik, commonly thought to be the father of American Modern-Orthodoxy, believes as Rabbi Kook does that the State of Israel represents the obvious hand of God working in history. While not nearly as messianic as Kook, Soloveitchik believes that divine will was the only way to account for the seemingly miraculous events that enabled the State of Israel to be created. Thus, while Soloveitchik does not see the

---

10. Leibowitz, "Ahistorical Thinkers," 96.

11. David Hartman, *A Living Covenant: The Innovative Spirit in Traditional Judaism* (Woodstock: Jewish Lights, 1997), 285.

12. Hartman, *Living Covenant*, 285.

modern Jewish nation state as heralding the end of history, he does see religious meaning in the State of Israel as the direct creation of God. Soloveitchik spells this view out in his famous essay Kol Dodi Dofek (The Voice of my Beloved Knocks), in which he enjoins the American Jewish community to heed the miracles worked by God in the creation of the State of Israel. Soloveitchik even goes as far as enumerating what he believes to be the six major miracles that the Lord preformed when He "suddenly manifested Himself"[13] in 1948, the year of Israel's birth.

Yet, while maintaining his belief that the birth of the modern state of Israel is a manifest miracle, Soloveitchik also finds a halakhic basis for the religious significance of the Jewish State. Soloveitchik finds this basis in the commandment to settle the Land of Israel (*Yishuv Ha'aretz*), from which he extrapolates an obligation to create Jewish sovereignty in the land as well. "We said, this mitzvah is fulfilled not only by building up the country . . . but also by our sovereignty there."[14] Soloveitchik bolsters his position that the commandment of *Yishuv Ha'aretz* includes the notion of sovereignty by citing the Biblical source of the decree[15] and the commentary of Nachmanides,[16] both of which can be read as advocating Jewish rule of the Holy Land. These traditional sources, the Rav claims, show that the mitzvah has long been understood as obligating Jews to pursue autonomy in the Holy Land.

Despite Soloveitchik's attempt to couch his extrapolation in traditional terms, he was certainly aware that his reading an obligation to establish sovereignty into the mitzvah of *Yishuv Ha'aretz* was a major innovation in halakha, and one that broke with the traditional understanding of the mitzvah. In his major work on Zionism, Fir Droshes, Soloveitchik notes that although his illustrious and pious grandfather Rabbi Chaim of Brisk dreamed of "settl[ing] in the land of Israel . . . and fulfill[ing] the commandments pertaining to the land,"[17] he was opposed to the idea of Jewish sovereignty. "His love of Zion and Jerusalem had no relation to the Zionism of Chaim Weizmann,"[18] Soloveitchik writes. Rabbi Soloveitchik's prominent rabbinic family was far from neutral when it came to the issue of Zionism. Indeed,

---

13. Joseph Soloveitchik, "Kol Dodi Dofek," in *Fate and Destiny: From Holocaust to the State of Israel* (Hoboken, NJ: Ktav, 2000).

14. Joseph Soloveitchik, *The Rav Speaks: Five Addresses on Israel, History and the Jewish People* (New York: Judaica Press, 2002), 137.

15. "And ye shall drive out the inhabitants of the land, and swell therein" (Numbers 33:53, translation from Scherman, *Stone Edition Tanach*).

16. Nachmanides writes that Jews are obligated to "possess the land . . . and not forsake it in the hands of others."

17. Soloveitchik, *Rav Speaks*, 35.

18. Soloveitchik, *Rav Speaks*, 35.

the Rav's great-grandfather vigorously denounced the fledging movement as early as 1889.

It is surprising, then, that Soloveitchik pays so little attention to his halakhic innovation and its implications in his writings. There is no discussion of the legitimacy of his relocating of the locus of *Yishuv Ha'aretz* from the individual to the collective, nor is there discussion about the validity of a corporate actor fulfilling a commandment issued to individuals.

Moreover, Soloveitchik does not discuss the implications that follow from grounding the halakhic nature of the state in the mitzvah of *Yishuv Ha'aretz*. By so basing the state, Soloveitchik makes immigration to Israel, or aliyah, the primary goal of Jewish sovereignty, and he raises a standard by which we are to religiously judge aspects the Jewish nation-state. The elements of Jewish sovereignty that promote immigration are to be considered holy, those which do not are not. This dichotomy, I believe, does not fit well with the empirical religious valuations most Jews make about the State of Israel. For example, Jews tend to see Israel's victories in 1948 and 1967, but not the fifth Aliyah, as religiously significant events. Soloveitchik's method would also require Jews to strenuously oppose Israeli settlements in the Golan Heights, which may not hold the status of the Land of Israel according to the halakha. Lastly, one wonders how Soloveitchik's method can hold meaning for the millions of Jews in the Diaspora who do not plan on emigrating. According to Soloveitchik, these Jews must find religious meaning in the State of Israel in that it facilitates their fulfillment of a commandment that they do not plan to fulfill. This method forces Diaspora Jewry to maintain a hypocritical approach to the state's religious nature, and I personally feel that a better understanding of religious Zionism can be found.

Emil Fackenheim's Moral Imperative to Self-Defense and the Beginnings of a Second Option

The formative years of Religious Zionism have come during a period of history in which the Jewish people have been forced to realize the dangers that lie in powerlessness. Emil Fackenheim, one of Judaism's first post-Holocaust theologians, addresses the issue of the Holocaust by positing a "first priority" for the Jewish people, namely "safety of their children."[19] Fackenheim believes that Jews were "morally required to seek independence" and "safety" and that this requirement preceded any relationship the Jewish people would establish with either God or with the Christian world. Fackenheim

---

19. Emil Fackenheim, *To Mend the World: Foundations of Post-Holocaust Jewish Thought* (Bloomington: Indiana University Press, 1994), 284.

articulates this need for Jewish self-defense in his famed six-hundred-and-fourteenth commandment, which emanated from the "commanding Voice of Auschwitz, forbidding the post-Holocaust Jew to give Hitler posthumous victories."[20] Fackenheim believes that this "commandment," this moral imperative, was best fulfilled by the creation of a Jewish State. Therefore, Fackenheim writes, "except among the theologically or humanly perverse, Zionism—the commitment to the safety and genuine sovereignty of the State of Israel—is not negotiable."[21]

Building on Fackenheim

While Fackenheim's sentiments about the need for Jewish self-reliance in the form of a Jewish state are immensely popular, Fackenheim fails to locate a religious or divine source for his "moral imperative." For Fackenheim, self-defense and its manifestation in Zionism, are not religious values but rather things that precede religious value or stand outside of it. Thus, Fackenheim locates the significance of the Jewish State in the Holocaust rather than in traditional Judaism: "solely because of the connection of the events ... with Auschwitz did a military victory acquire an inescapable religious dimension."[22] Yet this need not be the case.

The Torah provides a religious locus for the moral imperative to Jewish communal defense in the book of Leviticus: "do not stand idly by your brother's blood." Put in another way, the Bible commands Jews to defend one another. The lesson of the Holocaust, as Fackenheim notes, is that such defense is impossible without a nation-state and sovereignty. Numerous books, articles and publications have documented how the large, stateless Jewish community of the United States was forced to literally stand by as the Holocaust killed more than six million of its brethren.[23] Thus, it may be possible to consider Zionism and the modern State of Israel as the collective Jewish fulfillment of the ancient halakhic charge not to stand idly by.

Identifying the State of Israel as the Jewish people's movement toward self-defense also fits nicely with the stated aims of Zionism and the State of Israel. Israel's Declaration of Independence cites the defenselessness of the Jewish community during the Holocaust as a "clear demonstration of the

20. Fackenheim, *To Mend the World*, 299.
21. Fackenheim, *To Mend the World*, 284–85.
22. Emil Fackenheim, "Jewish Faith and the Holocaust: A Fragment," *Commentary* (August 1968).
23. An example of this literature is Arthur Morse, *While Six Million Died* (London: Secker and Warburg, 1968).

urgency of solving the problem of [its] homelessness by reestablishing in Eretz-Israel the Jewish State." The Declaration proclaims that Israel is the response to the Jews' need for self-defense; that is, it is a fulfillment of their halakhic obligation toward self-defense.

Benefits and Challenges of the New Approach

The possibility of locating Zionism's religious significance within the framework of the commandment not to "stand idly by" yields, I believe, a number of important benefits to those seeking a religiously relevant Jewish State. The primary benefit is, of course, the ability to celebrate Israel's victories in intellectually honest religious terms. The War of Independence, the Six Day War and even Israel's current war on terror can be seen as religiously significant acts through this lens as all were fought or are being fought for the purpose of defending Jewish lives. Looking at the modern Jewish national movement as the fulfillment of this specific commandment from God justifies the language used and the attention given to the State of Israel in most American synagogues.

There is, however, another equally important advantage to locating Zionism's religious message within the context of this commandment of *Lo Ta'amod*. By placing the religious value of Zionism in the context of fulfilling a single mitzvah, one can not only celebrate Israel's victories, but can also classify what aspects of Israel are indeed religiously significant. In other words, by locating the religious meaning of Zionism within the commandment of Jewish communal defense, only the aspects of Israel that further that goal ought to truly be considered religiously relevant. Thus, one does not necessarily need to support policies to make the machinery of the state more compliant with halakha, for the machinery is not relevant because it enforces halakha generally but rather because it fulfills a single, discrete commandment. Zionism looked at as the fulfillment of the mitzvah of *Lo Ta'amod* can be religiously significant without the need to advocate a theocratic, halakha-enforcing state. More generally, finding the religious locus of the state within a single commandment allows one to designate as "holy" only the aspects of the state that fulfill that commandment.

Additionally, this new basis for Religious Zionism allows for a more stable approach to the existence of the Jewish State, I believe, than does the approach of Rabbi Kook. Kook's view tempts one to view every mundane event concerning Israel as a highly charged part of the meta-historical drama of an impending Messianic age. This temptation could have disastrous consequences and is neutralized by defining Israel's religious meaning in a non-messianic way.

This is not to say, however, that the new method is not without its difficulties. Reading a halakhic backing for the state out of a verse in Leviticus, like Soloveitchik's innovation, requires an active interpretation of the commandment at odds with the traditional reading. Even the fairly early commentary of Rabbi Shimon Yitzhaki (Rashi) interprets the commandment as applying only once a person is in the position to save a fellow's life. That is, Rashi did not see the commandment as a blanket requirement for Jews to place themselves in the position to save their fellows. Yet, in a post-Holocaust world, stretching the traditional commandment hardly seems unreasonable. Other difficulties to be worked out include, again as with Soloveitchik's approach, the transfer of the onus of the commandment from the individual to the community and the validity of a Jewish corporate actor.

Though this is merely the beginning of a new approach to Religious Zionism, I hope that this article will generate some new thought on the subject. Israel is under attack today not only physically, but also intellectually. It is incumbent upon us to find new and workable approaches to all branches of Zionism.

> **Daniel Shoag** is an associate professor of public policy at Harvard Kennedy School, a visiting professor at Case Western Reserve University, and an affiliate of the Taubman Center for State and Local Government. Daniel received his BA and PhD in economics from Harvard University and lives in Newton, MA and Cleveland, OH with his wife and four sons.

Sefer BeMidbar—The Daughters of Zelophehad

Supplemental Reading

Loving the Land of Israel

—Rabbi Ephraim Z. Buchwald

In this coming week's parasha, parashat Phinehas, we learn the fascinating tale of five trail-blazing young women: Mahlah, Noah, Hoglah, Milcah, and Tirzah—the daughters of Zelophehad. On Thursday, June 27, 2002, Jews all over the world will observe the Fast of *Shiv'ah Asar B'Tamuz,* the 17th day of Tamuz. This fast commemorates the breaching of the walls of Jerusalem by the Babylonian army during the siege of the city in 586 BCE, leading to the destruction of the Temple and the city of Jerusalem. As we shall see, there is a striking confluence between the request of the daughters of Zelophehad and the mourning for the loss of the Temple and Jerusalem.

Who are these five women? In Numbers 27:1–2 we read: *Vah'tik'rav'nah b'not Zelophehad ben Chefer ben Gilad ben Machir ben Menashe la'mish'p'chot Menashe ben Yosef . . . Va'ta'ah'mod'nah lif'nei Moshe,* These women, who were direct descendants of forefather Joseph, approached Moses with a claim about the legal rights to their father's property in the land of Israel.

In Genesis 50:25 the Bible quotes Joseph as saying to his family before his death, *Pakod yif'kod Eloh'kim et'chem . . . V'ha'ah'lee'tem et atz'mo'tai mee'zeh,* G-d will surely remember you, and you shall carry up my bones from here [Egypt], and bring them to the land of Israel. By identifying the women as descendants of Joseph, scripture underscores that these five women were spiritual as well as physical descendants of Joseph—a person with an abiding commitment to the land of Israel. Although Joseph was certainly a greatly admired hero in Egypt, he knew that Egypt was not his land, and insisted on being taken out of that land to be buried in the land of Israel.

Numbers 27:3–4 fills in the details of the womens' claim: "Our father died in the wilderness, and he was not in the company of them that gathered themselves together against the Lord in the company of Korah. But he died in his own sin, and he had no sons. Why should the name of our father be eliminated from his family because he has no sons? Give to us a possession among the brethren of our father." Clearly, these women were passionately committed to the Holy Land.

G-d's response (Numbers 27:7): *Kain b'not Zelophehad dovrot*, the daughters of Zelophehad speak correctly. They shall surely be given a possession of inheritance among their father's brethren. And thou shall cause the inheritance of their father to pass to them. The women's passionate commitment to Israel was rewarded!

When contrasted with the great love of Zion of the daughters of Zelophehad, contemporary Jewry's commitment, despite all the fretting over the security of Israel, rather pales. Frankly, one of the greatest lies of contemporary Jewry is the statement that diaspora Jews pronounce at the end of Yom Kippur and toward the close of the Passover seder, *L'shanah ha'ba'ah b'Yerushalayim*, next year in Jerusalem.

When the so-called Oslo Peace Agreement was feted on the White House lawn in 1993, together with President Clinton, Prime Minister Rabin and Yasser Arafat, I had a nightmare. I had a nightmare that the Al-mighty tried to clarify to the world the purpose of the Oslo accords by exclaiming to the Jewish people. "For 2,000 years you have been badgering and nudging me with prayers and petitions. *V'lee'Yerushalayim eer'cha b'rachamim tah'shuv*, restore Your presence to Zion, Oh Lord, *V'teh'cheh'zeh'nah ay'nay'noo b'shuv'chah l'Tzion b'rah'chah'mim*, may our eyes soon behold the return of the presence of G-d to Zion. In bentching, in the Grace after meals, you cried out, *Ooh'v'nay Yerushalayim eir hakodesh*, rebuild Jerusalem, the Holy city. Every year at the seder and the conclusion of Yom Kippur you exclaimed, *L'shah'nah ha'ba'ah b'Yerushalayim*, next year in Jerusalem." "So," said G-d in my nightmare, "in 1948, against all odds, I restored the Jewish people to their land. And you know what happened? No one came! Only a few *chalutzim*—pioneers. In fact, most of those who came to Israel were refugees, expelled from Arab lands, with nowhere else to go. Almost no one came from the lands of comfort, from the United States, from Canada, from Europe, South Africa, Australia, except a few crazies."

"And I said to myself," said the Al-mighty, "What's wrong? Perhaps, they are not coming because they had no access to the *Kotel*, the Western

Wall, *Mah'ahrat Hamachpela*, the cave of the Patriarchs in Hebron, the sepulcher of Joseph in Nablus, in Shechem. So in 1967 I restored the Old City, I gave them Hebron, the entire West Bank, and I even threw in Sharm El Sheik for scuba diving and the Hermon mountains for snow skiing! I waited and waited, and no one came. So, 25 years later, I said to Myself, *Oib ah'zoy*, if that's the case, I'm going to give the land to people who really love the land, and those are the Palestinians! Hamas, Hezbola, the PFLP—they are willing to die for the land."

We say in our Amidah prayer and in the Grace after meals, *V'to'lee'chay'nu ko'm'mee'yut l'artzay'nu*, restore us upright to our land—upright does not mean in a coffin. The land of Israel is intended to be a homeland for living Jews. It should not become a dumping ground for dead Jews. When we fast on the 17th of Tamuz, it is imperative for us to bear in mind as well that peace for the Jewish people has always been a factor of the Jewish peoples' relationship to G-d. If we truly desire peace, we must return to G-d, and He will return to us, and in this way the land as well will be restored to the people of G-d.

May you be blessed.

Rabbi Ephraim Buchwald is one of the leaders in the movement of Jewish return in America today. He has pioneered and developed many of the most dramatic and effective outreach programs in this country. Ordained at Yeshiva University, where he was a student of Rabbi Dr. J. B. Soloveitchik, Rabbi Buchwald served for fifteen years beginning in 1973 as the director of education at Lincoln Square Synagogue in New York, which became one of the largest and most successful centers for adult Jewish education programs in America during his tenure. He also established and coordinated Lincoln Square's celebrated outreach program. Since 1975, Rabbi Buchwald has led the now-renowned "Beginners Service," a special Sabbath service for people with little or no synagogue experience.

Sefer BeMidbar—The Daughters of Zelophehad

Supplemental Reading

The Daughters of Zelophehad: Legitimate Feminist Claims

—Rabbi Ephraim Z. Buchwald

In this coming week's parasha, parashat Phinehas, we learn of the precedent-shattering request of the daughters of Zelophehad.

The Torah, in Numbers 27, records that the five daughters of Zelophehad came before Moses, Eleazar the Priest, the Princes of the Israelite tribes, and the entire congregation at the door of the Tabernacle. The women claimed that their father had died in the wilderness and had left no sons (Numbers 27:4). *T'nu la'nu achuzah b'toch achei avinu,* Give us a possession among our father's brothers, they asked.

The Torah relates that since Moses did not know the immediate answer, he brought the question before G-d. G-d told Moses (Numbers 27:7) that the claim of the daughters of Zelophehad was justified and instructed Moses to transfer the inheritance of their father to them. In further clarification, G-d states that if a man dies and leaves no sons, his property shall first transfer to his daughters, and only afterwards, if there are no female heirs, to other close relatives.

This scriptural portion is indeed remarkable. After all, why didn't the Torah just include this law, that the property of a man who leaves no male heirs transfers to his daughters, as part of the regular legal portions that appear throughout the Torah? Why was it necessary for the daughters to approach Moses, and why was Moses incapable of responding, making it necessary for him to get the answer directly from G-d?

We live in an age where many disenfranchised, or so-called disenfranchised, people make claims about historic injustices. They demand that the discriminatory practices cease and often request compensation for the previous injustices. While surely many of these claims are legitimate, the practice of discriminatory claims has become so widespread and in certain instances has gotten so out of hand, that it's been quipped, only half in jest, that soon left-handed people will start class-action suits against public accommodations which have staircase rails only on the right.

Distinguishing between a legitimate claim and a non-legitimate claim has become an art. And with the factor of "political correctness" often being added into the mix, woe unto the person that does not show proper respect to those claims—legitimate or not!

It is fascinating that the Torah has included the episode of the daughters of Zelophehad in a featured parasha, rather than having us learn it from some textual exegesis, as are many other important laws. It underscores that Judaism is really light years ahead of other civilizations in establishing fair and equitable parameters for Jewish women. But, it's not so surprising after all, since already in Genesis (2:27) the Torah declares that both husband and wife should become one flesh, and just as one would not hurt or mistreat oneself, so one may not hurt or mistreat one's spouse.

The Torah was the first universal document to insist that a man provide for and adequately support his wife, as we learn from Exodus 21:10, *Sh'era, k'sutah, v'onatah lo yig'rah*, Men must provide their wives with food, clothing and sexual pleasure.

Furthermore, the entire narrative of the book of Exodus indicates that, were it not for the women, the Jewish people would never have been redeemed from Egypt—in each case citing the errant behavior of the men and the faithful behavior of the women. The Torah (Deuteronomy 24:1) is also the first document in human history to provide for divorce for unsuccessful marriages. Similarly, the Torah (Deuteronomy 21:15) insists that if a man has multiple wives, he may not favor one's children over the other's. In fact, the Torah clearly looks down on multiple wives; after all, each case of polygamy cited in the Bible is riddled with pain and unhappiness. The Bible (1 Samuel 1:6) intentionally calls the second wife a *tzara*—literally a "pain" to the first wife and the origin of the venerable Yiddish word *tsuris*—travail! The Talmud (Sanhedrin 76b) states movingly that one must love one's wife as much as oneself and honor her more than himself. It is indeed fascinating to note that the male-dominated Halakhic hierarchy of Jewish law has worked assiduously over the millennia to expand the rights and privileges of women, particularly remarkable since this was done at the time when other civilizations were limiting the rights of women. It was not so long ago that women in some countries of the Orient were expected to jump into the grave and be buried alive after their husbands died. Jewish tradition teaches that an older women [sic] in the house is a treasure and a blessing (Talmud, Arakhin 19a).

Now back to the earlier question. Why indeed was the law of inheritance of daughters not included in the general legal sections of the Bible? Why was it necessary to ask G-d to render a decision? Perhaps because *Halakha*, Jewish law, is an evolving law. Clearly the social status and positions of both men and women change as society evolves. Could it be that the Al-mighty was signaling us that as the role of women changes in secular society, the role of women needs to be reevaluated in the religious society. But, of course, there is a caveat—if the laws of secular society controvert any of the values and laws of the Torah, they must not be followed. To the contrary, they must be rejected. However, when the laws and customs of society do not clash with Jewish law, then by all means Jews must take a leading stand in the efforts to expand women's rights and privileges.

I think it is fair to say in retrospect, especially in light of some of the excesses we have seen in the contemporary feminist movement in America, that it is quite obvious that women, even passionately feminist women, do not really seek to be men. To the contrary, we have learned that women for the most part truly want to be *women*, but resent being disenfranchised from rights and privileges that should legitimately be theirs. Women are entitled to equal pay for equal work. Women are entitled to have the opportunity to properly nurture their children, to be granted maternity and paternity leave, and, of course, women are entitled to equal education.

The ancient laws that we learn from the episode of the daughters of Zelophehad were a revolutionary breakthrough in society and family. They exist to help us understand the nature of Torah and the nature of the Torah's perspective on women. The fact that Moses had to seek G-d's opinion clearly indicates that the Al-mighty wanted this area of Jewish life to evolve. The Al-mighty wants more than anything else for us to explore His Torah, find new insights, and discover new patterns. It is G-d's fervent wish that through this continuing search, all of G-d's creatures will be able to develop in a healthful and constructive manner for the betterment of all of humankind.

May you be blessed.

Rabbi Ephraim Buchwald is one of the leaders in the movement of Jewish return in America today. He has pioneered and developed many of the most dramatic and effective outreach programs in this country. Ordained at Yeshiva University, where he was a student of Rabbi Dr. J. B. Soloveitchik, Rabbi Buchwald served for fifteen years beginning in 1973 as the director of education at Lincoln Square Synagogue in New York, which became one of the largest and most successful centers for adult Jewish education programs in America during his tenure. He also established and coordinated Lincoln Square's celebrated outreach program. Since 1975, Rabbi Buchwald has led the now-renowned "Beginners Service," a special Sabbath service for people with little or no synagogue experience.

Final Thoughts

We read in the second chapter of Pirqe Avot about Rabbi Yohanan ben Zakai and his five disciples: Rabbi Eliezer ben Hyrcanus, Rabbi Joshua ben Hananiah, Rabbi Yossei the Kohen, Rabbi Shimon ben Nethanel, and Rabbi Elazar ben Arach. Their Rebbe, Rabbi Yohanan ben Zakai, would recount their praises and ultimately challenged them to "go and see which is the best trait for a person to acquire" (Avot 2:10). Here is what they reported back:

> Said Rabbi Eliezer: A good eye. Said Rabbi Joshua: A good friend. Said Rabbi Yossei: A good neighbor. Said Rabbi Shimon: To see what is born [out of one's actions]. Said Rabbi Elazar: A good heart (Avot 2:10).

After hearing their findings, Rabbi Yohanan ben Zakai concluded that he preferred the advice of Rabbi Elazar, "for his words include all of yours."

In a sense, that is the goal of this book when used to teach *Sefer BeMidbar*: to use the book of Numbers to engage and force students (as did Rabbi Yohanan) to reflect on the character traits they hope to embody and those they understand they need to avoid.

To this end, we have examined a broad range of character traits and have seen how fine a line it can be between a particular trait being positive or detrimental. Like Rabbi Yohanan ben Zakai, teachers who adopt the pedagogy set forth in this book will be asking their students to "go and see which is the best trait for a person to acquire." My hope is that they will reach the same conclusion as Rabbi Yohanan ben Zakai, that is, to find one that includes and cultivates them all.

Appendix

Sample Rubric for *Middot* Essays

As will be clear from day one, our studies of *Sefer BeMidbar* will be theme-based. Specifically, we will study the main characters in the book (many of whom have entire *parshiyot* named for them) and attempt to determine which character traits (*middot* in Hebrew) they personify. This will be a major focus of our in-depth reading of various chapters throughout the book, and this will be reinforced by the specific commentaries we will study on each chapter.

To further deepen our understanding of and appreciation for the *middot* portrayed in *Sefer BeMidbar*, students will be required to craft a written analysis for each unit. In brief, these will be 500-word essays that address each of the following:

1. Define the character trait that is the focus of each chapter or narrative we study.

2. Describe how the main character(s) embodies this character trait, being sure to support your analysis with verses and commentaries from the chapter in question.

3. Analyze the chapter's presentation of the character trait. Is it set forth in a positive light or is it portrayed as a negative trait? Again, be sure to support your analysis with verses and commentaries from the chapter in question.

4. Discuss whether this is a character trait to be emulated or avoided. If, emulated, how so? If avoided, why? While this part of the essay is opinion based, you must support your opinion with verses from the chapter, with commentaries studied on the chapter, and/or with material from our class discussions.

These essays will *generally* be due the *day before* the unit test on the chapter, thereby allowing us to discuss these essays in class and to use these discussions as a review session for the unit test. Each of these written assignments are worth 100 points.

About the Author

RABBI TRAVIS SPENT FIFTEEN years as an advertising and marketing executive working both for large Fortune 500 firms such as Georgia-Pacific and Ogilvy & Mather and as a consultant. He developed strategic business and marketing plans for a variety of consumer packaged goods and financial services companies. Twenty years ago, Rabbi Travis changed professions and started his career as an educator. In that time he has taught a wide range of classes, including Jewish Law, Bible, Jewish history, Zionism and the Shoah, Israel advocacy, American history, and Advanced Placement U.S. government.

Rabbi Travis earned his bachelor's degree from Dartmouth College, where he graduated Phi Beta Kappa with a double major in French literature and political science. He holds a Masters of Judaic Studies from Spertus College and a Masters of Teaching from Mercer University. He received his rabbinic ordination from Rabbi Michael J. Broyde, dean of Atlanta Torah MiTzion Kollel, after spending four years studying with Rabbi Broyde and the members of the kollel.

In 2013, Rabbi Travis was named the Distinguished High School Educator of the Year by the Georgia Commission on the Holocaust for his instruction on civil rights in his American History courses. That same year, he was also named as a Natalia Twersky Award finalist by the Jewish Women's Archive.

Bibliography

"Adolescence: Developing Independence and Identity." Chapter 6.3 in *Introduction to Psychology*. https://doi.org/10.24926/8668.1201.

Artson, Bradley Shavit. "Sotah: Trial by Ordeal." Ziegler School of Rabbinic Studies, American Jewish University. 9 Sivan 5767. http://ziegler.aju.edu/default.aspx?id=5507.

Bazak, Amnon. "Why Are the Laws of the Nazir and the Sota Juxtaposed?" Israel Koschitzky Virtual Beit Midrash. http://etzion.org.il/en/why-are-laws-nazir-and-sota-juxtaposed.

Bellows, Amy. "Your Teen's Search for Identity." PsychCentral. July 17, 2016. https://psychcentral.com/lib/your-teens-search-for-identity/.

Bick, Ezra. *In His Mercy*. New Milford, CT: Magid Books, 2010.

Broyde, Michael J. "Orthodox Women Clergy?" *Jewish Press*, July 22, 2009, http://www.jewishpress.com/indepth/opinions/orthodox-women-clergy/2009/07/22/.

Burton, Neel. "Is Greed Good? The Psychology and Philosophy of Greed." *Psychology Today*. October 6, 2014. https://www.psychologytoday.com/us/blog/hide-and-seek/201410/is-greed-good.

Efron, Joshua. *Studies on the Hasmonean Period*. Leiden: Brill, 1987.

Eisenberg, Ronald L. *Essential Figures in the Talmud*. Lanham, MD: Jason Aronson, 2013.

Etshalom, Yitzchak. "Rav Soloveitchik's Lecture on Leadership." Torah.org. https://torah.org/torah-portion/mikra-5774-behaaloscha/

Fox, Bernie. "Lessons from the Nazir." Torah New York. https://www.ou.org/torah/parsha/rabbi-fox-on-parsha/lessons_from_the_nazir/.

Friedman, Hershey H. and Abraham C. Weisel. "Should Moral Individuals Ever Lie? Insights from Jewish Law." Jewish Law. 2003. http://www.jlaw.com/Articles/hf_LyingPermissible.html.

Gilbert, Sophie. "The Movement of #MeToo: How a Hashtag Got Its Power." *Atlantic*. October 16, 2017. https://www.theatlantic.com/entertainment/archive/2017/10/the-movement-of-metoo/542979/.

Ginzberg, Louis. *The Legends of the Jews*. 1909. http://www.sacred-texts.com/jud/loj/index.htm.

Goldman, Shalom L. *Zeal for Zion*. Chapel Hill: University of North Carolina Press, 2014.

Goldwater, Barry. "Goldwater's 1964 Acceptance Speech." Washington Post.com Archives. https://www.washingtonpost.com/wp-srv/politics/daily/may98/goldwaterspeech.htm.

Gordis, Daniel. "Why Many American Jews Are Becoming Indifferent or Even Hostile to Israel." *Mosaic*. May 8, 2017. https://mosaicmagazine.com/essay/2017/05/why-many-american-jews-are-becoming-indifferent-or-even-hostile-to-israel/.

Graves, David E. "Bonus 38—Deir 'Alla Balaam Inscription." Biblical Archaeology (blog). December 29, 2014. https://biblicalarchaeologygraves.blogspot.com/2014/12/bonus-38-deir-alla-balaam-inscription.html.

Grossman, Y. "'How Good Are Your Tents, Yaakov'—On the Arrangement of the Shekhina's Chariot," http://www.etzion.org.il/vbm/archive/9-parsha/39bemidbar.rtf.

Hailparn, D. F. and M. Hailparn. "Four Dimensions of Envy: Strategies for Managing its Manifestations in Psychotherapy." *Journal of Contemporary Psychotherapy* 27, no. 1 (1997): 49–60, accessed online at http://ron-sheese.wikidot.com/group-ik10.

Halberstam, Chaya T. *Law and Truth in Biblical and Rabbinic Literature*. Bloomington: Indiana University Press, 2010.

Herodotus. *On the Customs of the Persians*. Ancient History Encyclopedia. January 18, 2012. https://www.ancient.eu/article/149/herodotus-on-the-customs-of-the-persians/.

Hirsch, Samson Raphael. *The Pentateuch. Volume II: Exodus*. Translated by Isaac Levy. Gateshead: Judaica Press, 1982.

"Historical Rankings of Presidents of the United States." Wikipedia. https://en.wikipedia.org/wiki/Historical_rankings_of_presidents_of_the_United_States.

Hitler, Adolf. *Mein Kampf*. Translated by James Murphy. Project Gutenberg of Australia. http://gutenberg.net.au/ebooks02/0200601.txt.

Hoftijzer, Jacob, and Gerrit van der Kooij. *Aramaic Texts from Deir 'Alla* (Leiden: Brill, 1976).

Israel, Alex. "The Book of Bamidbar: An Introduction." Alexisrael.org. http://www.alexisrael.org/the-structure-of-sefer-bemidbar-

Katz, Ari. "The Sin of the Spies." Yeshivat Kerem B'Yavne. http://www.kby.org.il/english/torat-yavneh/view.asp?id=3797.

King, Martin Luther, Jr. "Letter from a Birmingham Jail." African Studies Center, University of Pennsylvania. https://www.africa.upenn.edu/Articles_Gen/Letter_Birmingham.html.

Kulp, Joshua. "Nazir, Chapter 9, Mishnah 5." USCJ: Conservative Yeshiva in Jerusalem. http://learn.conservativeyeshiva.org/nazir-chapter-nine-mishnah-five/.

Lamm, Norman. *Torah Umaddah*. Lanham, MD: Rowman and Littlefield, 1990.

Lee, Robert E., to Mary Anna Randolph Custis Lee, December 27, 1856. Lee Family Digital Archive. https://leefamilyarchive.org/9-family-papers/339-robert-e-lee-to-mary-anna-randolph-custis-lee-1856-december-27.

Leff, Zev. "Do Not Separate Yourself from the Community." Aish.com. http://www.aish.com/tp/i/oai/48966856.html.

Leibowitz, Nehama. *Studies in Bamidbar (Numbers)*. Jerusalem: Ahava Press, 1980.

Leibtag, Menachem. "Tehillim Perek 78 and Sefer Bamidbar." Tanach.org. http://www.tanach.org/bamidbar/th78.txt

Levy, Yitzchak. "Shiur #27: The History of the Resting of the Shekhina (Part XIII)—The Dedication of the Mishkan (Part III)." Israel Koschitzky Virtual Beit Midrash.

http://etzion.org.il/en/shiur-27-history-resting-shekhinapart-xiii-dedication-mishkan-part-iii.

Lichtenstein, Mosheh. "The Crisis of Leadership." Israel Koschitzky Virtual Beit Midrash. http://etzion.org.il/en/crisis-leadership.

Loevinger, Neal J. "Seeing Beneath the Surface." MyJewishLearning.org. https://www.myjewishlearning.com/article/seeing-beneath-the-surface/.

McAlpine, Fraser. "Lost in Translation: Five British Stereotypes That Are True." Anglophenia (blog). http://www.bbcamerica.com/anglophenia/2011/09/lost-in-translation-five-british-stereotypes-that-are-true

Meiselman, Moshe. *Jewish Woman in Jewish Law*. New York: Ktav, 1978.

Myatt, Mike. "15 Ways to Identify Bad Leaders." *Forbes*. October 18, 2012. https://www.forbes.com/sites/mikemyatt/2012/10/18/15-ways-to-identify-bad-leaders/#74e3e56115da.

Nachshoni, Yehuda. *Studies in the Weekly Parashah: BeMidbar*. Brooklyn, NY: Mesorah, 1989.

O'Connor, Evelyn. "Othello—Virtues and Flaws." leavingcertenglish.net. February 20, 2014. http://leavingcertenglish.net/2014/02/othello-virtues-flaws/

Olson, Carl. "'The 'Angry God' and the 'Loving God.'" *Our Sunday Visitor*. April 4, 2013. https://www.osv.com/Article/TabId/493/ArtMID/13569/ArticleID/9385/The-"Angry-God"-and-the-"Loving-God"-.aspx

Orlansky, Harold. "The Study of Man: Jewish Personality Traits." *Commentary* (online). October 1, 1946. https://www.commentarymagazine.com/articles/the-study-of-man-jewish-personality-traits/

"Parshat Naso: Sota and Nazir: Why are They 'Out of Place?'" Tanach.org. http://www.tanach.org/bamidbar/naso/nasos1.htm

Ramban. *Commentary on the Torah—Numbers*. Translated by Charles B. Chavel. New York: Shilo, 1975.

Rettew, David. "Nature versus Nurture: Where We Are in 2017." *Psychology Today*. October 6, 2017. https://www.psychologytoday.com/us/blog/abcs-child-psychiatry/201710/nature-versus-nurture-where-we-are-in-2017.

Roosevelt, Franklin D. "Address at Oglethorpe University in Atlanta, Georgia, May 22, 1932." American Presidency Project, http://www.presidency.ucsb.edu/ws/?pid=88410.

Sabato, Haim. *Seeking His Presence: Conversations with Rabbi Aharon Lichtenstein*. Tel Aviv: Yedioth Books, 2016.

Sacks, Jonathan. "Parshat Shelach: Without Walls." Torah New York. https://www.ou.org/torah/parsha/rabbi-sacks-on-parsha/covenant_and_conversation_withoutwalls/.

Sacks, Jonathan. "Pinchas (5772)—The Zealot." Jonathan Sacks. July 9, 2012. http://rabbisacks.org/covenant-conversation-5772-pinchas-the-zealot/

Sacks, Jonathan. "The Zealot." Torah New York. https://www.ou.org/torah/parsha/rabbi-sacks-on-parsha/the_zealot/.

Safran, Eliyahu. "Jealousy Rots, Envy Can Redeem." Torah New York, https://www.ou.org/torah/parsha/parsha-from-ou/jealousy-rots-envy-can-redeem/.

Samet, Elchanan. "The Sota (5:11–31)." Israel Koschitzky Virtual Beit Midrash. http://etzion.org.il/en/sota-511-31.

Schäferhoff, Nick. "9 German Stereotypes That Are Straight Up True." FluentU (blog). https://www.fluentu.com/blog/german/german-stereotypes/

Sforno, Ovadiah ben Yaacov. *Commentary on the Torah*. Translated by Raphael Pelcovitz. Brooklyn, NY: Mesorah, 1987.

"Shlach (Numbers 13–15): The Spies." May 24, 2000. Aish.com. http://www.aish.com/tp/i/moha/48925052.html.

Soleveitchik, Joseph B. *Kol Dodi Dofek" My Beloved Knocks*. New York: Yeshiva University, 2006.

Swindoll, Charles. "Numbers." The Bible-Teaching Ministry of Charles R. Swindoll. https://www.insight.org/resources/bible/the-pentateuch/numbers

Tamari, Meir. *The Challenge of Wealth: A Jewish Perspective on Earning and Spending Money*. North Vale, NJ: Jason Aronson, 1995. Cited portion available online at https://www.myjewishlearning.com/article/judaism-on-greed/.

Terracciano, Antonio, and Robert R. McCrae. "Perceptions of Americans and the Iraq Invasion: Implications for Understanding National Character Stereotypes." *Journal of Cross Cultural Psychology* 38, no. 6 (2007): 695–710. Author manuscript available online at https://www.ncbi.nlm.nih.gov/pmc/articles/PMC2447921/#!po=24.0909

Thayer, Ernest Lawrence. "Casey at the Bat." Poets.org. https://m.poets.org/poetsorg/poem/casey-bat.

"Top 100 American Speeches of the 20th Century." https://news.wisc.edu/archive/misc/speeches/.

Viola, Frank. "God Behaving Badly: Is the God of the Old Testament an Angry, Racist, Sexist Masochist?" The Deeper Journey (blog). August 14, 2013. http://www.patheos.com/blogs/frankviola/godbehavingbadly/

Wegner, Judith Romney. "Women in Classical Rabbinic Judaism." Page 84 in *Jewish Women: Historical Perspective*, edited by Judith R. Baskin. Detroit: Wayne State University Press, 1991.

Wiggins, Grant, and Jay McTighe. *Understanding by Design*. Vanderbilt University Xenter for Teaching. https://cft.vanderbilt.edu/guides-sub-pages/understanding-by-design/.

Zhu, Lin. "A Comparative Look at Chinese and American Stereotypes: A Focus Group Study." *Journal of Intercultural Communication* 42 (November 2016). https://www.immi.se/intercultural/nr42/zhu.html

www.ingramcontent.com/pod-product-compliance
Lightning Source LLC
Chambersburg PA
CBHW071145300426
44113CB00009B/1096